Hong Guk-Pyoung
Judah's Desire and the Making of the Abrahamic Israel

Beihefte zur Zeitschrift für die alttestamentliche Wissenschaft

Edited by
John Barton, Reinhard G. Kratz, Nathan MacDonald,
Sara Milstein, and Markus Witte

Volume 559

Hong Guk-Pyoung

Judah's Desire and the Making of the Abrahamic Israel

A Contextual and Functional Approach

DE GRUYTER

This work was supported by the Yonsei University Research Grant of 2022.

ISBN 978-3-11-137600-4
e-ISBN (PDF) 978-3-11-137655-4
e-ISBN (EPUB) 978-3-11-137775-9
ISSN 0934-2575

Library of Congress Control Number: 2023950309

Bibliographic information published by the Deutsche Nationalbibliothek
The Deutsche Nationalbibliothek lists this publication in the Deutsche Nationalbibliografie;
detailed bibliographic data are available on the internet at http://dnb.dnb.de.

MIX
Papier | Fördert
gute Waldnutzung
FSC
www.fsc.org FSC® C083411

For my parents,
Hong Soon-young and Park Hye-sun

Contents

Part II: Judah Rewrites Israel's Past

Acknowledgements

This book embodies a decade of my research, ignited by a fascination with the North-South dynamics in Israel. What began as an academic endeavor transformed into a profound journey of self-reflection as a Korean biblical scholar, illuminating my motivations for studying the Old Testament/Hebrew Bible, my approach to teaching, and the direction I envision for my career. This book stands as a testament to my belief that scripture derives its significance from the engagement of its readers. Thus, it explores questions inherently rooted and driven by my Korean heritage, which would naturally provoke a question, "What does Korea have to do with the Hebrew Bible?" The book turns the question back to the readers, encouraging a reflection on if not the same applies to them, or how their cultural background shapes their interpretation of the Hebrew text. Ultimately, my aim is to demonstrate how diverse cultural heritages actively contribute unique insights to biblical interpretation. In anticipation of the skeptic's "So what?" – which questions the broader significance of context-specific meanings – I strive to strike a balance between personal context and universal relevance. In doing so, I endeavor to demonstrate how my context-driven perspective finds resonance with readers across diverse backgrounds.

This book incorporates materials previously featured in other publications. I am thankful to the respective publishers for granting permission to include them. Chapter 2 is a revised version of "United Yet Divided: Reading Judah and Israel in the Context of Two Koreas," which appeared in the *Oxford Handbook of the Bible in Korea* (2021), edited by Won W. Lee. Chapter 3 is an update of "Once Again: The Emergence of 'Biblical Israel'," published in *ZAW* 125 (2013). Chapter 10 is a condensed version of "Abraham, Our Father, the Father of All: A Perspective from Ancient Korean History," originally from *JSOT* 43 (2019).

I am deeply indebted to those who have supported me throughout this journey. My colleagues at Yonsei University, especially Dong-Hyuk Kim and Sung Uk Lim, who share the responsibility of leading biblical studies with me, have provided steadfast encouragement and support. I am grateful to my students – undergraduates, graduates, and those in the GIT program – who have been the foundation of my inspiration and an essential test ground for my ideas. Special thanks go to my tireless assistant, Hong Yoonbin, for her constant support and meticulous attention to detail, as well as to Kim Minji for her thorough indexing and neat illustrations.

My sincere appreciation goes to the editors of the BZAW for their faith in this unconventional manuscript and for accepting it into the series. I am also grateful to Dr. Albrecht Döhnert, Katrin Mittmann, and Sabina Dabrowski for their editorial guidance. This book has benefitted from insights and constructive

https://doi.org/10.1515/9783111376554-203

criticism from colleagues, including Marvin Sweeney, Bob Coote, Jaeyoung Jeon, Mark Hamilton, Kah-Jin Jeffrey Kuan, Andrew Tobolowsky, Hye Kyung Park, Meira Polliack, Soo Kim-Sweeney, Paul Hyunchul Kim, Won W. Lee, Paul K.-K. Cho, Roger S. Nam, Shuichi Hasegawa, Grace Hui Liang, Sonia Kwok Wong, Sang-Won Lee, JiSeong Kwon, Johannes Unsok Ro, Daewook Kim, Hyunwoo Kim, and Yitzhak Lee-Sak.

The cornerstone of my life is my family. My wife, Mikyoung, has been an unwavering pillar of strength, enriching every step of my journey. This book is a tribute to our blissful 25 years of marriage, and I look forward to many more years of meaning-making together. This book's evolution has mirrored the growth of our daughter, Sungwon. Her presence in our lives is a continuous fountain of joy, and my hope is that she will one day understand the depth of happiness she brings to our lives. Finally, I dedicate this book to my parents, the guiding lights in my life. Words fail to capture the immensity of their love, and each day forward will serve as an expression of my love and gratitude. Thank you.

List of Tables and Figures

https://doi.org/10.1515/9783111376554-204

List of Abbreviations

AASOR	*Annual of the American Schools of Oriental Research*
AB	Anchor Bible
ABS	Archaeology and Biblical Studies
AIL	Ancient Israel and Its Literature
ANEM	Ancient Near East Monographs/Monografías sobre el Antiguo Cercano Oriente
BA	*Biblical Archaeologist*
BASOR	*Bulletin of the American Schools of Oriental Research*
BETL	Bibliotheca Ephemeridum Theologicarum Lovaniensium
Bib	*Biblica*
BibInt	*Biblical Interpretation*
BJS	Brown Judaic Studies
BTB	*Biblical Theology Bulletin*
BZ	*Biblische Zeitschrift*
BZABR	Beihefte zur Zeitschrift für altorientalische und biblische Rechtsgeschichte
BZAW	Beihefte zur Zeitschrift für die alttestamentliche Wissenschaft
CBQ	*Catholic Biblical Quarterly*
ConBOT	Coniectanea Biblica: Old Testament Series
CurBR	*Currents in Biblical Research*
DBAT	*Dielheimer Blätter zum Alten Testament und seiner Rezeption in der Alten Kirche*
FAT	Forschungen zum Alten Testament
FRLANT	Forschungen zur Religion und Literatur des Alten und Neuen Testaments
HeBAI	*Hebrew Bible and Ancient Israel*
HS	*Hebrew Studies*
HSAO	Heidelberger Studien zum Alten Orient
HSM	Harvard Semitic Monographs
IEJ	*Israel Exploration Journal*
JBL	*Journal of Biblical Literature*
JEA	*Journal of Egyptian Archaeology*
JHebS	*Journal of Hebrew Scriptures*
JSOT	*Journal for the Study of the Old Testament*
JSOTSup	Journal for the Study of the Old Testament: Supplement Series
LHBOTS	Library of Hebrew Bible/Old Testament Studies
NEA	*Near Eastern Archaeology*
OBO	Orbis biblicus et orientalis
OTL	Old Testament Library
OtSt	*Oudtestamentische Studiën*
RB	*Revue biblique*
RHR	*Revue de l'histoire des religions*
SBT	Studies in Biblical Theology
SemeiaSt	Semeia Studies
SJOT	*Scandinavian Journal of the Old Testament*
SJT	*Scottish Journal of Theology*
SSN	Studia Semitica Neerlandica
TA	*Tel Aviv*
TSJTSA	Texts and Studies of the Jewish Theological Seminary of America

https://doi.org/10.1515/9783111376554-205

UF	*Ugarit-Forschungen*
VT	*Vetus Testamentum*
VTSup	Supplements to Vetus Testamentum
WMANT	Wissenschaftliche Monographien zum Alten und Neuen Testament
WO	*Die Welt des Orients*
ZAW	*Zeitschrift für die alttestamentliche Wissenschaft*
ZDPV	*Zeitschrift des deutschen Palästina-Vereins*
ZTK	*Zeitschrift für Theologie und Kirche*

1 Introduction: Why Judah and Israel Again?

1.1 Social and Psychological Nature of Identity

Did early Judahites perceive themselves Israelites? If they did, was this identity adopted over time, or was it an inherent part of their self-perception from the onset?[1] On the flip side, how were they perceived in return by the *Israelites* in the North? And how did Judah's self-perception impact their understanding of the past, present, and future as a people?

For a long time, biblical scholars, historians, and archaeologists have studied Judah and Israel primarily from historical and objective perspectives, focusing on questions like who the first Israelites were, where the Israelite tribes originated, and how the two kingdoms grew out of them. While these inquiries provide valuable insights, they often overlook the subjective and psychological aspects of the intergroup dynamic between Judah and Israel. As someone who grew up in South Korea, I have always been acutely aware of the social and psychological dimensions of political rivalry, which cannot be fully captured by historical and objective investigations alone.

The Hebrew Bible assumes the primordial unity of Judah and Israel, grounded in their shared Abrahamic kinship and Yahwistic worship. However, throughout much of the monarchic era, the two kingdoms remained divided and never achieved unity again. As a Korean, living in a country with an ongoing reality of political division among "one people," I have a heightened sensitivity to the reality of unity in division. Thus, I believe I can contribute to the discussion on the complex intergroup dynamics between Judah and Israel in the Hebrew Bible. Although the biblical text presents Judah and Israel as descending from a common ancestor, this kind of origin myth is common in the construction of political identities. The key question is not whether their unity is real, but how and by whom that unity was constructed and maintained, and what consequences it had for the development of the Israelite identity, as we know it.

---

1 I am well aware of the complexities associated with the term "identity," an issue illuminated by Brubaker and Cooper's critique. Rogers Brubaker and Frederick Cooper, "Beyond 'Identity,'" *Theory and Society* 29 (2000): 1–47, https://doi.org/10.1023/A:1007068714468. They underscored the ambiguous nature of "identity" as a term that is both encompassing, capturing a wide array of experiences and affiliations, and yet can be limiting, often reducing complex dynamics into overly simplified constructs. Their insights point to the tension between the term's general applicability and the necessity for specificity and precision in nuanced social and analytical contexts. Despite these challenges, I continue to maintain the use of "identity," in the absence of a more nuanced substitute, albeit with a measured approach and due consideration to its limitations.

https://doi.org/10.1515/9783111376554-001

The premise behind these questions is that one's self-perception is crucial in determining social behavior. To illustrate, consider the question, "Who is Hispanic?" The term itself can be ambiguous, and while there is no universally agreed-upon definition, two primary perspectives often compete. Some believe that being Hispanic revolves around self-identification, with individuals personally identifying as Hispanic regardless of their precise ethnic or cultural background. In contrast, others contend that being Hispanic necessitates tangible ties, whether those are rooted in Spanish heritage, ethnicity, specific territories (like countries from Latin America), or cultural traditions. The historical evolution of the term "Hispanic," originally referring to people from Spain and later encompassing Spanish-speaking individuals from Latin America, adds depth to this already complex debate.[2] This dilemma should be relevant beyond just the Hispanic context. When applied to biblical Israel, profound implications emerge. Historically, scholars appear to have leaned towards the latter viewpoint, leading many to recognize the Northern Kingdom as the "historical Israel." However, if we shift our focus to the former perspective, our conclusions could be markedly different. The key idea I promote in this book is that while Judah believed they were Israel, most Israelites thought differently. Recognizing this gap in perspective, I contend, provides invaluable insights into the multifaceted nature of "biblical Israel."[3]

Let me illustrate the significance of the gap between one's own and social perceptions. If someone asks me, "are you Korean?" it would have little significance to me. In South Korea, where the population is predominantly ethnically Korean, my identity as a Korean is socially taken for granted. However, for a Korean living in Japan (a Zainichi Korean[4]) during the early twentieth century, such a question could have been a life-or-death matter.[5] In fact, for a Zainichi Korean, the question necessarily entails the other side, "are you (not) Japanese?" because they were seen as different from Japanese people around them, who re-

---

2 See, e.g., Suzanne Oboler, *Ethnic Labels, Latino Lives: Identity and the Politics of (Re)Presentation in the United States* (Minneapolis: University of Minnesota Press, 1995).
3 For example, a number of recent scholars have suggested the existence of two distinct forms of Israel, an intriguing concept that my proposition can further elucidate. See Section 3.3 below. As for the notion of "biblical Israel," see Philip R. Davies, *In Search of 'Ancient Israel,'* JSOTSup 148 (Sheffield: JSOT Press, 1992). For a history of research on the notion, see Philip R. Davies, *The Origins of Biblical Israel*, LHBOTS 485 (New York: T&T Clark, 2007), 5–24.
4 "Zainichi" literally means "residing in Japan," which is often used as a simple form of "Zainichi Koreans (在日韓国人, Zainichi Kankokujin)," ethnic Koreans who have permanent residency status in Japan.
5 One can now read, or watch, Min Jin Lee's *Pachinko*. Min Jin Lee, *Pachinko* (New York: Grand Central Publishing, 2017). Noah, a Zainichi Korean and the son of the main character Sunja, strikingly kills himself when his Korean identity is revealed.

garded them as outsiders. Zainichi Koreans in Japan had to endure persecution and derogatory perceptions, and for some of them, persuading themselves and others of their Japanese identity was a crucial part of their social life and survival. Important here is to understand that this is not a legal matter but of social perception. A mere document that proves citizenship would not have answered this question.

Similarly, "are you American?" may not be a critical question for a middle-class white American who considers themselves a true American and is socially perceived as such. However, for second and third-generation Korean American youths struggling with their identity, this could be the most crucial question of their lives, at least at the moment. While legally they hold American citizenship, socially they are made to question their degree of Americanness, for their perceived difference. In any society, the perception of Self and Others inevitably involves power dynamics between the majority and minorities. The majority seeks to maintain the status quo, while the marginalized try to elevate their status through various means, such as assimilation, imitation, and self-promotion.

These illustrations may be overly dramatic, but they do underscore the fundamental importance of social reality in shaping one's self-perception that underpins my questions. The significance of my question becomes clearer when compared with other Israelite tribes, such as the Ephraimites. There is little indication in biblical literature that casts doubt on the status of this elite clan, which was home to Joshua (Num 13:8), Deborah (Judg 4:5), and Samuel (1Sam 1:1–2). In contrast, Judah's presence within early Israel is minimal before the rise of David. If we consider that the era of David is largely a later idealization, as most historians today acknowledge, then the early status of Judah within Israel becomes more problematic. Could it be an overstatement to say that Judah's identification with Israel was fundamentally no different from that of a Zainichi Korean seeking Japanese identity? Could we argue that "Israel" was an aspired identity for Judah similar to how "American" is for some second-generation Korean Americans?

There is no shortage of examples in human history of culturally inferior conquerors taking over the superior legacy and identity of the conquered. Most European nations or Westerners in general, appear to think they inherit a Roman heritage. What inheriting Rome does to their "barbaric" origins cannot be more apparent. Romans created barbarians, but later, those Romanized barbarians "reinvented Rome" to carve out their noble origin.[6] By virtue of their claim to inherit Rome, the long-deceased empire continued to be revived. Zeus's striking omni-

---

6 See Patrick J. Geary, *Before France and Germany: The Creation and Transformation of the Merovingian World* (New York: Oxford University Press, 1988).

presence in Greek hero lineages, likely reflects regional communities vying for prestige, each eager to weave their local heroes into the intricate fabric of Zeus's divine lineage.

The primary aim of this book is to demonstrate the vital role Judah played in reshaping Israel's past, redefining the very concept of "Israel." I argue that this transformative process was fueled by Judah's sense of inferiority to, and desire for, Israel. I examine how biblical ancestral traditions have served as discursive tools for imagining Israel's origins, and how originally competing identities (behind the Jacob and Abraham narratives) have been presently harmonized into a coherent image of "Abrahamic Israel." I emphasize the constructed nature of this process as against the underlying "Jacobean Israel" – also an appropriation from Israel of the underlying indigenous heritage.[7] I conceive Judahites' reimagining Israel's past as an essential element of their identity politics. By reorienting Israel's ancestral past in Abraham, the southern ancestor, Judah has cultivated a new mythic space in which they could establish their newly imagined identity, Judah as "the new Israel."[8] Understanding this is critical given the ubiquity of materials that are related to the Israel-Judah, or North-South, relationship in biblical traditions.

1.2 Context Matters

This project is rooted in my personal experiences and questions that stem from my Korean context, which calls for an explanation of how I came to be grasped by this subject. It was about two decades ago, when I was finishing up my master's study in the U. S. as an international student. I think I was reading Ernest Nicholson's *Deuteronomy and Tradition* on a bench near the Charles River. As a South Korean, his description of how the northern prophets brought down the endangered tradition to Jerusalem instantly captured my attention. The way he assumed the northern prophets' role in forming Judah's religious reform was intriguing, but it left me with a sense of discomfort. My eyes stayed with one sentence.

> Deuteronomy originated among a northern circle who fled south to Judah after the destruction of the northern kingdom in 721 B.C. and there formulated their old traditions into a programme of reform and revival which they intended to be carried out by the Judaean authorities with whom they believed the future of Israel to lie. In composing their work the authors had in mind Jerusalem as the cultic and political centre of the reformation movement

---

7 See Section 9.4 below.
8 Cf. Lemche's use of the term. Niels Peter Lemche, *The Israelites in History and Tradition*, Library of Ancient Israel (London: SPCK, 1998), 20–21.

and made certain concessions to the Jerusalem cult tradition. Such a view would obviously present a plausible solution to the problem for it would account for Deuteronomy's north Israelite background as well as its presence in Jerusalem in Josiah's reign.[9]

I thought this could be true, but only when the northern prophets willingly accepted Jerusalem as their new home. I immediately thought of North Korea and the people there. If one of the Koreas were to fall, would the elites eagerly transfer their national treasures and documents to the other thinking that the destiny of the Korean people now depends solely on them? My immediate answer was, "it really depends." I see these as the question about the complex interplay between ethnic and political identities. Although the two Koreas share a common ethnic identity as one people, they construe each other as political foes, and which dimension of their dual relationship becomes salient at a particular moment depends on numerous internal and external factors. This book emerged from my ongoing efforts to articulate the nature and source of this initial hesitation.

The 2016 International Meeting of Society of Biblical Literature at Yonsei University further developed my interests in contextual biblical studies. As the secretary in the local committee, I was tasked with showcasing Korean biblical scholarship, but it was surprisingly difficult to define exactly what that meant. The earlier generations of Korean biblical scholars made worthy attempts to contextualize theology and biblical studies, but such efforts have ironically diminished in today's increasingly globalized world. Regrettably, Minjung theology,[10] after more than a half century, still appears to remain the main window through which Korean theology, as well as biblical studies, is known to the outside world. Today, Korean biblical scholars seem more content than before to repeat Western scholarship, unwittingly engaging in academic and theological colonization. Recognizing the increasingly colonized landscape of Korean biblical studies has reignited my interest in posing context-oriented questions to the Bible.

As I recall, during my studies in the U.S., some of my teachers asked me questions such as "What do you think as a Korean?" or "I don't see anything Korean in your paper." They were attempting to encourage me to bring my Korean identity and perspectives into my work. However, like many of my Korean

---

9 Ernest W. Nicholson, *Deuteronomy and Tradition* (Philadelphia: Fortress, 1967), 94.

10 See, e.g., Yong-bok Kim, ed., *Minjung Theology: People as the Subjects of History* (Singapore: Christian Conference of Asia, 1981); Yung Suk Kim and Chin-ho Kim, eds., *Reading Minjung Theology in the Twenty-First Century: Selected Writings by Ahn Byung-Mu and Modern Critical Responses* (Eugene, OR: Pickwick, 2013); Jinkwan Kwon and Volker Küster, eds., *Minjung Theology Today: Contextual and Intercultural Perspectives*, ContactZone 21 (Leipzig: Evangelische Verlagsanstalt, 2018).

colleagues, I did not respond positively at the time. Instead of accepting their well-intentioned call to contribute as a Korean student, my vulnerable self would insist that I could perform as well as other students in non-Korean, conventional ways. Self-censorship was innate as an international student, and I was willingly seeking approval from Western scholarship.

Looking back, I realize that I was stubborn to admit what was going on. Instead, I insisted that my interests were in more traditional subjects, which was partly true. As a young student, I was fascinated by the ways in which historical critics such as Julius Wellhausen, Hermann Gunkel, and Martin Noth could uncover hidden meanings and historical contexts behind the biblical text. Their probing of issues like authorship, settings, and textual growth opened up new vistas for me. And my full embrace of critical scholarship led me to experience even greater surprise as I discovered subsequent scholars challenging some of the fundamental tenets of critical scholarship, resulting in a gradual expansion of the horizons of biblical studies towards new directions. However, as I equipped myself with "methods" in biblical studies, I did not realize that I was donning a persona that was not mine. I was maturing as a biblical scholar along the exact same path as Western scholarship developed. My doctoral thesis might have gone unnoticed as being authored by a Korean if not for my name and the personal notes in the acknowledgments.[11]

---

11 A recent introspection on this matter led me to embrace "Hong Guk-Pyoung" as my academic name, transitioning from the previously used "Koog P. Hong" or "K. P. Hong." In essence, "Koog" was derived from the central syllable of my three-letter Korean name. Much like the Chinese, most Koreans have three-letter names, each letter bearing a distinct meaning. My given name, 국평 (Guk-Pyoung), is formed from two Chinese characters: 國, symbolizing "nation," and 平, meaning "peace." This name is a testament to my father's aspirations. Having witnessed the ravages of war firsthand, he named his second son with a hope for peace in our nation. Upon our initial, temporary move to the U.S. in the early 1980s for his academic pursuits, my father registered my name as "Koog-Pyoung." I believe no consideration was given to the derogatory connotation of "Gook," which is the same word with Guk or Koog. For that, see Bruce Cumings, "American Orientalism at War in Korea and the United States: A Hegemony of Racism, Repression, and Amnesia," in *Orientalism and War*, ed. Tarak Barkawi and Keith Stanski (New York: Columbia University Press, 2012), 45. I used "Koog" ever since as my first name (since Koog-Pyoung is too long and difficult to pronounce), and when I came back later to the U.S. for my own study, it was only natural for me to go by that name. All my American friends and colleagues call me as Koog, which led to several funny mix-ups. When they discussed me with other Koreans, almost none of the Koreans could associate the name "Koog" with me, whom they knew as "Hong Guk-Pyoung." In that way, my Self has been torn part, or practically lost in translation. Additionally, the Americanized name fails to convey the intended meaning of the name. Now, the thought of presenting my father with a copy of this book, which I dedicate to him, bearing the name he meant me to carry and embody in this world, fills me with joy.

I came to realize that I was embracing others' questions. Gadamer promotes the importance of knowing the question by introducing Collingwood's remark, "we can understand a text only when we have understood the question to which it is an answer."[12] For long, I have merely adopted "their" answers without fully understanding "their" questions. This is not a path for a healthy relationship with the text that I love. Which questions I pose defines "who I am" as a scholar. I realized that in following others' questions passively, I could risk losing the opportunity to develop my own character as a Korean biblical scholar. I began to ask what makes me unique as a biblical scholar and what genuine contributions I, as a Korean, can bring to the field. I must cultivate my own questions, questions that are rooted in my own context. However, if those questions bring about answers that are meaningful only to Koreans, my studies' value will be confined in my own context. Thus, I began to look for questions that only Koreans can ask but entailing general implications to biblical scholarship.

It is at this point that I have become increasingly disillusioned with simply following traditional questions. It is not because their questions became suddenly meaningless. I could see more clearly than before that those major questions posed by the giants of our field, as I have always been trained to recognize, were also products of their contexts. They were meaningful in their time and space, but their significance cannot be merely translated into different contexts. As a Korean scholar, I must also consider cultural factors in addition to the time factor that Western scholars typically consider. Therefore, before transplanting traditional questions into a new context, they must first be *processed* properly. In my view, this presents a chance to uncover the degree to which Western scholars have projected a largely Western-oriented framework and perspective onto this *oriental* text.[13] I aim to move beyond the constraints of "their" questions, reframe my interpretation of the Bible within my cultural context, and share my insights with biblical scholars across the globe. Fortunately, Korea boasts a long and vibrant history with abundant cultural assets that can contribute to this cause.

Finally, my teaching experience, both at undergraduate and graduate levels, was another critical factor that gave form to my struggle for Korean biblical scholarship. Initially, I strove to help my students recognize the academic and practical significance of modern biblical scholarship and to replicate my astonishment, both in its own right and the way it was later challenged. However, as I

---

12 Hans Georg Gadamer, *Truth and Method*, 2nd ed. (London: Continuum, 2004), 363–71. See R. G. Collingwood, *An Autobiography* (London: Oxford University Press, 1939), 29–43.
13 Cf. Uriah Y. Kim, *Decolonizing Josiah: Toward a Postcolonial Reading of the Deuteronomistic History* (Sheffield: Sheffield Phoenix Press, 2005); idem, *Identity and Loyalty in the David Story: A Postcolonial Reading* (Sheffield: Sheffield Phoenix Press, 2008).

was developing my thoughts on cultivating contextual questions, I became increasingly dissatisfied with my pedagogy. My students in general are less invested in the Bible than students of my generation. The result is a growing disinterest in this ancient and unfamiliar text. While this may be a universal problem in today's world, it is more pressing for Koreans due to their cultural distance from the West. From the outset, they were naturally less likely to be intrigued by the way critics like Wellhausen posed questions about the authorship of the Bible. The bigger problem, of course, is that today's students in general are more familiar with post-modern perspectives, and thus naturally more receptive to new ideas such as the polyphony of the text. Without considering the growing distance between my students and critical scholars, I was continually striving to equip them with critical scholarship only to debunk it later. It was only a matter of time before I began to question if this was the right way to teach the Bible in Korea today.

I began to explore a new way of teaching the Bible, inviting students to engage with the text by posing context-oriented questions. For instance, when introducing the Pentateuch, I would begin by posing a simple question, "what makes you a Korean?" Students at first take this puzzling because most of them take their national identity for granted and see no connection to the Pentateuch. Koreans believe that they have cohabited on the Korean peninsula for thousands of years, which offers a more tangible basis to imagine biological and cultural commonalities than in most other countries. Despite the popular belief, it is clear that this unity cannot be proven biologically. A simple DNA test would suffice to expose the genetic diversity behind this claimed unity. Slowly, students understand that the meaningfulness of an ethnic origin is called for and shaped by the social and political contexts in which the origin story is received and utilized. Whether we acknowledge it or not, today's Koreans must include descents from various ethnic groups, including Chinese, Mongols, and Japanese, among others, who somehow found ways into the Korean peninsula in different times.[14]

---

14 Nationalist sentiments are still prevalent in today's South Korean society, perhaps because of the conflict-laden recent history and the present geo-political circumstances that remind persistent external threats from neighboring countries like Japan and China, on top of Korea's own political division. Such sentiments are surprisingly dominant among the younger generations as well. This prevalence among the youth may be attributed to their increased exposure to Others through the internet – a space where they spend more time compared to older generations. The heightened interaction with people from other nations often paradoxically reinforces national boundaries, making their national identity more salienced over other levels of identity. As a result, when I challenge the idea that the boundary between Korea, Japan, and China is clear-cut, it inevitably leads to a strong nationalist backlash, as I have experienced in the classroom.

Thus, I would often ask students what they would do if their DNA tests revealed deeper connections to China or Japan. Such questions may be familiar to those who live in a multiethnic community, but not to students in Korea, which is largely conceived as a monoethnic country. With little help, students engage in a lively debate about what it means to identify themselves as Koreans. Thus far, none of them has answered that their identity as Korean would be affected. This question is effective in shattering my students' naïve assumptions about their political identity.

This naturally leads to the question of how Koreans' sense of being "one people" has been constructed. Most of their answers are related to common biological and cultural traits, such as language, appearance, food, and the land. As we continue the discussion, students begin to see that the experiences that make them feel the strongest sense of Korean-ness are sports, travel, and war movies. And what shapes these experiences is the contact with Others, both near and distant. Importantly, many of these contacts with Others are experienced and expressed in narrative forms. For example, in the case of the national soccer competition against Japan, Korea's greatest rival, the game is not simply viewed as a soccer match, but rather as the latest chapter in a larger narrative that previous matches have built. Additionally, it is perceived in the context of the historical narrative of Japanese colonization, which imbues the match with a symbolic significance.

I then equip them with theoretical languages and tools, such as Fredrik Barth's "ethnicity and boundaries," Benedict Anderson's "imagined communities," Eric Hobsbawm's "invention of traditions," and Bruce Lincoln's "discourse and the construction of society."[15] I discuss how stories from the distant past, which commemorate heroic mythic figures and momentous events such as war, persecution, or liberation, serve as instruments for bonding disparate social units that collectively claim their origin in the mythic past.[16]

This helps students realize that historical and scientific inquiries are inadequate when it comes to examining the origin of an ethnic group. Instead, stu-

---

15 Fredrik Barth, ed., *Ethnic Groups and Boundaries: The Social Organization of Culture Difference* (Boston: Little, Brown and Co., 1969); Benedict Anderson, *Imagined Communities: Reflections on the Origin and Spread of Nationalism*, Rev. ed. (London: Verso, 2006); Eric Hobsbawm and Terence Ranger, eds., *The Invention of Tradition*, Past and Present Publications (Cambridge: Cambridge University Press, 1983); Bruce Lincoln, *Discourse and the Construction of Society: Comparative Studies of Myth, Ritual, and Classification* (New York: Oxford University Press, 1989).
16 Jacob Wright has been investigating the function of war commemoration in this regard. See Jacob L. Wright, *David, King of Israel, and Caleb in Biblical Memory* (New York: Cambridge University Press, 2014); idem, *War, Memory, and National Identity in the Hebrew Bible* (Cambridge: Cambridge University Press, 2020).

dents come to understand the heuristic force of the "shared belief"[17] in a common origin, and how this sense of unity is constructed and sustained through a shared culture and education. These scholars also observe how significant stories from the past provide a concrete foundation for envisioning a primordial unity, all the while masking *many* faces of real Koreans.[18] After recognizing the ideological and discursive nature of their own identity, my students can then engage with the Pentateuch with a new perspective and genuine interest. At this point, I introduce the scholarly proposition that we can read Genesis and Exodus as fundamentally different types of origin myths and guide them to compare them with other foundation myths, including some from our own culture, and they begin to see the Pentateuch in a new light. Finally, I present the enduring efforts to redefine "Israel," as they are presented in the Hebrew Bible and continue to resonate throughout history, culminating in Paul's pivotal, Christian reinterpretation. When one comes to understand that their engagement with the Old Testament has fundamentally been through the interpretive lens in the process of redefining Christian identity, I see some true learning commences in young minds.

I cannot assert that my contextual approach to teaching the Bible is less challenging for students from conservative backgrounds compared to employing critical theories, such as the documentary hypothesis, as a guiding principle. However, I can say with certainty that this approach has added value because it helps my students to understand the why and how of reading the Old Testament as Christians. When approached from a traditional perspective, students tend to view Israel's ancestral tradition as objective historical facts from the past. They may wonder why they should read this ancient history that belonged to others. However, as students learn that this text served as Israel's identity narrative, they come to understand how they too, without even realizing it, are embracing this text as their own identity narrative, albeit in different ways. This also opens their eyes to recognize the importance of the thousands of years of interpretive endeavors that have strived to make this ancient text relevant to so many people, even modern Koreans, who desire to embrace the much-valued identity of God's chosen people.

This book is a product of my ongoing struggle to find myself as a Korean biblical scholar and teacher, and to find a way to contribute to the field as my authentic Self. Throughout the years, I have examined various issues and different parts of the Hebrew Bible from this perspective, and this book only touches

---

[17] Daniel Bar-Tal, *Shared Beliefs in a Society: Social Psychological Analysis* (Thousand Oaks, CA: Sage, 2000).

[18] Cf. Anthony P. Cohen, *The Symbolic Construction of Community* (Chichester: E. Horwood and Tavistock, 1985), 44.

on one of them. As initially stated, the focus of this book is the North-South dynamic in Israel and Judah's eventful history, which is informed by my experiences in Korea. Upon reflecting on my encounter with Nicholson's perspective, I now see with greater clarity that my initial hesitation to fully embrace his view stemmed from my dissatisfaction with his simplistic perspective, which appears to uncritically accept the biblical text's portrayal of Judah and Israel's primordial unity. My Korean background has made me more skeptical of essentialist perspectives that assume origins determine intergroup relations.[19] My life experience in Korea has made me acutely aware that the past is not a fixed space but rather an arena of struggle. When two or more parties are entangled in conflicting relationships, there are more crucial factors than claimed origins. I believe that biblical scholars often underestimate the significance of the rivalry between Judah and Israel in *realpolitik*, instead accepting their claimed unity at face value.

This is the background that prompted my initial question about how Judahites felt about their Israelite identity. The implications of this question should now be clearer. Informed by my context, I am interested in exploring the subjective element of Judah's self-perception, moving beyond an objective investigation of Judah or Israel's origins. Specifically, I focus on Judah's perceived inferiority to Israel, shifting attention from historical facts to the social and psychological aspects of Judah's relationship with Israel.

In venturing into this exploration, I am acutely aware that the choice of subtitle, "a contextual approach," may prompt reservations among some readers. To many, especially in a series that has traditionally celebrated historical, critical, and philological dimensions, the term "contextual" could be seen as hinting at a personal or ideologically skewed reading. To some, it might even appear as an autobiography masquerading as objective interpretation, suggesting it incommensurable with "critical" readings. Such critiques, while anticipated, underscore the very complexities and challenges this work seeks to navigate. I contemplate the essence of what truly constitutes "critical" thought. Does it lie more in the candidness with which I recognize the context that shapes my insights or in the tendency to remain entrenched in a "normative" paradigm, blinded to one's own biases, while relegating alternative perspectives to the status of "contextual" or "peripheral"? It is paramount to emphasize that my invocation of context is not an abandonment of critical rigor but rather an enrichment of it. In today's scholarly landscape, it is universally understood that historians and interpreters do not operate from a

---

19 It is not claimed that Koreans are generally more drawn into such skepticism. Given the dominant conservative sentiments in Korean Christianity, doubting the historical veracity of biblical traditions would engender serious criticism especially from the popular level. It is only that my contemplations on my context presented me heightened sensitivity on these issues.

vacuum; their unique contexts invariably shape their perspectives. Yet, all too often, this insight is merely acknowledged in passing, while the march towards "objectivity" proceeds with minimal self-examination. This work, in its candid recognition of its contextual underpinnings, underscores the necessity for all scholarship to engage introspectively with its own biases, bridging the often-perceived divide between "committed" and "scientific" interpretations.

Conversely, some might defend my approach, emphasizing that despite its contextual guise, its nature is ultimately historical given that it aims to solve an established historical question on Judah's relationship with Israel. While I appreciate their efforts, if that is the sole avenue through which they can appreciate my work, I will have to respectfully decline that defense. My research does not shy away from its contextual roots, nor do I intend to retrofit it to fit into a historical mold. I fully recognize that my perspective is a product of my unique context. I would add that other scholars, even the most rigorous historical critics, also inevitably draw upon their own backgrounds when conducting their research.

Many readers, while resonating with my critical stance, might still find its content and perspectives too foreign to their own experiences, thus feeling justified to set it aside as not applicable to them. I deeply understand this sentiment, as that feeling is hardly foreign to me. My point simply is that most non-Western scholars do not have the luxury to dismiss what is unfamiliar to them. Instead, they are expected to internalize the discourse of Western scholars – not only the main thesis but all the contextual illustrations and all else that come with it – regardless of its unfamiliarity.[20] It is only just that I, too, should have the liberty to incorporate my own examples without fearing them being seen as a sign that sanctions conventional readers to dismiss my work as deviating from the standard modus operandi in our field.

1.3 Narrative as a Tool

I understand identity as a social process influenced by the dynamic interplay between the Self and Others.[21] However, most traditional biblical scholars in the past have treated collective identities, such as "Israel," as inherently fixed, static, and unchanging, rendering it ill-equipped to address the social and psychological

---

20 Of course, I am not asking others to engage in hyper self-censorship or to strive for an ultra-neutral tone in their scholarly discussions. But I simply have to let this out because I often feel quite scary how I am becoming more familiar with those *foreign* examples than my own.
21 One finds a concise discussion in Richard Jenkins, *Social Identity*, 3rd ed., Key Ideas (London: Routledge, 2008), 1–15.

aspects of my inquiry. Scholars debated on the classification of "Israel" as either an ethnic, religious, or class-based group, but most of them viewed the matter through a historical lens and approached it like any other empirical fact that could be verified through available evidence.

Today, the situation has changed drastically. On the one hand, biblical scholars are no longer confident in embracing the "positivist" perspective regarding the historical value of biblical traditions, especially those related to foundational eras. Half a century ago, Thomas Thompson's challenge to the historicity of the Abraham tradition caused a serious controversy, but I wonder how many biblical historians would consider the patriarchal history as part of Israel's historical era today.[22] Related is the increasing tendency to date Israel's foundation traditions to a late period. The Pentateuchal tradition played an instrumental role in shaping the idea of "one people," and dating these texts to exilic or post-exilic eras undermines the ground for the perceived unity as one people. Recent archaeological discoveries support these observations. The majority of archaeologists now agree that the ancestral tradition described in the text is likely reflective of the Iron-age material world. The glorious era of David and Solomon is also largely considered a late idealization. As a result, an increasing number of scholars today start their historical presentation of Israel with the Omrides in the North.[23]

On the other hand, significant progress has been made in social science, and one of the most important changes is the widespread acceptance of the social construction of identity.[24] Thus, most social scientists today agree to define "ethnicity" in social terms, that is, "not a thing or a collective asset of a particular group" but as "a social relation in which social actors perceive themselves and are

---

22 See now Israel Finkelstein and Thomas Römer, "Comments on the Historical Background of the Abraham Narrative: Between 'Realia' and 'Exegetica,'" *HeBAI* 3 (2014): 4, https://doi.org/10.1628/219222714X13994465496820. For a broader survey of the changing perspective in Israel's early history, see Megan Bishop Moore and Brad E. Kelle, *Biblical History and Israel's Past: The Changing Study of the Bible and History* (Grand Rapids, MI: Eerdmans, 2011), esp. 63; Lester L. Grabbe, *Ancient Israel: What Do We Know and How Do We Know It?*, Rev. ed. (London: Bloomsbury T&T Clark, 2017); Andrew Tobolowsky, "Israelite and Judahite History in Contemporary Theoretical Approaches," *CurBR* 17 (2018): 34, https://doi.org/10.1177/1476993X18765117.
23 E.g., Emanuel Pfoh, *The Emergence of Israel in Ancient Palestine: Historical and Anthropological Perspectives*, Copenhagen International Seminar (Abingdon, Oxon: Routledge, 2009), 161–87. One finds a renewed interest in exploring the real face of the Northern Kingdom. Daniel E. Fleming, *The Legacy of Israel in Judah's Bible: History, Politics, and the Reinscribing of Tradition* (New York: Cambridge University Press, 2012); Israel Finkelstein, *The Forgotten Kingdom: The Archaeology and History of Northern Israel*, ANEM 5 (Atlanta: Society of Biblical Literature, 2013).
24 For a foundational work of this subject relating to biblical history, see Barth, *Ethnic Groups and Boundaries*. For a helpful summary and discussion of ethnic studies from the perspective of the Hebrew Bible, see James C. Miller, "Ethnicity and the Hebrew Bible: Problems and Prospects," *CurBR* 6 (2008): 170–213, https://doi.org/10.1177/1476993x07083627.

perceived by others as being culturally distinct collectivities."[25] This perspective is vastly different from the traditional approach, introducing an entirely new way of comprehending a people, kingdom, or nation. Ethnic groups share a belief that they originated with a single figure. But no ethnic group, despite their claims, owns a genuine united past. People are only *made* to believe so, because they need to.[26] Diverse groups happen to live together, and their social reality of sharing the space, culture, and time requires stories that explain who they are and where they came from. In the same vein, no group entity begins with a remarkable, unique, and splendid origin; every origin is humble and ordinary. It is what they later become that demands a narrative that matches its grandeur and obscures the forgettable origin.[27] Many scholars who study Israel's origin begin with a discussion of the Merneptah Stele, but how ironic is it that one initiates the quest for an ethnic group's origin in an inscription that declares its extinction?[28]

Assigning our detailed discussion on the theoretical side of the functional approach to below (Chapter 7), let me briefly summarize what I aim to achieve by adopting this perspective. Firstly, the past is a constructed space. The notion that the past is constructed aligns with evolving perspectives of contemporary historians and incorporates social-scientific concepts such as the "invented past," "imagined communities," and "discursive construction of society."[29] It is important to clarify that the main emphasis is not on highlighting the fictitious nature. Instead, I aim to underscore the inherently constructive nature of recounting the past, even when grounded in facts. Secondly, acknowledging the constructed nature of the past directs attention to its impact on the identity formation of the present. Remembering our origins inevitably shapes our sense of Self. This means, I understand the text not merely as history but place it within the sphere of identity discourse. My aim is to shift from a linear perspective of historical progression and preservation, and instead explore how the ongoing negotiation

---

25 Siniša Malešević, *The Sociology of Ethnicity* (London: Sage, 2004), 4.

26 Cf. James Richard Linville, *Israel in the Book of Kings: The Past as a Project of Social Identity*, JSOTSup 272 (Sheffield: Sheffield Academic Press, 1998), 31.

27 See Peter Machinist, "Outsiders or Insiders: The Biblical View of Emergent Israel and Its Contexts," in *The Other in Jewish Thought and History: Constructions of Jewish Culture and Identity*, ed. Laurence J. Silberstein and Robert L. Cohn, New Perspectives on Jewish Studies (New York: New York University Press, 1994), 51.

28 See Aren Maeir, "On Defining Israel: Or, Let's Do the Kulturkreislehre Again!," *HeBAI* 10 (2021): 127, https://doi.org/10.1628/hebai-2021-0010. Cf. Michael G. Hasel, "Israel in the Merneptah Stela," *BASOR* 296 (1994): 45–61, https://doi.org/10.2307/1357179; K. W. Whitelam, "'Israel Is Laid Waste; His Seed Is No More': What If Merneptah's Scribes Were Telling the Truth?," in *Virtual History and the Bible*, ed. J. Cheryl Exum (Leiden: Brill, 2000), 8–22.

29 Hobsbawm and Ranger, *The Invention of Tradition*; Anderson, *Imagined Communities*; Lincoln, *Discourse and the Construction of Society*.

of the present continually reshapes the past.[30] This approach shifts the focus of biblical narratives away from merely being objective accounts of "what actually happened," and instead encourages us to embrace the subjective aspect of "who we are," which is inherently woven into how we remember the past. Thirdly, identity is often expressed in narrative forms and we can interpret past narratives as tools for identity formation, highlighting their instrumentality in (re)shaping the past. Through this lens, I aim to investigate how the stories of Jacob and Abraham portray Israel's origins in distinct ways, and to discern how their negotiation contributed to pivotal transformations in the course of the growth of biblical ancestral tradition.

My goal is not to offer a groundbreaking literary-critical reading of the Jacob and Abraham traditions. Instead, the merit of my take on the Jacob and Abraham narratives should be evaluated within the broader scope of my project, which aims to understand the growth of the ancestral traditions as mediums for identity discourse. For this undertaking, diving into new insights in literary-critical readings could dilute the focus. Instead, I choose to adopt an established reading, primarily based on Blum's block model, and showcase how a fresh perspective can provide insights into understanding the functionality of these narratives within the context of Israel's and Judah's identity discourse.

Choosing to foreground identity discourse over history carries some heuristic, and much more radical, implications for me. It suggests a shift from traditional author-centered methods to a reader-focused hermeneutical lens. While my primary question might still be perceived as objective, namely, what relationship did Judah maintain with Israel, it concurrently connects to a new realm of inquiry: What does this relationship signify for diverse readers living in the twenty-first century? If Judah indeed appropriated Israel's identity, and rewrote Israel's past, that means Judah was among the first readers of Israel's traditions. Then, one can relate Judah with many other empirical readers in history who also participated in their own acts of appropriation of Israel. Western readers might not prioritize such insights, assuming their innate right in owning this text albeit on problematic grounds, but for someone like me, living on the peripheries, pondering the significance of "their" Bible to "me" provides a critical point of divergence for introspection.

---

30 In essence, this is why I am deeply interested in the field of reception history. Hans Robert Jauss, *Literaturgeschichte als Provokation* (Frankfurt am Main: Suhrkamp, 1970); idem, *Toward an Aesthetic of Reception*, Theory and History of Literature 2 (Minneapolis: University of Minnesota Press, 1982); idem, *Aesthetic Experience and Literary Hermeneutics*, Theory and History of Literature 3 (Minneapolis: University of Minnesota Press, 1982); Anthony C. Thiselton, "Reception Theory, H. R. Jauss and the Formative Power of Scripture," *SJT* 65 (2012): 289–308, https://doi.org/10.1017/S0036930612000129.

Overall, this shift in perspective resonates well with biblical scholars' efforts to sociologically (broadly defined) expand or adapt historical criticism using social-scientific approaches. Between the two, there is no *better* way; rather, the suitability of a method hinges on the nature of the question being explored and the nuances of the text under scrutiny. In this book, as we delve into topics such as the self-perception of Judah and Israel, their intertwined identities, and their mutual interactions, it is clear that both historical and sociological viewpoints are indispensable. It is this reason I aim to broaden historical insights through social-scientific lenses.

1.4 Brief Review of Scholarship

My work builds upon major precursors, from a range of methodological orientations, that have brought fresh perspectives to the understanding of Judah's relationship with Israel. By selectively reviewing major works from various perspectives, let me illustrate where my functional approach fits in and how it can strengthen, rather than oppose, existing scholarship.[31]

I must begin with Daniel Fleming's masterly display of the Israelite legacy in Judah's Bible.[32] Unlike other scholars who tended to view Northern Israel as a mere part of the history of Israel, Fleming clearly recognized it as a subject for investigation in its own right. Like my project, Fleming primarily investigates Israel's textual tradition as his main source, though he puts greater emphasis on situating it in the wider context of the Ancient Near East. He also introduces other relevant contexts that he deems appropriate to compare.[33] Fleming's investigation covers the entire biblical text, and within the ancestral tradition, which is my focus, he too identifies the Jacob tradition as the core of the northern legacy. Still, his method is historical with a particular interest in the political dimension. He attempts to retrieve the genuine Israel traditions and use it as a basis for a deeper understanding of the nature of Israel. He focuses on the decentralized power as the characteristic of Israel, which he elaborates with the concept of "collaborative politics," illustrating it in comparison with both within and outside Near Eastern context. Still, his overall trajectory of interpretation falls within a largely traditional and evolutionary perspective that traces Israel from herdsmen to decentralized Israel to highly centralized Judah. Thus, the Israelite kingdom is characterized as a more "corporate" and "egalitarian" polity, which he pits against the more

---

31 Regarding the scholarly review on the subject matter of Judah's assumption of the Israel identity, I address it separately in Chapter 3.
32 Fleming, *The Legacy of Israel*.
33 Fleming, 193–201.

centralized and hierarchical Judah in the South.[34] While his objective and cultural observations on the differences between Northern Israel and southern Judah may be noteworthy, the subjective and psychological dimension of Judah's self-perception as a minor entity has not received sufficient attention. He indeed discusses the Israel-Judah dynamic in a section specifically entitled "Judah's Appropriation of Israelite Identity."[35] But his discussion in this section mainly is a review of biblical texts, charting through expressions of Israel in texts like prophetic literature and Chronicles to demonstrate divergent ways in which Judahites embraced the title. Still, when it comes to explaining the motivation of Judah's appropriation of Israel, he tends to fall back on traditional views that some blocks of the David narrative are old and find the root of Judah's aspiration from the authentic memory as "onetime rulers over Israel."[36] Thus, although my project has a lot in common with Fleming's *Legacy of Israel*, there is a considerable divergence between his and my perspectives. I perceive that our differences stem from the divergent methodologies we employ. His is fundamentally rooted in historical pursuit of the origin, of course, on an objective ground, whereas mine is a pursuit of the subjective side as to how Judah's desire as an inferior party drove the entire process of cultural appropriation of the superior Israel.

Israel Finkelstein's revisionist approach, aimed at reinterpreting Israel's history from the archaeological perspective, deserves special mention.[37] Despite our different methodological orientations, I find myself in agreement with much of Finkelstein's interpretation of Judah and Israel. His low chronology, in particular, has been one of the major catalysts for me to rethink the nature of the kingdom of David and Solomon, as well as the history of Israel in general.[38] However, I

---

31 Fleming, 189–92.

35 Fleming, 47–55.

36 Fleming, 49. This idea is further elaborated in Fleming's recent collaborative works with Lauren Monroe, wherein they strive to uncover traces of an earlier Israel before the Omrides. Daniel E. Fleming, "The Bible's Little Israel: Terminological Clasts in a Compositional Matrix," *HeBAI* 10 (2021): 149–86, https://doi.org/10.1628/hebai-2021-0011; Lauren Monroe, "On the Origins and Development of Greater Israel," *HeBAI* 10 (2021): 187–227, https://doi.org/10.1628/hebai-2021-0012.

37 Israel Finkelstein and Neil Asher Silberman, *The Bible Unearthed: Archaeology's New Vision of Ancient Israel and the Origin of Its Sacred Texts* (New York: Free Press, 2001); idem, *David and Solomon: In Search of the Bible's Sacred Kings and the Roots of the Western Tradition* (New York: Free Press, 2006); Israel Finkelstein and Amihai Mazar, *The Quest for the Historical Israel: Debating Archaeology and the History of Early Israel*, ed. Brian B. Schmidt, ABS 17 (Atlanta: Society of Biblical Literature, 2007).

38 Israel Finkelstein, "The Date of the Settlement of the Philistines in Canaan," *TA* 22 (1995): 213–39, https://doi.org/10.1179/tav.1995.1995.2.213; idem, "The Archaeology of the United Monarchy: An Alternative View," *Levant* 28 (1996): 177–87, https://doi.org/10.1179/lev.1996.28.1.177; idem, "Hazor and the North in the Iron Age: A Low Chronology Perspective," *BASOR* 314 (1999): 55–70, https://doi.org/10.2307/1357451; idem, "A Great United Monarchy?: Archaeological and Historical Perspec-

diverge from Finkelstein on a particular, yet critical issue: the significance of the moment after Israel's fall in the making of "biblical Israel."[39] Our disagreement is a matter of nuanced interpretation, as we both agree on the constructed nature of Judah's Israel and the discontinuity between the old "Israel" of the North and the new "Israel" recreated in the South. Unlike his other innovative ideas, at this moment, Finkelstein goes with the traditional way, accepting the influx of mass migrants from the North.[40] He does so because he sees the archaeological evidence of the rapid expansion of Jerusalem cannot be explained other than by a mass migration. I understand his reasoning, and I can accept that there were some refugees. But my problem lies with the effect of uncritically accepting the alleged impact of the refugees because doing so, I see, can be perilous to undo many of his important insights that are conducive to embracing the constructed nature of Judah's Israel. This carries methodological implications. His view is based on archaeological evidence, but I fundamentally believe that, when it comes to discussing "identity" the text must take precedence over material remains. Pig bones can be used as identity markers for non-Israelites, but that is because we know Israel's text tradition that bans pork consumption.[41] In contrast, my functional approach emphasizes Judah's perceived inferiority as the driving force behind its adoption of Israel's identity, thereby spotlighting the discontinuity and revolutionary aspects of this process. To that end, I provide more detailed evidence from the text (in Part II) of how the rewriting of Israel's past contributed to the unlikely success of this identity project.

Kenton Sparks's *Prolegomena* offers a groundbreaking ethnographic approach, tracing ethnic expressions in the Hebrew Bible from the pre-monarchic to the exilic period.[42] There is much to commend in his work, as he attempts to ground his

---

tives," in *One God, One Cult, One Nation: Archaeological and Biblical Perspectives*, ed. Reinhard Gregor Kratz and Hermann Spieckermann (Berlin: Walter de Gruyter, 2010), 3–28; Israel Finkelstein and Eli Piasetzky, "The Iron Age Chronology Debate: Is the Gap Narrowing?," *NEA* 74 (2011): 50–54, https://doi.org/10.5615/neareastarch.74.1.0050.

39 For discussion, see Chapter 3 below.

40 Fleming (*The Legacy of Israel*, 49, 172) also alludes to refugees, though in a more cautious manner.

41 Additionally, Maeir's recent critique of Faust on this matter is worth noting. Maeir, "On Defining Israel," 135. He references recent studies revealing the presence of pig bones in some Israelite and Judahite sites; see Israel Finkelstein, Yuval Gadot, and Lidar Sapir-Hen, "Pig Frequencies in Iron Age Sites and the Biblical Pig Taboo: Once Again," *UF* 49 (2018): 109–16. Maeir then criticizes Faust's argument that pig bones in Israelite regions indicate non-Israelite presence at those sites, labeling it a blatant example of "self-referencing circular argument." For Maeir's discussion of self-referential circularity as a universal problem in the field of archaeology, see Maeir, "On Defining Israel," 122–25.

42 Kenton L. Sparks, *Ethnicity and Identity in Ancient Israel: Prolegomena to the Study of Ethnic Sentiments and Their Expression in the Hebrew Bible* (Winona Lake, IN: Eisenbrauns, 1998).

review of literature in social-scientific studies of ethnicity and gives careful attention to the fluidity and social construction of ethnic identity. While Sparks's theoretical survey may not be the most up-to-date, he was well ahead of his time
when he published his work, at least among biblical scholars. Especially, Sparks's
interpretation of the early expressions of ethnic identity, which he traces through
classical prophecy, as more prominent in the North and the later emergence of
Judah's identity aligns with the essential framework of my study. However, there
are divergences that call for further exploration. First, Sparks excludes the Pentateuch and Deuteronomistic history from his investigation, influenced by his teacher Van Seters who dates them to post-monarchic eras.[43] As a result, Sparks's survey
only indirectly examines the foundational traditions of Israel, by extracting information from scattered references in prophetic literature. Second, Sparks makes
an erroneous dichotomy in his analysis of identity expressions in the monarchic
era, categorizing the North as ethnic and the South as religious and social in
nature. This perspective is largely informed by his reliance on classical prophecy,
citing Hosea for the North and Isaiah and Amos for the South. As I shall demonstrate in part II of this book, ethnic identity expressions are also pronounced in
Judah, which is well displayed through the Abraham narrative as against Israel's
Jacob narrative. Thirdly, my critique of Finkelstein's approach to the transitional
period from Israel to Judah also applies to Sparks. Like Finkelstein, Sparks assumes that the transmission of northern materials to the south and the emergence
of Judah's identity can be explained by the movement of northern refugees.

Carly Crouch's anthropological approach demands attention, insofar as her
work is entitled "The Making of Israel" and purportedly examines the construction of "Israel" in seventh-century Judah.[44] Despite the title, Crouch gives surprisingly little attention to the socio-political dynamic between Judah and Israel. That
is so, even when Deuteronomy consistently uses "Israel," the name *owned* by the
recently fallen Northern Kingdom, as the term for Judah's communal self-definition. The reason goes back to the nature of her study, which is essentially a study
of Deuteronomy.[45] Crouch argues that the book functioned as an identity project
for the Judahites during the seventh century, a period marked by an identity crisis
triggered by increased cultural interaction in the southern Levant as a result of
the *pax Assyriaca*. Crouch argues that her focus on the internal Levantine dynamic is justified by an anthropological observation that intense identity threats tend

---

43 Sparks, 14–16, 329.
44 Carly L. Crouch, *The Making of Israel: Cultural Diversity in the Southern Levant and the Formation of Ethnic Identity in Deuteronomy*, VTSup 162 (Leiden: Brill, 2014).
45 The subtitle proves to be more fitting than the main.

to come from proximate Others rather than distant ones.[46] While I entirely agree with this point itself, her application of it within this specific context raises questions. If similarity is as much a cause for identity struggle, then the lack of attention given to the alterity/similarity to the Northern Kingdom – the most crucial proximate Other to Judah – is all the more striking.[47] Throughout the book, Crouch makes few passing references to the Northern Kingdom, which are made only in reference to material culture. There are two-fold reasons. First, her anthropological survey of the seventh century Levant provides little need to pay heed to North Israel given its fall several decades prior, but doing so overlooks the lingering effect of the superior rival on Judah's psyche. Second, another point worth noting is Crouch's interpretation of Deuteronomy's use of "Israel" as a sign of the Deuteronomic author's pan-Israelism, which, for her, discounts the old political division as a factor.[48] Here, Crouch combines an established perception of the Deuteronomic Israel's idealized nature and her theoretical categorization of this Israel as an "ethnic" concept, which, she argues, must be detached from the nationalist concern of Judahite state.[49] As a result, despite employing various

---

46 Crouch, 94–97.

47 That is, let alone the larger political threat posed by Assyria, the effect of which Crouch plays down next to its consequence in increased cultural interaction within the region. She criticizes earlier scholars for the oversight, who formed their investigation around Assyrian threats. Norbert Lohfink, "Culture Shock and Theology: A Discussion of Theology as a Cultural and a Sociological Phenomenon Based on the Example of a Deuteronomic Law," *BTB* 7 (1977): 12–22, https://doi.org/10.1177/014610797700700104; Louis Stulman, "Encroachment in Deuteronomy: An Analysis of the Social World of the D Code," *JBL* 109 (1990): 613–32, https://doi.org/10.2307/3267366; Peter Machinist, "The Rab Šāqēh at the Wall of Jerusalem: Israelite Identity in the Face of the Assyrian 'Other,'" *HS* 41 (2000): 151–68, https://doi.org/10.1353/hbr.2000.0039. For my perspective on Judah's struggle with North Israel, see "The Golden Calf of Bethel and Judah's Mimetic Desire of Israel," *JSOT* 47 (2023): 359–71, https://doi.org/10.1177/03090892231168657.

48 Similarly, Sparks, *Ethnicity and Identity in Ancient Israel*, 235.

49 Crouch (*The Making of Israel*, 6) places a great deal of emphasis on the distinction between ethnicity and nationalism. Cf. Fleming's understanding of Israel as a polity, not an ethnicity. Fleming, *The Legacy of Israel*, 18–23. There are several problems. First, applying such a strict distinction between ethnicity and nationalism risks imposing modern concepts onto an ancient context. In my view, modern European concepts of ethnicity and nationalism are not applicable to ancient contexts. I believe that the ancient Israel encompasses elements of both ethnicity and nationalism, yet it cannot be perfectly defined by either. As an Asian, I have seen enough how the modern European concepts of ethnie or nation have been abused as an analytic category to evaluate polities in other regions and time, including those of East Asia. As a result, I refrain from using them as normative categories. The matter becomes more complex when a term from one linguistic context is applied to other contexts. This problem is evident in the fact that both ἔθνος in Greek and *natio* in Latin cover comparable meanings that encompass modern understanding of both nationalism and ethnicity. I believe ethnic studies must be primarily a descriptive analysis insofar as the idea of people and nation differed in each context. Cf. Clifford Geertz,

theories, Crouch appears to fall back on the conventional view of Israel and Judah's unity, which I find disappointing.[50] To me, more important than the question of whether Deuteronomy's "Israel" is an ethnic or national term is discerning *who* was behind this concept.[51] This ideal Israel could have served Northern Israel's cultic identity, the seventh century Judahites or the exilic and post-exilic Judeans, if they repurposed it for their causes. It is more productive to observe how

---

The Interpretation of Cultures: Selected Essays (New York: Basic Books, 1973); Anthony D. Smith, *Nationalism and Modernism: A Critical Survey of Recent Theories of Nations and Nationalism* (London: Routledge, 1998). Second, Crouch's sharp distinction between ethnicity and nationalism is solely based on Calhoun, but one must wonder if Calhoun intended to draw such a clear distinction. Craig Calhoun, "Nationalism and Ethnicity," *Annual Review of Sociology* 19 (1993): 211–39, https://doi.org/10.1146/annurev.so.19.080193.001235. Crouch repeatedly makes a quote from this paper's abstract: "Nationalism, in particular, remains the pre-eminent rhetoric for attempts to demarcate political communities, claim rights of self-determination and legitimate rule by reference to 'the people' of a country. Ethnic solidarities and identities are claimed most often where groups do not seek 'national' autonomy but rather a recognition internal to or cross-cutting national or state boundaries." However, Crouch leaves out the subsequent sentence from her quote, which, in my judgment, forms an integral element of Calhoun's thesis: "The possibility of a closer link to nationalism is seldom altogether absent from such ethnic claims, however, and the two sorts of categorical identities are often invoked in similar ways." The reality is that ethnic and nationalist sentiments are intricately related, as national entities frequently employ ethnic sentiments, and ethnic groups evoke nationalist sentiments when necessary. What is more important is to observe the strategic ways in which human groups adopt and mobilize different aspects and levels of their multilayered identity in specific situations, rather than rigidly categorizing them as either ethnic or national groups.

50 More recently, Crouch has promoted a more radical proposal that "Israel" began to designate the first wave exiled group (in 597 BCE), whereas "Judah" was taken to indicate those who resided in the land. Carly L. Crouch, *Israel and Judah Redefined: Migration, Trauma, and Empire in the Sixth Century BCE*, Society for Old Testament Study Monographs (Cambridge: Cambridge University Press, 2021). I will have to address this elsewhere.

51 Rather, the dialectic between "ethnic" and "civic" concepts of nationhood (see Chapter 5 for discussion and literature) appears to be more significant. While applying this modern framework to the study of ancient texts may present its own challenges, it offers valuable insights for understanding Genesis and Exodus-Deuteronomy as distinct expressions of "ethnic" and "civic" identity, respectively. The ancestral tradition, based on a concrete sense of kinship terms, is more appropriate for "ethnic" identity, as Deuteronomy promotes an abstract and idealized depiction that is better suited for a more religious and ideological side of identity. I do not view this as a matter of importance, but rather as an issue of different functions for each tradition. While the ancestral tradition imagines Israel as being rooted in the lineage of Abraham, Isaac, and Jacob, Exodus-Deuteronomy fundamentally presents a different perspective. "Israel" is not a given but made by those loyal to the "constitution" and that is how a group of slaves, or "the mixed multitude" could become the covenantal community of Yhwh's people. I see these as two major social voices in determining "what makes one Israelite," both of which were always present in social negotiations, constantly competing yet ultimately balancing each other.

these traditions were utilized as discursive tools to serve specific agendas of different times, rather than trying to fix them to a specific historical juncture.

Lastly, Andrew Tobolowsky's works align more closely with my approach. Drawing parallels with classical Greek mythology studies, Tobolowsky contends that the twelve-tribe system is a late Judean construct from the post-exilic period.[52] In particular, his focus on the constructed nature of the past – termed the "cultural invention" method in his word – resonates well with my functional approach.[53] Nevertheless, our methodologies differ in nuanced ways, reflecting the distinct subject matters and time period we each prioritize. While both of us acknowledge the constructed nature of history, Tobolowsky focuses primarily on Judah's late invention of the twelve-tribe system. In contrast, I spotlight the merging of the Abraham and Jacob traditions before the establishment of the twelve-tribe ideal. My assertion is that the making of the Abrahamic Israel demands a separate attention, which might have entailed its own significance before or in relation to the emergence of the pan-Israel ideal.[54] For the sake of clarity, throughout this book, I will refer to Tobolowsky's subject as "pan-Israelism" (twelve-tribe Israel) as he often terms it, while designating mine as the "Abrahamic Israel" (Abraham-Isaac-Jacob).

The most important distinction between our works lies in the focus on North Israel.[55] Tobolowsky's analysis, anchored in a later time frame, tends to sideline

---

52 Andrew Tobolowsky, *The Sons of Jacob and the Sons of Herakles: The History of the Tribal System and the Organization of Biblical Identity*, FAT 2/96 (Tübingen: Mohr Siebeck, 2017).

53 Andrew Tobolowsky, *The Myth of the Twelve Tribes of Israel: New Identities Across Time and Space* (Cambridge: Cambridge University Press, 2022), 45–59. This book delves into how Israel became an object of appropriation for various groups, a point aligns seamlessly with the core premise of my research.

54 This historical alignment remains open to interpretation. While I maintain that the tribalization portrayed in the text emerges from a literary layer subsequent to that of the Abrahamic Israel, it does not dictate a rigid chronological progression for the foundational ideas behind these dual representations of Israel. One interpretation positions Judah as simply another tribe within Israel, while the other, as I argue in this volume, seeks to amplify Judah's prominence vis-à-vis Israel, highlighting Abraham as the forefather of Jacob. In the latter perspective, there exist numerous potential ways to integrate Judah into Israel's genealogy, of which the current form might not necessarily be the most straightforward one. It is plausible that these interpretations either competed or coexisted independently, ultimately merging into the current text. On the other hand, our understanding of historical sequencing could be further complicated by the potential existence of earlier, distinct tribal configurations, including those of the Northern Kingdom, predating Judah's conception of a twelve-tribe Israel.

55 Naturally, another distinction lies in his emphasis on genealogy, whereas I am more drawn to the broader narrative depiction of identity. Specifically, note his critique of Robert Wilson's older model in light of the contemporary social-scientific understanding of genealogy. Tobolowsky, *The Sons of Jacob and the Sons of Herakles*, 2–11.

North Israel.[56] Consequently, within his exploration, Israel's influence on Judah's conceptualization of pan-Israelism is not brought to the fore.[57] The oversight aligns with contemporary critics who view Judah's identity formation as constrained to the Persian and Hellenistic periods. In contrast, I underscore the necessity of acknowledging the stage predating this late idealization. The pre-exilic era is saturated with Judah's rivalry with Israel. Although these sentiments might have receded in Judah's subsequent pan-Israelite ideal, they were once paramount and indelibly left their marks on the text. These nuances risk being overlooked if our analysis is confined to the later periods.

Most of these scholars, perhaps with the exception of Tobolowsky, lean towards the traditional perspective of viewing Israel and Judah as brethren to varying extents. My aim is to contest this perspective by employing a functional approach to explore how this perception of unity between Israel and Judah was a social and discursive construct, out of their prolonged social interaction, rather than a given reality. Thus, I do not regard this as a matter of excavating Israel's true origin, where they came from or who they really were, or determining whether Israel was a nation, an *ethnie*, or a social class. It is true that Judah and Israel came to become significant Others to each other,[58] more so than with other neighbors in the region, but simply attributing it to an innate bond would ignore the constructed nature of their unity. Rather, it is important to ask how this sense of unity was constructed and who played a role in driving it.

I conceive identity as a social function, with Tobolowsky and more so than the other scholars discussed before him, and it is through this perspective that I aim to explore my initial question concerning the self-perception of the Judahites. I stress that identity is mainly expressed in narrative forms. Thus, I highlight narratives' functionality in constructing the collective self-understanding. Naturally, the primary resource for my approach is the text rather than archaeological or cultural observations, which cannot contain direct information on the subjective side of Judah's relationship with Israel. In particular, I choose the ancestral tradition. Drawing upon the insights of historians who emphasize the instrumen-

---

56 This also led him to embrace the origin of the Jacob narrative, to which the tribalization owes much, as a late southern Judean construct. In this, he accepts Liverani and Na'aman's arguments of the Jacob tradition's post-exilic southern origin. Tobolowsky, 100–101. See Mario Liverani, *Israel's History and the History of Israel* (London: Equinox, 2005); Nadav Na'aman, "The Jacob Story and the Formation of Biblical Israel," *TA* 41 (2014): 95–125, https://doi.org/10.1179/0334435514Z.00000000032.

57 But see his interest in later recurrence of the North's influence in the form of Judah's relations with the Samaritans. Tobolowsky, *The Myth of the Twelve Tribes of Israel*, 66–106.

58 Most would take their common religion as a deciding factor, but that could also be a product of one party's imitation of the other rather than a reflection of their innate connection.

tality of the past in shaping the present, I believe that the past is a formative space for the present, and that past narratives play a critical role in constructing the identity of present-day groups. I stress the heuristic effect of remembering figures such as Jacob and Abraham as ancestors. The historical accuracy of these stories is not the only important factor, but also the value they instill in those who claim them. In my view, Jacob and Abraham were remembered not simply because their stories were available and collected by historians, but because the Israelites and Judahites required a discursive basis to imagine their origin as a group.

Like other scholars, I assume that the Jacob story was the original foundation of "Jacobean Israel" in the North. My focus lies in exploring how the Abrahamic expansion fundamentally reoriented the underlying Jacob tradition and its implications – taking it not as a natural growth but a strategic reformulation.[59] I will emphasize the causal chain of this narrative reorientation of "Abrahamic Israel" and its impact on Judah's collective self-understanding.

Of course, this Abrahamic reorientation was not a one-time event but underwent retouching in subsequent eras, and each literary manifestation may reflect the much bigger and complex social and discursive dimensions behind the scenes. Through my analysis of the "Abrahamic Israel" as a Judahite construct, I argue that this identity shift was one of the most significant and successful programs in the history of Israel and Judah. Its enduring influence, palpable even today, reveals Judah's deepest identity complex that drove this project.

1.5 Summary of Chapters

The book unfolds over two parts, designed to illuminate how Judah's past serves its present self-perception. Part I delves into Judah's desire for Israel, emphasizing the perceived inferiority as an underlying driving force. Part II examines the ways in which this desire is reflected in Israel's ancestral narratives. As described, the focus is on Judah's rewriting of Israel's ancestral narrative, particularly how the foundational Jacob narrative was reoriented by the Abraham tradition. This reworking redefined the old Israel and ushered in a new, Abrahamic Israel.

---

59 Milstein's concept of "revision through introduction," supported by "hard evidence" from Mesopotamian and biblical texts, reflects my understanding of the "forward expansion" of Israel's ancestral past. Sara J. Milstein, *Tracking the Master Scribe: Revision Through Introduction in Biblical and Mesopotamian Literature* (New York: Oxford University Press, 2016). Although her case studies do not include Genesis, I maintain that reframing the Jacob tradition by placing Abraham at the beginning of Israel's lineage serves as a fitting example of "revision through introduction."

In Chapter 2, I set forth the reasoning for the contextual and functional approach adopted in this project by examining the dual conceptions of "Israel" in biblical literature and how they are reconciled into a coherent narrative. While the text emphasizes the ultimate unity of Israel and portrays the political division as a temporary issue to be resolved, I question the tendency to overstate the value of the claimed unity in real-life intergroup dynamics, using the example of the division between North and South Korea despite their extensive shared history, culture, and land. I make a critical juxtaposition, highlighting that while North and South Korea's relationship might superficially echo that of Judah and Israel, the underpinnings differ significantly. North and South Korea's dynamic is underlined by ethnic and political rifts, representing one people divided into two nations. Conversely, while Judah and Israel are ostensibly represented as such, they were fundamentally distinct entities in real. It was only from the vantage of the inferior Judah that they envisaged themselves as integral to, and eventually as a leading tribe of, Israel. This underscores that, contrary to the Korean situation, the salient issue lies in the gap between Judah's ideal and reality. This sets the stage for the subsequent discussion, positioning the gap between Judah's idealized Self and its real Self as both a catalyst for its perceived inferiority and a motivating force for rewriting Israel's past as a discursive tool to bridge it.

Chapter 3 provides a scholarship review regarding the emergence of a unified Israel as portrayed in the present form of the Bible. There is a growing consensus among scholars today that Judah was a separate entity from Israel, and the concept of a unified "Israel" presented in the Bible is largely a construct of Judah. However, the specifics of when and why Judah adopted Israel's legacy and name continue to spur diverse scholarly interpretations. I assess the competing perspectives of key contributors to this ongoing debate, examining their strengths and weaknesses, with an aim to promote the appropriation model. I demonstrate how Philip Davies has driven a shift in scholarly perspective towards the exilic era, moving away from the prevailing perspective that situated the emergence of "biblical Israel" in the pre-exilic post-722 era. However, I argue that the *when* question should not overshadow the matter because it is intertwined with the subjective aspects of the *why* question. I present Nadav Na'aman's cultural patrimony model as a compelling alternative, one that supports a pre-exilic origin. Yet I also take note of the lingering traditional perspective that clings to Judah's primordial tie to Israel. I offer this as a point that underscores the enduring challenges posed to the appropriation model, necessitating further efforts to defend it.

Chapter 4 delves into the refugee theory, which stands out as the most robust alternative to the appropriation model. Despite recent challenges, this theory enjoys widespread acceptance as the most suitable framework for explaining matters concerning North-South transmission. While Jerusalem's westward expansion has long been taken as a tangible basis for the influx of northern refugees, alternative explanations have been offered for it. Due to the cultural affinity, exactly where the source of the expansion came from cannot be pinpointed. Influx from the North is not improbable, but how much it contributed to the expansion and the formation of Judahite society largely remains conjectural. These uncertainties do not mean the migration of refugees must be discounted, but they do call for caution when grounding other theories on this premise. By examining some Korean empirical cases of refugees, both ancient and modern, I argue for a more cautious and balanced perspective. Exaggerating the role of refugees from the North oversimplifies what could be a far more complex situation, with many other sources for cultural and popular interactions. Doing so also runs the risk of overshadowing the active engagement of the Judahites, who could have played an instrumental and deliberate role in shaping their identity during this tumultuous era.

Chapter 5 emphasizes the Judahites' sense of cultural inferiority as the driving force behind their desire to appropriate Israel's legacy and identity. This addresses the lingering question of why Judah would willingly adopt Israel's identity – a question that has deterred many scholars from embracing the appropriation model, often leading them back to accepting the biblical narrative of a single people divided into two kingdoms. Though this formal answer embedded in the text may offer a convenient solution, there was a reason behind revisionists' initial decision to steer clear of it. Among others, I take seriously Judah's contradictory stance against Israel apparent in the text – both of desire and resentment. To embrace the text's explanation that Israel was deemed detestable due to their sins strikes me as overly simplistic. Instead, I suggest that Judah, perceived as culturally inferior, sought recognition as a member of Israel, but repeatedly faced denial from Israelites. To highlight Judah's perceived inferiority, I emphasize the relative shallowness of Judah's own founding traditions, as well as the conspicuous Canaanite influences that pervade the few traditions they can claim as their own. I maintain that this rejection cultivated within the Judahites a profound yearning for Israel, a longing that could finally be satisfied when the Northern Kingdom ceased to exist. By elucidating the complex and contradictory nature of Judah's attitude towards Israel, I provide novel insights into the contradictions inherent in "biblical Israel."

Chapter 6 tackles a follow-up question whether Judahites' desire for Israel was strong enough to compel them to adopt Israel's identity. I conduct a comparative analysis with East Asian contexts, where neighboring ethnic groups have held strong aspiration for China's prestigious position, which often did compel them ultimately equate them with China. However, in emphasizing inferiority and desire, my aim is not to cast Judah in a negative light as a subservient entity devoid of character. Quite the opposite, the focus is on how these factors turned into a lasting source of strength and creativity, propelling Judahites with unwavering resolve in their pursuit of supremacy. To make this point, I introduce a recent movement in the field of Chinese history, called "New Qing History," and demonstrate its relevance in understanding Judah's desire for Israel. While traditional historians had downplayed the foreign rulers' ethnic identity, recent scholars have acknowledged the role that their ethnic and hybrid identity played in the empire's success. Insights from China and its interactions with its marginal Others provide a fresh perspective for understanding not only Judah's appropriation of Israel but also its rigorous efforts to redefine it.

Chapter 7 begins Part II of the book that aims to demonstrate how Judah's perceived inferiority drove their identity project of the past to redefine their own "Israel." Before delving into the rewriting of Israel's ancestral tradition, I first promote a functional approach to the ancestral traditions, focusing on how past narratives function as discursive tools to construct the past. While traditional critics have been mainly concerned with historical accuracy, I stress the import of recognizing traditions' utility, understanding how the invented past cooperates with the factual past in service of the present needs. Building on Stephen Cornell's theory of identity formation as a narrative process, I argue that collective stories function as tools to create and maintain a coherent identity. This necessitates a shift in focus from the historical realities described in the tradition to the impact these stories have on the later community that remembers them as their own past. While recent studies on identity formation within the Hebrew Bible predominantly center on the Persian period, I argue for the need for a diachronic analysis, treating identity formation as a continuous process.

Chapter 8 demonstrates how I understand Jacob and Abraham traditions as northern and southern ancestral origin myths. I begin by reviewing Pentateuchal scholarship to examine how northern and southern ancestral traditions have been discerned, and how the Jacob and Abraham traditions have been understood within that framework in competing composition models. I explain how the block model serves well today's understanding of ethnicity and collective identity, and how we can turn the rich historical-critical assets into a means for examining Judah's identity formation as a narrative process. But instead of focusing on how the text grew into the present form in stages, the functional approach guides me to pose different questions as to what impact this reformulated past effectuated in the context of Judah's identity formation. By viewing the Jacob and Abraham traditions as distinct identity narratives, I emphasize their role in shaping the self-perception of those who embraced them as their origin stories, rather than merely serving to convey past information.

Chapter 9 demonstrates how the early Jacob tradition functioned as a self-sufficient identity narrative for the Northern Kingdom, which provides a necessary backdrop for my subsequent discussion how Judah has reoriented it. On top of the northern orientation of the Jacob tradition that scholars have long observed, I argue that the default plot structure of the Jacob-Laban narrative is built to emphasize the dominance of Joseph, the father of the leading clans of Northern Israel. Additionally, I propose that the Jacob tradition was one part of Northern Israel's dual origin myths, operating in conjunction with the Exodus tradition. While the Exodus tradition served as an origin myth that defined Israel's origin as coming from outside the land, the Jacob tradition established Israel as indigenous to the land. I explore the possibility that this trickster tradition predates the formation of Israel, suggesting it originated from the land's indigenous inhabitants. As these inhabitants became part of the Israelite kingdom, their traditions came to merge with the exodus myth, likely brought by the group who conceived their origins from outside the land. I explore the implications of this, especially in relation to Judah's subsequent adoption of this tradition, as I perceive Judah as exhibiting more indigenous traits.

In Chapter 10, a cross-cultural comparative study of the biblical ancestral tradition is conducted with ancient Korean history to highlight the significance of Abraham's principal position in the present form of the ancestral tradition. I demonstrate how the united polity emerged in ancient Korean history, which was earlier divided into three or more political entities. Each of these kingdoms had their own origin myths, but a new story was positioned prior to the era of division and effectively implanted a sense of primeval unity for the united Korea. Highlighted is the functionality of the past to the present. I apply this insight to the Abraham narrative, examining how its principal position serves Judah's agenda to take control of Israel's past.

In Chapter 11, I analyze the impact of the Abrahamic expansion on the Jacob narrative and its implications on Judah's redefinition of "Israel." The merging of the two narratives is not just about preserving past traditions. The Abraham narrative is made as the new foundation for the "Israel" reimagined by Judah. By examining the functionality of these narratives in relation to the intergroup dynamic between Israel and Judah, it becomes clear that the Abraham narrative was used as a tool by Judah to redefine their identity by rewriting the ancestral past of Israel. I show how the Abraham narrative claims key sites and elements of the Jacob narrative, negates key aspects of Jacob's identity, and distances from the land to which Jacob had deeper connections. Jacob's trickster aspect and lack of birthright are highlighted, and Abraham is promoted as a remedy for Jacob, who must find a proper wife in Abraham's land that purifies him to be the legitimate heir of Abraham's chosen line.

Ultimately, my goal is to investigate how Judah's rewriting of Israel's past, fueled by its sense of inferiority and desire for Israel, significantly contributed to redefining "Israel." This perspective sheds new light on conflicting representation of "Israel" in the present text and underscores the significance of understanding how the past serves to shape identity in the present. In essence, this was an act of claiming and appropriating what initially belonged to a superior rival. This desire-driven appropriation has left lasting imprints on biblical literature, which is replete with traditions tracing back to northern origins. Among them, we observe only one, but seminal, reorientation as an illustration, which is the Abrahamic expansion of the Jacob tradition. I will show how this added tradition has completely changed the way the underlying Jacob tradition originally was meant to function in North Israel. To view them not simply as preservation of earlier traditions but as active appropriation and repurposing requires a radical shift in how we interpret Judah's Bible.

Part I: **Judah Desires Israel**

2 United yet Divided: Reading Judah and Israel in the Context of Two Koreas

The people of Korea boast more than a thousand years of unity, but they have been severed to become part of two hostile independent political entities. The sense of tragedy inherent in this ongoing political standoff offers South Korean biblical scholars a unique viewpoint to approach Israelite history, which features its own North-South division – that of Judah and Israel. At a cursory look, the similarity of these two divisions – Israel and Korea – might seem apparent. However, a deeper dive reveals significant underlying distinctions as well. Notably, the two Koreas regard each other more as equal competitors, devoid of the persistent and pronounced power imbalance seen between Judah and Israel.[60]

Thus, it is imperative to clarify from the outset that my aim is not to draw a direct parallel between the two Koreas and Judah and Israel. In fact, the dynamics of superiority and inferiority seen between Israel and Judah find a closer mirror in China's position within its marginal Others (including Korea) in Sinocentric East Asia, a subject I delve into separately in Chapter 6. My primary takeaway from the backdrop of the two Koreas is a sheer recognition of the socio-political complexities inherent to such circumstances. As a Korean biblical scholar, I am keenly attuned to the delicate balance in relationships between closely situated political entities, a relationship that perpetually oscillates between perceptions of brotherhood and hostility. Yet, each ethnic conflict, I believe, is marked by its unique complexity, demanding tailored and judicious scrutiny. Consequently, my objective is to use this comparative perspective to sharpen our grasp of biblical Israel's formation, rather than superimposing the Korean context onto Judah and Israel.

This chapter, using Korea as a comparative lens, underscores the duality in Judah's relations with Israel: united in ideal but divided in real. Too often biblical scholars assume "oneness" as a default framework for addressing vexed North-South relations, but it is critical to distinguish between ideal and reality. The biblical presentation of "one Israel," as I argue in this book, is a late Judean construct that reveals more of Judah's desire for supremacy than of historical facts.

---

60 The power dynamics between the Koreas have shifted over the years. While South Korea currently wields more substantial economic, cultural, and military influence, there was a post-war phase when North Korea dominated both economically and militarily.

https://doi.org/10.1515/9783111376554-002

2.1 Two Conceptions of Israel

Two different conceptions of "Israel" coexist in the Bible.[61] As a whole, the biblical literature presents "Israel" as "one people," descended from common ancestors: Abraham, Isaac, and Jacob. The collective memory of Exodus and their unique covenantal relationship with the one God Yhwh, consummated at Sinai, bond them together as Yhwh's people. The land to which Yhwh has led them presents an enduring sense of belonging, and a shared dynastic legacy puts them on firm historical ground. Moreover, ancient Israelites shared a common language and culture, at least as the text portrays. Cumulatively, this "Israel" – both north and south – has almost every criterion that social scientists employ to define an ethnic nation.[62] However, biblical texts also present another image of "Israel." Biblical history, as depicted in Samuel-Kings for instance, presents "Israel" as synonymous with the distinct political entity of Israel, which opposed a rival kingdom, Judah, for most of its monarchic history. Outside the rather idealistic depiction of the initial unity of David's kingdom, the two have largely remained as independent entities.

In biblical literature, in sum, "Israel" is conceived either as a unity, originating in the twelve-tribe league of a common ancestral root and shared experiences, or as nomenclature for the Northern Kingdom set against the southern Judah of Jerusalem. Judah is within Israel in the former and against it in the latter. Judah's ambivalent position begs questions for the origin of such dissonance and its implications for Judah's relation to Northern Israel.

The formal answer to this duality provided by the primary narrative of the biblical text is clear: One people split into two polities when the northern tribes seceded from the United Monarchy. It is the secession of the northern tribes, a tragic moment in Israelite history, that ultimately ruined the innate unity of Yhwh's people. This explanation may appear quite familiar to most readers of the Bible, but it is important to recognize what it actually achieves. It provides a discursive logic that harmonizes the above-mentioned two conceptions of Israel by categorizing one in ethnic and the other in political terms. Despite the ongoing political division, it argues, the two were still "one people." Most readers process this categorization historically: one in the distant past and the other in the more recent past. The present division is an anomaly and ought to be temporary until the past unity is restored in the future.

---

61 Biblical scholars have long struggled with this issue. See, e.g., Reinhard Gregor Kratz, "Israel als Staat und als Volk," *ZTK* 97 (2000): 2.

62 John Hutchinson and Anthony D. Smith, eds., *Ethnicity*, Oxford Readers (Oxford: Oxford University Press, 1996), 6–7.

If one gives it some thought, however, it becomes evident that this explanation does not quite resolve the problem. If unity was original, one would expect to find two "Israels" after the division: one in the North and the other in the South, similar to the case of Korea. But what we find is quite different. One maintains the name, while the other, Judah, is left outside "Israel." Despite this, the formal explanation has been tremendously successful in persuading most readers of the Bible. This includes critical scholarship.[63] In a sense, traditional scholars were more vulnerable due to their dominantly historical frame of reference and their pursuit of historical origins. The predominant mode of inquiry for critical scholars has thus generally been whether Israel and Judah were originally one or two.[64] Their questions therefore centered on debating the historical veracity of the United Monarchy, the tribal confederacy, Exodus, and the Patriarchal age. Alternatively, others have asked when different concepts of Israel emerged, attempting to trace the trajectory of Israel's evolution over time.[65] Although I do not underestimate the significance of such historical inquiries, it is certain that the underlying political dynamic is frequently overshadowed by the dominant historical interests.

Claims of ethnic unity typically assume a primordial look. While presented as factual claims, they recede far back in time, to a mythic past. Unbound by facts, myths hold a distinct power in shaping societies. No two groups in society own or can demonstrate a biologically and historically verifiable common origin. Instead, social scientists illuminate that ethnic identity is a social product.[66] People happen to live together, and out of that social coexistence emerges a necessity to search for and reinforce a sense of cohesiveness, for which a story of a common origin of the constituent groups – families, clans, even kingdoms – is useful. Simply, ethnic unity is never something factually proven. It is something claimed, which, when enough people accept it, elevates to the level of "fact." In essence, it is a "shared belief," a constructed reality. People make use of ethnic claims to maintain and justify their political realities. What is factual is the sociopolitical reality that requires people to make such claims of ethnic "oneness." People evoke

---

63 For recent advocates, see Kristin Weingart, *Stämmevolk – Staatsvolk – Gottesvolk?: Studien zur Verwendung des Israel-Namens im Alten Testament*, FAT 2/68 (Tübingen: Mohr Siebeck, 2014). For more discussion, see Chapter 3.

64 See Gary N. Knoppers, *Two Nations under God: The Deuteronomistic History of Solomon and the Dual Monarchies. Vol. 1. The Reign of Solomon and the Rise of Jeroboam*, HSM 52 (Atlanta: Scholars Press, 1993), 1–10.

65 E.g., H. G. M. Williamson, "The Concept of Israel in Transition," in *The World of Ancient Israel: Sociological, Anthropological, and Political Perspectives*, ed. R. E. Clements (Cambridge: Cambridge University Press, 1989), 141–61.

66 Barth, *Ethnic Groups and Boundaries*.

a sense of unity to erase more recent histories of real division, which is often forced by common external threats.

For complex social entities like Israel and Judah, asking if they were historically one or two is helplessly simplistic. The biblical texts' claim of Israel's one origin apparently belongs to the space of the mythic past. It is a political ideal that must not be mistaken for a historical fact. That is, to claim an ethnic unity of two groups is as much a political act as describing and justifying their political separation. Understanding how the ideal and reality interact, or how we draw the past and use it for the present, is the first step towards gaining a better understanding of the nature of the biblical presentation of Judah and Israel.[67] Comparing with the Korean context will bring this point into sharper focus.

2.2 One People, Two Polities?

One can make a germane case for Korea being one people temporarily broken into two polities. Korean people today, both North and South, maintain a remarkably high sense of homogeneity. We Koreans have a distinct language. We have occupied a relatively segregated land for thousands of years. We have successfully defended our land, despite innumerable invasions that have continually threatened our autonomy, for centuries. We share a concrete history of political unity, featuring only one change of royal dynasty over the entire millennium up to the dawn of the modern era.[68] All these have contributed to producing and maintaining an indestructible sense of ethnic unity. Indeed, Korea stands as one of the few countries that can make a case for a premodern "nation."[69] However, it was startling how quickly and inexplicably this long-standing unity could be shattered.

At the end of World War II, Korea, which had been occupied by Japan since 1910, was on the verge of gaining independence. However, as the war neared its end, the United States, anticipating the challenges of managing post-war territories and keen on ensuring the swift defeat of remaining Japanese forces, called upon the Soviet Union, then an ally, for support. In a rapid response, the Soviets occupied the northern part of Korea in just about a week. While Japan succumbed

---

67 Hobsbawm and Ranger, *The Invention of Tradition.*
68 My deliberate use of "we" here, which may have bothered some of the Western readers, reflects Korean language custom in which "we/us" is much more frequently employed than "I/ me." One might take this as a trace of Korean people's collective mind being ingrained in the linguistic custom.
69 See Hutchinson and Smith, *Ethnicity,* 11.

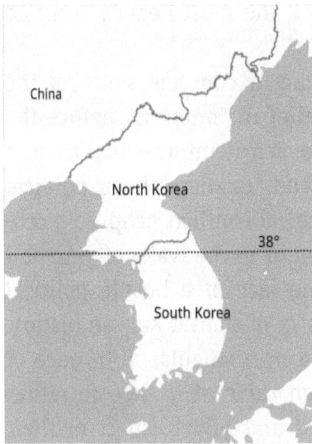

Fig. 1: Division of Korea around the Korean War. Illustration by Kim Minji.

Tab. 1: Timeline Surrounding the Division of Korea.

1910–1945.8.15	Japanese Colonial Rule
1945.8.15	Korea is divided along the 38th parallel
1948	Establishment of Distinct Regimes in North and South Korea
1950.6.25	Outbreak of the Korean War
1953.7.27	End of the Korean War with the Korean Armistice Agreement

with ease, the real challenge emerged from the Soviets' push southward. To counteract this, the U. S. was forced to accept a division at the 38th parallel (Fig. 1). This split, more impromptu than planned, was initially seen as a temporary measure, at least by most Koreans. As Cold War tensions between the two superpowers escalated, attempts by the Korean people to mend the division proved futile. By 1948, despite fervent efforts to avert such an outcome, two separate governments emerged: the Republic of Korea in the South, backed by the United States, and the Democratic People's Republic of Korea in the North, endorsed by the Soviet Union.[70]

Only two years afterwards, in 1950, the Korean War broke out, which perpetuated the division of the land that was meant to be temporary. After three years of brutal war, an armistice agreement in 1953 halted active combat, but a formal peace treaty was never signed. The Demilitarized Zone (DMZ) was established as

---

70 See Michael J. Seth, *A Concise History of Korea: From Antiquity to the Present*, 2nd ed. (Lanham, MD: Rowman & Littlefield, 2016), 325–59.

a buffer, and this border stands to this day as one of the most heavily fortified in the world.

This experience provides Korean biblical scholars a concrete sense of the futility of claims of ethnic unity and the shared belief in "oneness" before the political reality of division. The current state in Korea clearly informs that a sense of ethnic unity on its own is hardly enough to defend "oneness" from political tensions. Koreans have vividly witnessed how ideological conflicts eclipsed a centuries-old sense of ethnic unity, how helpless "we" were in the wake of war, and how useless the rhetoric of ethnic unity was in the face of a hostile political reality. What is striking is how the deep-rooted tapestry of shared Korean history, culture, and language was completely overshadowed by a singular difference of ideology in such a short span of time. Even though their allegiance to either democracy or communism was an entirely external and novel aspect of their relationship, the two Koreas agreed to rally around this sole difference, transforming brethren into enemies and allowing their homeland to become a theater for the ideological clashes of foreign superpowers. This emphasis on ideological difference at the exclusion of their deep-rooted shared history and culture is a profound testament to the power of socio-political reality. When socio-political conflict required them to oppose the other side, they actively sought differences, even fabricating arbitrary ones, mobilized around them, and reinforced the division. In Korea's case, ideology was the difference, but in other cases, it could be anything else, be it religion, color, or language.

However, this is not to say that the sense of division is now fixed and permanent in Korea, or that the political division has completely destroyed the sense of unity among Koreans. While international media coverage may highlight the military tension around the border of South Korea and North Korea, outsiders would be surprised how many Koreans hold fast on to the notion of "one people" and stay calm through most tensioned political upheavals.[71] Since its division, the pursuit of reunification has remained a central collective yearning in Korea,[72] which may remain a potential force that might, I hope, restore unity in the future.

---

71 The sense of unity is most often exhibited in the context of sports events. The unified ping pong team of Korea's gold medal win at the 1991 World Table Tennis Championships left an indelible mark of hope for Korean people that one day the divided nation will be reunited. See Woongbee Lee, "The North and South Korean gold medal ping pong pals separated for ever," BBC News, 10. 02. 2018, https://www.bbc.com/news/av/world-asia-42999448/ [accessed 30. 05. 2019].
72 See, e.g., Nick Eberstadt, *Korea Approaches Reunification* (Armonk, NY: M. E. Sharpe, 1995); Jongmin Park et al., "How Has the Republic of Korea Viewed 'North Korea' and 'Reunification' Over the Past 20 Years?," *Korean Journal of Journalism & Communication Studies* 64 (2020): 161–201, https://doi.org/10.20879/kjjcs.2020.64.6.005 [박종민 외, "대한민국은 지난 20 년간 '북한'과 '통일'을 어떻게 보았는가? 언론 보도 빅데이터 분석 및 국민 인식 종단연구"].

There have been continual negotiations for reunification between the two Koreas, but they simply failed to reach an agreement. What each side envisages as a proper union differs drastically, and unless one party cedes control to the other, reunification talks will always hit a deadlock.

Instead, a dual mode of sentiment, divided yet united, has become a distinctive feature of the two Koreas' mutual relationship. While the Korean War has left a big scar in the minds of Koreans, down under, there remains a deep-rooted sentiment of "we are one."[73] As such, the two sentiments, one in ethnic and the other in political terms now coexist in tragic dissonance and continue to clash with each other, each seeking to influence the other. One argues "We are brethren" and the other retorts "They are communists, our enemy." Then, which is the true of the two? The point that I am striving to make here is that it is impossible to discern which is the true sentiment. So many factors can affect how one feels about the Self and the Other. Thus, South Koreans' sentiment towards North Korea

---

[73] A recurring debate in South Korea on *Ju-jeuck* (the Enemy or "the primary enemy") demonstrates well such a dual sense. This is a debate whether to identify North Korea as "the Enemy." After the Korean War, North Korea has been recognized as a primary threat to South Korean national security. At one point when North Korean threat was pressing, a clause to identify North Korea as "the Enemy" has been inserted into South Korea's Defense White Paper. Afterward, there have been rounds of heated debate on this issue. South Korea's political right and left wings, and also older and younger generations, tend to maintain very different perspectives on this particular issue. Later, when a peace mood ripened, the clause of North Korea as an "enemy" was removed. See Hyung-Jin Kim, "For First Time Since 2010, South Korea Defense Report Doesn't Refer to North Korea as 'Enemy'," USA Today, 15. 01. 2019, https://www.usatoday.com/story/news/world/2019/01/14/south-korea-north-korea-relations-no-enemy-designation/2578073002/ [accessed 30. 05. 2019].

One simple question unravels the problem under the notion of the enemy: "Are all the people of North Korea our enemy?" This question unsettles South Koreans' notion of the enemy, between their ethnic and political identities. Even the most rigorous right-wing supporters would hesitate to affirm this question because doing so will invite a backlash from the left wing that *Minjung* (common people) in North Korea are "brothers and sisters" who happen to suffer from a malicious regime. But, still, the right-wing party would stress not to forget what happened in the Korean War. To foolishly trust North Korea will repeat the tragic war. Their caution is legitimate. The price may be high to let the ethnic sentiment unduly override a political decision. The rhetoric of "we are one" is useless, if not deceptively dangerous, when the other side aims the gun at us. I am sure the debate on "the Enemy" will continually reinstate itself in the coming eras of Korean politics, shifting back and forth between the two poles, a debate that reflects the cyclical dynamic between the two contrasting modes of sentiments. In fact, most recently in 2023, the political drama has made another turn as Korea's new government tries to reinstate North Korea's state as the enemy. See Je-hun Lee, "Leaders of Two Koreas Engage in Perilous Game of Chicken," Hankyoreh, 05. 01. 2023, https://english.hani.co.kr/arti/english_edition/e_north korea/1074579.html [accessed 20. 01. 2023].

is not fixed but is constantly in motion, oscillating between ethnic ideals and political reality.

When set against the backdrop of Korea, the ephemeral nature of Judah and Israel's unity stands out starkly. Their alleged political union lasted merely for about a century, during the infancy of the monarchic history. Beyond this fleeting unity, there was no restoration of union. Outside of Benjamin, which was later incorporated into Judah,[74] other northern tribes – including the powerful northern clans Ephraim and Manasseh – largely disappeared from Judeans' postmonarchic life. This is a problem because the beginning is the period most susceptible to later embellishment, warranting caution in accepting it as factual. Challenges to this portrayal of original unity have persistently emerged from critical scholars.[75] Recent archaeological discoveries have radically changed our perspective on the era of David and Solomon. The glorious depiction of the Davidic monarchy is increasingly seen as a late idealization, representing it as a golden age for Judah's vision of Israel.[76]

The fundamental difference between the two contexts of Israel and Korea can be demonstrated in all phases of Israel's monarchic history. For instance, compare the scene of the United Monarchy's breach with Korea's division. Unlike the Korean case that was largely driven by the complex international dynamic, the way Israelites seceded from David's rule was driven by the seemingly innate division between Judah and other Israelites. Most noteworthy is the slogan that the northern people ("all Israel") cried out at the moment of separation (1Kgs 12:16): "What share do we have in David? There is no portion for us in David. No inheritance in the son of Jesse! To your tents, O Israel! Now take care of your house, David!" This is almost identical to the slogan that was proclaimed in the Sheba incident (2Sam 20). That incident was quickly subdued, but this one leads to a permanent rupture between Judah and Israel. Notably, the slogan summons David, not Rehoboam or Solomon, which reminds us of David's covenant with Israel (2Sam 5).[77]

---

74 See Yigal Levin, "Joseph, Judah and the 'Benjamin Conundrum,'" *ZAW* 116 (2004): 223–41; Philip R. Davies, "The Trouble with Benjamin," in *Reflection and Refraction*, ed. Robert Rezetko, Timothy H. Lim, and W. Brian Aucker, VTSup 113 (Leiden: Brill, 2007), 93–111; Nadav Na'aman, "Saul, Benjamin and the Emergence of 'Biblical Israel' (Part 1)," *ZAW* 121 (2009): 211–24, https://doi.org/10.1515/ZAW.2009.014; idem, "Saul, Benjamin and the Emergence of 'Biblical Israel' (Part 2)," *ZAW* 121 (2009): 335–49, https://doi.org/10.1515/ZAW.2009.023.
75 See Knoppers, *Two Nations under God 1*, 1–10.
76 See, e.g., Moore and Kelle, *Biblical History*; Grabbe, *Ancient Israel*; Finkelstein and Mazar, *The Quest for the Historical Israel*.
77 A notable characteristic of David's establishment of the United Monarchy is his anointment in two distinct steps: initially by the tribe of Judah (2Sam 2:1–4a), followed by all Israel (2Sam 5:1–3). Critics tended to read the two-step anointment of David as a natural process within the larger story of David's rise to power (1Sam 16:1–2Sam 5:3). Cf. e.g., P. Kyle McCarter, *II Samuel: A New*

This reveals the nature of the summit at Shechem between Rehoboam and Jeroboam. The foundational tie between the northern tribes and Judah was David's covenant with Israel (2Sam 5:1–3). Faced with the Israelites' dissatisfaction, they aimed to renegotiate the terms.[78] A fruitful negotiation would have refreshed

Translation with Introduction, Notes, and Commentary, AB 9 (Garden City, NY: Doubleday, 1984), 133–34; Walter Brueggemann, *First and Second Samuel*, Interpretation (Louisville, KY: John Knox, 1990), 236; Robert Alter, *The David Story: A Translation with Commentary of 1 and 2 Samuel* (New York: W. W. Norton, 1999), 202. For instance, Alt famously described the kingdom of David as a product of the "personal union" achieved by his military and political prowess. See Albrecht Alt, "The Formation of the Israelite State in Palestine," in *Essays on Old Testament History and Religion* (Oxford: Blackwell, 1966), 172–237, here 218–19, 233; see also Martin Noth, *The History of Israel*, 2nd ed. (New York: Harper & Row, 1960), 187. For Alt, David's kingdom was "an amalgam of the popular monarchies of Israel and Judah, the city-state monarchies of Ziklag and Jerusalem, and in addition, directly or indirectly, of the popular monarchies of the eastern mountain states and the city-state monarchies of the Philistines" (p. 233). Therefore, Alt reads David's first anointment with Judah as a personal union between Ziklag and Judah and the second anointment with Israel as a personal union between the Ziklag-Judah and Israel. Soon afterward, Jerusalem and other city-states and kingdoms were included. Alt's keen observation that David's prowess played a key role in bringing disparate entities together is of paramount importance in understanding the nature of David's kingdom. However, as to why the two *kin* groups Judah and Israel needed such a union, as if they were unrelated, Alt could only adumbrate: "even the unity of the Israelite tribes in the worship of Yahweh did not apparently prevent the free control of their own private affairs, and as regards communal business, imposed a moral obligation rather than a political authority" (p. 180). There might be some truth in this observation, but the surprising independence of Judah implied in the text is not fully explained. Alt's overarching scheme of the now defunct Israelite amphictyony appears to hinder him from fully endorsing the division between Judah and Israel that the text suggests (pp. 179–80). Noth argued that Israel's federation of twelve or six tribes could be understood based on the model of the amphictyonies established in ancient Greece and Italy. Martin Noth, *Das System der zwölf Stämme Israels* (Darmstadt: Wissenschaftliche Buchgesellschaft, 1930); Noth, *History*, 87–89. For a brief summary of his argument see C. H. J. de Geus, *The Tribes of Israel: An Investigation into Some of the Presuppositions of Martin Noth's Amphictyony Hypothesis*, Studia Semitica Neerlandica 18 (Assen: Van Gorcum, 1976), 40–42.

78 Alt ("The Formation of the Israelite State in Palestine," 237) views the secession as an attempt to restore the ideal of charismatic leadership in Israel. The Israelites, who did not accept the dynastic principle until the time of Omri, could not accept Solomon's kingship (cf. 1Sam 12, Deut 17:14–20). For them, the legitimate king is the one chosen by Yhwh. This influential idea shaped a significant volume of scholarly research on the various aspects of the nature of Israelite kingship. However, it has been challenged by scholars, who showed that a dynastic principle of kingship was a basic feature of ancient Near Eastern, including Israelite, kingship. See, e.g., Giorgio Buccellati, *Cities and Nations of Ancient Syria; an Essay on Political Institutions with Special Reference to the Israelite Kingdoms* (Rome: Istituto di Studi Del Vicino Oriente, Università di Roma, 1967); Tomoo Ishida, *The Royal Dynasties in Ancient Israel: A Study on the Formation and Development of Royal-Dynastic Ideology*, BZAW 142 (Berlin: Walter de Gruyter, 1977). It is difficult to conclude that what Israel wanted was a Yhwh-chosen, charismatic leader when their initial request betrayed their willingness to continue serving Rehoboam if the burden was low-

this bond, which only underscores the gravity of Rehoboam's misjudgment in letting this chance slip. His lapse effectively severed the legal affiliation David had established with Israel.[79] The Israelites walked away from the covenant, and they each took their own ways.[80] Thus, the rise and fall of the United Monarchy is *presented* as a failed attempt to unite two independent groups, rather than as a schism between brothers.[81]

One may wonder to what extent this narrative is based on actual events and how much is mere exaggeration. It is entirely plausible that the underlying event was a localized affair around Judah – with Benjamin and perhaps Ephraim – later amplified to glorify David's reign as Israel's golden age.[82] However, the crux of the matter lies in the intentions behind the present formation of the narrative. If one accepts that the stories of David and Solomon were added by the Judahites as a golden era in which David is portrayed as the founding ruler of all Israel, Israel's division is not a genuine rupture of ethnic ties, unlike that of Korea, but rather a fracture made only within Judah's ideal.

---

ered. This is also implied in the stark contrast between the two key words, "today" and "forever," in the elders' suggestion: "If you become a servant of this people today ... then they will be your servants to you forever" (2Kgs 12:7). Cf. Georg Fohrer, "Der Vertrag zwischen König und Volk in Israel," *ZAW* 71 (1959): 8, https://doi.org/10.1515/zatw.1959.71.1-4.1; Abraham Malamat, "Organs of Statecraft in the Israelite Monarchy," *BA* 28 (1965): 36, 39, https://doi.org/10.2307/3211054; Tryggve N. D. Mettinger, *King and Messiah: The Civil and Sacral Legitimation of the Israelite Kings*, ConBOT 8 (Lund: LiberLäromedel/Gleerup, 1976), 139–40.

79 Malamat ("Organs of Statecraft in the Israelite Monarchy," 39) calls it "covenant nullification." In comparison, no covenant renewal between Solomon and Israel is reported. Perhaps such a covenant was not necessary every time the throne changed hands, but only in exceptional circumstances, such as when the succession was interrupted, like in the case of Joash. See Malamat, 36–37.

80 Alt, "The Formation of the Israelite State in Palestine," 237. As Alt correctly points out, it is not a conventional split or division of the kingdom; it is "the voluntary withdrawal of the kingdom of Israel from its form of personal union with the kingdom of Judah" (p. 236). Cf. Malamat, "Organs of Statecraft in the Israelite Monarchy," 39; Fohrer, "Der Vertrag zwischen König und Volk in Israel," 8.

81 What I mean to say is not that one should take the textual representation at face value, as if historical events occurred precisely as described. Rather, the manner in which David's united kingdom is presented in the text is significant in its own right, as there must have been a reason the later author/redactor chose to depict the scene in this specific way.

82 Cf. Compare with Fleming and Monroe's recent proposal of distinguishing between "little" and "greater" Israel, together with Sergi's similar idea of two separate houses of Israel – southern and northern. Lauren Monroe and Daniel E. Fleming, eds., "Israel before the Omrides," *HeBAI* 10 (2021): 97–227, https://doi.org/10.1628/hebai-2021-0009; Omer Sergi, *The Two Houses of Israel: State Formation and the Origins of Pan-Israelite Identity* (Atlanta: SBL Press, 2023). See Section 3.3.

Indeed, following their split, the two parties' interactions mirrored those of neighboring kingdoms,[83] without any particular drive to restore their ancient unity. An illuminating example of this is the confrontation between Amaziah and Jehoash (2Kgs 14; 2Chr 25). Jehoash triumphs, capturing Amaziah and tearing down Jerusalem's walls; then, after plundering the temple and palace, he simply departs. Considering the deep-rooted desire for reunification within the Korean mindset, the absence of a push towards unification is striking to me. It appears that no moment in the history of these divided kingdoms presented a more opportune moment for reunification. Yet, his actions, or lack thereof – like neglecting to seize the Ark – suggest a different narrative. This would have been a golden opportunity to return the Ark of Moses to where it originally belonged to. However, the text says nothing of the Ark in Jerusalem, the most prized booty from the city, when the plundering of the temple is specifically mentioned (2Kgs 14:13–14).[84] It seems even when Israel held the upper hand, restoring old ties with Judah was not a priority for northern monarchs. Did Jehoash miss a golden opportunity to etch his name in history, or are we reading into the text expecting something that was simply not there?

Granted, the unification theme is not entirely lacking in biblical literature. In prophetic literature, for example, the restoration of the ideal past is a common motif, and such evocation of the past often takes a form of restoring the North-South union. Yet, such yearning stems out exclusively of Judean prophets (e.g., Isa 11; Jer 3; Ezek 23, 37).[85] In contrast, northern prophets like Hosea set their ideals in the restoration of the Mosaic era, accentuating Israel's special relationship with Yhwh, with little attention given to the North-South union. This differ-

---

83 There was a time when Judah appears to have served Israel as a vassal. Yet scholars have frequently exaggerated Judah's vassalhood as its kinship with Israel. One often comes across a remark that Jehoshaphat's military aid to Ahab (1Kgs 22) or his son Jehoram (2Kgs 3) reflects Judah's brotherhood with Israel. Yet, Jehoshaphat's word "My people are your people, my horses are your horses" can just as easily be interpreted as a diplomatic language. A weaker ally's desire to stress kinship with the stronger partner is a gesture common in diplomatic settings. See Lee E. Patterson, *Kinship Myth in Ancient Greece* (Austin: University of Texas Press, 2010); Angelika Berlejung, "Family Ties: Constructed Memories about Aram and the Aramaeans in the Old Testament," in *In Search for Aram and Israel: Politics, Culture, and Identity*, ed. Omer Sergi, Manfred Oeming, and Izaak J. de Hulster, Orientalische Religionen in der Antike 20 (Tübingen: Mohr Siebeck, 2016), 355–77. The fictive relationship between David and Israelites is a case in point. The Israelite elders claimed, "We are your bone and flesh" (2Sam 5:1) when they needed David's assistance, but later on they said, "What share do we have with David?" (1Kgs 12:16).

84 There is a stark contrast between Jehoash's disinterest and David's great interest in promoting his legitimacy by transferring the Ark (2Sam 6). I think it self-evident which of these is idealistic, aimed at laying a propagandistic claim of legitimacy.

85 Cf. Finkelstein and Silberman, *The Bible Unearthed*, 149–50, 168.

ence in emphasis suggests that the motif of reunification primarily originated from late Judean circles as a political ideal.[86] The unity in the Davidic era serves as its foundation, which is then projected into the prophetic vision of an idyllic future.

2.3 Judah's Invention of One Israel

If the "one Israel" in the present text is primarily a construct of Judah's making, it is important to delve into how this identity was constructed, as it could illuminate the core intentions behind Judah's identity project. An invention of identity is usually achieved by rewriting the past, myth or history.[87] Then, important here is to remember that Judahites did not invent "Israel" but built upon the northerners' existing conception of Israel. A question might immediately follow as to why Judah, if independent from Israel, chose to adopt Israel's identity. I shall address that in subsequent chapters, but I first establish what it took for Judahites to appropriate Israel's legacy as their own. Two reorientations of Israel's past were pivotal: one monarchic and the other ancestral.[88]

On the one hand, Judah's rewriting of Israel's monarchic past played a pivotal role, and it entails two distinct aspects. The first is the synchronization of the two

---

86 It is important to realize that this "Israel" constructed by Judah's rewriting does not align with the Israel imagined by northern Israelites. The Davidic monarchy, as envisioned in the present text, was hardly a golden age for northern Israelites. It was only for Judahites. In other words, Judahites' invention of the golden age of David was the very part of Judah's strategy to claim their right to inherit the legacy of both southern and northern kingdoms: Israel was originally one and ruled by "our king."

Thus, the rhetorical nature of Judah's call for the restoration of the "one Israel" must be recognized as well. By making an appeal to "one Israel" in antiquity, Judahites hardly intended to restore the northern version of Israel. This is a very different Israel, wherein Judah's predominant status is granted. What is going on here essentially is the politics of inheriting, or Judahite supersessionism. The claim that Judahites inherited the old "Israel" in its *entirety* necessitates the annexation of its original members. In reality, therefore, this inclusive-looking rhetoric of "one Israel" entails just as much exclusivity – perhaps not very different from the "exclusive inclusivity" Rom-Shiloni has pointed to in Judean identity politics. Cf. Dalit Rom-Shiloni, *Exclusive Inclusivity: Identity Conflicts between the Exiles and the People Who Remained (6th-5th Centuries BCE)*, LHBOTS 543 (London: Bloomsbury, 2013), 29.

87 Hobsbawm and Ranger, *The Invention of Tradition*. Cf. Anderson, *Imagined Communities*, 11–12; Berlejung, "The Gilead between Aram and Israel," 356–58.

88 To forge a new identity, one must revisit and reinterpret the past, present, and future. While biblical texts encompass all these facets of identity discourse, I choose to hone in on the past in this book. After all, our origins play a pivotal role in shaping our self-perception.

kingdoms' royal accounts.[89] To the average biblical reader, this may seem to be standard, but in reality, this joint presentation might be quite revolutionary. If a royal chronicle were to be discovered in Samaria, I doubt it would encompass the history of the Judahite kingdom. In that regard, I believe it worth inquiring whether the Chronicler's portrayal of Judah's past stays truer to the norm, while the Deuteronomist's integrated presentation might be an outlier. While I must spare this topic for another occasion, I have to emphasize here the profound effect of the synchronized presentation of Israel and Judah's histories. By inter-twining their histories, readers are imbued with a sense of idealized unity over against their actual divisions. The second is the promotion of Judah as Yhwh's chosen. The Deuteronomistic History (DtrH) presents Judah as the sole and legiti-mate remnant of Israel that must carry on the cause Northern Israel left unful-filled. The Deuteronomist (Dtr) deliberately depicts Northern Israel as rejected by Yhwh, who punished them for their unfaithfulness to Yhwh's covenant. Utilizing the vassal treaty motif, Northern Israel is labeled as a failed vassal of Yhwh, a position then claimed by Josiah in his faithful deeds. David embodies both of these aspects and plays a paramount role as a prototype for the Judahite Israel.[90] The kingdom of David serves as the golden age that orients Judah and Israel in a common root, while the divine choice of David secures Judah's leading role.

On the other hand, the reorientation of Israel's ancestral past played as sig-nificant role. Israel's ancestral past has been also reframed by the addition of the Abraham tradition to the existing Jacob tradition. Scholars have perhaps under-stated the importance of this shift, but this project has been equally influential in redefining Israel. Prior to this addition, Judahites may have yearned for their place in Jacobean Israel, which eventually materialized in the present form of Jacob's genealogy. The birth reports of the eleven sons of Jacob (Gen 29:31–30:24) appear to have been updated at one point to reflect the Judean perspective.[91] This insures Judah's place within Israel's ancestry. Yet, as I will detail below (Sec-

---

89 See Kratz, "Israel als Staat," 8–9.

90 R. E. Clements, *Abraham and David: Genesis XV and Its Meaning for Israelite Tradition*, SBT 2/5 (Naperville, IL: Allenson, 1967).

91 See, e.g., Kratz, "Israel als Staat," 13; idem, *The Composition of the Narrative Books of the Old Testament*, trans. John Bowden (London: T&T Clark, 2005), 266; Israel Finkelstein and Thomas Römer, "Comments on the Historical Background of the Jacob Narrative in Genesis," *ZAW* 126 (2014): 335–36, https://doi.org/10.1515/zaw-2014-0020. Kratz proposes that Judah's designation as Jacob's son is secondary, reflecting the Judahites' endeavor to position Judah as Jacob's legitimate successor. While precisely tracing the evolution of the current birth report proves challenging, its alignment with other tribal lists, predominantly associated with P, hints at a later origin. Cf. Tobolowsky (*The Sons of Jacob*, 100–101), who contends that the list was a late Judean product rather than a revision of a pre-existing list.

tion 9.2), the Jacob tradition is a tightly structured narrative that are innately designed to endorse the leadership of the Joseph clans, which leaves little room for Judahites to bolster their state within the Jacob tradition.[92]

In this regard, the Abrahamic expansion takes added significance. The Judahite revision expands the ancestral history by adding the Abraham tradition, which is apparently of southern origin. Adding new traditions inevitably results in a change to the existing group identity. Abraham's principal position in Israel's lineage serves as a counterweight, diminishing Jacob's original prominence in the early northern Israelite identity narrative, while promoting Abraham as the principal figure in Israel's ancestry.[93] Granted, Jacob's legacy has not been completely erased. Yet for those who formerly traced their ancestry solely to Jacob, the ramifications of this redefined lineage of Israel must be profound. As a result, the revision of the ancestral past ensures Judah's membership in Israel and, at the same time, justifies Judah's leading role in it.

Together, these reorientations shift the foundation of the northern traditions, originally in Jeroboam and Jacob, towards their southern counterparts, David and Abraham. As a result, the monarchic project constructs a "Davidic Israel," whereas the ancestral project produces an "Abrahamic Israel." One can easily see how these identity projects contributed to promoting the formal biblical answer to Judah and Israel's relationship as that of one people being temporarily severed for political reasons. The unity of Judah and Israel is secured in both the ancestral and monarchic past, one based on Abraham and the other on David. This unity is severed when Jeroboam led Israelites fall astray from the Davidic leadership.

If the alleged unity in Abraham and David was only later imagined by Judahites, these reorientations of the past cannot be treated outside considerations of what was aimed at in their historical present. Notably, they would have resonated well with the spirited aspiration to reclaim Israel's vacant heritage reflected in the alleged reformation program of Josiah. For instance, bracketed by David and Josiah, the northern kings, spearheaded by the emblematic Jeroboam ben Nebat, are blamed for forfeiting Yhwh's covenant, which paves the way for Judah's ascension as Yhwh's elected covenantal partner. In addition, the same dynamic is observed also in the "Abrahamic Israel," wherein Abraham takes precedence over Jacob, paralleling David's overshadowing of Jeroboam. In doing so, the monarchic and ancestral pasts work in tandem to bolster Judah's position in Israel's ideal

---

92 See Chapter 9.

93 As scholars have observed, undermining the first three sons' authority might have played a role, but that is secondary. Within the narrative grammar of the Jacob-Joseph tradition, Joseph's authority is granted not by virtue of birthright.

past. It is the enormous success of these identity projects, which continually evolved afterward, that gave a lasting impression that Israel was originally "one."

2.4 Israel in Ideal and Real

Now, the essential distinction between the two contexts becomes clear. The Korean people's identity struggle oscillates between two poles: their ethnic and political sides of identity. Both ethnic unity and political division are as tangible as it gets, rooted in palpable realities.[94] This naturally intensifies the tragic sense of division and the yearning for reunification. At first glance, Judah's conception of "Israel" may appear to mirror the ethnic-political dichotomy seen in Korea. However, the alleged ethnic unity, as we saw above, resides in Judah's ideal, with little reflection in the actual political interactions between the two kingdoms during the so-called "divided monarchy."[95] Then, in contrast to Korea, Judah's identity struggle is not anchored in the ethnic unity and political division. Instead, the crux of the issue lies in the gap between Judah's ideal and reality. That is, Judah's identity discourse against Israel, at any point of their history, must be addressed within the continuum of Judah's two selves: ideal and real.[96] Objectively, Judah and Israel operated as separate entities, but they were reimagined to own primordial unity in Judah's ideal. That this union was only a construct in Judah's ideal explains why mutual yearning for reunification between Judah and Israel is absent.

The gap between these two selves constitutes the very essence of my understanding of the subjective side of Judah's self-perception. I believe that Judah's sense of inferiority serves as the crucial bridge that connects these two sides of Judah's identity. Out of the desire for the superior Israel, the inferior Judah (real) constructed the ideal unity in the mythic past, while painting themselves as the more superior party (ideal). Yet, at a deeper level, the Judahites were acutely

---

94 Of course, these are all relative. No ethnic sentiment is absolute. I am simply stating that the profound history of Koreans provides a more substantial basis to their ethnic identity compared to many other nations.

95 The term "divided monarchy" itself is misleading, which presupposes the division of the United Monarchy as factual.

96 The underlying assumption is that social phenomena such as identity negotiation do not necessarily take a linear and evolutionary form but rather a cyclical form as society immerses itself in the recurring debate of "who we are." The clashing voices are preserved in the text precisely because they offer much-needed versatility, like a living organism, as each group strives to maintain its coherent identity while responding to challenges posed by changing realities. As for the concept of the "Self," I am employing them in a more general sense, rather than within the specific framework of social psychology. Cf. Daniel M. Wegner and Robin R. Vallacher, eds., *The Self in Social Psychology* (New York: Oxford University Press, 1980).

aware of the reality, in which they were continually perceived as outsiders by the *truer* Israelites. I see this internal struggle between the two selves emblematic of Judah's enduring schizophrenia, having lived for long in the shadow of the powerful Israel. This dynamic might also clarify why a dominant characteristic of Judah's identity discourse is its defensive nature, leading them to project an excessive aggression towards Israel, the very object of their desire.

2.5 Conclusion

How can the Korean experience of division shed light on the intricate North-South dynamics in biblical history? While there are ostensible parallels between the two situations, a closer examination revealed key distinctions. The Korean case is marked by a deep-seated ethnic unity, tragically fractured by political conflict. The ties between Israel and Judah, in contrast, were far more tenuous. Strictly speaking, the notions of primordial unity, its tragic breach, and the hope for restoration under a Davidic heir are all born out of Judah's idealization.

This observation offers key takeaways. Above all, when analyzing the *realpolitik* between Judah and Israel during the monarchic era, it is crucial not to blur their reality with the later ideal. A much more realistic approach is required when it comes to reconstructing historical relations between Judah and Israel. Koreans' bitter experience of political division provides Korean biblical scholars a heightened sensibility to the powerlessness of alleged ethnic bonds before political turmoil. If the sense of unity among Koreans, sustained by more than a thousand years of political union and social commingling, was so vulnerable to a political conflict, much more so would have been true for the case of Judah and Israel. Their relationship must have been dictated not by the claimed unity but by their often-conflicting reality, or uneven political power dynamic.

On the other hand, in examining Judah's identity expressions, it is crucial to interpret their varied voices as indicative of an internal struggle between the envisioned and the lived reality. The tension between the unity in ideal and the division in reality is palpable throughout. While biblical texts endeavor to bridge this gap by positing a single people divided into two kingdoms – akin to the two Koreas – accepting this as a historical fact raises more questions than it resolves. Instead of seeking to uncover the real or original relations between Judah and Israel as something fixed, we might be better served by embracing the dual nature born out of this constant negotiation between Judah's two selves – real and ideal. Thus, the portrayal of Judah and Israel in biblical literature may not be as useful for restoring historical reality behind the text. Instead, it reflects more of Judah's constructed reality, wherein multiple concepts of "Israel" were in competition.

3 Recent Debate on the Emergence of Biblical Israel

Recently, a growing consensus among biblical scholars posits Judah as distinct from Israel, implying that Judah adopted the Israelite identity in a subsequent period. Interpretations of this development vary widely.[97] Two main debates exist among proponents of this view. One pertains to *when* this sentiment arose, and the other explores *why* – the motivations behind Judah's assumption of the Israelite identity. While scholars paid more attention to the question of *when*, I agree with Philip Davies that the question of *why* deserves equal, if not greater, attention.[98] This is so because the *when* is intrinsically linked to, and often contingent upon, the *why*. Also, this aligns with my contention that focusing on the subjective aspect is crucial for understanding Judah's appropriation of Israel. Insofar as I see Judah's desire for Israel as deeply rooted, simply asking when they began to imagine themselves as Israel misses the point. Instead, what matters is when they managed to, finally, convince themselves and others of this constructed reality. An identity is a social phenomenon, and not all claimed identities are accepted. In this chapter, I underscore this point by engaging with major participants in the current debate on Judah's assumption of the Israel identity, while also addressing recent challenges posed to it.

3.1 Current Debate on Judah's Assumption of Israel Identity

It would be apt to begin with the seminal works of Philip Davies. Davies stands as a paramount figure in the conversation surrounding Judah's appropriation of the Israel identity. His groundbreaking *In Search of 'Ancient Israel'* (1992) fundamentally shifted our understanding of the term "Israel." He called for a distinction between "historical Israel" from the "biblical Israel," by which he means the conflicting depictions of Israel nested within biblical literature.[99] In 2007, Davies pub-

---

97 For a succinct summary, see now Tobolowsky, "Israelite and Judahite History in Contemporary Theoretical Approaches," 37–39.
98 See Philip R. Davies, *The Origins of Biblical Israel*, LHBOTS 485 (New York: T&T Clark, 2007), 3.
99 Davies, *In Search of 'Ancient Israel.'* Kratz (*The Composition of the Narrative Books*, 309) has also alluded to this distinction: "The Israel of the literary tradition is not the Israel of history. As in the New Testament a distinction is made between the historical and the kerygmatic Christ, so in the Old Testament the historical and the biblical Israel must be kept separate." See now Reinhard G. Kratz, *Historical and Biblical Israel: The History, Tradition, and Archives of Israel and Judah*, trans. Paul Michael Kurtz (Oxford: Oxford University Press, 2015). As is well known, Davies further set apart "ancient Israel" from these two forms of Israel, defining it as a modern

https://doi.org/10.1515/9783111376554-003

lished another significant work, *The Origins of Biblical Israel*, where he directly addressed an important question that he admittedly had overlooked: why did Judah take on the name "Israel"?[100]

His position is a radical one. In contrast with most other participants in the conversation, who maintain biblical Israel's pre-exilic origin, Davies led the scholarly tide towards accepting its late (post-exilic) origin. Thus, Davies is largely responsible for the divided landscape of the current debate around biblical Israel.

Davies rejects all propositions for a pre-exilic origin of biblical Israel, but not because he has an utterly different understanding of the nature of biblical Israel. It is because he fails to find an appropriate historical setting for Judahites' alleged assumption of Israelite identity during the pre-exilic period. Like many other scholars today, Davies does not consider Judah's assumption of Israelite identity a given. For anyone who accepts Judah's autonomy from Israel, it becomes extremely challenging to rationalize why Judah would embrace the rival's name. This is more so during the period of divided monarchy. Then, this title Israel belonged to the Northern Kingdom when it maintained its political life – i.e., the "historical Israel." Therefore, during that time, he deems it unlikely that the Judahites could claim that title. Most scholars agree on this point and thus think Judah's assumption of the Israel identity happened sometime after Samaria's fall, but Davies finds that unlikely after considering two pre-exilic scenarios.[101] The first is the common solution via the northern refugee theory. The second is the possibility that the name "Israel" was imposed on Judah when it served Israel as a vassal. Davies immediately dismisses the latter, given the premise that Judah would have gotten rid of the imposed name when they later achieved independence from Israel. Davies addresses the former extensively, mainly taking up the argument promoted by Israel Finkelstein and Neil Silberman, which he considers as "the most powerful alternative" to his own theory.[102]

---

scholarly construct. He critiqued the ideological implications of accepting "ancient Israel" as factual, arguing – much like Whitelam – that doing so neglects or erases the actual history of Palestine. Cf. Keith W. Whitelam, *The Invention of Ancient Israel: The Silencing of Palestinian History* (New York: Routledge, 1996).

100 Philip R. Davies, "The Origin of Biblical Israel," in *Essays on Ancient Israel in Its Near Eastern Context: A Tribute to Nadav Na'aman*, ed. Yaira Amit et al. (Winona Lake, IN: Eisenbrauns, 2006), 141–48; idem, *The Origins of Biblical Israel*; Davies, "The Trouble with Benjamin."

101 Davies, *The Origins of Biblical Israel*, 20–21.

102 Davies, 147. Finkelstein and Silberman's model, given its popularity, stands as a significant counterpoint to my position as well, and I have dedicated Chapter 4 specifically to their position.

Finkelstein and Silberman's position is rooted in the archaeological interpretation of the westward expansion of Jerusalem that it was mainly caused by the influx of refugees from the North,[103] which brought about needs for Judahite elites to control and reconcile the resulting mixed demography.[104] Out of various strategies for incorporating northern legacies, including cultic centralization and literary propaganda, the first "pan-Israelite idea" emerged in the context of Hezekiah's reformation.[105] Hence, the motivation behind the alleged adoption of Israel's identity was the need to cater to the increasingly influential northern populace, and Judahites were, in a sense, forced to embrace the identity of these migrants. Davies rejects their theory upon several grounds.[106] Firstly, there is no concrete archaeological evidence that confirms an influx of northern Israelites into Jerusalem. Secondly, the available demographic data does not necessarily pinpoint the expansion specifically to Hezekiah's reign; it might have been a more gradual process. Thirdly, Davies challenges the idea that fear of deportation would have compelled the northerners to relocate. Also, if that were the case, they would have likely returned home when Jerusalem later faced similar threats. Lastly, he suggests that the supposed Ephraimite refugees would have likely sought refuge in Benjaminite towns rather than Jerusalem, given that the Benjaminites seem to have evaded the crisis. For Davies, therefore, this is not the time when the alleged merging of identity took place. Without refugees, there is no need for the alleged "remaking" of the nation promoted by Finkelstein and Silberman.[107]

Reinhard Kratz is another scholar that Davies interacts with, who has also posited a pre-exilic origin for pan-Israelism, independently of Finkelstein and Silberman. Kratz's model is grounded in his detailed literary studies and, thus, is contoured very differently from Finkelstein's. Kratz also thinks that "Israel" originally was a politically and territorially defined kingdom, and the broader concept of "Israel" that includes Judah, which naturally could be conceived only outside

---

103 E.g., Finkelstein and Silberman, *The Bible Unearthed*, 243–45; idem, "Temple and Dynasty: Hezekiah, the Remaking of Judah and the Rise of the Pan-Israelite Ideology," *JSOT* 30 (2006): 259–85, https://doi.org/10.1177/0309089206063428; idem, *David and Solomon*; Israel Finkelstein, "The Settlement History of Jerusalem in the Eighth and Seventh Century BC," *RB* 115 (2008): 499–515, https://doi.org/10.2143/RBI.115.4.3206463.
104 See Finkelstein and Silberman, "Temple and Dynasty," 269–79; idem, *David and Solomon*, 134–44. Similarly, William M. Schniedewind, *How the Bible Became a Book: The Textualization of Ancient Israel* (Cambridge: Cambridge University Press, 2004), 191. Na'aman calls this a "melting pot" policy. Na'aman, "Saul, Benjamin and the Emergence of 'Biblical Israel' (Part 1)," 214.
105 Finkelstein and Silberman, "Temple and Dynasty," 279.
106 For his critique, Davies, *The Origins of Biblical Israel*, 147–50.
107 Finkelstein and Silberman, "Temple and Dynasty," 279.

the political terms, developed gradually after the fall of Samaria.[108] Kratz finds the beginning of this broader Israel in the "theological reflection" of northern escapees, who struggled to understand the significance of Israel's fall, while the same Yhwh-worshipping Judah has survived. Here, a particular theological reflection emerged among the prophetic circle that it was not the failure of Yhwh but the failure of the Northern Kingdom; hence Yhwh's judgment. It is in this context that Kratz claims, "Under the impact of the downfall of Israel … there emerged among the prophets for the first time, or at any rate for the first time explicitly, a notion of the unity of Yhwh and his people transcending the oppositions between Israel and Judah."[109] This concept of a broader Israel, which originated in classical prophecy,[110] was embraced and expanded upon in other literary works. This progression encompasses the combination of Saul and David materials,[111] the synchronization of the pre-Dtr history of Judah and Israel,[112] and the redefinition of Israel in terms of the common patriarchs in his Yahwistic patriarchal history.[113] When Judah later joined the same fate after Jerusalem's fall, out of the common experience a similar theological reflection arose, and the pan-Israelite identity was further developed.

Here, Judah's motivation to adopt the Israelite identity arose from their adoption of the theological contemplations of the northerners. The northerners had navigated this reflection ahead of the southerners, and they realized that Yhwh's people would persist despite the decline of monarchies. In the aftermath of the monarchy's demise, therefore, stories of the patriarchs and the Exodus crystallized as new bedrock narratives, spurring the restoration of the ethnic and religious notion of Israel and replacing the political notion of Israel.[114] When the Judahites later encountered similar adversities, they found resonance with this ideal and deemed it appropriate to embrace. While Kratz emphasizes the theological aspect, the primary mechanism of identity convergence mirrors Finkelstein

---

108 Kratz, "Israel als Staat," 3, 15–17; idem, *The Composition of the Narrative Books*, 265.

109 Kratz, *The Composition of the Narrative Books*, 314.

110 Kratz supports this early origin of pan-Israelism in his study of Isaiah, in which he demonstrates that the use of the title "holy one of Israel," together with the strategic parallel use of Jacob and Israel, began in the pre-exilic layer of the book. Reinhard Gregor Kratz, "Israel in the Book of Isaiah," *JSOT* 31 (2006): 103–28, https://doi.org/10.1177/0309089206068845.

111 Kratz, "Israel als Staat," 9; idem, *The Composition of the Narrative Books*, 314.

112 Kratz, "Israel als Staat," 8–11.

113 Kratz, 13–15. Kratz defines this as the "Legitimationsschrift" for the union in the kingdom of Judah.

114 This interpretation diverges from mine, which views the patriarchal and Exodus narratives as dual origin myths stemming from the monarchic era – one "ethnic" and the other "civic" in nature. See n. 51.

and Silberman's perspective: the North shaping the South. The distinction lies in that Finkelstein and Silberman saw northerners entering Jerusalem, while Kratz perceived them remaining on the fringe of the city.[115]

However, Davies approaches Kratz's proposition with cautious skepticism, given their methodological divergence.[116] Firstly, he critiques Kratz's heavy focus on the theological aspect of the issue, advocating for a more comprehensive consideration of wider social, cultural, and political factors, which, in his view, would have given Judah many reasons to distance itself from the defeated Israel. Secondly, Davies questions Kratz's assumption of a common cult in Judah and Israel, suggesting it might have been a historical outcome rather than an original state. Most significantly, Davies asks why Judah would adopt the name Israel: "Kratz has not explained why Yhwh should be specially regarded as the god of Israel rather than of Judah, or why Samarians should not have been encouraged to worship Yhwh as the god of Judah who had abandoned Israel."[117] As such, Davies rejects both Finkelstein and Kratz as "wrong answers" to the question of the emergence of "Judah's 'Israelite' identity."[118]

This is not to say that Davies rejects their ideas outright. He is sympathetic to many aspects of their positions but simply does not think this occurred in pre-exilic Judah. For Davies, it does not make sense that Judahites would take up the name of the recently doomed Israel. For Davies, this means that the entire pre-exilic era must be removed from consideration,[119] because he cannot account for the alleged motivation for the pre-exilic Judah to claim the fallen Israel's identity. So, even if we accept that refugees from the North migrated into Jerusalem, or anywhere else, one still must answer why Judahites were willing to embrace the name "Israel." It is one thing for Judah to take advantage of Israel's rich religious and cultural heritage. It is entirely another to adopt the title of their fallen neighbor.[120]

Consequently, Davies needs to find a more appropriate setting sometime after the fall of Jerusalem – when Judah became *weaker* than the northern remnants. It is certainly not natural to find a fitting moment when Judah was inferior to

---

115 Kratz (*The Composition of the Narrative Books*, 269) theorizes, based on Gen 35:21, that these northerners settled beyond Migdal-eder, where they produced their history (J).

116 Davies, *The Origins of Biblical Israel*, 23–24.

117 Davies, 24.

118 See Davies, 20–24, 142–50.

119 Davies, *The Origins of Biblical Israel*, 150; idem, "The Origin of Biblical Israel," 8.

120 This is why later Finkelstein ("The Settlement History," 507) had to adumbrate that while Judah held a dominant position, it was not powerful enough to turn away incoming refugees or dismiss their traditions. But just how weak would Judah have had to be to go so far as adopting the identity of the refugees?

Israel, since by then Israel as a political entity had long ceased. Here comes in the unique position of Benjaminites between Israel and Judah: Benjaminites belonged first to Israel, before they were annexed by Judah.[121] For Davies, Benjamin's dual membership holds the key for solving this riddle. Judeans' assumption of Israel identity arose out of a post-exilic power struggle between Judah and Benjamin. According to his theory, after the fall of Jerusalem, Benjaminites remained in the land around Mizpah, which was saved from the Babylonian raid and functioned as an administrative center of the area for over a century, and there they produced their history largely following their *Israelite* (not Judahite) identity around their hero Saul. This argument is based on Davies's assumption that Benjaminites retained their northern identity even after its inclusion to Judean district (which he thinks occurred after 722 BCE).[122] When Judeans later returned to their land from exile, they had to face this established Benjaminite/Israelite history. The broader concept of Israel (including Judah in it) arose out of negotiation with this Benjaminite history.[123] For Davies, this was the inception of the pan-Israelite identity. Later, when Judeans rose once again as the center of Yehud, they created a countermemory (he calls it "the First History"[124]) against it, which accounts for the strong polemical stance against Benjamin/Saul present in the final text of the story of David's rise over Saul.[125]

---

121 Unlike Na'aman, Davies considers Benjamin's claimed southern orientation from the beginning of the divided monarchy (1Kgs 12:16–21) a retrojection of the later Judah-Benjamin union. Davies, "The Origin of Biblical Israel," 2; idem, "The Trouble with Benjamin," 103.

122 About the alleged Benjaminites' northern sentiment, see the interesting case made in Davies, "The Trouble with Benjamin," 94–97.

123 Davies, "The Origin of Biblical Israel," 8; idem, *The Origins of Biblical Israel*, 174. Similarly, Guillaume, "Jerusalem 720–705," 203.

124 It encompassed the conquest narrative under Joshua, the "book of saviours" in Judges, and the history of Saul. Davies, *The Origins of Biblical Israel*, 104–5.

125 Davies, *The Origins of Biblical Israel*, 174. Na'aman tackles precisely this matter of Benjamin's dual membership in order to undermine Davies's idea of Benjamin's alleged bridging role played between Israel and Judah. Na'aman, "Saul, Benjamin and the Emergence of 'Biblical Israel' (Part 1)"; idem, "Saul, Benjamin and the Emergence of 'Biblical Israel' (Part 2)." Na'aman (p. 347) argues that "the district of Benjamin always had a southward orientation" and that "the stories of Saul and his house are no less Judahite than those of David." Against Davies's claim for a post-exilic origin of biblical Israel, then, Na'aman (p. 348) formulates a theory that the rise of biblical Israel came about almost as an aftereffect of the pre-Dtr literature (hence, pre-exilic) in which "Israel" is used as a "literary designation" describing territories ruled by Saul, David, and Solomon. However, Na'aman's claim for Benjamin's southern orientation is not without problem. Debating the role of Benjamin is replete with complexities and ambiguities. While its pivotal role in the North-South transmission is undeniable, concrete evidence detailing Benjamin's position between Israel and Judah is scarce. Thus, it is difficult to ascertain unequivocally the exact moment of Benjamin's inclusion in Judah. Even more elusive is the question of how Benjaminites

At this point of the debate, therefore, it may seem that Davies carries the day: none of the scenarios for a pre-exilic origin for biblical Israel is convincing, because they all fail to answer his basic question, "why would Judeans want to adopt the title Israel after Israel was defeated?"[126]

However, in my view, Davies too falls short of answering this question. Despite Davies's extensive critique of Finkelstein and Silberman, there seems to be a fundamental affinity in their explanatory paradigms. Davies's challenge of Finkelstein focuses on the factual basis of the influx of mass migrants but not on the underlying premise: that these refugees could impose their identity to the Judahites. Thus, when explaining why Judah chose to adopt Israel's identity and traditions, they both search for a context wherein Judah was *forced* to adopt the Israel identity. Both invoke the presence of mediating groups between the North and South. Essentially, Davies has simply substituted northern refugees with the Benjaminites. This leads me to question whether he has really answered the *why* question. Even if we accept the premise that the Benjaminites held more sway than the Judahite returnees, does this convincingly explain Judah's calling themselves "Israel"?[127] One can insist that the Judahites were forced to adopt the domi-

---

actually felt about their identity between Israel and Judah. In any case, even though Benjamin's southern membership in later period is irrefutable, its earlier, northern origin is difficult to ignore. In the end, there are reasons why Levin called it the "Benjamin conundrum." See Levin, "Benjamin Conundrum." If so, regardless of the exact point of its inclusion to Judah, one can agree with Davies that Benjaminites may well have retained an identity somewhat different from that of Judahites.

Na'aman's essays, then, have been challenged by Finkelstein. Israel Finkelstein, "Saul, Benjamin and the Emergence of 'Biblical Israel': An Alternative View," *ZAW* 123 (2011): 348–67. In reaction, I composed an essay which formed the basis of this chapter, elucidating Finkelstein's shortcomings in his endeavors. As previously discussed, Finkelstein's theory faced challenges from different angles. What he required was a compelling rebuttal to the critiques specifically aimed at his own theory. For that, see Koog P. Hong, "Once Again: The Emergence of 'Biblical Israel,'" *ZAW* 125 (2013): 278–88, https://doi.org/10.1515/zaw-2013-0017.

126 See Davies, *The Origins of Biblical Israel*, 1.

127 This applies also to Finkelstein. Why did the Judahites in Jerusalem adopt the refugees' identity? Here, note Finkelstein's oversight of the psychological nuances underpinning the purported combination of traditions, which is fraught with anti-northern polemic. Finkelstein and Silberman ("Temple and Dynasty," 279) suggest that the merged tradition – the "History of David's Rise (HDR)" and the "Succession History" – was created in order to appease the newly incorporated northern population: "they had to cater to the large northern population in Judah." To me, the fact that a Saulide memory was preserved seems less critical as *how* it was preserved. In HDR, Benjaminites' hero Saul is shamed, and Benjamin's pride as the holder of the first scepter of Israel is diminished. Attributing Saul's fall to divine judgment guaranteed the legitimacy of David's rise. How could such a device cater to Benjaminite, and Israelite, interests? If this is how the Judahites incorporated Benjaminite memory, then the Benjaminites, in my view, would rather have their memory forgotten. Davies has made a similar critique. See Davies, *The Origins of Biblical Israel*, 149.

nant Israel identity, but one must still wonder about its surprising durability of this forced identity. When the balance of power subsequently shifted back, would that not have afforded the Judahites an opportunity to rewrite the past and finally discard it in favor of their own identity?[128] And this is why I think Davies remains tentative on his conclusion, admitting that this is not presented as "a definitive 'solution.'"[129]

3.2 Na'aman and Struggle for Patrimony

In this context, Nadav Na'aman's new proposition merits special attention. It introduces a distinct approach to interpreting the situation, thus laying the groundwork for my own proposition.[130] Drawing upon striking parallels with the Mesopotamian case of patrimonial struggle between Assyria and Babylonia, Na'aman has recently proposed another argument (cf. n. 125), elaborating particularly on Judah's motivation in adopting the Israel identity. "The adoption of the Israelite identity by the Judahite scribes and elite was motivated by the desire to take over the highly prestigious vacant heritage of the Northern Kingdom,"[131] he claims, "just as Assyria had sought to take possession of the highly prestigious heritage of ancient Mesopotamia."[132] Na'aman takes up Machinist's thesis "literature is essentially a political act, created to explain and justify major political and cultur-

---

128 For example, Davies (*The Origins of Biblical Israel*, 104–5) posits that Judahites later formed the "first history" that is polemical to Saul. Then, in this version, why not discard Israel altogether and return to a true Judahite history? The same must apply to Finkelstein.

129 Davies, *The Origins of Biblical Israel*, 172.

130 As shall be apparent in Part II, it turns out there are more differences between his and my approach. While he appears to promote a pre-exilic origin of Judah's appropriation of Israel, his more recent publication on the formation of the Jacob narrative, in which he argued for its sixth century Judahite origin, has complicated the matter. Rejecting to see the Jacob tradition's function as North Israel's identity narrative, and limiting its functionality to later Judean context, he brings his position much similar to Davies. See, esp. Na'aman, "The Jacob Story and the Formation of Biblical Israel," 117–19. To me, it is not clear enough how his position put forward in articles on Saul, David, and Josiah relate to the conclusion drawn from his study on the Jacob narrative.

131 Schütte rejects Naaman's notion of the "vacant heritage." Wolfgang Schütte, "Wie wurde Juda israelitisiert?," *ZAW* 124 (2012): 52–72, https://doi.org/10.1515/zaw-2012-0004. Schütte contends that cultural and religious transmission cannot occur without human intermediaries. For discussion, refer to Section 4.2.1.

132 Nadav Na'aman, "The Israelite-Judahite Struggle for the Patrimony of Ancient Israel," *Bib* 91 (2010): 17, https://doi.org/10.2143/BIB.91.1.3188850. I have previously discussed Na'aman's model in some of my earlier publications, and this section draws heavily from them. See esp. Koog P. Hong, "The Deceptive Pen of Scribes: Judean Reworking of the Bethel Tradition as a Program for Assuming Israelite Identity," *Bib* 92 (2011): 427–28, 440–41, https://doi.org/10.2143/BIB.92.3.3188816.

al shifts" and freshly applies it to Josiah's program of northern expansion.[133] In comparison with the friction between Assyria and Babylonia, Na'aman tries to account for Judah's assuming Israelite identity in terms of a struggle for Israelite "patrimony."[134] Laying out the strategies that Assyrians employed in their attempt to take over Mesopotamian cultural patrimony, he highlights similarities between these strategies and Josianic reform strategies. When Assyrians managed to overcome Babylonia, they employed several typical strategies for legitimating their conquests and supremacy. Assyrians moved the statue of Marduk to Ashur and celebrated a major religious festival in Ashur, actions that were both conscious attempts to shift the Mesopotamian cultural center to Assyria. They also transported Babylon's large literary collection to Assyria, created original propagandist work, and reworked the foundational epic to serve Assyrian interests.[135]

Na'aman demonstrates that this sequence of events is similar to that of Josiah's reform and argues that the Josianic period in the last third of the seventh century BCE was the era when the new "ethno-religious-cultural identity of 'Israel'" that embraced inhabitants of both kingdoms emerged.[136] Na'aman interprets Dtr's presentation of Josiah's reform in 2Kgs 23 as a program of identity reformulation that aimed to embrace the northern identity and traditions. First, he promotes Josiah's northern expansion (2Kgs 23:15–18) signifies his aspiration for the newly realized pan-Israelite identity. Against Davies and Knauf, who proposed earlier dates for the annexation of Bethel's southern region, Na'aman contends that it was Josiah who conquered and annexed this northern shrine – a move he believes holds significant implications for the identity politics of that era. He also rejects Van Seters's wholesale denial of the historicity of Josiah's northern campaign,[137] and suggests that his northern operation was the reason for his death at Megiddo.

---

133 Machinist, on the other hand, had applied it to the time of David and Solomon. See Peter Machinist, "Literature as Politics: The Tukulti-Ninurta Epic and the Bible," *CBQ* 38 (1976): 478.

134 Na'aman, "The Israelite-Judahite Struggle for the Patrimony."

135 For more, see Na'aman, 9–12.

136 That is, Na'aman rejects the Hezekian era, or the late eighth–early seventh century BCE to be precise, as the incipient period of the pan-Israelite identity because of the remaining Assyrian influence. It was only after the Assyrian withdrawal from Syria-Palestine that allowed Josiah to "operate with no organized resistance in the highlands areas north of his kingdom and expand into the former Israelite territories." Na'aman, 20.

137 Na'aman, 19. Whether there is a *fondamentum in re* to this literary claim is another question, however. I do not share the confidence in the historicity of Josiah's northern campaign that Na'aman displays. My reservation about the historicity does not, however, diminish the significance of this literary presentation of Josiah's campaign. Important for our purposes is the sheer fact that such literary claims have been made, insofar as they exhibit the political motivation behind such propaganda. See n. 231.

Following the Assyrian withdrawal from Palestine and the new political opportunities opened up before the Kingdom of Judah, Josiah expanded northward and conquered several Israelite territories, conducted cult reform in his kingdom, and eliminated what was considered an "Assyrian" cult – namely, one that contemporaries associated with the Assyrian empire. The creation of a new ethnic-religious-cultural identity for the inhabitants of Judah fits in well the objects of the reform. Thus, the appropriation of the patrimony of the former Kingdom of Israel as part of the formation of a new identity might be regarded as an integral part of the reform.[138]

Second, Na'aman suggests that Josiah "may have plundered scrolls deposited in the temple of Bethel, just as Tukulti-Ninurta I and Ashurbanipal seized the scholarly tablets of Babylon."[139] This is the way Na'aman understands how some of northern traditions found their ways to Judah. He further argues that the name "Israel" used in these northern scrolls was later adopted by Judahite scribes as a new inclusive identity marker.[140]

Third, Josiah then celebrates the major Israelite religious festival, Passover, in Jerusalem (2Kgs 23:21–23). Na'aman assumes that Exodus was a central tradition in Northern Israel, whereas its trace in pre-exilic Judah was minimal at best.[141] Given the way the text presents Josiah's celebration of Passover in Jerusalem as an innovation, Na'aman argues that the feast of Passover was "part of his efforts to integrate northern Israelite traditions into his kingdom, just as Tukulti-Ninurta's and Sennacherib's celebration of the Akitu festival in Ashur was a way of integrating the Babylonian festival into Assyria."[142]

Then, one can expand this observation to the entire Dtr program. It is not only 2Kgs 23 that served Judah's program to take over Israel's position. In fact, one can argue that DH1, or the Josianic edition of the DtrH, is a program to justify Judah's takeover of Northern Israel's position as Yhwh's covenantal partner.[143] Every single king of Israel followed the sins of "Jeroboam ben Nebat" and forfeited the covenant with Yhwh (2Kgs 22:15–17). Based on the treaty motif, Dtr claims that the fall of Samaria is a manifestation of divine abandonment of northern Israelite monarchy (2Kgs 17:7–24) and promotes the idea of a divine choice of Judah, perhaps as an ideal covenant partner with Yhwh, through Josiah's faithfulness (2Kgs 23:21–25). The pure covenantal relationship with Yhwh could be restored only by the removal of the rival's sins. Josiah finally wipes out Jeroboam's

---

138 Na'aman, 20.
139 Na'aman, 20.
140 Na'aman, "Saul, Benjamin and the Emergence of 'Biblical Israel' (Part 2)," 342–48.
141 Na'aman, "The Israelite-Judahite Struggle for the Patrimony," 21.
142 Na'aman, 21.
143 Marvin A. Sweeney, *King Josiah of Judah: The Lost Messiah of Israel* (Oxford: Oxford University Press, 2001).

sins, which justifies his and Judah's promotion to the true heirs of the Mosaic Law (2Kgs 23:25). The treaty motif constitutes the heart of Deuteronomy. What makes Israel the people of Yhwh is the fidelity to the mutual covenant, the breach of which will only forfeit Israelhood. Noteworthy in this regard is that the Assyrian Tukulti-Ninurta epic frequently relies on a treaty motif as well to highlight the divine abandonment of the Babylonian king.[144]

Granted, the Mesopotamian analogy may not align precisely with the situation between Judah and Israel. The power dynamics between the two were quite distinct from those of Babylonia and Assyria, with Judah significantly weaker than Israel. Also, while Babylonia and Assyria contested over cultural patrimony, neither assumed the other's name.[145] This means, we should further take into consideration the power imbalance when we address Judah's relationship with Israel.

Still, compared to other theories, Na'aman's patrimony model is better equipped to address the elusive question of *why* the Judahites adopted the legacy of the defeated Israel. This challenges Davies's wholesale rejection of the pre-exilic origin of Judah's identity appropriation.[146] Even though Judahites were in a position superior to Israel after Samaria's fall, the possibility that they wanted to take over Israel – not for its present attraction but for its nostalgic appeal of past glory – still remains.

3.3 Recent Challenges to Appropriation Model

Recently, there has been a growing tendency to challenge the late origin of the unified Israel, reviving the traditional perspective, one way or the other, that the notion of "one Israel" had roots in Judah and Israel's early unity established in David's *Israelite* kingdom. Given the concerted efforts of several scholars in this direction, I see it necessary to address this before delving into my appropriation model.

Firstly, Kristin Weingart has challenged the recent tendency to interpret "Israel" as a political or religious concept, instead reviving the conventional position

---

144 Machinist, "Literature as Politics," 458, 464. Cf. the Cyrus edict for the employment of the same motif.

145 There are instances where one party attempting to embrace the other's name or title, particularly during periods of shifting power dynamics. One such example is the Assyrian King Tiglath-Pileser III (reigned 745–727 BCE), who, after conquering Babylon, adopted the title "King of Babylon" as a strategic move to consolidate and legitimize his dominion over Babylonia.

146 Yet in his subsequent publication, Na'aman argues for the Jacob tradition's post-exilic origin, which potentially undercuts his own theory of Judah's pre-exilic appropriation of Israel's legacy. See discussion in Section 8.2.

to see it as an ethnic designation that from earlier on included Judah.[147] She poses the same question as Davies: who would adopt the name of a loser to bolster their own position?[148] But unlike Davies, she searches for an answer from a pre-exilic ethnic unity between Judah and Israel. Weingart's approach is a semantic analysis of the term "Israel" in biblical writings. She underscores that both expansive and narrow concepts of "Israel" were present in texts predating the fall of Samaria in 722 BCE, from both northern and southern traditions.

However, the problem of her argument lies in her choice of early southern and northern texts, which is questionable, particularly with respect to whether they are free from later retouching. On the one hand, her primary source for the southern pre-722 text is the succession narrative (along with Isaiah and Micah).[149] Weingart's key observation is that "Israel" in the succession narrative often betrays the broader sense, including Judah. Here, Weingart's early dating of the succession narrative is conspicuous. Of course, there is no doubt that "Israel" in this text often encompasses Judah, but it is problematic to equate them with the contemporary perception of "Israel" in the early Judahite society. Above all, with the Davidic era seen as an idealization of the late period, one cannot rule out the possibility that the expanded sense of Israel was a product of a later imposition.[150] To me, what requires more attention is the recurring hints of Israel's narrow sense in this segment of the text, as reflected in the well-known phrase "Judah and *all* Israel."[151]

---

147 Weingart, *Stämmevolk – Staatsvolk – Gottesvolk?*; idem, "What Makes an Israelite an Israelite? Judean Perspectives on the Samarians in the Persian Period," *JSOT* 42 (2017): 155–75, https://doi.org/10.1177/0309089216677664.

148 "Wer schmückt sich mit den Namen eines Verlierers, um die eigene Postion [sic!] zu stärken?" Weingart, *Stämmevolk – Staatsvolk – Gottesvolk?*, 363–64.

149 Weingart, 171–89.

150 Weingart complains that other scholars are taking all the instances where a broad sense of Israel appears as a late text, which is a circular argument. Yet, a certain degree of circularity is almost unavoidable in most critical inquiries. The crux rather lies in how one defends their stance with additional supportive arguments.

151 See James W. Flanagan, "Judah in All Israel," in *No Famine in the Land: Studies in Honor of John L. McKenzie*, ed. James W. Flanagan and Anita Weisbrod Robinson (Missoula, MT: Scholars Press, 1975), 101–16. James Flanagan examined the usage of the technical term "all Israel" in the Saul narrative and demonstrated that Judah was not considered part of Israel during Saul's time. Let us briefly review a few of the passages that Flanagan presents as evidence that "all Israel" did not include Judah at that time. (1) "But all Israel and Judah loved David" (1Sam 18:16a). "All Israel" and Judah are juxtaposed; the former does not include the latter. (2) "But the prophet Gad said to David, 'Do not stay in the stronghold; go at once to the territory of Judah'" (1Sam 22:5). The land of Judah does not seem to be considered part of the area over which Saul reigned. (3) "So Saul took three thousand picked men from all Israel and went in search of David and his men in the direction of the rocks of the wild goats" (1Sam 24:3). "All Israel" appears to exclude Judah, insofar as the people of Judah were unlikely to go against their kin, David. Flanagan also

While the broader sense of Israel in this text can be attributed to later modifications, explaining the persisting narrow sense of Israel poses a greater challenge.

The same critique applies to her observation on the pre-exilic northern Jacob narrative. Weingart relies primarily on the birth report of Jacob's sons in Gen 29:31–30:24 to substantiate Judah's inclusion in "Israel."[152] Yet, again, this very text has been instrumental in shaping the pan-Israelite concept, and its dating remains a matter of debate. Weingart defends the coherence of the birth report against Levin, Kratz, and Fleming, arguing that removing certain elements would disrupt the narrative flow of what she regards as a well-crafted composition.[153] This argument might counter the staged reconstruction of this passage's growth,[154] but it falls short when confronted with propositions for the late origin of the present list, whether or not drawing from earlier listings.[155] One can still postulate that Judah was not included in the original version of the tribal list (or simply in the earlier perceptions).

Secondly, Omer Sergi makes a similar claim based on archaeological findings. He, too, interprets "Israel" as an ethnic concept encompassing both Judah and Israel.[156] Sergi points out that the archaeological findings of the sedantarization of the Iron Age I and II central highland mirror the textual portrayal of Saul and David's reigns.[157] This means that unlike others who saw Saul's reign as the beginning of the Northern Kingdom, now separated by the inserted Judahite David-Solomon traditions, he sees the Saul-David traditions represent a southern perspective of early Israel in the Benjamin-Jerusalem area, which is different from the territorial polity of the North developed from the time of Omrides.[158] Given that this group always is designated as Israel in the text, he concludes that there

---

observes that, in 1Sam, Judah is not frequently mentioned except in the section related to David. Saul is anointed by "all Israel," which does not include Judah. Most battle accounts do not mention Judah's role either. There are a few mentions of Judah's participation in Saul's warfare (1Sam 11:8; 15:4), but they are Deuteronomistic glosses. See Flanagan, 105. With few exceptions, "Judah" is used as a geographic term (1Sam 22:5; 23:3, 23; 27:10; 30:14, 16) or describes an entity separate from "all Israel" (1Sam 18:16, 30:26); it also appears in another Dtr gloss (1Sam 27:6).

152 Weingart, *Stämmevolk – Staatsvolk – Gottesvolk?*, 236–44.
153 Weingart, 238–41.
154 E.g., Kratz, *The Composition of the Narrative Books*, 266.
155 E.g., Tobolowsky, *The Sons of Jacob and the Sons of Herakles*.
156 See Omer Sergi, "Israelite Identity and the Formation of the Israelite Polities in the Iron I–IIA Central Canaanite Highlands," *WO* 49 (2019): 206–35, https://doi.org/10.13109/wdor.2019.49.2.206. Also, see now Sergi, *The Two Houses of Israel*.
157 Omer Sergi, "Saul, David, and the Formation of the Israelite Monarchy: Revisiting the Historical and Literary Context of 1 Samuel 9–2 Samuel 5," in *Saul, Benjamin, and the Emergence of Monarchy in Israel: Biblical and Archaeological Perspectives*, ed. Joachim J. Krause, Omer Sergi, and Kristin Weingart, AIL 40 (Atlanta: SBL Press, 2020), 57–91.
158 This echoes Na'aman's stance discussed earlier.

were two different Israels, first in the South and then in the North.[159] However, the challenge lies in the fact that archaeological evidence does not elucidate the self-perception of these emerging highlanders in the Benjamin-Jerusalem area.[160] Thus, the matter pivots back to how much we can trust identity expressions in the text. Yet, in scrutinizing the text, Sergi seems predisposed to take the text at face value.[161] Simply, Sergi's primary argument for Judah's early assumption of the Israelite identity stems from his simplistic reading of the Saul-David narrative, which portrays David as an Israelite and labels his kingdom as Israel.[162] In doing so, he hardly accounts for the possibility that these portrayals might have been influenced by subsequent viewpoints, when others may take these as the very discursive instrument to construct the glorious, united past. That the Saul-David narrative fits the archaeological evidence is not insignificant, but that does not mean that minute details like text's depiction of the group identity also can be taken at their face value.

Finally, Daniel Fleming and Lauren Monroe have charted a distinct path in exploring Judah's early connection to Israel. Earlier in *The Legacy of Israel in Judah's Bible*, Fleming already articulated his challenges with understanding Judah's appropriation of the Israelite legacy and identity. While he devoted significant attention to the appropriation model,[163] he ultimately found it unlikely that

---

159 In this, Sergi is similar to Fleming and Monroe's position that we discuss shortly.
160 Our divergence stems from distinct methodological orientations. As an archaeologist, Sergi seems to be confident that archaeological findings of the settlement patterns in the Benjamin-Jerusalem region in the Iron IIA supports the idea that the early Judah-Benjamin polity formed a distinct entity – materially, politically, and economically – from the polity north of Bethel. See Omer Sergi, "The Emergence of Judah as a Political Entity between Jerusalem and Benjamin," *ZDPV* 133 (2017): 1–23; idem, "Israelite Identity and the Formation of the Israelite Polities in the Iron I–IIA Central Canaanite Highlands." Also, his refined presentation is found in Sections 3.1., 4.2., and 4.3. of Sergi, *The Two Houses of Israel*. In contrast, I hold reservations about using this material evidence as a primary source to infer the residents' self-perception concerning their ethnic or socio-political identities. See n. 41 in the introduction and n. 179 in Chapter 4 below. As maintained throughout this book, I believe such perceptions are dynamic and context-dependent, shaped by the shifting socio-political landscape than being etched in stone.
161 Sergi, "Saul, David, and the Formation of the Israelite Monarchy," 81–83. For his conservative view of the early period of Judah, see Sergi, "The Emergence of Judah as a Political Entity between Jerusalem and Benjamin."
162 E.g., Sergi ("Saul, David, and the Formation of the Israelite Monarchy," 81) posits that David's kinship identity was not Judahite but Ephrathite (hence, Israelite) that settled in Bethlehem. Cf. Leonard-Fleckman's argument that the house of David was distinct from the tribe of Judah. She also contends that David was originally a king of Israel, and it was only through later editorial interventions that the Judahites presented him as their monarch. Mahri Leonard-Fleckman, *The House of David: Between Political Formation and Literary Revision* (Minneapolis: Fortress, 2016).
163 Fleming, *The Legacy of Israel*, 47–57.

the Judahites would take on the name of their rival without genuine historical ties. Consequently, Fleming gravitated towards a traditional perspective, positing that there persisted an authentic recollection of David ruling over Israel.[164]

This perspective is further elucidated in Fleming's recent collaborations with Lauren Monroe.[165] Fleming and Monroe adopt a nuanced, yet unmistakably positivist stance. I describe their approach as holistic, aiming to integrate all available evidence – historical, archaeological, and textual – to provide a cohesive answer. They contend that, contrary to the dominant academic inclination to downplay the value of biblical texts as historical records, the extant biblical narratives can, albeit selectively, offer insights that complement other historical and archaeological data.[166] Their vision is commendable, but I harbor reservations about its pragmatic outcomes.

With this, what they promote essentially is a dual Israel theory: an initial southern "little Israel" and a subsequent northern "greater Israel." The southern "little Israel," distinct from Judah, encompasses the central highlands of Ephraim, Benjamin, and Judah, where Saul and David's reigns over "Israel" were anchored in Gibeah and Jerusalem. In contrast, the "greater Israel" represents the political and territorial expanse of the Northern Kingdom, stretching from its center in Samaria all the way to its northern boundaries in the Galilean frontiers. Following the fall of Samaria, Judahite scribes creatively re-envisioned this "greater Israel," realizing their aspirations for Israel that they have never fully given up. The implications of this position are well articulated by Monroe's summary statement:

> At the same time, it is worth noting here that Judah's identification with the name Israel was *neither contrived nor artificial.* As the Merenptah inscription indicates, the name Israel was tied to populations residing in the southern Levant prior to the establishment of any kingdom that bore this name. It is entirely plausible that a population called Israel resided

---

164 Fleming (*The Legacy of Israel*, 49) states: "Although I am not persuaded that the early David material includes Judah, the notion that David's fame derived from rule of Israel forges an ancient bond between the founder of the southern kingdom and the northern realm. By speaking of 'the two houses of Israel,' the writer of Isa. 8:14 appears to echo a claim that the house of David never gave up its heritage as onetime rulers over Israel. Such a claim would lie at the root of Judah's eventual appropriation of the Israel name, never fully abandoned by the house of David. ... Once the kingdom of Israel was removed from the scene, it is very likely that its own survivors strove to *preserve* a sense of identity, and this effort may have contributed to bodies of Israelite material that found their way into the Bible."
165 Fleming, "The Bible's Little Israel"; Monroe, "On the Origins and Development of Greater Israel." See also Lauren Monroe and Daniel E. Fleming, "Earliest Israel in Highland Company," *NEA* 82 (2019): 16–23, https://doi.org/10.1086/703322.
166 See, especially, Fleming, "The Bible's Little Israel," 150; Monroe, "On the Origins and Development of Greater Israel," 189.

in both northern and southern spaces, so it was just as natural for a Saul or David to establish rule over Israel in the southern central highlands as it was for a Jeroboam or his successors to rule over Israel from Tirzah, though this scenario would differ considerably from the one we find in the books of Samuel and Kings. If this is the case, the claim to the name Israel made by Judah's scribes would not have been simply a matter of appropriation; rather it would have reflected an authentic and deeply embedded identification with the name that has been obscured by the later distinction between "Israel" and "Judah."[167]

Monroe's assertion that the adoption of the name Israel was "neither contrived nor artificial" captures the nature of their solution. They want to seek the basis for Judah's unlikely claim for Israel's identity.[168] In the end, they arrive at the remarkable conclusion that the division we observe in the text between Judah and Israel is a later invention, precipitated by the inclusion of Judah's own history, whereas originally there were merely two distinct "Israels."

I can resonate with many of their observations.[169] Yet, again, the crucial question is whether we can interpret this text as a reliable reflection of early historical reality. The challenge lies in the fact that Saul and David appear in a period of history that stands sharply contested between Judah and Israel. The identity portrayed in the text might very well be more a product of this dispute than a reflection of actual history. Within such a context, no fact stands neutral. Even if David's regional dominion held true, that version of Israel differs from the subsequently expanded Israel. Thus, such a claim becomes moot if the northern Israelites choose not to honor David's alleged rule over them.

Instead, I see it more profitable to see echoes of different Israels in the text as reflections of different claims, i.e., as claimed reality rather than historical reality. That an early text evinces a "semantic" range of a broad "Israel" does not necessarily mean that such a well-defined *entity* with clear boundaries existed. Instead, it suggests that particular groups were staking their claims on those

---

167 Monroe, 191. Italic added.

168 In a way, this mirrors the model proposed by Kratz ("Israel als Staat," 17), who also perceived that the ancient ideal of ethnic and religious Israel was reinstated following the collapse of the monarchy.

169 My own perspective has always been that the tales of Saul and David emanate from a southern local tradition, set apart from the northern monarchic narratives linked to figures like Jeroboam, Omri, and Jehu. That is, the Israel that Judah actually engaged with was largely confined to tribes in the central highland region, namely Benjamin and Ephraim. Since their contact was mainly through Benjamin and Ephraim, Judah's appropriating Israel's legacy is mainly spelled out in terms of their connections to Benjamin and Ephraim. Entities of farther north, with whom their actual contact was limited, necessarily was not incorporated into the core of Judah's Israel heritage. It seems evident that these original local stories have been reimagined and cast into the grand foundation narrative of the United Monarchy.

identities. I simply accept that there were multiple definitions of Israel, and I see no reason to assume a continuity among them. Both Judah and Israel had their own constructs of Israel, and even before them, there appear to be entities that staked a claim to the name Israel, as evinced in Mernephtah. The present text must be understood within this framework, representing Judah's definition of Israel, wherein Israel's definition is very much obscured.

Consequently, the issue at hand is not about which claim is historically more genuine or authentic, but rather who possesses the greater power behind these claims. I assume that while the Northern Kingdom persisted, its claim of Israel was significantly more dominant than Judah's, rendering the latter's claim virtually inconsequential. However, with the demise of Samaria, Judah's ideal could finally come to fruition. This is how I understand Judah's appropriation of Israel, which, in my view, provides a more pragmatic perspective than seeking historical reality behind different claims of Israel.

3.4 Conclusion

Biblical scholars have debated much on *when* and *why* Judah assumed Israel's identity. In addressing the *when*, debate persists between those advocating for a pre-exilic origin and those favoring an exilic one. Yet the resolution to that question mostly hinges on one's interpretation of the *why*. As for the *why*, we observed that some believe Judah was forced to adopt Israel's identity, while others think it stemmed from Judah's aspiration. While Davies dismissed all pre-exilic explanations, the appropriation model appears to have a potential to support a pre-exilic origin. However, many remain skeptical that such aspiration would be strong enough to spur Judah to adopt the legacy of a now fallen Israel, leading them to revert to the traditional perspective that Judah was simply rekindling an ancient unity. The present state of scholarly research thus points to a remaining challenge: to delve deeper into understanding the impetus behind Judah's unlikely adoption of Israel's identity, and that is what I aim to tackle in the rest of Part I.

4 Rethinking Northern Refugees

Before exploring Judah's motivation to assume the identity of Israel, I will have to first address the northern refugee theory, a prevailing view that offers a strong alternative perspective. As discussed earlier (Section 3.1.), the theory championed by Israel Finkelstein and Neil Silberman has been criticized by Philip Davies. Subsequently, Nadav Na'aman has emerged as a prominent challenger to Finkelstein,[170] resulting in a series of spirited debates between the two Tel Aviv scholars.[171] Yet even with the significant critiques presented by Na'aman and others, Finkelstein's hypothesis continues to find substantial support. That is in part because these

---

170 Na'aman offered a programmatic analysis of Jerusalem's expansion from the *la longue durée* perspective, attributing it to gradual economic prosperity under the Assyrian empire. Nadav Na'aman, "When and How Did Jerusalem Become a Great City? The Rise of Jerusalem as Judah's Premier City in the Eighth-Seventh Centuries B.C.E.," *BASOR* 347 (2007): 21–56, https://doi.org/10.1086/BASOR25067021. He also presented pointed arguments against an influx of mass refugees, framing it against the political landscape of the Assyrian empire and the specific condition of Jerusalem's economic system. (1) Against the international politics, Na'aman cites how political refugees were treated in Ancient Near Eastern kingdoms and argues that Judah was not in a position to accept Israelite refugees, which "would have amounted to an open provocation against the king of Assyria," a risk Hezekiah was unlikely to take (p. 35). (2) Against Jerusalem's economic system, he questions if Jerusalem could manage the sudden influx of large-scale refugees within the structure of a self-supporting agrarian society. The large influx of refugees would have caused a supply-demand imbalance, collapsing Jerusalem's economic system and creating social chaos, putting Judah into great trouble (p. 36).

171 Finkelstein, "The Settlement History"; Nadav Na'aman, "The Growth and Development of Judah and Jerusalem in the Eighth Century BCE: A Rejoinder," *RB* 116 (2009): 321–35, https://doi.org/10.2143/RBI.116.3.3206430; idem, "Saul, Benjamin and the Emergence of 'Biblical Israel' (Part 1)"; idem, "Saul, Benjamin and the Emergence of 'Biblical Israel' (Part 2)"; Finkelstein, "Saul, Benjamin: An Alternative View." Finkelstein's defense against Na'aman has centered on stressing the unprecedented rapidity of the expansion based on archaeological grounds. "If we are not contemplating the arrival of extra-terrestrials," Finkelstein ("The Settlement History," 511) claims, "we are dealing with refugees." Granted, the rapidity of the expansion increases the likelihood that it resulted from a sudden demographic move, but archaeology simply does not reveal if the migrants came from the North. See Guillaume, "Jerusalem 720–705," 197. In addition, Finkelstein stresses the rapid decrease in settlement in the North. Yet, the decrease of population does not necessarily indicate the inhabitants came to Jerusalem rather than to other places. For other sporadic comments against the refugee theory, see Davies, *The Origins of Biblical Israel*, 20–24; idem, "The Origin of Biblical Israel," *JHebS* 5 (2005): 7, https://doi.org/10.5508/jhs.2005.v5.a17; idem, "The Trouble with Benjamin," 109; Ernst Axel Knauf, "Bethel: The Israelite Impact on Judean Language and Literature," in *Judah and the Judeans in the Persian Period*, ed. Oded Lipschits and Manfred Oeming (Winona Lake, IN: Eisenbrauns, 2006), 293–95; Niels Peter Lemche, "Did a Reform like Josiah's Happen?," in *The Historian and the Bible: Essays in Honour of Lester L. Grabbe*, ed. Philip R. Davies and Diana V. Edelman, LHBOTS 530 (New York: T&T Clark, 2010), 16–17.

https://doi.org/10.1515/9783111376554-004

critiques remain under-recognized. Yet, it is fundamentally because scholars in general, still presuming an innate tie between Judah and Israel, find the refugee theory offers the most economic explanation for phenomena relating to North-South transmission. Given its popularity, I find it necessary to dedicate further attention to this theory.[172]

I take no issue with scholars theorizing a potential influx of northern refugees; speculation is a natural element of academic discourse. My reservations arise from the widespread belief that concrete material evidence exists for these northern refugees. That is to say, most scholars who embrace the northern refugee theory today lean heavily on Magen Broshi's classic interpretation of the "broad wall"[173] discovered in the western hill of Jerusalem by Nahman Avigad.[174] While the significance of this discovery in biblical archaeology is substantial,[175] the inconvenient truth is that Jerusalem's expansion alone does not prove or disprove the said migration. Here, Broshi's argument for the migration from the North uses eight lines, mostly of speculation without hard facts.[176] Additionally,

---

172 Not only Finkelstein, but also many other significant interlocutors that I interact with in this book accept this view, one way or another, making it crucial for me to clarify. See, e.g., Sparks, *Ethnicity and Identity in Ancient Israel*, 38, 40, 43, 223–24, 233–35, 271, 283; William M. Schniedewind, "Jerusalem, the Late Judahite Monarchy, and the Composition of the Biblical Texts," in *Jerusalem in Bible and Archaeology: The First Temple Period*, ed. Andrew G. Vaughn and Ann E. Killebrew, Symposium Series 18 (Leiden: Brill, 2003), 380, 385–86; idem, *How the Bible Became a Book*, 94–95; Fleming, *The Legacy of Israel*, 172, 310; Weingart, *Stämmevolk – Staatsvolk – Gottesvolk?*, 14–21, 268, 363–64.
173 The wall is originally called "the Israelite wall." Later Avigad identifies the wall with the "broad wall" of Neh 3:8. Nahman Avigad, *Discovering Jerusalem* (Nashville: Thomas Nelson, 1983), 62; Hillel Geva, ed., *Jewish Quarter Excavations in the Old City of Jerusalem: Conducted by Nahman Avigad, 1969–1982*, vol. 1 (Jerusalem: Israel Exploration Society, 2000), 81.
174 The discovery of the wall, with an overall length of 65 meters and a width of approximately 7 meters, was made possible by a rare archaeological excavation of the Jewish Quarter of the old city of Jerusalem, conducted from 1969 to 1982. Despite initial doubts, after a painstaking examination of the stratigraphy and the pottery, the excavators concluded that the broad wall belonged to the First Temple period. See Avigad, *Discovering Jerusalem*, 49; Geva, *Jewish Quarter Excavations*, 61–80.
175 This is especially so pertaining to the debate between the maximalists and minimalists on the size of Jerusalem in the First Temple period. For a detailed description of the debate, see Avigad, *Discovering Jerusalem*, 27–31.
176 Magen Broshi, "Expansion of Jerusalem in the Reigns of Hezekiah and Manasseh," *IEJ* 24 (1974): 25. It starts with a conjecture that "the sharp decline of the formerly Israelite provinces might have caused a mass immigration to the south." The argument ends with another conjecture that "it is quite reasonable to assume that the reduction of the population of these places [Dan, Bethel, Hazor, and Shiqmona] can be explained by forced exile and by emigration of people seeking refuge in independent Judah."

for Broshi, northern refugees represented one of two probable avenues for the influx with the other stemming from the Judean Shephelah.[177]

Following Broshi, many others have entered the discussion, including Finkelstein and Na'aman. To my knowledge, however, there has been limited progression from Broshi's initial findings in terms of direct and tangible evidence; instead, there has been a reliance on speculation and circumstantial evidence. I believe most participants of the debate acknowledge this limitation.[178] While discussions on potential scenarios can continue, I doubt that would yield any substantial results. The material evidence can tell us only so much, especially considering the consistent material culture shared between Judah and Israel.[179] Even if evidence indicates some presence of northern materials in Jerusalem, it does not necessarily confirm a refugee influx; such materials could be attributed to different forms of interchange. Even if, against expectations, sweeping evidence affirms their arrival, it does not automatically indicate their pivotal influence on Judahite society. Invoking refugees as a catch-all solution for subsequent transformations in Judah is oversimplification.

In this chapter, I take a distinctive route. By referencing empirical instances from Korean history involving refugee movements, I aim to highlight the complex dynamics that typically characterize such situations. In particular, I challenge the tendency to overstate the role of northern refugees, while casting the Judahites in a passive light. This is most evident when explaining the transmission of northern traditions to the South and their incorporation into Judah's Bible. My goal is to underscore the need for a nuanced approach, steering clear of oversimplifications in what could be a very complex situation.

---

177 Broshi, "Expansion of Jerusalem."

178 Finkelstein also admits this point. See Finkelstein and Silberman, "Temple and Dynasty," 266.

179 There is a larger debate among scholars of various disciplines on how archaeology can, or cannot, serve our understanding of changes taking place in group identities. For long, scholars relied on archaeology on explaining matters on cultural identity; but as soon as we recognize that identity is a social phenomenon, the efficacy of archaeology becomes questionable – especially when we deal with peoples of cultural affinity. Because matters of identity are most pronounced precisely among contingent groups, one must question what material discoveries can provide in our quest for people's perceptions of "who we are." The perception of "who Israel is" is probably one of the most complex cases within this context, and it is crucial to exercise caution when interpreting evidence from the material realm, avoiding uncritical assumptions or the imposition of established perspectives. See, e.g., Siân Jones, *The Archaeology of Ethnicity: Constructing Identities in the Past and Present* (London: Routledge, 1997). Cf. Maeir, "On Defining Israel"; Omer Sergi, "(Re)Constructing Identities in the Bronze and Iron Age Levant: Introduction," *WO* 49 (2019): 146–50, https://doi.org/10.13109/wdor.2019.49.2.146.

4.1 Some Observations on Refugees in Korean Contexts

As a way of cautioning against overconfidence in our analytical prowess, I propose examining empirical scenarios from other analogous cases to supplement the ambiguous material evidence available. Although arriving at a definitive answer might still be challenging, this approach enables us to investigate various potential explanations and ultimately select the most reasonable one for our specific context. I will offer two examples from the Korean context, one ancient and one modern, each serving a unique purpose in my argument. Again, this is not to assert that these Korean examples have exclusive value over others; rather, I present them as an invitation for others to incorporate their own contextual insights.[180]

4.1.1 Koguryŏ Refugees to Silla

Tab. 2: Concise Timeline of Ancient Korean History.

57 BCE–668 CE	*Three Kingdoms Period*
668–935 CE	United Silla
918–1392 CE	Koryŏ
1392–1910 CE	Chosŏn

The first example comes from Korea's Three Kingdoms period, a seminal era in ancient Korean history.[181] During the Three Kingdoms period, which spanned

---

180 Cross-cultural analysis between ancient Israel and ancient or modern Korean contexts has not been widely pursued. But a notable recent attempt can be found in Hyun Chul Paul Kim, "'The Myth of the Empty Exile': A Comparative Exploration into Ancient Biblical Exile and Modern Korean Exile," *JSOT* 45 (2020): 45–64, https://doi.org/10.1177/0309089219875157.

181 The following content does not offer groundbreaking or academically cutting-edge insights. As I am not an expert in Korean history, my presentation aims to provide a general overview rather than specialized analysis, covering knowledge typically found in textbooks. For an accessible history in English, see Seth, *A Concise History of Korea*. Nonetheless, I have consulted recent academic research to ensure accuracy, and my work has benefited much from the following studies. Sun-Yoh Chung, "The Goguryo Refugees Who Move to the Silla Kingdom – Focused on the Settlers in Bodeokguk," *History and Discourse* 56 (2010): 71–106 [정선여, "신라로 유입된 고구려 유민의 동향"]; Mi Kyoung Lee, "Silla's Policy for Ruling Bodeokguk," *Daegu Historical Review* 120 (2015): 101–32, https://doi.org/10.17751/DHR.120.101 [이미경, "신라의 보덕국 지배정책"]; Gyu-ho Lee, "Dang's Policy to Deal with Goguryeo Refugees, and the Situation of the Refugees,"

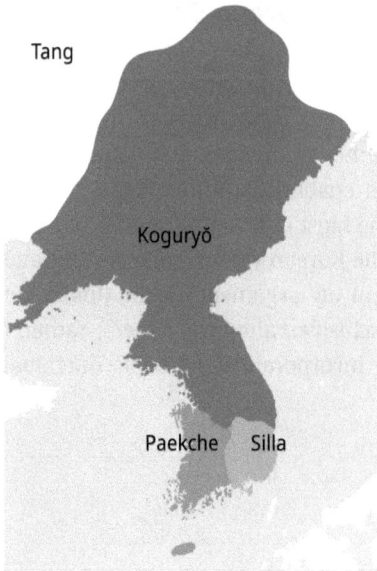

Fig. 2: Korean Peninsula (5th cent CE). Illustration by Kim Minji.

from 57 BCE to 668 CE, the kingdoms of Koguryŏ, Paekche, and Silla held sway over the Korean peninsula. Koguryŏ, located in the northern region of the peninsula, was renowned for its military prowess, acting as a buffer against powerful Chinese empires and dangerous nomadic tribes from the north. Paekche was situated in the southwestern part of the peninsula, while Silla occupied the southeastern region. The political dynamics among the three kingdoms were often contentious, characterized by frequent wars and shifting alliances, but there were also periods of cooperation and cultural exchange, particularly between Paekche and Silla in the south.

Quarterly Review of Korean History 101 (2016): 141–72 [이규호, "당의 고구려 유민 정책과 유민들의 동향"]; Yong-chul Bang, "The Outbreak and Characteristics of Goguryeo Revival War," *Daegu Historical Review* 133 (2018): 115–49, https://doi.org/10.17751/DHR.133.115 [방용철, "고구려 부흥전쟁의 발발과 그 성격"]; Eun-yi Shin, "The Foundation and Meanings of Bodeokguk," *Daegu Historical Review* 132 (2018): 237–73, https://doi.org/10.17751/DHR.132.237 [신은이, "보덕국의 탄생과 그 의미"]; Ho-won Choi, "Geommojam and Anseung Forces of Goguryeo and Their Relationship with and Perception of Silla," *Sillasahakpo* 49 (2020): 171–206 [최호원, "고구려 검모잠·안승 세력과 대신라관계 인식"]; Chang-hyeok Kwon, "A Review of Silla's Strategy to Support Goguryeo Revival Movement in 670–673," *Sillasahakpo* 51 (2021): 165–205 [권창혁, "670~673 년 신라의 고구려 부흥운동 지원 전략에 대한 검토"].

It was Silla that eventually defeated the two other kingdoms and united the Korean Peninsula (668 CE). That was partial unification though; Silla achieved it only in alliance with the Tang Empire of China, and they had to pay hefty price for that. Most of the Koguryŏ region fell back into Tang's hands. The fall of Koguryŏ in the north bears some resemblance to the conquest of North Israel by Assyria. Though Judah did not engage militarily as Silla did, it influenced the chain of events that ultimately precipitated Israel's downfall (2Kgs 16:7–9). Like Assyria conquered Israel and deported major population (2Kgs 17:6), Koguryŏ suffered a similar situation by Tang. This prompts the inquiry into what happened to the remnants of Koguryŏ. Contrary to the ancient Israelite situation, we possess some evidence and historical accounts detailing the fate of some of the remnants, offering a compelling point of comparison.

Historians have observed that the movements of the remnants have taken place in several directions.[182] Firstly, some were forcibly relocated to China by Tang, which bears resemblance to the mass deportations in the Israelite context by Assyria or Babylonia.[183] Following the fall of Pyongyang-seong, Koguryŏ's capital, the Tang Empire relocated approximately 28,000 people, including a significant portion from the royal family and the ruling elite. Those transported to Tang were spread across various provinces,[184] with the royal family and the nobility primarily settled in the Tang capital, which underscores the tight control the empire maintained over them during this era.

Secondly, many Koguryŏ people continued to reside in the northern area. Following the relocation of numerous residents to China, local resistance to Tang oppression emerged. Despite the fierce opposition, the resistance ultimately faltered and was quelled by the Tang forces. The Tang Empire then gradually stabilized and took control of the region, with their efforts including the repatriation of Koguryŏ's last king, who ended up conspiring against Tang and faced exile once again.

---

182 I would like to thank my student, Kim Hanbit, for a helpful review of scholarship on this topic among Korean historians.
183 See Lee, "Dang's policy to deal with Goguryeo refugees, and the situation of the refugees."
184 Recent discoveries of ancient burial sites, featuring tombstones inscribed with the names of Koguryŏ people brought to Tang, have sparked numerous studies on the lives of these displaced individuals. See, e.g., Su-Jin Kim, "Recognition of Goguryeo by Bureaucrats in Tang Dynasty Through the Epitaphs of Displaced People in Goguryeo," *Humanities Studies East and West* 54 (2018): 41–84 [김수진, "고구려 유민 묘지명에 나타난 당인 관인의 '高句麗' 인식"]; Byung-jin Jang, "Stories of Goguryeo described in Tomb Epitaphs Made for the Goguryeo Refugees in Dang," *Quarterly Review of Korean History* 117 (2020): 225–56, https://doi.org/10.35865/YWH.2020.09.117.225 [장병진, "고구려 유민 묘지명의 고구려 관련 전승과 그 계통"].

Thirdly, some Koguryŏ people migrated to Silla. This occurred in multiple phases and was complicated by intricate political developments. Initially, many remained in their homeland and participated in the aforementioned resistance movement. However, an intriguing turn of events took place when a member of Koguryŏ's royal family (안승/보덕, Anseung/Bodeok), who was leading the resistance, was forced to seek refuge in Silla. There, he reestablished the kingdom and sought recognition from Silla. Remarkably, Silla not only acknowledged them but also facilitated their relocation to Silla, granting them a territory to rule as an independent revived state – known as the State of Bodeok (보덕국, Bodeokguk) – albeit temporarily (674–683 CE).[185]

This complex situation requires further elaboration. After Tang and Silla defeated Paekche (660 CE) and Koguryŏ (668 CE) in sequence, Tang sought to exert control over the peninsula, apparently more than what their agreement with Silla had stipulated. This posed a threat to Silla, and the last phase of Silla's unification campaign makes an ironic turn to repel against Tang that they allied to conquer Paekche and Koguryŏ. This is called the Silla-Tang war (670–676 CE). For that cause, Silla could use effectively the military prowess of the remaining Koguryŏ soldiers. In an effort to resist Tang, Silla strategically reassessed their stance and decided to embrace the remnants of Koguryŏ. This alignment enabled Silla to support their resistance. Koguryŏ soldiers had substantial combat experience against China and other northern adversaries, which make them useful for Silla's fight against Tang. United, Silla and Koguryŏ forces fought against Tang and ultimately drove out Tang. This not only showcases Silla's astute political decision-making but also serves as a reminder that political affairs during times of turmoil can take unexpected turns, rendering reasoned conjectures unreliable.

Fourth, studies reveal that aside from these movements of the rulers and military elites, commoners were scattered to various nearby areas. Some migrated to the northwestern region in the broader area towards Mongolia. Others relocated to the eastern Manchuria and lived among tribal groups with whom they had prior connections. These movements primarily consisted of scattered

---

185 As previously mentioned (n. 170), Na'aman posited that Hezekiah's welcoming of northern refugees might have incited Assyrian retaliation. A similar situation occurs here. When Tang learned that Silla had embraced Anseung and supported the State of Bodeok, Tang removed Silla's King from office. See Shin, "The Foundation and Meanings of Bodeokguk." Yet, note that Finkelstein has denied that the northern refugees were similar to the political fugitives described in Na'aman's examples. Finkelstein ("The Settlement History," 506) claims that they were commoners, "refugees fleeing from the advancing Assyrian army in a mountainous, frontier area." However, if most of them were commoners, their migration to the South could not be as impactful as Finkelstein envisions it.

flows of refugees in small groups from various directions, rather than organized mass migration.[186]

From this comparison, we can glean several insights. First, both cases involve forced relocation of ruling elites to the conquering country and the dispersion of the common populace. Second, the fact that many Koguryŏ people remained in their land differs from the claimed scenario of Israel. This could be due to the distinct imperial policies employed by Tang and Assyria. Yet, it also raises the possibility that biblical scholars might have hastily embraced the biblical portrayal of Israel's total displacement (2Kgs 17:6–18), a narrative likely influenced by Judah's ideological standpoint. Third, some Koguryŏ remnants indeed found their way to Silla. This observation reveals that during times of political turmoil, alliances can quickly change, making it imprudent to assume that past foes will always remain enemies. Of course, caution is necessary in applying this observation to Israel's case at face value. The Silla-Koguryŏ relationship developed in a peculiar manner in response to their shared adversary, Tang, but no analogous situation unfolded between Judah and Israel against Assyria. Nonetheless, it is possible to speculate that military leaders from the North might have brought their forces to the South, and Judah might have strategically welcomed them for their military experience, which could be useful in the struggle against Assyria. Fourth, it appears likely that commoners from the North may have dispersed in various directions, with Jerusalem being just one of the numerous potential destinations for refuge. The number who entered Jerusalem and stayed there permanently is, however, open to speculation.

4.1.2 Lessons from North Korean Migrant Settlers

As such, one can accept that some refugees found their way to Jerusalem, yet it is critical to carefully assess the extent of their impact on the receiving society. To illustrate this point, I would like to move forward to the modern era and introduce some recent studies on North Korean migrant settlers ("월남민") in the post-war South Korean context.[187] Again, the situations are vastly different, which

---

186 But there in Manchuria, about thirty years after the fall of the kingdom, an eventual revival of Koguryŏ occurred (Balhae/Parhae, 698–926 CE) led by a former general of Koguryŏ, forming another North-South era in Korea's history (Silla in the South, Balhae in the North). See Seth, *A Concise History of Korea*, 71–73.

187 I am using the term "North Korean migrant settlers" to refer to "Wollammin (월남민)," which literally means "people who crossed over to the South." This term encompasses both refugees, defectors, and displaced persons for various reasons, voluntarily and involuntarily.

requires an additional measure of caution when making cross-cultural comparisons across time. However, I maintain that this comparison provides valuable insights into a key aspect: the experiences of refugees in the receiving society are more complex and ambiguous than the simplified stereotypes often imposed upon them by popular perceptions.

The point I aim to underscore here is that, even if refugees from Northern Israel did arrive, we must be careful not to make broad assumptions about their impact on their new home. As observed in the case of the remnants of Koguryŏ, their lives within the receiving society tend to be dictated by how their value is perceived by that society. Thus, individuals could be successful in adapting to a new society but mostly when they cater well to the needs of the receiving society. But simply how probable is it to posit that the migrants became the driving force behind the transformation of the receiving society, or that their presence exerted sufficient influence to compel the ruling elites to modify their governing social narrative?[188]

Let me provide a brief background on North Korean migrant settlers. Before and after the Korean war (1950–53), a significant number of North Korean people migrated to South Korea for various reasons. Numerous individuals sought refuge from the war, while others left before the outbreak due to Communist persecution. As the primary targets for persecution were landowning elites and Christians,[189] a significant portion of the refugees were elite Christians.[190] Following the closure of the border after the war, thousands of northern individuals found themselves settling in South Korea, awaiting the day they could return home and reunite with family members left behind in the North. This enduring separation of innumerable families remains a heartrending aspect of the ongoing tragedy involving the two Koreas.

In the post-war South Korean society, the prevailing view of these migrants from the North was that they were "anti-communist fighters" seeking freedom in the South, and they were primarily composed of the elite and middle class

---

188 Regarding the second point, I have already presented an argument against it, as the predominantly negative portrayal of Northern Israel in the Hebrew Bible does not align well with the notion that Judah's elites were compelled to cater to their views.

189 To explore this context in a fictional work, see Richard E. Kim, *The Martyred* (New York: G. Braziller, 1964).

190 It is important to consider the historical backdrop of Christianity's early prevalence in North Korea when examining this topic. For the broader history of Korean Christianity, see Sebastian C. H. Kim and Kirsteen Kim, *A History of Korean Christianity* (New York: Cambridge University Press, 2015).

from the North.[191] However, recent studies of oral history have challenged these perceptions.[192] An interesting finding from recent reports is that individuals of North Korean heritage in South Korea have notably diverse self-perceptions and varied lives, challenging the polarizing stereotypes that dominated social perceptions of this population.

Allow me to present the findings of Kim Gwiok's study, *The Life Experiences and Identities of North Korean Migrant Settlers*. Kim's work focuses on the experiences and identities of North Korean migrants from a grassroots perspective. She undertook comprehensive studies on notable settlements like Cheongho-dong's "Abai Village (아바이마을)" in Sokcho and "Yongji Farm (용지농원)" in Gimje. Her analysis covered the reasons for migration, settlement processes, living conditions, and identity formations of the North Korean migrant settlers. Her findings challenge prevalent beliefs, suggesting that it is a misconception to broadly label North Korean migrants as anti-communist fighters or to assume that the majority of North Korean migrants belonged to the elite or middle class.

First, Kim demonstrates that their motivations were mostly due to war-time circumstances. The tragic situation during the Korean War occurred in the context of the piston movement, with mutually hostile military forces crossing borders back and forth. Many people were killed, and others were forcibly taken to either the South or the North against their will.

---

191 Certainly, these stereotypes are not fixed. During periods of heightened political tensions, an alternative stereotype quickly emerges, replacing the dominant one. In such instances, all those who came from the North might be stigmatized as communists, and the slogan "you the reds!" becomes a devastating and often lethal label used to demonize North Korean migrants. It is true that these migrants cannot fully embrace South Koreans' extreme anti-North sentiments, as their family members still reside in the North. Accepting a propaganda that demonizes one's own family is challenging. Consequently, their emotions remain torn between the two Koreas, regardless of the self-image they present to the outer society.

192 Oral historians gather information through first-hand accounts, interviews, and personal narratives, and their focus is often on the experiences and perspectives of individuals and groups that have been historically underrepresented. See Donald A. Ritchie, *Doing Oral History*, 3rd ed. (Oxford: Oxford University Press, 2014). North Korean migrants have naturally been the subject of several recent studies by oral historians. E.g., Gwiok Kim, *The Life Experiences and Identities of North Korean Migrant Settlers: A Grassroots Study of North Korean Migrant Settlers* (Seoul: Seoul National University Press, 1999) [김귀옥, 월남민의 생활 경험과 정체성: 밑으로부터의 월남민 연구]; idem, *Separated Families, Neither "Anti-Communist Fighters" nor "Communists"...: A New Perspective on the Issue of Separated Families* (Seoul: Yukbi, 2004) [김귀옥, 이산가족, '반공전사'도 '빨갱이'도 아닌...: 이산가족 문제를 보는 새로운 시각]; A Ram Kim, "Beyond the 38th Parallel, Across the Sea, to Hallasan – The Settlement Process and the Lives of North Korean Refugees," *Critical Studies on Modern Korean History* 35 (2016): 207–51 [김아람, "38선 넘고 바다 건너 한라산까지, 월남민의 제주도 정착 과정과 삶"].

Second, Kim argues that the majority of North Korean migrants became anti-communists due to their ideological, social, and economic conditions after their arrival in South Korea. As a survival strategy, they were compelled to conform to the expectations set by the dominant anti-communist ideology in South Korean society. It is not difficult to understand this dynamic. In an unfamiliar and hostile context, the most socially useful role these migrants could adopt was to demonstrate their loyalty to their new society by publicly expressing their disgust with the communism they had experienced first-hand. In doing so, South Koreans would perceive them as true allies and valuable tools for propaganda, reinforcing the message: "Listen to what the North Koreans have to say about communism." Thus, an intriguing aspect of North Korean migrants' integration into South Korean society is their frequent employment in the police and military sectors – the most ardent fighters against communism.

Third, the assumption that most North Korean migrants were the elite or middle class is also incorrect. Kim's extensive interviews disclosed that the majority of North Korean migrants belonged to the lower socio-economic tiers, with only a small fraction experiencing a middle-class lifestyle. The point is that the prevailing perception on the North Korean migrants was a product of South Korea's ideological agenda. Only a select few North Korean migrants, who managed to ascend to prominence by aligning with the expectations of South Korean society, were remembered. Stereotypes then crystallized around the narratives of these few migrants, overshadowing the majority and their diverse experiences.[193]

4.2 From Transmission to Appropriation

The foregoing observation leaves some pragmatic implications on how heavily biblical scholars have relied upon the refugee theory. Much like the oversimplified perceptions Koreans held about northern migrant settlers – relying on broad stereotypes rather than nuanced understanding – biblical scholars seem to be treading a similar path. Yet, the burden of speculation that biblical scholars have

---

[193] This can be linked to the earlier observation on the Koguryŏ remnants. It is true that some remnants of Koguryŏ were strikingly adept in bargaining their value with Silla, even obtaining land and independence when they could negotiate with Silla for their experienced warriors against Tang. However, it is evident that this was part of Silla's strategic move given that Silla did not continue to support the State of Bodeok. After defeating Tang, the utility of the Koguryŏ state within Silla had vanished; consequently, its people were encouraged to assimilate into Silla society. When the dissatisfied remaining members rebelled, they were forcibly suppressed, and the State of Bodeok was erased from existence.

placed on these refugees far surpasses the stereotypes South Koreans held for their northern migrant settlers. They are practically made the linchpin in explaining several key aspects of the post-722 Judahite society – from identity to religion and textual traditions: (1) As for the complex question of Judah's assumption of Israel's identity, the answer has been sought in the influx of refugees. (2) These same refugees are presented as the driving force behind the alleged religious reform in Hezekiah's time. (3) Most composite texts that include northern traditions are attributed to the mediation of the arriving refugees. Simply, refugees seem to neatly fit into our knowledge gaps, providing just the right pieces absent from our historical puzzle. This is almost too convenient to be true. After all, reality tends to be less dramatic than what speculations suggest.

Instead of investing entirely in this romantic view, it is prudent to explore alternative explanations and treat this as one of several possible scenarios, given the vast uncertainties. In promoting the appropriation model as a prime alternative, as featured in this book, I spotlight two shortcomings of the transmission model.

4.2.1 Masking Judah's Agency

First, it casts a subdued, passive portrayal of Judahite redactors. Let us use textual transmission as a lens to highlight this point. The presence of northern traditions in Judah's Bible forms one of the primary reasons that scholars gravitate towards the idea of northern refugees. Indeed, many see the very existence of these northern traditions as indirect proof of either the refugees' arrival or a mediating role they may have assumed. There is no doubt that resorting to the refugee theory provides an easy route to explain this integration. Yet, a significant gap lies between this romantic perception and our knowledge of reality. There is no documentation of any prominent individuals relocating south after the fall of Samaria that influenced the ensuing transformations in Jerusalem or its fight against Assyria. The notion of an integration of a substantial number of northern refugees rests mostly on academic conjectures.

Scholars continue to lean on this view not because they have evidence but because they feel the integrated northern traditions require an explanation. Yet human mediation is not the only way for cultural dissemination. While it is conceivable that some northern scribes, priests, or prophets introduced their texts, this is but one of several plausible scenarios. It is equally possible that Judahites accessed northern archives,[194] or that these traditions spread orally or were part

---

194 E.g., Na'aman ("The Israelite-Judahite Struggle for the Patrimony," 20) suggests that the scrolls in Bethel have been taken by Josiah during his northern campaign.

of pre-existing popular traditions. Textual transmission is more required in some texts, with highly technical details, but there are other types of text, like folk tales, that humans could carry equally well. Especially when delving into narratives such as those of Abraham and Jacob, as highlighted in this book, it is crucial to also weigh other potential modes of transmission. I see both written and oral transmission as natural part of Judah's cultural interaction with Israel, which was not necessarily confined to a specific mediating group or strictly constrained by political boundaries.[195]

My primary concern centers on the consequent passive portrayal of Judahites when it comes to the assumption of Israel's identity. Despite the paucity of concrete knowledge, all too often, biblical scholars merely assumed that a few northern elites drifted south with their endangered manuscripts and passed the torch to their brothers in the South, who carried on the sacred duty. In this romantic depiction, the northern tradents are presumed to be active guardians of traditions, whereas the southerners are pictured as passive recipients.[196] Yet, few questioned how the Judahite agency is unduly overlooked in this perception. To draw a stark analogy, it is akin to suggesting that Romans could embrace Hellenic heritage only because the Greeks benevolently shared and transferred their cultural heritage. While the Romans' extensive adoption of Hellenic culture is well-recognized, which began even before its political subjugation, it would be inaccurate to describe the Romans merely as passive recipients of Greek heritage.[197] Instead, the Romans, admiring Greek civilization, proactively selected, imitated, and adopted elements from it, turning them into integral part of their own legacy.

Against this, biblical critics would insist in questioning how then the northern traditions and documents were transmitted.[198] However, akin to the relationship

---

195 A perfect example of such cross-cultural spread of local tales is depicted in the scene where Gehazi, a non-professional storyteller, recounts tales of Elisha, the Israelite miracle worker, to the Aramean royal court (2Kgs 8:4–5). All that was needed was the captivation and curiosity elicited by the stories; with an enthralled audience, such tales could easily propagate. The stories of Jacob and Abraham, central to my project in Part II, are equally captivating and meaningful for the target audience.

196 Nicholson's classic theory on the origin of Deuteronomy (*Deuteronomy and Tradition*, 94), as we have reviewed in the introduction, is a good example of such. See also Sparks, *Ethnicity and Identity in Ancient Israel*, 283. For Nicholson's recently changed position, see Ernest W. Nicholson, "Reconsidering the Provenance of Deuteronomy," *ZAW* 124 (2012): 528–40, https://doi.org/10.1515/zaw-2012-0037.

197 See, e.g., Erich S. Gruen, *Culture and National Identity in Republican Rome*, Cornell Studies in Classical Philology 52 (Ithaca, NY: Cornell University Press, 1992).

198 For instance, Schütte ("Wie wurde Juda israelitisiert?," 55–56) assumes that a cultural transmission of such requires a human medium. See also Wolfgang Schütte, *Israels Exil in Juda: Untersuchungen zur Entstehung der Schriftprophetie*, OBO 279 (Fribourg: Academic Press Fri-

between Rome and Greece, I perceive such mediation no requisite – not that it never occurred – as cultural influence naturally extends to neighboring cultures.[199] The appropriation model, while not assuming innate unity, presumes cultural interaction as a basis. The point is that on-going social interaction with Israel, not their kinship, provided the real backdrop for Judah's identity appropriation. Social entities both exert and absorb influences. More often than not, influence flows from a dominant culture to a subordinate one, but not strictly along bloodlines. As a minor group living in the shadow of Israel, I posit Judah had a sustained cultural dependence, a point I further develop in the following chapter.[200]

---

bourg, 2016). He moves on to pinpoint the Shaphanids as the ones who could have transferred northern traditions to Judah. Following Israel's downfall in 720 BCE, he argues, northern scribes who sought refuge in Judah became integral figures in its intellectual and social fabric. They shaped an "Israelite exile theology" to integrate incoming refugees and redefine Israel's broader concept, with David becoming a symbol of unity between Judah and Israel. This theology gained prominence during Josiah's reign, and the Babylonian Exile intensified its influence. In essence, Schütte synthesizes the main ideas of Nicholson (refugees) and Kratz (theological reflection).

199 Although Josiah's discovery of the hidden scroll has been regarded as a pivotal event, it does not embody a characteristic mode through which Israel influenced Judah, nor does it imply complete ignorance of Israelite traditions among the Judahites. This narrative ought to be seen as a form of propaganda, strategically devised with the precise aim of exalting Josiah as a chosen leader, endorsed by divine authority, who ultimately fulfilled the requirements set by the Dtr to become a just ruler in alignment with Mosaic stipulations.

200 A Korean experience of Japanese colonialism might provide an interesting analogy. Since Japan annexed Korea (then Chosŏn) in 1910, the shadow of Japan's colonial legacy has continued to cast a long and palpable influence over modern Korea. For instance, many of Korea's legal terms are identical to Japanese terms because they were borrowed from Japan in the first place, and Koreans failed to get over it completely. Such a problem is not limited in legal matters; it pervades from practically all aspects of our culture, including how we speak, dress, and even think. With Korea's sudden independence in 1945 after Japan's defeat in the Pacific War, one of the first orders of business was to rid the country of Japanese influence. However, erasing external cultural influences is a daunting task, especially when such influences have been ingrained in society for over half a century. The imposed foreign system became not only familiar but also deeply ingrained in our daily lives.

What is unsettling is that the Japanese shade did not dissipate after the end of imperial colonization in 1945. Japan has left, but curiously, its influence has endured. It is surprising to see that, in many ways, Koreans have continued to imitate and borrow Japanese customs, conventions, and systems long after independence. This type of borrowing extends far beyond large structures and seeps into the minutiae of society. It took several decades for Koreans to mobilize social awareness to curb such imitations, though one can never say that we are now fully free from the influence.

Remarkably, this sustained imitation was undercurrent even in the face of prevailing anti-Japanese sentiments within Korean society. It is a testament to how cultural currents often defy societal wills but follow natural laws, flowing from high to low. That is part of the dynamic that imposes a sense of contradiction to the mimicking Self, which Homi Bhabha has described "colo-

Yet, in scenarios where two rival entities engage, situations rarely remain straightforward; even the simplest matters can take on nuanced interpretations. That is, in my thinking, even if refugees brought northern scrolls, it is not a given that the Judahites would readily assimilate them into their own tradition. These were not just any tales but identity narratives with profound political stakes and divisive undertones. Judahites were not absent-minded collectors who gathered whatever traditions available to them.[201] That is to say, for the refugee theory to hold, one must concede that the Judahites were bereft of sovereign will, becoming entirely subservient to the refugees who, on the other hand, despite being stateless, tenaciously held onto their own identity, refusing to give in to the receiving society. They are not merely perceived as settlers but as puppeteers commandeering the socio-political apparatus of Jerusalem, seeking to fulfill in the southern kingdom what they could not achieve in the North. In such a representation, the role of the Judahites is diminished, rendering them mere spectators of their own reformation.

While my portrayal may seem overly dramatic, it encapsulates the essence of the unfairness inherent in the refugee theory. I find parallels with how Chinese historians interpret the Jurchens, the ethnic conquerors of China that established the Qing Empire. Their triumphant narrative is often overshadowed by claims of the overwhelming influence of Han Chinese culture, which they supposedly adopted for success. Such interpretations, in my view, seem grossly unfair to the ethnic conquerors and their remarkable achievements (see Sections 6.3 & 6.4).

It is not entirely implausible that migrants played a part in introducing new cultural or religious impetus, but that must not overshadow the Judahites' agency. Embracing the appropriation model therefore uncovers nuances that the trans-

---

nial mimicry" or "hybridity." Homi K. Bhabha, *The Location of Culture* (London: Routledge, 1994). The notion of colonial mimicry touches on the strategies that colonized populations use to imitate or adopt the language, culture, behaviors, and attitudes of their colonizers. This imitation acts as a double-edged sword: it is both a form of resistance, challenging the colonizer's authority, and a form of submission, recognizing their dominance. In parallel, Bhabha's idea of hybridity delves into the creation of new cultural forms and identities that emerge from the interaction of the colonized with their colonizer. It emphasizes the production of new meanings and identities that are neither the one nor the other, but something in-between. While the dynamics between Judah and Israel might not correspond as closely to these post-colonial concepts as those between Korea and Japan, the pronounced influences from the dominant Israel and the subsequent hybrid identity of Judah echo Bhabha's concepts.

201 This is my response to the popular assumption that the mere presence of northern traditions in our texts testifies to the arrival of northern tradents. While numerous alternative explanations can account for that, the more important is discerning who spearheaded the initiative. There is a marked difference between a text being supplied and it being appropriated.

mission model might obscure, leading to a more tempered and balanced understanding.

4.2.2 Masking Jerusalem's Complex Composition

Second, the uncritical adoption of the transmission model might entail a reductive view of Jerusalem under the Assyrian hegemony. By spotlighting Israelite immigrants, it potentially sidelines the city's broader diversity. Since this carries far-reaching implications beyond this chapter's scope, I will address it only briefly here. In focusing on proving or disproving northern refugees, little attention has been given to potential refugees from other nearby areas and the resulting mixed population of Jerusalem. It would be an oversight to assume that refugees from the North were the sole group seeking refuge in Jerusalem or integrating into the Judahite society in the face of the Assyrian crisis. This view rests in part on the enduring but simplistic assumption that the shared Yhwh cult would only permit demographic convergence between Judah and Israel. However, we must be careful not to naively equate ancient practices of ethnic and social boundary maintenance with the rigorous controls of modern nation-state border patrols. Given the significant upheaval that the entire southern Levant underwent during and after the Assyrian campaign, it seems inevitable that Judah during this period faced transformation that they have never experienced, including diversification of its population and increased cultural interaction with neighboring areas.[202] If so, biblical scholars' tendency to limit the influence to that from the North, neglecting other factors, mirrors the biblical text's ideological portrayal of a singular, pure Israel. The sociocultural evolution precipitated by such demographic changes, including their identity narratives, warrants far more comprehensive and nuanced attention.

4.3 Conclusion

Jerusalem's expansion alone provides little tangible evidence for the influx of northern refugees. Of course, one can, and perhaps should, contemplate on what must have happened to northern Israelite people in the aftermath of the Northern Kingdom's fall. Our examination of Korean history has shown that many unexpected events can occur around wartime, challenging our preconceived notions.

---

202 See Crouch, *The Making of Israel.*

In view of these considerations, I stress the need to shift our focus towards the often-underestimated role of the Judahites in proactively appropriating the northern legacy during this tumultuous time. Regardless of what the purported northern refugees might have introduced to Jerusalem, it was ultimately the Judahites who held the key to determining how to capitalize on these opportunities. It was their decisions on how to respond to the external impetus that ultimately made differences, which warrant greater scholarly attention.

5 Inferiority, Desire, and Judah's Contradictory Self

In the scholarly quest to elucidate Judah's Israelite identity, the prevailing discourse has overlooked Judah's inferiority vis-à-vis Israel as a factor. In lieu of this subjective side, scholars tend to lean towards furnishing a rational explication for what is construed as a natural and objective phenomenon. Stated or not, this perspective pivots upon an underlying assumption of "one people divided into two polities," thus framed within the idea of transmission (of shared legacy) and restoration (of ancient unity). Contrary to the romanticized perspective, as observed earlier, reality does not conform to the ideal of a singular ethnic group invariably coalescing while disparate groups maintain their separateness. Adopting a more realistic standpoint, which conceives every nation or *ethnie* as a social product out of strategic discernment of assimilation and differentiation, necessitates an investigation into the motivations and mechanisms behind the emergence of Judah's Israelite identity: why did an autonomous Judah choose to adopt the legacy and identity of Israel?

In answering this question, I find myself drawn to Na'aman's cultural patrimony model as a viable alternative to Finkelstein's and other prevailing models (see Section 3.2).[203] Unlike others, his model illuminates the psychological dimension of Judah's appropriation of Israel, viewing it through the lens of rivals' contestation. Nevertheless, I see potential for further refinement. Unlike the relatively even rivalry between Assyria and Babylonia, North Israel's historical lineage, cultural richness, and socio-political influence overshadowed Judah in almost every conceivable aspect. Judah may have desired equal recognition as a rival, but the reality diverged significantly. The gap between Judah's ideal and reality (Section 2.4), I suggest, markedly impacted Judah's self-perception. This calls for greater emphasis on Judah's minor status when analyzing its cultural appropriation of Israelite legacy.

Inferiority encompasses two faces, positive and negative, and each warrants due consideration. Inferiority can act as a powerful source of drive for supremacy, while it can also foster aggression towards the superior. This dynamic is not limited to individual competition but, to a degree, extends to the collective sphere.[204]

---

203 Na'aman, "The Israelite-Judahite Struggle for the Patrimony."
204 In the realm of political science, the impact of the ontological (in)security of secondary states in their struggle for survival and recognition through engagement with superior powers has garnered considerable attention. E.g, Ayşe Zarakol, "Ontological (In)Security and State Denial of Historical Crimes: Turkey and Japan," *International Relations* 24 (2010): 3–23, https://doi.org/10.1177/0047117809359040; Joseph MacKay, "The Nomadic Other: Ontological Security and the Inner Asian

https://doi.org/10.1515/9783111376554-005

I suggest that both aspects are manifest in Judah's appropriation of Israel. Judah not only displayed exceptional determination in pursuing Israel but also imposed excessive blame upon Israel – an aspect that presents a challenge in models that perceive them as mere brothers or rivals.

In this chapter, I argue that Judah's long-standing cultural inferiority to Israel must be counted as a principal factor, which provides a social backdrop for Judah's unlikely move to embrace the legacy of Israel. This offers a cogent alternative that can explain Judah's Israel identity without relying on an assumption of primordial unity. Within the context of the skewed power dynamic between Judah and Israel, it is likely that the complexities of desire played a role, contributing to a contradictory mindset that simultaneously desires and resents Israel.

5.1 Inferiority as Source of Desire

Judah's sentiments towards Israel appear far from straightforward. On the surface, Judah blames Israel's sinful ways, yet in the end, they adopt Israel's legacy, traditions, cultic symbols, and even name. As noted, the traditional scholarly explanation for this phenomenon is that after Israel's fall, Judah underwent a theological reflection to understand the reasons behind it. Israel's disloyalty to Yhwh caused its downfall, and Judah's condemnation of Israel reflects their determination not to follow in Israel's footsteps.[205] However, it is curious that Judah appears to have followed that precise path. Yes, they may have simply failed, but I wonder if there is more to this dynamic.

What captures my attention is the level of blame posed on the Northern Kingdom. Every single king of Israel is depicted as sinful. Even when Samaria has fallen, a sense of loss for the fallen brothers is completely absent (2Kgs 17). I find this perplexing. Of course, kin groups can become entangled in conflicts of such, but even in such instances, if one is killed by others, the natural response is to express lament and anger – at least for public perception and image, if not anything else. Yet, Judah seems to lack just that.

Instead, Dtr strives to wipe out any remaining hope for the Northern Kingdom, strategically employing the politics of defilement.[206] Exaggerating the impact

---

Steppe in Historical East Asian International Politics," *Review of International Studies* 42 (2016): 471–91, https://doi.org/10.1017/S0260210515000327; Jelena Subotić, "Narrative, Ontological Security, and Foreign Policy Change," *Foreign Policy Analysis* 12 (2016): 610–27, https://doi.org/10.1111/fpa.12089.

205 E.g., Knoppers, *Two Nations under God 1*, 4.

206 Lauren A. S. Monroe, *Josiah's Reform and the Dynamics of Defilement: Israelite Rites of Violence and the Making of a Biblical Text* (Oxford: Oxford University Press, 2011).

of mass deportation and painting the remnants as the mix-blooded bunch are typical strategies to negate their existence. By promoting the myth of the empty land, they can deny legitimacy for any claim from the remnants, which prepares their own claim of Israel and its legacy. How can we account for the discrepancy between this superficial blame and the underlying appropriation?

Portraying Judah's response merely as a theological reflection on their brothers' misfortunes paints Judahites as detached, cold-blooded historians. Of course, sin is detestable, but expressing such exaggerated resentment towards fallen brethren seems unnatural and unrealistic.[207] What made Judah so tense that they could not acknowledge a single northern king, appreciate the vibrant legacy of Israel, or even mourn their tragic fall? This is a complex question, and there may not be a single explanation. Nevertheless, I propose that one compelling way to addressing this issue involves examining Judah's profound sense of insecurity: Judah had to attribute blame to Israel in order to legitimize its appropriation, while concealing its longing for Israel.[208]

By stressing Judah's perceived inferiority, I aim not to emphasize their subjugated or passive stance in relation to Israel (see Section 4.2). Rather, my argument posits that this perceived inferiority acted as an endless wellspring of desire, motivating them to continually champion their ideals and resolutely pursue them to fruition. I see this unwavering commitment as culminating in the production of one of the most resilient and triumphant identity narratives in human history. On the other hand, what Judahites have done with Israel's legacy, regardless of their justification, must be construed as "identity theft"[209] from the perspective of the Israelites.

---

207 One could observe that both northern and southern kings encounter negative portrayals in the biblical narrative. Yet, there is a distinct nuance in the nature and purpose behind these critiques. The criticism aimed at the northern kings is tinged with elements of demonization and stark vilification. In contrast, the scrutiny of figures like David and Solomon is deeper, leaning into introspection and imbued with moral and theological reflection.

208 Interpreting these contradictory sentiments, I draw insights from Girard's mimetic theory. Some of his key works that have informed my thoughts include René Girard, *Deceit, Desire, and the Novel: Self and Other in Literary Structure* (Baltimore: Johns Hopkins University Press, 1965); idem, "Mimesis and Violence: Perspectives in Cultural Criticism," *Berkshire Review* 14 (1979): 9–19; idem, *A Theater of Envy: William Shakespeare*, Odéon (New York: Oxford University Press, 1991).

209 Cf. Lemche's use of the term, which he applies to the conflict between Jews and Samaritans in the second century BCE. Niels Peter Lemche, "Too Good to Be True? The Creation of the People of Israel," *WO* 50 (2020): 268–69, https://doi.org/10.13109/wdor.2020.50.2.254.

5.2 Judah's Inferiority

My interest in Judah's inferiority originated from my observation of the surprisingly limited depth and breadth in Judah's traditions. This is particularly significant because I hold that a community's cultural heritage is intrinsically tied to its collective self-worth. Given that the present form of the Hebrew Bible is fundamentally shaped by Judeans, I assume that Judeans had the power and interest to include their traditions as much as they wanted. It is natural for human groups to base their origin stories on their own stories, and the yearning is stronger for secondary states. That not many Judahite stories of their noble origins are included in early biblical traditions must be considered seriously and requires explanations.

5.2.1 North Israel's Mythic Past

It is well established that Northern Israel was the home of many foundational biblical traditions.[210] Scholars have long recognized the northern orientation of the Jacob tradition, which is mainly based in major northern sites. The Jacob story provides a firm foundation in Israel's ancestral past.[211] Scholars have also recognized the prominence of the Exodus motif in early northern texts. The Exodus narrative provides a shared historical experience in the mythic past and an ideological basis upon which diverse groups and popular segments are coalesced into the people of Yhwh. Israel's covenant-making with Yhwh at Sinai forms a definitive moment when Israel becomes the people of Yhwh and Yhwh as the God of Israel. Critics have also noted the northern orientation of Deuteronomy in its early form.[212] Deuteronomy accentuates the covenantal nature of "Israel" by means of the treaty motif, which – by nature – increases the focus on imposing the covenantal duty to Israel as Yhwh's people. Together with the Exodus narrative, Deuteronomy describes how the "mixed multitude" (Exod 12:38) from Egypt became the people of Yhwh at Sinai and provides a firm definition of what it means to be Israel. Undoubtedly, the present forms of all these traditions include

---

210 See Harold Louis Ginsberg, *The Israelian Heritage of Judaism*, TSJTSA 24 (New York: Jewish Theological Seminary of America, 1982); Fleming, *The Legacy of Israel*.
211 See Chapters 8 and 9 for details.
212 E.g., Adam Cleghorn Welch, *The Code of Deuteronomy: A New Theory of Its Origin* (London: J. Clarke & Co., 1924); Albrecht Alt, "Die Heimat des Deuteronomium," in *Kleine Schriften zur Geschichte des Volkes Israel*, vol. 2 (München: C. H. Beck, 1953), 250–75. For a review and a critical appraisal, see Reinhard Müller and Cynthia Edenburg, "A Northern Provenance for Deuteronomy? A Critical Review," *HeBAI* 4 (2015): 148–61, https://doi.org/10.1628/219222715X14453513581333.

many traces of Judean revisions.[213] However, there is little dispute that the core elements of these traditions originated in the North.

Scholars have tended to use these observations in their attempts to reconstruct the traditional and literary growths of biblical texts, but my observation centers on their functionality as origin myths. I posit that the earlier forms of the Jacob and Exodus traditions functioned as the Northern Kingdom's dual origin myths.[214] I pay particular attention to the balance of seemingly conflicting perspectives, both indigenous and external, within this origin tradition. As scholars have widely suggested, the Jacob story promotes Israel's indigenous origin, whereas the Exodus story promotes Israel's external origin.[215] Moreover, each tradition represents "ethnic" and "civic" arguments for the Israelite identity.[216] One defines "Israel" as a people of a shared lineage, whereas the other promotes "Israel" as a constitutional entity formed by a pledge to the covenant. Historical critics might be inclined to assign these contrasting voices to different eras or settings, but I believe doing so is unnecessary and misleading. In my opinion, ethnic and political communities are primarily shaped by the composition of these two sides of the identity argument, although their distribution may differ in each group. I propose that the dual perspective in Israel's major origin myths reveals the complexity of the popular composition of the Northern Kingdom. As a centralized polity, Northern Israel possessed a well-balanced mythic support system in which two voices constantly debated "who we are."

5.2.2 Judah's Superficial Past

By contrast, Judahites could boast little of their noble origins to match this rich northern Israelite heritage. It is generally accepted that the amount of southern

---

213 For instance, Judah is depicted as rescuing Joseph (Gen 37:26). Yet, this portrayal overlaps with a comparable role attributed to Reuben. Considering the pro-Judahite bias, the Judah layer appears a late addition. The promise layer, rooted in the Abrahamic promise that tradition-historical critics observed as a linking device of originally separate tradition blocks, is another segment that betrays Judah's revisionist efforts. See Rolf Rendtorff, *The Problem of the Process of Transmission in the Pentateuch*, trans. J. J. Scullion, JSOTSup 89 (Sheffield: Sheffield Academic Press, 1990).

214 E.g., Finkelstein and Römer, "Comments on the Historical Background of the Jacob Narrative," 329; Finkelstein, *The Forgotten Kingdom*, 141–51.

215 See Konrad Schmid, *Genesis and the Moses Story: Israel's Dual Origins in the Hebrew Bible*, trans. James Nogalski, Siphrut 3 (Winona Lake, IN: Eisenbrauns, 2010).

216 Previous scholars often emphasized the distinction between the two models, using the opposition to contrast "western" and "eastern" European ideas of nationhood. However, this binary distinction is now widely dismissed. Instead, the two ideals are construed as part of any movement of nation building or nationalism. See among others, Anthony D. Smith, *The Ethnic Origins*

tradition is noticeably limited in pre-exilic literature.[217] This is particularly true in origin stories that directly address Judah's roots. Most of the Judean origin stories are late additions to the existing northern Israelite tradition. The Abraham tradition is probably the only major tradition that can be definitively placed in the South. Otherwise, the entire Pentateuch is framed by the original northern traditions, to which Judah's materials are later added. The Priestly materials, such as Leviticus and tabernacle traditions, occupy substantial space in the current shape of the Pentateuch, but they are late additions.[218] Even for the Abraham traditions, scholars date most of them to the late period. Although it is difficult to know the exact origin and date of the early Abraham tradition in its local context, its incorporation into biblical texts occurred relatively late, which contrasts clear traces of Jacob in pre-exilic traditions.[219]

Outside the Abrahamic and Priestly traditions, Gen 38 is perhaps the only extensive Judahite tradition within the Pentateuch. However, the type of narrative presented in this problematic episode is strikingly unfit for the origin story of the home clan of David.[220] This episode serves as the origin story for Judah's leading clans, the Perezites and Zerahites, but it comes with the indelible mark of their incestuous beginnings. Curiously, this makes Judah's origin not different from that of Moab and Ammon, which is derided by Judah's text (Gen 19:30–37). Considering Lot's circumstances were beyond his control, Judah's situation might

of Nations (Oxford: Blackwell, 1987), 149–52; Michael Keating, *Nations Against the State: The New Politics of Nationalism in Quebec, Catalonia, and Scotland* (Basingstoke: Palgrave Macmillan, 1996), 3–8; Rogers Brubaker, *Ethnicity Without Groups* (Cambridge, MA: Harvard University Press, 2004), 132–46.

217 Cf. Kratz's point (*The Composition of the Narrative Books*, 261) on the Abraham and Isaac traditions as against the Jacob tradition.

218 Except that the Jerusalem school would disagree, which holds onto the notion of P's foundational place in tradition history. See Moshe Weinfeld, *The Place of the Law in the Religion of Ancient Israel*, VTSup 100 (Leiden: Brill, 2004); A. Hurvitz, "The Evidence of Language in Dating the Priestly Code," *RB* 81 (1974): 24–56; Menahem Haran, "Behind the Scenes of History: Determining the Date of the Priestly Source," *JBL* 100 (1981): 321–33, https://doi.org/10.2307/3265957; Ziony Zevit, "Converging Lines of Evidence Bearing on the Date of P," *ZAW* 94 (1982): 481–511, https://doi.org/10.1515/zatw.1982.94.4.481; Israel Knohl, *The Sanctuary of Silence: The Priestly Torah and the Holiness School* (Minneapolis: Fortress, 1995); Baruch J. Schwartz, "The Priestly Account of the Theophany and Lawgiving at Sinai," in *Texts, Temples, and Traditions: A Tribute to Menahem Haran*, ed. Michael V. Fox, James L. Kugel, and Frank Moore Cross (Winona Lake, IN: Eisenbrauns, 1996), 103–34.

219 Thomas Römer, "Abraham Traditions in the Hebrew Bible Outside the Book of Genesis," in *The Book of Genesis: Composition, Reception, and Interpretation*, ed. Craig A. Evans, Joel N. Lohr, and David L. Petersen, VTSup 152 (Leiden: Brill, 2012), 159–80.

220 See J. A. Emerton, "Some Problems in Genesis XXXVIII," *VT* 25 (1975): 338–61, https://doi.org/10.1163/156853375X00656.

be viewed as even more reprehensible. Also, Judah's behavior towards Tamar is far from honorable, offering little in the way of a worthy example for his descendants.[221]

Compare this with the origin story of the Joseph clans of the North. The Joseph novella directly supports the legitimacy of the Joseph clans, explaining how Joseph played a critical role in saving the endangered tribe of Jacob. Like his father, Joseph was not a firstborn. However, as Jacob's favorite son, he is also featured as Yhwh's chosen (Gen 49:22–26, 1Chr 5:1–2). Joseph's life journey, filled with conflicts and dramas, holds the key to the rest of the fate of Jacob's family. Simply, the Joseph clans own a well-structured narrative coherent with the preceding and following origin stories of Israel, which provides a firm mythic basis that legitimates their leading role in Israel.

5.2.3 Judah's Canaanite Connection

This observation segues into my second point. Judah's inferiority is evinced not only in the paucity of their origin traditions. Equally revealing is the Canaanite connection evident in the limited traditions that we identified as Judahite. Critical scholars have long observed Judah's Canaanite origin, and Gen 38 provided one of the bases.[222] Judah's marriage to the daughter of Shuah, "a certain Canaanite" (Gen 38:2) underscores this point. What I take interesting is the way the text presents this plainly, implying that in the original context of the tradition, Judah's Canaanite connection was not a problem. Granted, I take no issue with the Canaanite heritage by itself. As I argue in this book (Section 9.4), the Canaanite heritage is evident in both Judah and Israel. However, there is a difference be-

---

221 I assume that the episode was originally meant to be circulated within the tribe of Judah, as an ingroup narrative. Among competing ingroup clans within Judah, the point of the episode was not Judah's misdemeanor but the legitimation it allegedly brought to the Perez and Zerah clans.

222 For instance, Theodore Robinson long ago suggested Judah's Canaanite origin. Theodore H. Robinson, "The Origin of the Tribe of Judah," in *Amicitiæ Corolla: A Volume of Essays Presented to James Rendel Harris, D. LITT., on the Occasion of His Eightieth Birthday*, ed. Herbert George Wood (London: University of London Press, 1933), 265–73. Judah is not included in the ten-tribe federation in Judg 5, the Song of Deborah, which indicates that Judah was at that time "not yet recognized as one of the tribes of Israel" (p. 269). Robinson also examined the conquest narratives and argued that Judah did not appear in the oldest form of the tradition of the southern conquests (p. 272). In the ancestral tradition, he cited Gen 38, the story of Judah and Tamar, as evidence that Judah is of Canaanite origin. Cf. Emerton, "Some Problems in Genesis XXXVIII." Robinson ("The Origin of the Tribe of Judah," 272) concludes that only after the Philistines became a threat did Judah decide to join the "Aramaean YHWH-worshippers."

tween them. In the North, a robust Yahwistic tradition offsets the lingering Canaanite traces in Israel's cultural heritage, whereas Judah lacks a comparable Yahwistic foundation to provide a counterweight. This strange account in Gen 38 is the only text that features Judah as the protagonist within biblical ancestral traditions, which implies that the clan Judah owned no other story of origin to match Joseph's colorful tunic. Also, that perhaps was the reason why this problematic story of Judah's origin survived the eyes of later Judean redactors who are otherwise critical to Canaanite traces. They lacked alternatives to balance this problematic episode, and removing this story would have left a glaring void in Judah's origin.[223] I understand this as an indication of Judah's shallow roots as an *Israelite* clan. Before they *became* Israel, they were among the various tribes residing in this land, and this story reflects that indigenous origin.

Similar observations on Judah's shallow heritage, coupled with Canaanite connections, can be made in other parts of the biblical tradition. For instance, the lack of Mosaic heritage is striking in the major religious symbols and iconography of Judah, which instead have signs of Canaanite orientation. Their temple city is a well-known pagan city-state. Its Zadokite priesthood, architecture, and iconography all betray Canaanite roots. The text attempts to cover these Canaanite origins by means of the heroics of David and his band that acquired this ancient fortress (2Sam 5:6–9). However, the consequence of annexing the Jebusite city and turning it to Yhwh's temple city with the help of Phoenician architects is hardly addressed, which contrasts with the fatal accusation laid upon Jezebel, a Phoenician princess (1Kgs 16:29–31). In addition, although the present form of Israel's conquest narrative does begin with Judah, the featured hero is Caleb (Josh 14:6–15), whose ambiguous lineage indicates that he was not a figure from a pure Judahite lineage but only later adopted to the clan.[224] Also in the period of Judges, the only judge from the clan Judah is Othniel, Caleb's cousin (Judg 3:9–10). Hence, Fleming remarks, "The book of Judges is a biblical marvel, by itself a vivid signal that Judah grappled awkwardly sometimes with a tradition that was not finally its own … Judges offers little conceptual space for Judah, which seems to have preserved no old stories of its own as a contribution."[225]

---

223 Granted, not every undesirable story of origin is censored in the Hebrew Bible, both in Judah's and Israel's traditions; thus, my claim is not that this episode must have been removed. David's and Solomon's sins are not erased but are subject to self-critical discourse in Judah's Bible. The Moabite roots of David's line is openly acknowledged in the story of Ruth. Yet, what sets Judah apart is the notable absence of positive narratives otherwise, unlike David and Solomon. Erasing this account would have left no origin story for the leading clans of the house of Judah.

224 See Wright, *David, King of Israel, and Caleb in Biblical Memory.*

225 Fleming, *The Legacy of Israel,* 174.

5.3 Appropriation and Insecurity

Conventional readers might be inclined to interpret these within the traditional frame, taking these as indicative of Judah's being a peripheral tribe but still *within* Israel. Indeed, adopting this position by itself might be inconsequential.[226] Whether Judah was a peripheral clan within Israel or a complete outsider, their perceived inferiority could cultivate a desire for the core. Consequential, however, is the aftereffect of adopting that perspective. It subtly nudges us towards re-embracing the notion of primordial unity, which proves ineffective in explaining the dynamics of how ethnic groups merge and break away. I elect to direct my focus towards Judah's alterity, a perspective that prompts us to place greater emphasis on the power of Judah's aspiration – not membership – as a driving force behind Judah's assumption of Israel's identity.

The point I wish to underscore is that one's sense of membership to Israelite identity does not necessarily align with biological or societal status. Adopted children may intensely yearn for recognition as the father's own, while biological offspring often lack that, taking their status for granted.[227] As important as biological ties is the social dynamic, which compels groups to coalesce or break away – a fundamental takeaway from the thesis that identity is a social product. In instances where two groups operate within a skewed power dynamic, the minor party's perceived inferiority is a crucial social factor, instigating a desire for elevation. When an opportunity arises, they can fabricate an imagined unity in the past to align themselves with the superior.

In this context, one can envision how Judah's perceived inferiority found a crucial moment to materialize in the aftermath of Samaria's fall. Before then, the Northern Kingdom used to provide a buffer zone from international politics and

---

226 The identity, membership, and boundary of a marginal group vis-à-vis the core is a matter that belongs to an inherently contested realm, defying definitive characterization. It is never fixed but constantly shifting and contingent upon situational dynamics.

227 Indeed, none of the other Israelite tribes, or the *truer* members of Israel – like Ephraim and Manasseh – appears to have achieved the same level of success in preserving their Israel identity. Israelite tribes traversed a parallel path of adversity akin to the Judahites, either exiled or remaining in the land. Why they were less successful in retaining an Israelite identity remains elusive, given that we have limited understanding of the experiences of the dispersed and surviving Israelite groups. Yet when viewed in the context of the broader human history, what stands out is not the disappearance of the dispersed Israelite tribes. It is typical for defeated and dispersed political groups to assimilate into new environments. What stands out as truly remarkable is Judah's capacity to uphold its identity against all odds. I propose that the persistence and determination exhibited by Judah can be, at least in part, elucidated by the power of its desire for supremacy.

served as a conduit to the outer world to isolated Judah. This allowed Judah to lead a relatively secure life in the Judean hill country, but also made them dependent on Israel in all aspects of their lives. At this stage, Judah's desire manifested as a longing for belonging, as they strove to integrate into the Israelite family. This aspiration was not reciprocated, as indicated by the limited attention paid to Judah within the northern tradition. Of course, I can see Israelites occasionally acknowledging Judah as "one of us" when it suited their interests, but more often than not, Judah remained outside the boundary of "us." This enduring sidelining only intensified Judah's longing. The fall of Samaria, juxtaposed against Jerusalem's miraculous survival (2 Kgs 19, Isa 37), marked a pivotal juncture heralding the initiation of a transformative journey in Judah's self-perception. From my perspective, therefore, the most consequential outcome of Israel's demise was not merely the influx of refugees or the introduction of new documents. Instead, it represented a momentous juncture for Judah to assert the heritage they had long been acquainted with and aspired to become part of. Judahites boldly staked their claim to Israel's identity, at last liberating themselves from the need for acknowledgment from the Israelites. In their pursuit of a renewed identity, the Judahites actively appropriated the rich legacy left by North Israel.

Looking at it from a modern perspective, one might question why Judah did not establish its identity around its own traditions. Yet, it was precisely in that aspect that Judah found itself lacking. Given their status as a minor entity existing under the shadow of Israel, it was not only pragmatic but also aspirational for them to build around the established system and repurpose it as their own.[228] I believe Judahites were immensely successful in achieving that. The result was a very different Israel though, in which Judah's position is secured through multiple strategies for self-promotion.

Despite their success, Judah's identity theft had profound and lasting effects on their collective psyche. Not unlike individuals, sentiments like shame and self-doubt exert strong influence over societies, frequently guiding collective actions. In that regard, it is important to remember that Judah's takeover of Israel was driven not by their own strength. Capitalizing on the unexpected turns of events, they were necessarily left with a lingering sense of self-doubt. This likely contributed to Judah's heightened focus on emphasizing Israel's transgressions, adopting an unusually harsh stance without the expected display of mourning for the fallen neighbor.

In another essay, I have made a case that the text's superficial condemnation of Jeroboam's cultus at Bethel in 1Kgs 12:25–34 can be seen as distorted reflections

---

228 Cf. Smith's notion of "translatability" of local deities. Mark S. Smith, *God in Translation: Deities in Cross-Cultural Discourse in the Biblical World*, FAT 57 (Tübingen: Mohr Siebeck, 2008).

of Judah's insecurity and mimetic desire.[229] While the text paints Jeroboam's golden calf as a fake replica of Jerusalem's cherubim, the monstrous depiction of the calf as a pagan idol may conceal Judah's insecurities on its own cherubim, which not only lacks genuine Yahwistic roots but could also be inspired by Bethel's icon.[230] The specific dynamic observed in Bethel's golden calf and Jerusalem's cherubim can be applied to Judah's general relations to Israel. Out of prolonged interaction with the superior Israel, Judah cultivated a mimetic desire for Israel. Following Israel's downfall, Judah assumed its position and heaped heavy blame upon Israel as a way of rationalizing and legitimizing their takeover. Yet, Judah's overt condemnation of Israel veils a latent desire for Israel and reveals an insecurity as a supplanter.

5.4 Merits and Shortcomings of Appropriation Model

Through this, we can elucidate Judah's adoption of Israel's identity without invoking their primordial unity. The outcome is a model that aligns with modern interpretations of the ancient history of Judah and Israel, viewing them as separate entities, while also being receptive to an instrumentalist perspective, recognizing how Judah forged an imagined unity with Israel. Moreover, this approach aids in understanding Judah's contradictory psyche towards Israel: simultaneously casting blame and appropriating their heritage. An added benefit is that this model presents a viable option for a pre-exilic origin of Judah's Israelite identity, an option that eluded Davies, leading him to adopt a position of its post-exilic origin (see Section 3.1). The Judahite monarchic period, notably adorned with depictions of the reforms of Hezekiah and Josiah, must remain crucial for understanding Judah's identity reshaping, despite mounting challenges.[231]

---

229 Hong, "The Golden Calf of Bethel and Judah's Mimetic Desire of Israel."
230 On another level, the blatant polemic against the land and the indigenous population (e.g., Exod 3:8) or the emphasis on the purity ideology (e.g., Ezra 9:2) might also reflect Judah's Canaanite complex.
231 The historical authenticity of the proposed reform movements during this era remains a point of contention among scholars. See, e.g., Lowell K. Handy, "Hezekiah's Unlikely Reform," *ZAW* 100 (1988): 111–15; Nadav Na'aman, "The Debated Historicity of Hezekiah's Reform in the Light of Historical and Archaeological Research," *ZAW* 107 (1995): 179–95, https://doi.org/10.1515/9781575065694-025; Diana Edelman, "Hezekiah's Alleged Cultic Centralization," *JSOT* 32 (2008): 395–434, https://doi.org/10.1177/0309089208092. However, whether archaeological findings support Josiah's northern campaign remains a matter of secondary importance. What is paramount is the profound aspiration evident in his textual portrayals, which may reflect genuine sentiments that fueled this, even if it remains purely literary propaganda. Though Josiah's purported reforms might have been fictional or fleeting in political reality, the lasting imprint of identity

Granted, the appropriation model presents its own set of challenges. As we observed above (Section 3.3), scholars hesitated to embrace the appropriation model due to their struggle in comprehending Judah's eagerness to adopt Israel's identity if there was no basis.[232] Indeed, as soon as one removes a primordial tie as a basis, a question will follow, why Israel and not, say, Moab or Ammon? I recognize the weight of this question and do not claim to have an all-encompassing answer. But I also know that such questions by nature rarely have clear-cut answers in any instance of ethnic or political formation. It is like asking why one individual forms a unique bond with another amidst many potential relationships. Often, people lean on notions like destiny or divine purpose to validate such connections. Yet, at our core, we know these concepts are but tools to grapple with the fragile and arbitrary nature of human relationships.

Like personal bonds, group relationships often emerge from multifaceted socio-political factors that are not always rooted in demonstrable common genesis. In essence, there is no doubt that Judah has developed a special bond with Israel, it need not be considered innate. Judah's closer ethnic bonding with Israel is likely a product of their prolonged socio-political interaction, with geographical proximity playing a pivotal role.[233] While their shared worship of Yhwh acted as

---

reformation from this era cannot be understated. The exile did profoundly reshape Judah's Self, but the post-722 era remains a momentous precursor in Judah's identity journey.

Let me illustrate this with an interesting analogous case from ancient Korean history. During the Chosŏn Dynasty, an audacious proposal known as the "Northern Expedition Theory (북벌론)" emerged. It championed military ventures into northern terrains like Manchuria to counter the burgeoning Jurchen threats. This strategy arose amidst geopolitical shifts, notably the Jurchens' expansion and their eventual subjugation of Ming China, which I shall detail below in Section 6.1. While these bold campaigns largely remained on parchment and in passionate discussions, their ideological influence resonated across Korean society for centuries, molding identity and shaping political allegiances. Those rallying behind this theory were staunch traditionalists, often at odds with a rising pragmatic faction that emphasized ties with the Jurchens and the ascendant Qing Dynasty. As for the historical account of Josiah's supposed northern campaign, its factual veracity takes a backseat to its profound symbolic resonance. Josiah is portrayed as a figure who has actualized this northward ambition. Crafting such a narrative itself can be interpreted as an exercise in powerful, evocative propaganda.

232 Hence, Kristin Weingart critiques my position as to why Judah would embrace the Israelite identity if they were not Israelites and did not see themselves in Israel's traditions. "Was sollte Judäer veranlassen, die Identität des Unterdrückers anzunehmen, wenn sie sich nicht bereits als Teil Israels verstanden und in der Jakob-Tradition zugleich die eigene Geschichte fanden." Weingart, *Stämmevolk – Staatsvolk – Gottesvolk?*, 364 n. 308.

233 If one were to stress Judah's kinship with Israel as the basis of Judah's adoption of Israel heritage, one must remember that, in Israel's perceived world, most of the neighboring entities, perhaps except Philistines, were also perceived in kinship relations, though in different levels. Israelite genealogies do provide avenues to perceive Moab and Ammon as relatives. It is just that certain genealogical narratives became dominant over others. When we expand our per-

a critical factor binding them together and differentiating them from others,[234] it could well be a social outcome rather than the original reason.

5.5 Conclusion

Examining Judah's sense of inferiority offers fresh insights into its complex relationship with Israel. Modern sensibilities would lead us to question how Judah could willingly set aside its own identity in favor of embracing another's. Yet, one must remember that the takeover of the Israel identity did not necessarily cause Judahites to abandon their Judean identity. It only completed their long-yearned-for appropriation of Israel,[235] giving them a hybrid Self – Judean and Israelite – that endures to this day. This is the topic of the subsequent chapter.

---

spective to embrace the broader genealogical narrative, beginning with Adam, we all emerge as interconnected kin. In this, Judah's distinction from others is only relative. Yet, evoking this fundamental linkage carries limited practical resonance in political reality, which requires history, myths, and stories that lend it order and structure.

234 Biblical scholars have traditionally relied on Israel and Judah's common faith. Cf. Kratz's review ("Israel als Staat," 5–8) of the understanding of Israel as Yhwh's people in early scholarship.

235 Finkelstein and Silberman, *The Bible Unearthed*, 229–50.

6 Israel and Judah, China and its Others

Now, we must face the difficult question: does inferiority and desire really explain Judah's adoption of Israel's name? The real hurdle of the appropriation model lies in that Judah not only embraced Israel's legacy but also its name. To phrase bluntly, the situation could be compared to Romans, after dominating Greece, deciding to call themselves Hellenes.[236] Romans assimilated a great deal of Greek heritage, spanning mythology, literature, art, architecture, and philosophy, but not their name. Hence Daniel Fleming remarked:

> Given the ownership of the name by the kingdom north of Judah, it would be logical to conclude that the appropriation by Judah could have taken place only after 720. Yet this solution is still not entirely satisfying, because someone from Judah must have perceived a basis for the connection. Would it be enough simply to covet the reputation of the more powerful northern polity? Perhaps so, but the answer is uncertain.[237]

This comment captures well the general skepticism towards the appropriation model. As previously discussed (Section 3.3), Fleming thus sought to find a historical tether through the memory of David's ruling over Israel. Granted, this is an intricate issue, but I believe there is merit in exploring alternative solutions. Romans did not adopt names of other cultures they assimilated, but there were others who were more than willing to adopt Roman identity. Indeed, the inclination to align one's lineage with more esteemed families, peoples, or kingdoms is prevalent in human societies, highlighting one of the essential functions of genealogy.[238] This can be likened to the appeal of the "American" identity to immigrants. While Western scholars may be better suited to present that parallel, I intend to offer insights from the East Asian context.

I focus on the prestige China held in Sinocentric East Asia and make some relevant observations. First, I explore Korea's relations with China, illustrating how Koreans at one point in history developed a sense of voluntary subordination to China, to the extent that some of Korea's elites willingly identified their country as "Little China." Second, I emphasize China's prestige by examining the dual relations its "barbaric" conquerors, the Mongols and Manchus, maintained

---

236 Weingart (*Stämmevolk – Staatsvolk – Gottesvolk?*, 364 n. 309) makes a similar analogy against the German unification: "Angewandt auf die neuere deutsche Geschichte wäre ein analoger Vorgang, d. h. die Übernahme des Namens einer untergegangenen politischen Größe, die Umbenennung der Bundesrepublik in DDR im Zuge der Wiedervereinigung."
237 Fleming, *The Legacy of Israel in Judah's Bible*, 47. Similarly, Leonard-Fleckman, *The House of David*, 243. See also Kratz, "Israel als Staat," 12.
238 See discussion in Berlejung, "The Gilead between Aram and Israel," 356–58.

https://doi.org/10.1515/9783111376554-006

with respect to China. Upon conquering China, these ethnic outsiders seemed ready to assume the position of China. At the same time, I also underscore how these outsiders' ethnic and hybrid identities played a pivotal role in redefining China.

6.1 Korea, the Little China?

For pre-modern Koreans, China has been the preeminent regional powerhouse.[239] While Korea's contemporary relation to China has directly stemmed from a specific post-war context,[240] the current state is only a recent fraction when contextualized within the broader scope of the history of interactions between Korea and China. My discussion focuses on a specific period, the Chosŏn Dynasty, during which the perception of China experienced a significant elevation.[241]

Chosŏn (1392–1910 CE), Korea's final imperial dynasty before the onset of the modern era, was distinguished by its adoption of Confucianism as the state ideology. The adoption of Confucianism should be understood within the context of the founding elites' efforts to distinguish their regime from the incumbent Koryŏ Dynasty they displaced. Koryŏ was a kingdom deeply rooted in the legacies of Buddhism and Daoism, with its ruling class closely affiliated with Buddhist monasteries. Nonetheless, in the declining years of the Koryŏ Dynasty, an increasing sentiment arose that the nation had become excessively dependent on Buddhism, consequently weakening state authority and stability. This perception set the stage

---

239 For a review of China's influence to the region, see John King Fairbank and Ta-tuan Ch'en, eds., *The Chinese World Order: Traditional China's Foreign Relations*, Harvard East Asian Series 32 (Cambridge, MA: Harvard University Press, 1968); David C. Kang, *East Asia Before the West: Five Centuries of Trade and Tribute*, Contemporary Asia in the World (New York: Columbia University Press, 2010); Ji Young Lee, *China's Hegemony: Four Hundred Years of East Asian Domination* (New York: Columbia University Press, 2016); Odd Arne Westad, *Empire and Righteous Nation: 600 Years of China-Korea Relations* (Cambridge, MA: The Belknap Press of Harvard University Press, 2021).

240 At present, China's relationships with North and South Korea have emerged as a direct consequence of the specific political context during and after the Korean War. In this context, China and North Korea aligned with the Soviet Union, while South Korea formed alliances with the U. S. and other Western partners. Although South Korea's relationship with China has since progressed beyond hostility, China remains one of the few steadfast allies of North Korea. See Jian Chen, *China's Road to the Korean War: The Making of the Sino-American Confrontation* (New York: Columbia University Press, 1994).

241 For a review of this period, see John B. Duncan, *The Origins of the Choson Dynasty* (Seattle: University of Washington Press, 2000).

for the adoption of Confucianism, which was contemporaneously viewed as a more pragmatic and rational alternative for governance.

During the founding era of the Chosŏn Dynasty, Confucianism was actively promoted as the state ideology, and efforts were made to curtail Buddhist dominance.[242] Confucianism became intrinsic to Chosŏn's identity, providing a moral and ethical framework for the government while emphasizing social harmony, respect for authority, and the importance of education. Intriguingly, during the Chosŏn Dynasty, one can occasionally find self-expressions from the ruling elites referring to themselves as "Little China (小中華)."[243] Although this perception may appear absurd when compared to contemporary notions of sovereign states,[244] it is crucial to acknowledge that it was not simply an expression of self-deprecation. Instead, it was embedded in the context of a profoundly ingrained China-centered worldview, which constituted the core of Confucian ideology.

This self-subordination was deeply rooted in the hierarchical structure of Sinocentrism (中華思想), where nations were ranked according to their perceived levels of civilization and culture. Within this Sinocentric system, China was regarded as the center of the world, whereas regions beyond the Sinocentric sphere were perceived as uncivilized lands inhabited by "barbarians," strikingly similar to the world viewed from the Greek perspective of ἔθνη. The perceived inferiority, if not inhumanity, of these "barbaric" Others is evident. The Chinese language includes logograms akin to those found in Akkadian or Sumerian. There are logograms for animals, and – intriguingly – Chinese characters assigned as the names of China's neighboring ethnic minorities include animal logograms, calling each clan a different animal.[245] Within this system, for Chosŏn and other smaller entities surrounding China, presenting themselves as Little Chinas was a way to avoid

---

242 See John B. Duncan, "Confucianism in the Late Koryŏ and Early Chosŏn," *Korean Studies* 18 (1994): 78–81, https://doi.org/10.1353/ks.1994.0015.

243 Weiguo Sun, "An Analysis of the 'Little China' Ideology of Chosŏn Korea," *Frontiers of History in China* 7 (2012): 220–39, https://doi.org/10.3868/s020-001-012-0012-5.

244 No matter how one tries to justify it, this voluntary subordination troubles contemporary Koreans, and critical voices frequently arise regarding Chosŏn's disgraceful policy towards China. To make things worse, Japanese colonialists used Chosŏn's submissiveness as justification for Japan's annexation of Chosŏn. Japan ridiculed Chosŏn's blind subordination to China, arguing that Koreans were a people who lacked the purpose and ability to govern a sovereign state, contrasting it to their early adaptation to modern civilization as a characteristic of Japanese people's superiority over Koreans. As a result, any discussion of Korea's internal critical reflection can be targeted as pro-Japan rhetoric, making any self-critical discourse on Chosŏn a precarious business. Similarly, North Korea persistently condemns South Korea for its ongoing reliance on external power, portraying the U. S. as South Korea's new big brother.

245 Magnus Fiskesjö, "The Animal Other: China's Barbarians and Their Renaming in the Twentieth Century," *Social Text* 29 (2011): 57–79, https://doi.org/10.1215/01642472-1416091.

being relegated to "barbarians." Note well that from China's viewpoint, Korea had also been deemed part of the "four barbarians," identified as the Dōngyí (東夷, "Eastern Barbarians").[246] Chosŏn's self-perception as Little China must be understood in the context of China's deep-seated perception of them as barbarians.

For modern minds, this rigid, seemingly self-destructive, policy might seem like an unusual approach to diplomacy, as *realpolitik* often dictates that kingdoms and nations shift their loyalties as circumstances change. The explanation for this rigidity should be sought in the Confucian backdrop that shaped their understanding of vassalhood to China. In the Confucian worldview, relationships are governed by the principle of mutual obligation, and the most foundational relationship is the father-son relation. The king-vassal relationship is also understood in analogy to the father-son relationship, with the king taking on a paternal role for his vassal.[247] Naturally, Chosŏn saw itself in a filial relationship with the Chinese emperor, "the Son of Heaven (天子)."

Chosŏn's self-perception as Little China undergoes an intriguing shift when the Han Chinese Ming Dynasty falls to the hands of a "barbaric" Manchu clan, who establishes the Qing Dynasty. I will delve into this in more detail later, but when this transpires, a strong movement emerges among Chosŏn's elites to promote Chosŏn as the legitimate heir of China, refusing to recognize the authority of the new "barbaric" emperor of China.[248] Again, this must be seen against the Confucian world view. To betray Ming and accept Qing was regarded as the most heinous act of abandoning one's own father (cf. Isa 1:3).[249] Thus, Chosŏn is no longer perceived as Little China; rather, Chosŏn the Little China is re-envisioned as the true China (as the remaining sovereign state among China's vassals), which now must rise to the occasion and expel the "barbaric" usurper of the fallen Ming. This aspiration in ideal never transformed into a real campaign against

---

246 This perspective is called "Sino–barbarian dichotomy," dividing the world into China and its "barbaric" Others, an important scheme in support of Sinocentric system.

247 One also finds this father-son motif in Hittite vassal treaties as well as the biblical covenant bestowed upon David. See, e.g., J. W. McKay, "Man's Love for God in Deuteronomy and the Father/Teacher–Son/Pupil Relationship," *VT* 22 (1972): 426–35, https://doi.org/10.1163/156853372X00181; Moshe Weinfeld, *Deuteronomy and the Deuteronomic School* (Oxford: Clarendon, 1972), 69–81.

248 See, e.g., Seung Bum Kye, "A Criticism of the Contemporary Korean Scholarship on the Chosŏn Elites' View of the Chinese Confucian Culture (zhonghua) in the 1600s to the 1800s," *The Journal of Korean History* 159 (2012): 265–94 [계승범, "조선후기 조선중화주의와 그 해석 문제"]; Young-min Kim, "Reconsidering Sinocentrism In Late Choson Korea," *The Journal of Korean History* 162 (2013): 211–52 [김영민, "조선중화주의의 재검토: 이론적 접근"].

249 Consequently, when the Chosŏn king had to submit to the Qing emperor (1636 CE), which was perceived as the ultimate betrayal of Ming, Korean historians consider this incident as a symbolic turning point. It marks a moment when Chosŏn's elites witnessed the very foundation of their symbolic world being upended.

Qing, but the mere fact that such an ideal was conceived by the Chosŏn elites is noteworthy.[250] Korean historians refer to this phenomenon as "Chosŏn-Sinocentrism (朝鮮中華主義)," and numerous scholarly studies have been carried out on this subject, not least for its troubling implications for today's Koreans.

I find it intriguing that Judah exhibits both of these aspects observed in Korea and China in relation to Israel. On one hand, Judah perceives itself as a son of Jacob/Israel, and as a result Judah's position within the twelve tribes of Israel is firmly established within Jacob's lineage (see Section 2.3). On the other hand, Judah exhibits a significantly different level of aspiration. Instead of simply seeking a place within Israel, the Judahites begin to assert themselves as the new Israel, a process I aim to demonstrate in this book. In sum, Judah has portrayed itself both as Israel's offspring and as the authentic Israel. This pattern bears a striking resemblance to Chosŏn's relationship with China. Such parallels seem more than mere coincidence and further justify my decision to draw from China's case as a comparative lens for understanding Judah's complex relationship with Israel.

6.2 Foreign Rulers of China

In East Asia, China's cultural and political influence has been pervasive, and it was not limited to Korea. This influence permeates various cultural facets, encompassing language, religion, and philosophy. For thousands of years, China was the enemy and model for its surrounding ethnic kingdoms, including Korea. To accept China's dominance or to fight against it for long constituted a critical decision for rulers of these groups, most of whom China has perceived as "barbarians."

The aforementioned portrayal of Chosŏn might convey the impression that Koreans were always submissive to China. That is simply not true. Many kingdoms in Korea maintained conflicting relations with China throughout ages. Particularly, Koguryŏ, during the earlier Three Kingdoms Period, demonstrated military expansionism and posed a constant threat to China (cf. Sections 4.1.1 & 10.1). Admittedly, Korea's aspirations never culminated in a complete conquest of China. Intriguingly, however, there have been instances where China succumbed to foreign conquerors, and even more fascinatingly, to nomadic tribes whom they regarded as "barbarians." Therefore, examining the circumstances and consequences of these "barbaric" Others conquering China is a matter worthy of our attention.

---

250 See discussion in n. 231.

Tab. 3: Dynasties in Chinese History.

Han Dynasty	Foreign Dynasty	
Sui		581–618 CE
Tang		618–907 CE
Song	*Liao, Jin, Western Xia**	960–1279 CE
	Yuan	1271–1368 CE
Ming		1368–1644 CE
	Qing	1636–1912 CE

* Peripheral entities coexisting and contending with the Song Dynasty

Mainland China has been conquered twice by outsiders: first by the Mongols, leading to the Yuan Dynasty, and then by the Manchus, resulting in the Qing Dynasty. When these external conquerors occupied China, they redefined the boundary of "China" to include them in it and eventually equated their state with China.[251] For instance, Kublai Khan of the Mongol Empire, the grandson of the great Genghis Khan, after conquering the Song Dynasty, founded the Yuan Dynasty (1271–1368 CE) and proclaimed himself as its first emperor.[252]

In fact, this was not the first time that China's marginal Others established a state and asserted a Chinese identity. Previously, the Liao, Jin, and Western Xia were all founded by China's "barbaric" outsiders who proclaimed their state as China.[253] The difference was that none of them unified China; their dominion was confined to specific regions while the Han Chinese Song Dynasty persisted, albeit in a weakened state. Unlike them, Kublai Khan was able to conquer the entire territory of China extant at the time. The ruling Mongols and the subjected "Han Chinese" lived together in tension.[254] Each influenced the other but also

---

251 On the flexible boundaries of China, shaped by competing attempts to redefine "China," see Gang Zhao, "Reinventing China: Imperial Qing Ideology and the Rise of Modern Chinese National Identity in the Early Twentieth Century," *Modern China* 32 (2006): 6–14, https://doi.org/10.1177/0097700405282349.

252 See John D. Langlois, ed., *China Under Mongol Rule* (Princeton, NJ: Princeton University Press, 1981), 3–22; Morris Rossabi, *Khubilai Khan: His Life and Times* (Berkeley, CA: University of California Press, 1988), 115–52.

253 This indicates that "China 中國" (literally, "central state") was a contested identity, with several entities laying claim to it. Yet the crucial question was whether their claim to be China would gain recognition, particularly from the majority Han Chinese people.

254 "Han (漢)" is the term that Chinese people have used to identify themselves in both ethnic and cultural contexts. A wealth of research is dedicated to exploring the construction of Han identity. See Thomas S. Mullaney, *Critical Han Studies: The History, Representation, and Identity of China's Majority*, New Perspectives on Chinese Culture and Society 4 (Berkeley, CA: University of California Press, 2012); Agnieszka Joniak-Luthi, *The Han: China's Diverse Majority*, Studies on Ethnic

maintained their identities until the Han Chinese finally succeeded in driving the foreign rulers out of China.

With the establishment of the Ming Dynasty (1368 CE), the Han people's pride was restored. However, after approximately three centuries, Ming was again subjugated by another ethnic invaders. The Qing Dynasty (1636–1912 CE), the last imperial dynasty of China before the dawn of the modern era, was established by Nurhaci (1559–1626 CE), who was the chieftain of one of the Jurchen tribes, later called the Manchus.[255] Upon defeating China, Nurhaci established the Qing Dynasty, identifying his state with China, and proudly assumed the role of the emperor of China.[256]

Both Yuan and Qing were established by foreign founders, but my discussion below centers on Qing because of the peculiar position the Manchus have held in relation to China. Although the Mongols were also perceived as China's "barbaric" Other, they were a more distant nomadic group and, at the time, a formidable power that left deep scars across an incredibly vast region. As a result, China's fall to the Mongols was less surprising on a global historical scale. However, its fall to the Manchus was a shock and a much more humiliating blow to the Han Chinese. The Manchus were a semi-nomadic group situated in closer proximity to China, and they were direct part of its tributary system.

Significantly, this semi-nomadic tribe was also well known to Koreans, as the group resided in the regions between Korea and China. More importantly, within China's Sinocentric hierarchy, this tribe was categorized as part of the "barbaric" realm, ostensibly lower in status than Chosŏn (at least in Chosŏn's understanding), which asserted its position as Little China. Nurhaci originated from this "barbaric" clan, which was disdained by both China and Chosŏn. Upon unifying the Jurchen tribes, he invaded both Korea and China. Korea narrowly survived after making a disgraceful pact with him, while Ming China succumbed to defeat.[257]

Groups in China (Seattle: University of Washington Press, 2015); Kevin Carrico, *The Great Han: Race, Nationalism, and Tradition in China Today* (Berkeley, CA: University of California Press, 2017).

255 The intricate relationship between the inferior conquerors and their superior subjects in this context has recently sparked controversy among historians, a topic I will briefly discuss. See, e.g., James A. Millward et al., eds., *New Qing Imperial History: The Making of Inner Asian Empire at Qing Chengde* (London: Routledge, 2004). Still, there is no doubt that the "barbaric" rulers recreated their own identity by adopting and manipulating the existing powerful legacy of Han Chinese.

256 In addition, before invading Korea and China, Nurhaci had claimed to inherit the legacy of the Great Mongol empire, proclaiming himself as the Khan. Thus, his Qing Dynasty was to inherit the legacy of the Mongol Yuan Dynasty as well.

257 The relationship between the Qing Dynasty and Chosŏn is intriguing. As previously mentioned, the Chosŏn Dynasty was founded on Confucian principles, and the Chosŏn elites ideologically acknowledged Ming China's authority over Chosŏn. However, when Nurhaci's Manchus – a group perceived by Chosŏn as inferior to themselves and as one of China's "barbaric" others –

The aspiration of the Manchus to be identified with China did not emerge suddenly; instead, it evolved from a persistent and deep-rooted inclination to be affiliated with the political and cultural landscape of China. In fact, this was not the first time the Jurchen clans from Manchu established a Chinese dynasty. Several centuries ago, there was another Jurchen-led dynasty in China, the Jin Dynasty (1114–1234 CE), which Nurhaci initially proclaimed to inherit (as the Later Jin Dynasty, 1616–1636 CE) before renaming it to Qing. I find it difficult to say that these enduring endeavors to associate with China were unconnected to this marginal tribe's attempts to transcend the "barbaric" perception ascribed to them by the Han Chinese.

Of course, the point is not to suggest a direct parallel between the Manchus' China and Judah's Israel. The two situations differ in many aspects. Perhaps Judah was not as foreign to Israel as the Manchus were to Han Chinese, and Judah did not invade and conquer Israel. However, what connects them is that both were once considered inferior, marginalized groups, allegedly harboring aspiration for the superior, and later adopting the superior's identity. Thus, when used with due caution, this cross-cultural comparison can be helpful in explaining Judah's motivation to assume Israel's identity. If the Manchus, China's nomadic outsider, were willing to adopt China's cultural heritage and identity, it is not unusual or surprising for Judah, Israel's perceived outsider, to embrace the identity and legacy of the fallen Israel.

6.3 New Qing History and Judah

At this moment, I fear that my discussion of the Manchus could be construed as implying that they entirely surrendered their ethnic identity and eagerly assimilated into the ostensibly superior Han Chinese culture. Indeed, such a perspective dominated the understanding of Qing for a considerable length of time. However, a recent incisive challenge to this dominant viewpoint necessitates discussion to counterbalance the prior analysis on the Qing Dynasty. This reassessment will also bear significant implications for our comprehension of the nature of Judah's identity project.

A notable movement called "New Qing History" in recent scholarship in Chinese history might provide new insights into the significance of Judah's marginal-

---

conquered China, a potent anti-Qing movement emerged within Chosŏn, promoting Chosŏn as the legitimate heir of the Ming Dynasty. See Adam Bohnet, "Ruling Ideology and Marginal Subjects: Ming Loyalism and Foreign Lineages in Late Chosŏn Korea," *Journal of Early Modern History* 15 (2011): 477–505, https://doi.org/10.1163/157006511X604013. Cf. n. 231 above.

ized position in Israel.[258] New Qing History is a movement, largely led by Western scholars that attempt to redress the dominant one-dimensional perception of the Qing Dynasty by paying heightened attention to the persistence of the separate identity of the external ruling group and the role their ethnic identity played in Qing's success.[259]

The issue of the Qing Dynasty, of course, is that it was established by a "barbaric" Other of China. Thus, Qing's conquest of the Ming Empire, established after driving out the foreign Mongol Yuan Dynasty, was considered an ultimate disgrace for the Han Chinese, which once again lost control to ethnic invaders, similar to the fall of Rome by "barbarians." Not surprisingly, there has been a consistent tendency among traditional Chinese historians to downplay and minimize the impact of these ethnic rulers by highlighting the voluntary and large-scale assimilation into Han Chinese culture, "sinicization." Westerners have demonstrated that "barbarian" invaders assimilated into the dominant Roman culture; similarly, Chinese historians tended to construe that the Manchus lost their language, culture, and identity and became Han Chinese.[260] Additionally, the eventual fall of the Qing Empire to the West in the twentieth century is blamed for the remaining outsider identity of the ruling elites of the Qing, which hindered them from defending China from outsiders from the West. As a result, the "barbarian" impact is minimized, and the most disgraceful era of Chinese history is turned into proof of the superiority of Chinese culture that was powerful to transform the "barbarians" into humans. The subsequent disgrace of the defeat by the West is re-conceived as an eventual emancipation from the inferior Qing regime.

Even in this brief sketch, the contradictory perception is evident for the Qing. The Qing's success is ascribed to the influence of Han Chinese that erased the ethnic identity of the Qing, whereas its failure, which occurred centuries after

---

258 For the overview of the movement, see Millward et al., *New Qing Imperial History*, 1–4; William T. Rowe, *China's Last Empire: The Great Qing*, History of Imperial China (Cambridge, MA: Harvard University Press, 2010), 1–10.

259 The movement is driven by *la longue durée* of French Annals school. Major proponents of this movement include, Evelyn Sakakida Rawski, *The Last Emperors: A Social History of Qing Imperial Institutions* (Berkeley, CA: University of California Press, 1998); Pamela Kyle Crossley, *A Translucent Mirror: History and Identity in Qing Imperial Ideology*, Philip E. Lilienthal Asian Studies Imprint (Berkeley, CA: University of California Press, 1999); Mark C. Elliott, *The Manchu Way: The Eight Banners and Ethnic Identity in Late Imperial China* (Stanford, CA: Stanford University Press, 2001); Edward J. M. Rhoads, *Manchus and Han: Ethnic Relations and Political Power in Late Qing and Early Republican China, 1861–1928*, Studies on Ethnic Groups in China (Seattle: University of Washington Press, 2000).

260 Mary C. Wright, ed., *China in Revolution: The First Phase, 1900–1913* (New Haven: Yale University Press, 1968), 21–22; Rowe, *China's Last Empire*, 2.

the alleged assimilation, is blamed on the Qing's lingering ethnic identity. However, the Qing's success is difficult to explain only by the influence of Han Chinese. Moreover, it is unlikely that other Han Chinese dynasties, like Ming or Song, would have been successful in defending China from Western threats.

The New Qing historians aim to reveal the underlying nationalistic sentiments in this conventional perspective on the Qing empire and attribute some of the Qing's success to the Manchus' persistent ethnic identity. Although these ethnic invaders adopted and assimilated into the superior Chinese culture, that must not mean that their ethnic "Manchu" identity disappeared and played no part in Qing's success. Largely hidden beneath the nationalistic downplay of the impact of ethnic identity is the remarkable success of this ethnic group, which is demonstrated not only in the length of their regime that lasted for centuries but also by the unparalleled westward expansion. Namely, the large boundary of China in today's world map is possible because of the success of the Qing empire, which calls for attention to what role the Qing's ethnic and nomadic identity played in making possible the Qing's successful conquest of central Asia.[261] Unlike the preceding Han Chinese empires that despised and feared ethnic Others and segregated itself from the surrounding ethnic groups, a stance well symbolized in the Great Wall of China, the Qing Dynasty's "Manchu" identity enabled them to break out of the wall and annex many ethnic Others in central Asia into China.[262] Thus, challenging the predominant perception, the New Qing historians have promoted the "Manchu way" to highlight how their persistent ethnic identity provided rigor to the unparalleled success of the Qing.[263] One cannot deny that New Qing History has its bias embedded in the agenda of praising Western values of open-mindedness to the marginalized and minorities, which may not match the real face of the Qing empire. Still, the way these scholars call for attention to the significance of Qing's ethnic identity helps pose interesting questions regarding Judah's alterity and inferiority to Israel.

6.4 Sinicization, Israelization, and Judah's Hybridity

What role the sense of inferiority played in Judah's appropriation of Israel's traditions and identity has not received due attention. A reason for this overlook is that scholars largely construed Judah as part of "one Israel," failing to pay heed

---

261 See Peter C. Perdue, *China Marches West: The Qing Conquest of Central Eurasia* (Cambridge, MA: Belknap, 2005).
262 See Zhao, "Reinventing China," 6–14.
263 Elliott, *The Manchu Way.*

to Judah's separate identity. I interpret this perspective as a form of "Israeliza-tion" of Judah widespread among biblical scholars, akin to Chinese historians' "sinicization."

Similar to the Qing empire's success being reduced to the influence of Han Chinese, Judah's success (or failure) is largely viewed in the continuation of the legacy of "Israel" within biblical scholarship. In doing so, Judah is practically limit-ed to the "remnant" of Israel. It is true that Judahites themselves initially might have claimed that position.[264] However, describing Judah as the remnant falls short of capturing the profound impact this remnant has had, insofar as Judah's bold vision has led to a complete reinvention of "Israel." It was entirely up to Judah to reimagine "Israel" and shape the present form of the Bible. Historical critics have recognized the Judean layers in their analysis of the text's growth but have not always been keen on articulating how those layers served Judeans in constructing the past that they wanted and needed to imagine.

The comparison to New Qing History may prompt readers to recall Davies and Whitelam's assertion that "ancient Israel" is a modern scholarly construct.[265] Although the reception of this argument has not been favorable, they are making an important point. Ancient Israel may not be a complete invention by modern scholars, but they are guilty of uncritically accepting the biblical depiction of ancient Israel and failing to recognize its ideological nature and consequence. Davies and Whitelam have framed their arguments around silencing Palestine history, which may have some affinities to the perceived sinicization by New Qing historians. I can reiterate their point that biblical scholars were also guilty of silencing Judah's voice and identity. To what extent is Judah's "Israel" identical to the "Israel" conceived by the leading northern tribes?[266] Judah and Israel may have imagined "one Israel," but the "Israel" in the present text is Judah's construct that must be distinguished from Northern Israel's conception of "Israel."

What I deduce from New Qing History is that the reality is more complex than a scholarly reconstruction, which inherently includes prejudice and bias. While Chinese historians were prone to downplay the impact of the Qing rulers' alterity and embraced an easier, safer answer that served their nationalistic senti-ments, if the real Qing rulers returned and learned how traditional historians ascribed their success to the Han Chinese influence, they would have felt es-tranged from the depiction. I posit that their sentiment would be more complex.

---

264 Gerhard F. Hasel, *The Remnant: The History and Theology of the Remnant Idea from Genesis to Isaiah*, 2nd ed. (Berrien Springs, MI: Andrews University Press, 1974).
265 Davies, *In Search of 'Ancient Israel'*; Whitelam, *The Invention of Ancient Israel.*
266 Cf. now with Fleming and Monroe's idea of the smaller Israel in the South and the greater Israel in the North. Monroe and Fleming, "Israel before the Omrides."

They might feel satisfaction that they succeeded in covering up their ethnic roots and being accepted as authentic part of the Han Chinese that they admired. Yet at the same time, part of their Self might be saddened that little attention has been given to their Manchu identity. In my view, the same could be applied to the Judeans behind the invention of the "one Israel" in the present text. We need to place greater emphasis on the present form of the Bible as Judah's idealistic construct, which forces questions as to *how* that ideal has been constructed.

I call for a heightened focus on Judah's identity markers and identity narratives through which Israel has been reoriented in the present text. Similar to how New Qing historians have demonstrated the persistence of the "Manchu way," how Judah's separate identity played out in constructing Israel in the present text must be examined. Among New Qing historians, Mark Elliott, for instance, examined the "eight banners" as the Manchu clan's unique identity marker around which they strived to maintain their Manchu identity.[267] Similarly, as a marginalized party to Israel, Judah later invested much to promote Judah's own identity markers to reimagine Israel. Thus, figures like Abraham and David, along with traditions tied to places like Jerusalem, have added significance as Judah's unique identity markers.

Judah is heavily invested in the Zion tradition, around which the earlier Yhwh religion, deeply rooted in the Sinai tradition, is systematically reoriented. Although I agree with Jon Levenson that Zion and Sinai are intricately related in the final form of the text,[268] it is necessary to acknowledge that the two traditions originally had distinct origins. Then, the presently combined traditions may reflect Judah's hybrid identity. The Judahites strived to embrace the Sinai tradition as their past while striving to promote Zion as the new center of the Yahwistic heritage that balances the Sinai tradition. The innate tension between the motifs of covenantal duty and unconditional grant may originate – at least in part – from Judah's hybrid identity.

In addition, the Judahites reformulated Israel's ancestral past by orienting the existing Jacob tradition with the Abraham tradition. The Zion tradition has received more attention than the functional import of the southern Abraham narrative. I propose that human identities are expressed in narrative forms, and among many forms of narratives, past narratives have the most formative power to identity construction and maintenance. Thus, in the rest of the book, I focus on Judah's reimagination of the past and how this reimagination decisively altered Judah's self-definition and paved the way for Judah's emergence as the new Israel.

---

267 Elliott, *The Manchu Way.*
268 Jon Douglas Levenson, *Sinai and Zion: An Entry into the Jewish Bible* (Minneapolis: Winston, 1985).

6.5 Conclusion

Going back to Fleming's query, "Is it sufficient to merely covet the reputation of the more powerful northern polity?" my answer is that Israel represented more than just a "more powerful" polity for Judah, like China was for certain Koreans. Out of prolonged interaction, the minor Judah had somehow developed a profound yearning for the superior Israel. When Israel fell, the Judahites readily embraced Israel's legacy and identity, much like the barbaric conquerors did with China. The Jurchens, once perceived as a marginal Other, ultimately took over China, founding the Qing empire. Their lack of tangible connection to China suggests that sheer desire, anchored in a sense of inferiority, can be potent enough to drive a group to adopt the identity of the perceived superior. This scenario might seem to imply the marginal Other's absolute willingness to abandon their ethnic identities and assimilate into the dominant culture. To counter this perception, I have introduced New Qing historians' programmatic challenge, which emphasized the persistence of the Manchu ethnic identity and its pivotal role in fundamentally reshaping China.

The dynamics between Judah and Israel might not precisely mirror these observations, but they do provide illuminating perspectives on how Judah, as an outsider, seized the opportunity presented to it. What stands out is how Judah's appropriation of Israel mirrors these findings. In capitalizing on the opportunity, Judah first appropriated Israel's legacy and then profoundly reshaped it, a process I will illustrate in the subsequent discussion.

Part II: **Judah Rewrites Israel's Past**

7 Tradition, Narrative, and Identity: A Theoretical Discussion

In Part I, I have argued that Judah's relationship with Israel is complex and cannot be reduced to the simplistic depiction of "one Israel." I have emphasized how Judah's perceived inferiority to Israel motivated them to appropriate much of Israel's heritage and ultimately adopt Israel's identity, making the present text's construction of "one Israel" both a tool and a product of this Judean identity project. In Part II, I examine how the ancestral traditions in Genesis served the making of the "one Israel," with a focus on the instrumental aspect of the formation of the ancestral history. I demonstrate that the Abrahamic expansion of the Jacob tradition was not a natural product of growth of tradition, but rather Judahites' strategic move to subvert and reorient the underlying northern tradition.

Before delving into details, this chapter presents a theoretical exploration of my perspective on the ancestral traditions. I demonstrate how the functional approach shapes my understanding of biblical ancestral traditions as discursive resources for later polities to imagine and reimagine their collective identities.

7.1 Past and Present

Traditionally, biblical scholars viewed the ancestral traditions as historical resources, construing them as accumulations of past traditions. In other words, the stories were considered as vessels of past information. Perhaps this was inevitable because most historical critics earlier followed the Graf-Wellhausen legacy, approaching the text to reconstruct history, either of ancient Israel or their religion.[269] Their focus was set either on restoring the original scope of traditions and how they developed in stages into the present form or on seeking information about the historical context of the composition layers. According to this perspective, traditions were continuously revised over time as different traditions were added and necessary changes were implemented. While the accuracy of the information contained in these stories has been debated, early critics generally agreed that at least they were meant to convey historical information. The underlying assumption was that someone who possessed authentic knowledge and information about what had happened recorded it into writing to *preserve* it for

---

[269] See Ernest W. Nicholson, *The Pentateuch in the Twentieth Century: The Legacy of Julius Wellhausen* (Oxford: Clarendon, 1998).

https://doi.org/10.1515/9783111376554-007

future use. However, increased archaeological and cultural knowledge about the period described in the text has challenged this optimism. This is particularly true in the case of the ancestral traditions, which were documented centuries after the era they depict. Thus, the biblical ancestral traditions, or the book of Genesis as a whole, have been largely relegated to the realm of myth, which would help little historical critics' efforts to reconstruct real history.[270]

However, this only addresses one side of the past. From a utilitarian perspective, one can rediscover the value of the mythic past, even if its historical basis is problematic. Historians have repeatedly demonstrated that the past is a useful and essential space for the present. The past matters not only in itself but also in terms of its impact on the present.[271] Anthropologists echo this conviction, as concisely articulated by Thomas Eriksen, "history is not a product of the past but a response to requirements of the present."[272] Even if there is no tangible evidence, a remembered past can still influence the present if remembered by many. On the other hand, the past, regardless of its significance, loses its influence on the present when forgotten or not remembered.

People often remember the past not simply because it happened, but because it has positive or negative effects on their present reality. The problem is that human memory by nature is flexible and easily manipulated by internal and external stimuli. Willfully or not, people may forget the past or distort memories to serve their interests. Individuals may preserve accurate memories of life experiences, but specialists contend that even the most personal memories are socially constructed.[273] Furthermore, even if real memories are maintained, anthropologists assert that individual memories tend not to extend over three generations.[274] Anything that goes beyond three generations is regarded as mythic in practice.

---

270 See, e.g., Thomas L. Thompson, *The Historicity of the Patriarchal Narratives: The Quest for the Historical Abraham*, BZAW 133 (Berlin: Walter de Gruyter, 1974); idem, *Early History of the Israelite People: From the Written & Archaeological Sources*, Brill's Scholars' List (Leiden: Brill, 2000).

271 See, e.g., Hobsbawm and Ranger, *The Invention of Tradition*; George C. Bond and Angela Gilliam, eds., *Social Construction of the Past: Representation as Power*, One World Archaeology 24 (London: Routledge, 1994). For applications into biblical studies, see among others, Diana V. Edelman and Ehud Ben Zvi, eds., *Remembering Biblical Figures in the Late Persian and Early Hellenistic Periods: Social Memory and Imagination* (Oxford: Oxford University Press, 2013); Johannes Unsok Ro and Diana Edelman, eds., *Collective Memory and Collective Identity: Deuteronomy and the Deuteronomistic History in Their Context*, BZAW 534 (Berlin: Walter de Gruyter, 2021).

272 Thomas Hylland Eriksen, *Ethnicity and Nationalism: Anthropological Perspectives*, 3rd ed. (London: Pluto, 2010), 85.

273 Maurice Halbwachs, *On Collective Memory*, The Heritage of Sociology (Chicago: University of Chicago Press, 1992); idem, *The Collective Memory* (New York: Harper & Row, 1980).

274 See Jan Vansina, *Oral Tradition as History* (Madison, WI: University of Wisconsin Press, 1985); Jan Assmann, "Communicative and Cultural Memory," in *Cultural Memory Studies: An*

Thus, the distant past is, by nature, a mythic space, constructed by social and cultural memory. It is powerful in shaping collective identity but is also malleable and, thus, susceptible to manipulation.[275] All origin stories exploit the power of the distant past. Hence, today, it is no longer unusual to come across historians who claim that "'tradition' did not merely transmit the past, it created it."[276]

The changing perspective among classical historians offers a useful example, as they also devoted attention to foundation traditions similar to biblical scholars. Traditionally, classicists have assumed the positivist approach, viewing individual myths as sources containing some historical value. However, in the late twentieth century, a constructivist approach emerged, in which foundation myths are seen as social constructs of a later time.[277] Mac Sweeney provides a fitting illustration of the changing perspectives:

> Instead, it was argued that foundation myths should be seen as social and literary constructs and should be situated in the time in which they were written and circulated. This approach argued that foundation myths were shaped much more by the needs and agendas of those telling them in the historical present than by the objective facts of the historical past. It was argued that myths were altered, manipulated, and even created, for use in a strategic and political way. To return to the example of the Ionian Migration, instrumental interpretations of these myths have also been proposed. It is suggested that the idea that the colonists of the cities were originally migrants from Athens was promoted by Athens itself, as a means of justifying its expansionist ambitions in the eastern Aegean. If Athens could claim to be the mother city of the Ionians, this would give it a greater claim to influence over them.[278]

It is important to remember that the social consequences of remembering the past do not distinguish between fact and fiction. People's reception of the past as

International and Interdisciplinary Handbook, ed. Astrid Erll and Ansgar Nünning, Media and Cultural Memory 8 (Berlin: Walter de Gruyter, 2008), 109–18.

275 Alan Kirk, "Social and Cultural Memory," in *Memory, Tradition, and Text: Uses of the Past in Early Christianity*, ed. Alan Kirk and Tom Thatcher, SemeiaSt 52 (Atlanta: Society of Biblical Literature, 2005), 1–24; Astrid Erll and Ansgar Nünning, eds., *Cultural Memory Studies: An International and Interdisciplinary Handbook*, Media and Cultural Memory 8 (Berlin: Walter de Gruyter, 2008); Jan Assmann, *Cultural Memory and Early Civilization: Writing, Remembrance, and Political Imagination* (New York: Cambridge University Press, 2011).

276 M. I. Finley, *The Use and Abuse of History* (London: Chatto and Windus, 1975), 25.

277 See Naoíse Mac Sweeney, ed., *Foundation Myths in Ancient Societies: Dialogues and Discourses* (Philadelphia: University of Pennsylvania Press, 2015), 3–7.

278 Mac Sweeney, 4–5. Here, Mac Sweeney uses "constructionism" as an umbrella term that includes "instrumentalism." However, for some, constructionism might unnecessarily highlight the aspect of invention, while not all those on the constructionist side believe that the past is a total invention. Thus, I prefer using the term instrumentalism to highlight the past's strategic function for the present.

factual per se is a sufficient condition for its formative power to bind, or break, society. If factual pasts are forgotten and distorted, it is equally possible for fictional pasts to be remembered and consequential.[279] This is why I believe it essential to consider the instrumentalist perspective of the past when examining biblical ancestral traditions, in order to comprehend how the constructed past works alongside the factual past in service of present needs.

7.2 Narrative and Identity

My interest in the instrumentality of the past is closely tied to my interest in the formation of identity. Remembering the past might have many effects, but the focus here is its impact on human societies, particularly their identities. Memory is an important component of human minds, and how people remember their past, especially their roots, causes tangible consequences for their self-perception. There is growing recognition in diverse fields that the Self or identity is constructed in narrative forms.[280] Psychologists, for instance, have recognized the inherent link between the Self and narrative. Maintaining a coherent narrative of purpose and meaning is a critical part of maintaining the well-being of the Self, both at individual and collective levels. Naturally, the therapy of a disrupted Self requires an examination and modification of the narrative.[281]

For the purpose of this book, it is necessary to examine the functionality of narratives in forming a collective identity as a people. In that regard, Stephen

---

279 Using the primordialist-constructionist dichotomy might also entail an unnecessary impression of posing them as mutually exclusive categories when things are not that simple. Most of the past as we know it fall between the two poles, and most of today's historians' understanding of the past also fall between them. Even the most ardent critiques of constructionism have not denied some constructed nature of the past. Rather, the point of debate is the correct balance between tradition and invention; that is, whether the past is created or *recreated*. See David Carr, "Narrative and the Real World: An Argument for Continuity," *History and Theory* 25 (1986): 117–31, https://doi.org/10.2307/2505301.

280 E.g., Erik H. Erikson, *Identity, Youth, and Crisis* (New York: W. W. Norton, 1968); George C. Rosenwald and Richard L. Ochberg, eds., *Storied Lives: The Cultural Politics of Self-Understanding* (New Haven: Yale University Press, 1992); Margaret R. Somers, "The Narrative Constitution of Identity: A Relational and Network Approach," *Theory and Society* 23 (1994): 605–49, https://doi.org/10.1007/BF00992905; Dan P. McAdams, "The Psychology of Life Stories," *Review of General Psychology* 5 (2001): 100–122, https://doi.org/10.1037/1089-2680.5.2.100.

281 E.g., John D. Engel et al., *Narrative in Health Care: Healing Patients, Practitioners, Profession, and Community* (Oxford: Radcliffe, 2008); Jonathan M. Adler, Lauren M. Skalina, and Dan P. McAdams, "The Narrative Reconstruction of Psychotherapy and Psychological Health," *Psychotherapy Research* 18 (2008): 719–34, https://doi.org/10.1080/10503300802326020.

Cornell's recent essay is instructive, which cogently demonstrates that an ethnic identity tends to take a narrative form.[282] Several important points made by Cornell are worth considering. First, ethnicity is not merely a label, but a vessel of meaning: "Most ethnic labels have meanings attached to them that lend them power as organizers of relationships, resources, experience, and action."[283] Second, these organizing meanings are stored and conveyed in the form of a narrative.

> When people take on, create, or assign an ethnic identity, part of what they do – intentionally or not – is to take on, create, or assign a story, a narrative of some sort that captures central understandings about what it means to be a member of the group. It is a story that can be told in many ways, but ultimately it can be reduced to something along the lines of "we are the people who ..." (alternatively: "they are the people who ..."), in which the lacuna becomes a tale of some sort, a record of events. The story has a subject (the group in question), it has action (what happened or will happen), and it has value: it attaches a value to its subject.[284]

Third, "narrativization" typically involves three steps: selection, plotting, and interpretation,[285] and ethnic identity can be defined in terms of its social effect on others. "To the extent that selection, plotting, and interpretation take ethnic boundaries into account and use them as central organizing principles, the result is an ethnic identity narrative, the story of a particular ethnic 'us' or 'them.'"[286] Granted, narrative is not the only tool for collective identities to be constructed and maintained; segregating or integrating acts can occur by mere perceptions of differences or similarities on many forms of identity markers, such as language, appearance, or religion. Yet narrativizing them by selecting, plotting, and interpreting is most effective in controlling, magnifying, and perpetuating their effects. As discussed earlier, not every past story is memorable. If a certain event is narrativized, this not merely means that it occurred but also that someone at a later time deemed it memorable, thus, incorporating it into their collective past. Such strategic features of narrativization make narrative one of the most powerful tools for identity negotiation.

Fourth, identity narratives are fluid, adapting to new circumstances and needs. "As groups' understandings of themselves and others change, so do the narratives in which those understandings are encapsulated and through which they are given substance. Selection, plotting, interpretation – all or any may

---

282 Cornell, "That's the Story of Our Life," 41–53.
283 Cornell, 42.
284 Cornell, 42.
285 Cornell, 43.
286 Cornell, 44.

change over time."[287] Hence, any social change, derived from within or from outside, can trigger a change in the group's understanding of the collective Self, which in turn affects the group's identity narratives.

Fifth, what ultimately matters is not the truthfulness of the specific events recorded in the narrative, but the claims they make and their effects on the community. "What matters is not the validity of representations but their effects: the degree to which the narrative and its component parts are understood – by group members or by outsiders – as illustrative or exemplary, as capturing something essential about the group in question."[288] Not all true stories evoke collective sentiments, whereas invented narratives can be effective in binding diverse groups. To add a point, this also means not every group member needs to be innately linked to the narrative; once it becomes part of the collective past, other members can adopt it as their past by *participating* in that story. As Margaret Somers argued, "all of us come to *be* who we *are* (however ephemeral, multiple, and changing) by being located or locating ourselves (usually unconsciously) in social narratives *rarely of our own making*."[289] Sixth, the power of identity narratives lies in their "sense-making properties."[290] The problem of collective identity is creating an account of who "we" (or "they") are that makes sense of the larger matrix of social relations in which the group finds itself and of its place within that matrix and its experience of those relations. Narrative – which involves the relational ordering and framing of events and experiences – is peculiarly suited to these sense-making tasks.

As such, Cornell demonstrates how narratives, factual or fictional, serve ethnic groups in making sense of "who we are." Although the exact origins of ethnic groups may be elusive, the pursuit to understand their beginnings and their relevance to the present continues. In answering these questions, there is no better way than telling stories of origins. Then, past traditions' value can be analyzed in terms of their functionality and how they served later entities that strived to make sense of "who we are" by embracing them as their origins. This requires shifting attention from the reality that the traditions depict to the impact on the people who remember them as their past.

7.3 Identity Narrative and Instrumentality

My approach is to view biblical ancestral traditions as "identity narratives," a term that encompasses origin myths but also holds broader significance. In this

---

287 Cornell, 44.
288 Cornell, 44.
289 Somers, "The Narrative Constitution of Identity," 606.
290 Cornell, 44.

regard, Konrad Schmid has made a very important observation, that Genesis and Exodus functioned as independent traditions of "Israel's dual origins."[291] Despite his observation's social-scientific implications, however, Schmid assigns them only a subservient role to his primary goal of promoting the late dating of the literary merger of Genesis and Exodus, which he attributes to P.[292] It is also worth noting that his suggestion to approach this as a matter of form-critical classification is questionable. Building on proposals of earlier scholars like Albert de Pury and Moshe Weinfeld, he proposes a form-critical classification of these as the "tradition of origins."[293] Form criticism concerns a tradition's original setting, but I am interested in its impact on a later polity that embraces it. Technically speaking, Gunkel's concern lay in the *intended* genre, whereas my focus is on the *received* genre. A saga or legend in Gunkel's terms can function as an origin myth in later contexts.

When I classify biblical ancestral traditions as origin myths, I use the notion as part of the broader concept of identity narrative. Identity narratives entail temporal aspects. People struggle to define "who we are," which necessarily involves remembering "where we came from" and promoting "who we ought to be."[294] Origin myths are only part of this broader narrative representation of the collective Self, which centers on constructing the past as to "where we came

---

291 Schmid, *Genesis and the Moses Story.*

292 There is no doubt about the tremendous implications of this radical claim. However, there are more important things here than the matter of dating. If P was the first to combine Genesis and Exodus, this means there were two separate groups behind these traditions. Who were they? Schmid (*Genesis and the Moses Story*, 148) assigns the ancestral tradition to the South and the Exodus/Moses tradition to the North. If so, ascribing the merger to P means that the two major origin traditions of Israel remained independent from each other throughout the monarchic era, and combination came only after the fall of the monarchy. Biblical critics have long observed the northern orientation of the Jacob tradition, which contradicts Schmid's assignment of the ancestral tradition to the South. Furthermore, early northern traditions appear to show an awareness of both Jacob and Moses traditions. To what extent can we say that P was the first to combine the two traditions? Like other scholars, Schmid's attention here is fixed on the Persian period, which appears to prevent him from paying due attention to earlier contexts. P's literary combination of the ancestral and Exodus traditions is not insignificant, but it is likely just one late phase of many more mergers (and ruptures) of earlier stories. For a more detailed critique of his position, see my essay "Genesis and Exodus as Conceptually Independent, Competing Origin Myths?," *ZAW* 133 (2021): 427–41, https://doi.org/10.1515/zaw-2021-4001.

293 Schmid, *Genesis and the Moses Story*, 114–16, 147–48.

294 See Susan Condor, "Social Identity and Time," in *Social Groups and Identities: Developing the Legacy of Henri Tajfel*, ed. W. P. Robinson, International Series in Social Psychology (Oxford: Butterworth-Heinemann, 1996), 285–315; Marco Cinnirella, "Exploring Temporal Aspects of Social Identity: The Concept of Possible Social Identities," *European Journal of Social Psychology* 28 (1999): 227–48, https://doi.org/10.1002/(SICI)1099-0992(199803/04)28:2<227::AID-EJSP866>3.0.CO;2-X.

from." However, scholars often employ "origin myth" (or mythic history) merely to assign a mythic period to a quasi-historical era, as a preface to their historical presentation, in which the notion's innate functionality is not fully realized.

By construing biblical ancestral traditions as identity narratives, I aim to completely shift from the lingering historical framework to stress the traditions' instrumentality. The notion of identity narrative highlights the user's perspective, instead of focusing on the historical accuracy of the events described in the text. In addition, the concept of identity narrative enables me to effectively address the subjective aspect of the inquiry into Judah's self-perception that I initially posed in this book. The tradition is not just seen as a source of objective information; it is also a means of shaping the user's identity. For example, religious traditions serve as the cornerstone of personal and collective identity. These traditions' stories, rituals, and beliefs are central to shaping how individuals perceive themselves and their place in the world. They provide a sense of meaning in life and one's position within the larger story of the world. The focus shifts from the traditions' innate value or origins to how they are used as a narrative basis to construct "who we are."

Accordingly, my approach bears affinity to that of the minimalists.[295] For instance, I am in full agreement with Keith Whitelam's remark that "even if such origin traditions are late constructions, they remain valuable sources for the historian, not as witnesses to the earlier period they purport to describe, but rather to the later socio-political processes that shaped and adapted them."[296] It is no accident that the champions of the minimalist approach were among the first to embrace notions like "foundation myths" and "invention of tradition" or adopt approaches such as cultural memory.[297] However, these scholars tend to view most foundational materials as late literary inventions of the Hellenistic period, thereby limiting the "later socio-political processes" to only very late contexts. While the final form of the text must be dated late, I see no reason to deny earlier phases of the development of these traditions. Thus, we can exam-

---

295 See now Niels Peter Lemche, *Back to Reason: Minimalism in Biblical Studies*, Discourses in Ancient near Eastern and Biblical Studies (Sheffield: Equinox, 2022).

296 Whitelam, "Israel's Traditions of Origin," 31.

297 See Whitelam, *The Invention of Ancient Israel*. Niels Peter Lemche (*The Israelites in History and Tradition*, 86–97) also employs the notion of "foundation myth," considering the exile and exodus as two major myths upon which Israel's history has been constructed. Thomas Thompson (*The Mythic Past: Biblical Archaeology and the Myth of Israel* [New York: Basic Books, 1999], 208) likewise uses "origin myth" to highlight the constructed nature of Israel's past in service of later political and ideological agendas. Philip Davies (*The Origins of Biblical Israel*, 31–35) adopts "cultural memory" as a method in his investigation of the making of "biblical Israel," a move that shows his emphasis on those who remember past traditions.

ine how Israel's "origin traditions" were "shaped and adapted" in earlier periods, such as the monarchic era.[298]

Furthermore, viewing biblical traditions as identity narratives establishes a continuum that links the genesis of the tradition to its continued relevance, even until today. This is what I meant by the broader significance. Identity narratives are employed by people to construct and understand "who we are." These narratives serve as a foundation for individuals and groups to make sense of their experiences, define themselves in relation to Others, and articulate their values, beliefs, and aspirations. People from diverse backgrounds throughout history have embraced biblical traditions as part of their personal identity narrative, demonstrating the versatility and adaptability of these traditions that cannot be fully explained in historical terms. For instance, how can a modern Asian identify with and claim an Abrahamic heritage with confidence? One cannot explain this without taking into account the impact of participating into interpretive traditions that facilitated this remarkable leap of faith (see Gal 3:7). While this connection may be symbolic in nature, its effect is real in shaping the self-perception of believing Christians through Abraham's faith.

Therefore, perceiving biblical tradition as an identity narrative enables a deeper understanding of how this ancient narrative has become intertwined with personal and cultural identities, not simply as a retelling of history, but as a part of people's ongoing self-representation. The entire history of the Jewish and Christian religions can be characterized as continued efforts of identity redefinition through the act of "renarration" of the past. The production of the New Testament by Christians and the Mishnah and Talmud by Jews must be understood as part of their ongoing interpretive struggle to reinterpret ancient traditions in support of their present identity. These interpretive struggles are not isolated events but rather components of a larger process of identity formation that was already at work in the biblical time and is still ongoing today.

7.4 Identity Formation and Time

This leads me to question if Israel's identity formation should be a subject limited to certain settings, like the Persian period. Recent decades have witnessed a burgeoning interest in identity formation in biblical scholarship. As Carly Crouch has recently observed, however, studies on Israel's identity formation predominantly

---

298 The same point applies against Schmid. Schmid's investment in late dating makes him operate top-down, focusing on the final stage of literary cross-referencing between Genesis and Exodus tradition blocks. Instead, I operate bottom-up and focus on the division between the Jacob and Abraham traditions.

center on two periods.[299] While traditional discussions centered on the formative era of Israel, recent studies center on the Persian period and its literature, such as Second and Third Isaiah, Chronicles, Ezra-Nehemiah, Zechariah, and Haggai.[300] This leaves the Bible's foundational traditions, the Pentateuch and the Deuteronomistic history, largely unattended by inquiries of identity formation of Israel. Even in rare cases when scholars applied studies of identity formation in these texts, like E. Theodore Mullen Jr., R. Christopher Heard, and Mark Brett, their studies tended to focus on the final form, usually set against the Persian setting.[301] The unintended consequence is that, within biblical scholarship, studies of identity formation tend to be construed as a subject confined in Persian-period scholarship.[302]

---

299 Crouch, *The Making of Israel*, 1.
300 See, e.g., Louis Jonker, "Textual Identities in the Books of Chronicles: The Case of Jehoram's History," in *Community Identity in Judean Historiography: Biblical and Comparative Perspectives*, ed. Gary N. Knoppers and Kenneth A. Ristau (Winona Lake, IN: Eisenbrauns, 2009), 214; idem, *Texts, Contexts and Readings in Postexilic Literature: Explorations into Historiography and Identity Negotiation in Hebrew Bible and Related Texts*, FAT 2/53 (Tübingen: Mohr Siebeck, 2011); Rom-Shiloni, *Exclusive Inclusivity*; Jon L. Berquist, "Constructions of Identity in Postcolonial Yehud," in *Judah and the Judeans in the Persian Period*, ed. Oded Lipschits and Manfred Oeming (Winona Lake, IN: Eisenbrauns, 2006), 63. The Persian-period centrism is apparent also for those who adopt memory studies for similar purposes. See, e.g., Davies, *The Origins of Biblical Israel*; Ehud Ben Zvi, "Who Knew What?: The Construction of the Monarchic Past in Chronicles and Implications for the Intellectual Setting of Chronicles," in *Judah and the Judeans in the Fourth Century B.C.E*, ed. Oded Lipschits, Gary N. Knoppers, and Rainer Albertz (Winona Lake, IN: Eisenbrauns, 2007), 349–60; Ehud Ben Zvi, "Chronicles and Its Reshaping of Memories of Monarchic Period Prophets: Some Observations," in *Prophets, Prophecy, and Ancient Israelite Historiography*, ed. Mark J. Boda and Lissa M. Wray Beal (Winona Lake, IN: Eisenbrauns, 2013), 167–88.
301 As for the Pentateuch, see E. Theodore Mullen Jr., *Ethnic Myths and Pentateuchal Foundations: A New Approach to the Formation of the Pentateuch*, SemeiaSt (Atlanta: Scholars Press, 1997); Konrad Schmid, *Erzväter und Exodus: Untersuchungen zur doppelten Begründung der Ursprünge Israels Innerhalb der Geschichtsbücher des Alten Testaments*, WMANT 81 (Neukirchen-Vluyn: Neukirchener Verlag, 1999)=*Genesis and the Moses Story: Israel's Dual Origins in the Hebrew Bible*; Mark G. Brett, *Genesis: Procreation and the Politics of Identity* (London: Routledge, 2000); R. Christopher Heard, *The Dynamics of Diselection: Ambiguity in Genesis 12–36 and Ethnic Boundaries in Post-Exilic Judah*, SemeiaSt 39 (Atlanta: Society of Biblical Literature, 2001). As for the DtrH, see E. Theodore Mullen Jr., *Narrative History and Ethnic Boundaries: The Deuteronomistic Historian and the Creation of Israelite National Identity*, SemeiaSt (Atlanta: Scholars Press, 1993); Linville, *Israel in the Book of Kings*.
302 Not every biblical scholar confined Israel's identity formation to the Persian period though. Notable exceptions include Peter Machinist, Carly Crouch, and Kenton Sparks. Machinist and Crouch investigated the Israelite identity in the Assyrian period, though in very different manners. Machinist discusses the pre-exilic Israelite identity crisis in the face of the Assyrian threat, focusing on *Rab Šāqēh*'s psychological warfare. He ("The *Rab Šāqēh* at the Wall of Jerusalem," 166) argues that the biblical account of the Assyrian siege, found in 2Kgs 18–19 and

True, it is widely recognized that identity concerns are heightened in "periods of rupture," as individuals and groups are forced to confront significant challenges to their social and psychological well-being.[303] Thus, there is no denying that the Assyrian and Babylonian invasions and forced migrations brought about significant identity crises for Israel and Judah. However, that does not mean that there was no crisis of Israel's identity beforehand, or that the ownership of "Isra-

Isa 36–37, was written in response to the Assyrian threat and the challenge it posed to Israelite identity.

Unlike Machinist, who did not have a specific agenda against Persian-period centrism, Crouch actively challenged this perspective in order to shed light on pre-exilic identity formation through a close examination of Deuteronomy. However, she does not delve deeper into earlier periods and stays with the seventh century. After dismissing both the biblical account of Josiah's reformation (2Kgs 23) and the traditional linking with vassal treaty motif as proper reference point, however, Crouch (*The Making of Israel*, 106–14) simply states her aim to anchor the Deuteronomic core, which she later defines roughly as Deut 12–26, to the seventh-century. What she provides is a criticism of proponents of the book's exilic origin, mainly Nicholson, grounded in their failure to distinguish ethnicity from nationalism, which she deems critical. See n. 49 for my critique on this. At this point, I must question to what extent Crouch's anchoring this idealistic, perhaps *ahistorical* and *apolitical*, literature in the specific and tangible setting in seventh-century Judah is justified. Moreover, I find it curious that she pays no attention to the traditional critics' observations of Deuteronomy's deeper, northern origin, which would have provided a very different frame to understand the nature of Deuteronomy's Israel and its Judahite reception. Cf. e.g., Sweeney, *King Josiah of Judah*, 19; Sparks, *Ethnicity and Identity in Ancient Israel*, 222–67.

In contrast, Kenton Sparks (*Ethnicity and Identity in Ancient Israel*) has offered a comprehensive exploration of the ongoing process of identity formation by tracking the development and evolution of Israel's ethnic expressions throughout biblical literature, organizing them chronologically. However, as we noted above (Section 1.2), it is unfortunate that he leaves Israel's foundational traditions, both the Pentateuch and the Deuteronomistic History, out of his initial survey. This is unfortunate because the Pentateuch is widely recognized for its diachronic development, which, if given due attention, can provide insights into important aspects of the growth and changes in Israel's pre-exilic identity negotiations. That scholars no longer share a consensus view in reconstructing the text's prehistory does not categorically reject the existence of earlier forms of traditions and the possible roles they might have played in shaping Israel's and Judah's identity in earlier periods. Even Van Seters, who pushed back the date of J, does not deny that his exilic Yahwist, as an ancient historian, made use of existing materials.

303 Cornell, "That's the Story of Our Life," 45. However, Cornell's remark is not made to deny the narrative identity in ordinary, non-ruptured times. Rather, his point is to defend his thesis on the narrative nature of identity formation in the face of a predictable challenge: namely, why does the narrative aspect of identity appear to remain dormant in ordinary moments? Cornell explains this in line with Bruner's explanation of individuals' responses to a crisis, stating, "when things 'are as they should be,' the narratives of folk psychology are unnecessary." See Jerome S. Bruner, *Acts of Meaning* (Cambridge, MA: Harvard University Press, 1990), 40. Identity narratives are simply hidden beneath the "taken-for-grantedness" before resurfacing during the time of rupture.

el" and its boundary remained fixed and unchallenged before the threats of Mesopotamian empires. Nor the stories with which Persian-period Judeans constructed and understood their collective past were all created at the time. Cornell's introduction of Malkki's study of Hutu refugees from Burundi is illustrative on this point.

> Much of this effort took the form of narrating the Hutu past, from the colonial history of Burundi through ethnic warfare to the present period of exile. Hutus continually revisited past and present events, incorporating them into an evolving narrative, and in the process reinterpreted those events. The result was what Malkki calls a "mythico-history," replete with recurrent themes and pivotal episodes that added up to a highly standardized, collective Hutu narrative "which heroizes them as a distinct people with a historical trajectory setting them apart from other peoples." It is a narrative in which the Hutus "are the principal actors" and through which they recast historical events in moral terms. Narration is part of the way they deal with loss, with refugee status, with exile, and with discrimination at the hands of the Tanzanians, and it is how they construct themselves as a people. The Hutu label has not changed, but the identity it represents has been narratively reconstructed.[304]

I see many of these points applicable to the Judean exiles. Unlike Ezra/Nehemiah or Esther, which display clear indications of their historical contexts and are likely products of their time, the ancestral traditions of Abraham, Isaac, and Jacob, as well as many stories of the exodus and wilderness traditions, exhibit signs of more complex development, which discourages us from viewing them as coherent recollections of the past from a single vantage point. As most historical critics agree, these traditions had earlier origins and have gone through stages of growth, no matter how one understands it, of which the present text has taken its composite and complex shape. This suggests that the examination of composition/redaction history by traditional critics can prove invaluable resources that can shed light onto the diachronic process of Israel's efforts to *renarrate* the past as part of their ongoing identity formation.

In a similar vein, Bruce Lincoln emphasizes the social and historical aspects of identity formation, characterizing it as an ongoing social negotiation:

> Society is thus a synthesis ... the formation of any synthesis (intellectual, social, political, etc.) is never a final step. Any synthetic entity, having its origin in a prior dialectic confrontation, bears within it the tensions that existed between the thesis and antithesis involved

---

304 Cornell, "That's the Story of Our Life," 46. For the cited work, see Liisa Malkki, "Context and Consciousness: Local Conditions for the Production of Historical and National Thought among Hutu Refugees in Tanzania," in *Nationalist Ideologies and the Production of National Cultures*, ed. Richard G. Fox, American Ethnological Society Monograph Series 2 (Washington, DC: American Anthropological Association, 1990), 37, 34.

in its formation, and this residual tension remains ever capable of undoing the synthesis. Ultimately, that which either holds society together or takes it apart is a sentiment, and the chief instrument with which such sentiment may be aroused, manipulated, and rendered dormant is discourse.[305]

The Persian period or Assyrian crisis may have posed identity crises, but they must be understood in a continuum with the earlier phases of identity negotiation. This calls for a diachronic approach to investigating Israel's identity formation. Israel's identity formation was a continuous process that began with the initial claim of the designation to identify a group, rather than an abrupt occurrence after the fall of monarchic institutions. As seen in the Merneptah stele, the existence of Israel predates the appearance of Israelite kingdoms, and the first Israel was likely distinct from later iterations of Israel. The claim for the title of "Israel" was made by multiple groups, making it a contested and coveted identity, never a fixed reality. Therefore, limiting the formation of Israel's identity to specific periods, such as the exilic, post-exilic, or Assyrian era, is unnecessary and unhelpful. No matter how many different claimed "Israels" existed, so long as this designation served disparate entities in their efforts to secure their social place, one must say that the identity discourse on Israel remained a constant social negotiation.

7.5 Conclusion

Biblical critics have often assumed that the inclusion of biblical traditions in the text was simply to transmit information about notable past events, which were passed down by tradents, redactors, or authors. The past-depicting text is considered a resource for reconstructing history. This perspective tends to overlook the selection, plotting, and interpretation of narrativization. From an instrumentalist perspective, we can concentrate on those who utilized these traditions for their own purposes and ask how a particular version or segment of the ancestral tradition served their interests. Mythical pasts may be inaccessible, but the process of people's adopting, and adapting, these myths into their own narratives of the past are historical facts. Therefore, my interest is not in the historical past depicted in the text, but in the historical present that uses it for certain purposes. While many reasons for producing and circulating a text may exist, I focus on one of the most fundamental purposes: as a means of expressing, maintaining, and modifying the collective Self. Most scholars who study Israel's identity formation choose the Per-

---

305 Lincoln, *Discourse and the Construction of Society*, 10.

sian period as the historical present and take the final synchronic form of the text as an expression of identity at that time. Conversely, I aim to delve deeper into the pre-exilic, monarchic era of Judah and Israel, for which critical scholarly assets such as redaction or composition history are helpful. I focus on the era following the collapse of the Northern Kingdom, a time when the Judahites began to perceive themselves as the new Israel. I aim to demonstrate how this reshaped self-perception is mirrored in their renarration of Israel's ancestral past, which in turn provided a mythic foundation for Judah's bold vision of becoming Israel. I am aware of the potential pitfalls of relying on reconstructed pre-exilic traditions, but I will tread upon a basic and rough form of reconstruction upon which most critics would agree.

8 Jacob and Abraham, North and South

In the remainder of Part II, I demonstrate how Judah's longing for Israel has left lasting imprints on Israel's past. While earlier scholars have primarily addressed this issue through the Saul-David material or prophetic literature, I shift attention to ancestral traditions. The ancestral traditions, holding the seminal position in critical scholarship, have been dictated by the lens of prevailing methods of the time. Their dominant historical interests on dating and growth frequently over-shadowed their profound implications for identity formation. Critics' focus was set on addressing when and how these separate traditions were combined and which literary devices stitched them together, implying a natural growth or pro-gressive accretion of traditions. My perspective takes a different route. Regardless of their historical values, as long as these ancestral myths resonate with those who embrace them as their past, they are crucial in shaping their collective self-perception. This calls for an approach that emphasizes the effect of the reimag-ined past. I aim to demonstrate how Judah redefined "Israel" by reframing the northern Jacob narrative with their own Abraham narrative, a strategic move that I call the "Abrahamic expansion." In this context, ancestral traditions tran-scend mere preservation of the past; they serve as instruments to shape the past.

In this chapter, following a review of how Pentateuchal scholarship has inter-preted the Jacob and Abraham narratives, I illustrate how I understand them originally functioning as independent origin myths in the North and South, which will set the foundation for the subsequent discussion on their reorientation.

8.1 Jacob and Abraham in Critical Research

The idea that the traditions of Jacob and Abraham held separate origins, one in the North and the other in the South, has long been recognized,[306] but its fuller implications have been frequently blurred by the source-critical perspective. The problem was that, during the source-critical era, the North-South dichotomy was set to play out between J and E.[307] The divergent tradition-historical origins of

---

306 E.g., Albrecht Alt, "The God of the Fathers," in *Essays on Old Testament History and Religion* (Oxford: Blackwell, 1966), 51–55; Martin Noth, *A History of Pentateuchal Traditions* (Englewood Cliffs, NJ: Prentice Hall, 1972), 79–115; Roland de Vaux, *The Early History of Israel* (Philadelphia: Westminster, 1978), 169–75.

307 While the scholarly interests in the E source have significantly diminished, attempts to revive it have not ceased. See, e.g., Richard Elliott Friedman, *Who Wrote the Bible?* (New York: Summit Books, 1987); Robert B. Coote, *In Defense of Revolution: The Elohist History* (Minneapolis: Fortress, 1991); Axel Graupner, *Der Elohist: Gegenwart und Wirksamkeit des Transzendenten*

https://doi.org/10.1515/9783111376554-008

the Jacob and Abraham traditions played minimal role insofar as both J and E already embraced them. The result was that the disparate orientation of these traditions was taken as a matter limited to the pre-literate stage, which had already been combined by the time of the formation of the first "documents."

Elsewhere, I have argued that the source model is not well suited to the patriarchal narratives by highlighting methodological contradiction inherent in the Elohistic Abraham section in Gen 20–22.[308] The issue in analyzing this section arises from its conventional categorization as a northern E layer based on source-critical grounds. However, the traditions it encompasses, when seen from a tradition-historical standpoint, are fundamentally southern in origin. A simple review of scholarship demonstrates the uncritical nature in which early documentarians merely imposed source-critical criteria external to this text.[309] Similarly, the southern layers within the Jacob narrative are equally fragmentary, lacking any sign of a continuous southern Jacob tradition.

Thus, removing the E-J scheme as the basis for discerning North-South orientation must be the first step to identify northern and southern ancestral traditions. Instead, the identification of northern and southern traditions must be based primarily on the form- and tradition-historical criticism established by Hermann Gunkel and Martin Noth. Against the source model, scholars have often coined this as the "block model," which represents well its nature that is rooted in identifying smallest units and their contexts. However, both Gunkel and Noth fell short of realizing the full implications of the block model, subsuming their observations on pre-literate traditions as the pre-stage for the documentary formation.[310] For instance, Noth, though fully aware of the divergent geographic orientations in the Jacob and Abraham traditions, does not place them in the period of the northern and southern kingdoms. Instead, he locates them within the tribal eras, attributing the origin of the Jacob tradition to the central Palestinian tribes from the East and West sides of the Jordan,[311] while the Abraham and Isaac traditions are linked to the "southern and southernmost tribes."[312] His focus lies on demonstrating how these traditions coalesced under the rubric of one of

---

Gottes in der Geschichte, WMANT 97 (Neukirchen-Vluyn: Neukirchener Verlag, 2002); Tzemah L. Yoreh, *The First Book of God*, BZAW 402 (Berlin: Walter de Gruyter, 2010); Robert Karl Gnuse, *The Elohist: A Seventh-Century Theological Tradition* (Eugene, OR: Cascade Books, 2017).

308 Koog P. Hong, "Abraham, Genesis 20–22, and the Northern Elohist," *Bib* 94 (2013): 321–39, https://doi.org/10.2143/BIB.94.3.3186154.

309 Hong, 325–30.

310 See Noth, *Pentateuchal Traditions*, 38–41.

311 Noth, 79–101.

312 Noth, 102.

his five larger themes of the Pentateuch, "the promise to the patriarchs,"[313] before being incorporated into the foundational documents of the monarchic era.[314] One can clearly see that he presumes a common, negotiated identity of Israel already from the pre-monarchic era of the tribal confederacy.[315] The pervasive impact of the primordialist perspective of Israel as a unified ethnic group is evident.

It was Rolf Rendtorff who broke out of this methodological quandary.[316] He recognized a fundamental gap between the source and block models, and finally parted ways from the overarching source-critical scheme. Strictly following the methodological premise of tradition history, he aimed to trace the whole process of tradition's growth from its smallest units to larger units, and to the present form of the text. Blum developed this theory into a ground-breaking composition model with a rigorous treatment of the formation of the ancestral tradition, which he later expanded to the entire Pentateuch.[317] In his model, the root of Israel's ancestral tradition is construed as the Jacob tradition, which has been taken up and expanded by the pre-exilic ancestral history (*Vätergeschichte* 1) and the exilic ancestral history (*Vätergeschichte* 2), which is further developed by the Deuteronomistic (*Die vor-priesterliche Komposition*=KD) and Priestly compositions (*Die priesterliche Komposition*=KP).

Blum's take on the ancestral history has not enjoyed the recognition it deserved. Continental scholars gradually adopted his model, but for various reasons, their focus was set on later stages of his model, KD and KP.[318] Naturally, more

---

313 Noth, 54–58.
314 This point applies also to Cross's epic tradition. See Frank Moore Cross, *Canaanite Myth and Hebrew Epic: Essays in the History of the Religion of Israel* (Cambridge, MA: Harvard University Press, 1973); idem, *From Epic to Canon: History and Literature in Ancient Israel* (Baltimore: Johns Hopkins University Press, 1998). Cf. Lawrence E. Stager, "Forging an Identity: The Emergence of Ancient Israel," in *The Oxford History of the Biblical World*, ed. Michael David Coogan (New York: Oxford University Press, 1998), 123–75.
315 This was certainly influenced by his now-defunct theory of amphictyony. Noth, *Das System der zwölf Stämme Israels*. For the critique, see A. D. H. Mayes, *Israel in the Period of the Judges* (London: S.C.M. Press, 1974); Norman K. Gottwald, *The Tribes of Yahweh: A Sociology of the Religion of Liberated Israel, 1250–1050 B.C.E.* (Maryknoll, NY: Orbis, 1979), 345–86.
316 Rendtorff, *The Problem of the Process of Transmission in the Pentateuch*.
317 Erhard Blum, *Die Komposition der Vätergeschichte*, WMANT 57 (Neukirchen-Vluyn: Neukirchener Verlag, 1984); idem, *Studien zur Komposition des Pentateuch*, BZAW 189 (Berlin: Walter de Gruyter, 1990).
318 Perhaps, Blum's detailed study left little room for further discussion, or the emergent minimalist-maximalist debate rendered study of traditions of patriarchs, which were increasingly allocated into the mythic space, unappealing, if not precarious. See, esp. Thompson, *The Historicity of the Patriarchal Narratives*.

attention has been given to Exodus-Deuteronomy, and then Numbers,[319] and those remaining studies on the ancestral history tended to be pursued in relation to or under the context of broader literary and thematic context. On the other hand, Blum's model made much less impact to the English-speaking scholarship. When Blum's call for a fundamental reorientation left them confused, the discussion was largely driven by John Van Seters's call for a late date of the Yahwist.[320] There were attempts to introduce Blum's new model, most notably by David Carr,[321] but instead of genuine engagement with it, American scholarship was beginning to move towards a very different direction to adopt literary or ideological studies.[322]

While American scholars remained hesitant, continental scholarship shifted more swiftly towards a new consensus, making a critical reassessment of Blum's model and promoting the P source as the architect behind the earliest unified history of Israel.[323] This initially engendered a serious transatlantic debate on J,[324] but its true nature lies in reassigning many of the traditional pre-P texts to post-P

---

319 E.g., Matthias Köckert, *Vätergott und Väterverheissungen: Eine Auseinandersetzung mit Albrecht Alt und seinen Erben*, FRLANT 142 (Göttingen: Vandenhoeck & Ruprecht, 1988); Thomas Römer, *Israels Väter: Untersuchungen zur Väterthematik im Deutoronomium und in der deuteronomistischen Tradition*, OBO 99 (Freiburg, Schweiz: Universitätsverlag, 1990); Schmid, *Erzväter und Exodus*; Jaeyoung Jeon, *From the Reed Sea to Kadesh: A Redactional and Socio-Historical Study of the Pentateuchal Wilderness Narrative*, FAT 159 (Tübingen: Mohr Siebeck, 2022).

320 John Van Seters, *Abraham in History and Tradition* (New Haven: Yale University Press, 1975); idem, *In Search of History: Historiography in the Ancient World and the Origins of Biblical History* (New Haven: Yale University Press, 1983); idem, *Prologue to History: The Yahwist as Historian in Genesis* (Louisville, KY: Westminster John Knox, 1992). Also, Christoph Levin, *Der Jahwist*, FRLANT 157 (Göttingen: Vandenhoeck & Ruprecht, 1993).

321 David M. Carr, *Reading the Fractures of Genesis: Historical and Literary Approaches* (Louisville, KY: Westminster John Knox, 1996).

322 The late arrival of the so-called "Neo-Documentarians" further alienated American scholars from Pentateuchal criticism, not many finding it meaningful to return to a rigid literary criticism, often in a highly technical form of pre-Wellhausenian documentary theories. Joel S. Baden, *J, E, and the Redaction of the Pentateuch*, FAT 68 (Tübingen: Mohr Siebeck, 2009); idem, *The Composition of the Pentateuch: Renewing the Documentary Hypothesis* (New Haven: Yale University Press, 2012); Baruch J. Schwartz, "Does Recent Scholarship's Critique of the Documentary Hypothesis Constitute Grounds for Its Rejection?," in *The Pentateuch: International Perspectives on Current Research*, ed. Thomas B. Dozeman, Konrad Schmid, and Baruch J. Schwartz, FAT 78 (Tübingen: Mohr Siebeck, 2011), 3–16.

323 See Jan Christian Gertz, Konrad Schmid, and Markus Witte, eds., *Abschied vom Jahwisten: Die Komposition des Hexateuch in der jüngsten Diskussion*, BZAW 315 (Berlin: Walter de Gruyter, 2002).

324 Thomas B. Dozeman and Konrad Schmid, eds., *A Farewell to the Yahwist?: The Composition of the Pentateuch in Recent European Interpretation* (Atlanta: Society of Biblical Literature, 2006).

additions.[325] Naturally, an increasingly more contemporary studies on biblical ancestral traditions are pursued against the post-exilic background,[326] and division within the ancestral tradition before they were combined into a unit, especially with regards to the North-South relationship in the monarchic era, has been practically neglected.[327]

I see the diminishing interest in pre-Priestly ancestral traditions, and the tendency to date them post-exilic, regrettable, especially considering the immense potential in the block model in the face of today's growing instrumentalism. As is evident, instrumentalism was far from Blum's interests, who rather focused on demonstrating specific paths through which individual traditions grew into the larger whole in steps. Yet when we acknowledge that "Israel" is a social construct, and merging narratives and genealogies of disparate entities that came to make up Israel served as basic tools in the making of "one Israel," the rich assets left by tradition and redaction criticism can be turned into useful data for tracing the construction of Israel. Then, critical observations on the importance of the growth of biblical tradition blocks can be reassessed in terms of Israel's identity formation. This shift in perspective invites a reinvigoration of literary-critical observations, with a renewed appreciation for these foundational traditions as identity narratives of Israel and Judah. My objective is to unearth the significance of the Jacob and Abraham traditions in shaping Israel's and Judah's identity and to discern the implications of melding these traditions into a continuous patriarchal narrative for identity formation. In this endeavor, the North-South dynamic inherent in the Jacob and Abraham traditions becomes prominent, given that the relations between Israel and Judah were pivotal in the initial phase of Israel's sociopolitical life.

---

325 See, e.g., Federico Giuntoli and Konrad Schmid, eds., *The Post-Priestly Pentateuch: New Perspectives on Its Redactional Development and Theological Profiles*, FAT 101 (Tübingen: Mohr Siebeck, 2015); Jan C. Gertz et al., eds., *The Formation of the Pentateuch: Bridging the Academic Cultures of Europe, Israel, and North America* (Tübingen: Mohr Siebeck, 2016).

326 See among others, Matthias Köckert, *Von Jakob zu Abraham: Studien zum Buch Genesis*, FAT 147 (Tübingen: Mohr Siebeck, 2021); Na'aman, "The Jacob Story and the Formation of Biblical Israel"; Thomas Römer, "The Joseph Story in the Book of Genesis: Pre-P or Post-P?," in *The Post-Priestly Pentateuch: New Perspectives on Its Redactional Development and Theological Profiles*, ed. Federico Giuntoli and Konrad Schmid, FAT 101 (Tübingen: Mohr Siebeck, 2015), 185–201; Albert de Pury, "Abraham: The Priestly Writer's 'Ecumenical' Ancestor," in *Rethinking the Foundations: Historiography in the Ancient World and in the Bible: Essays in Honour of John Van Seters*, ed. Steven L. McKenzie and Thomas Römer, BZAW 294 (Berlin: Walter de Gruyter, 2000), 163–81.

327 Schmid, for instance, addresses the ancestral tradition in its entirety (Gen 12–50) and links it to the *'am ha'aretz* in Persian-period Yehud. See n. 390 in Section 9.3.

8.2 Abrahamic Expansion

Foundational to the block model, and a point we need to elaborate on, is the observation that the Jacob and Abraham traditions had distinct origins, and their present combination owes to Judah's rewriting of Israel's ancestral past (*Vg*).

Blum's Model	Literary Horizon	Political Orientation
Jakoberzählung	Jacob	Northern
Vätergeschichte	Abraham-Isaac-Jacob	Southern

Scholars have long observed that the Jacob tradition is rooted in northern regions, such as Bethel, Shechem, and Penuel,[328] whereas the Abraham tradition is rooted in southern locales, such as Hebron.[329] Another key observation is Jacob's prominence in early biblical texts, like those from classical prophets, where he tends to appear alone than in tandem with Abraham.[330] Conversely, Abraham begins to appear in later texts, more frequently alongside Jacob than in isolation.[331] Significantly, this pattern mirrors the progression of Israel's monarchic history, where the Northern Kingdom initially held prominence and Judah ascended to regional significance only after Samaria's fall.

The implications are clear from this observation. Initially, the Jacob tradition stood as an independent ancestral narrative for Northern Israel.[332] The Abraham tradition was subsequently introduced.

---

328 See, e.g., Blum, *Die Komposition der Vätergeschichte*, 171–75; Carr, *Reading the Fractures*, 204–15, 256–71, 298–300; Finkelstein and Römer, "Comments on the Historical Background of the Jacob Narrative," 321–30.
329 See, e.g., Clements, *Abraham and David*, 35–46; Finkelstein and Römer, "Comments on the Historical Background of the Abraham Narrative."
330 Jacob appears broadly outside the Pentateuch (134 times), and among them, only twice (2Kgs 13:23; Jer 33:26) does he appear as a part of the ancestral triad.
331 Outside the Pentateuch, Abraham appears much less than Jacob (25 times). Among them, only four times (Isa 51:2; 63:16; Ezek 33:24; Neh 9:7–8) is Abraham remembered independently of Jacob. See Römer, "Abraham Traditions in the Hebrew Bible Outside the Book of Genesis." Cf. Clements, *Abraham and David*, 61–63.
332 Contrary to the presently held views of the early and northern origins of the Jacob tradition, Nadav Na'aman ("The Jacob Story and the Formation of Biblical Israel," 109) has recently argued it to be a sixth century "Judahite exilic composition." There are some valid points in his observation of the late origin of the Jacob tradition, but most of them occur in passages widely accepted as late. Na'aman makes several observations. (1) The text's portrayal of Esau and Laban is more congruent with the post-exilic era. Regarding Esau, Na'aman accentuates the tension between Esau and Jacob, positing that this conflicting image mirrors the dynamics of a later context (pp. 103–4). However, Na'aman appears to exaggerate Esau's threat. While Esau might be seen as a rival, he remains depicted as a brother, and aside from Jacob's internal struggle, there is an

These are all well-established observations in literary criticism. However, the usual response from literary critics was to focus on matters of composition and dating. Hence, Reinhard Kratz when explaining the significance of Abraham's principal position bestowed in his J^G (the Yahwistic history), he focuses on eluci-dating the editorial rationale: "The way in which Abraham is put first is depend-ent all along the line on the redactional hinge in 12.1–3, which links the primal history and the patriarchal history, and in this converges with the Yahwistic revi-sion in Gen. 26–35."[333] The emphasis was on tracing the evolution of the biblical tradition alongside the growth of Yhwh's people, with the fundamental unity

---

absence of any overt hostility between them. Cf. Wöhrle considers the present text's depiction of Esau as positive, and hence rejects Na'aman's claim for the post-exilic dating. Jakob Wöhrle, "Koexistenz durch Unterwerfung: Zur Entstehung und politischen Intention der vorpriesterlichen Jakoberzählung," in *The Politics of the Ancestors: Exegetical and Historical Perspectives on Gene-sis 12–36*, ed. Mark G. Brett and Jakob Wöhrle, FAT 124 (Tübingen: Mohr Siebeck, 2018), 323. Similarly, concerning Laban, Na'aman dismisses prevailing scholarly opinions that view Laban as symbolic of Aram-Damascus during the monarchic period. Instead, he boldly proposes that the "Arameans of Upper Mesopotamia" personified by Laban are actually those Israelites deport-ed by the Assyrians, hence suggesting a post-exilic origin (pp. 104–6). Yet, this assertion seems purely speculative and lacks any basis. (2) He references Hurowitz's and Hamori's observations regarding the Mesopotamian influence in the Bethel and Jabbok episodes (pp. 100–103). See Victor Avigdor Hurowitz, "Babylon in Bethel-New Light on Jacob's Dream," in *Orientalism, Assyri-ology and the Bible*, ed. Steven W. Holloway, Hebrew Bible Monographs 10 (Sheffield: Phoenix Press, 2006), 436–48; Esther J. Hamori, "Echoes of Gilgamesh in the Jacob Story," *JBL* 130 (2011): 625–42, https://doi.org/10.2307/23488271. Nonetheless, the cultural influence of Mesopotamia on Syria-Palestine is not exclusive to the post-exilic period, as Na'aman himself admits, and remains, at best, a topic of debate. (3) Na'aman points out other southern traits. One is Rachel's tomb's location which is placed within Judah's territory (pp. 107–8). However, Gen 35 has widely been considered as a late Judahite editorial addition. Na'aman also points to the tribal order reflected in the birth report of Jacob's sons (Gen 29:31–30:24), which arguably reflects a Judah-oriented perspective (pp. 108–9). Yet, he seems to overlook that the Jacob narrative's default plot structure, which highlights Joseph's supremacy despite his low standing in genealogical order (see Section 9.2). Regarding the oft-discussed Hosea's reference to Jacob, Na'aman suggests that Hosea served as one of the sources that the author of the Jacob narrative drew from, but without paying enough attention to the opposite way of seeing the matter (pp. 110–12).

Overall, Na'aman appears to challenge the fundamental assumptions of literary criticism, pointing to its circularity (pp. 98–100). While no critique can entirely dismiss the presence of circular reasoning in criticism, in this particular instance, we seem to have enough evidence that suggests that tales of the heroic life journey of this eponymous ancestor were widely cir-culated, whether written down or not, during the prime of North Israel, say in the time of Jeroboam II, and played a role as part of Israel's origin myth. I believe that most of Na'aman's challenges can be ascribed to the ongoing evolution of the earlier Jacob tradition, and I find no reason to dismiss the existence of the Jacob story prior to its subsequent adaptations.

333 Kratz, *The Composition of the Narrative Books*, 273.

between the North and South presumed.[334] With this prevailing interest in charting the evolution, the question of dating naturally became paramount, such as whether the Abraham layer was incorporated during the pre-exilic or exilic period. Given the paucity of the direct literary ground for positing the pre-exilic layer, scholars were hesitant to speak of the pre-exilic Abraham tradition,[335] which was further corroborated by the fact that Abraham's role was more conspicuous in the exilic and post-exilic eras. But for my purpose, that poses no absolute barrier insofar as identity negotiation takes place in the discursive level. Stories do not need to be documented to take effect in identity discourse. It is sufficient to have reasonable grounds to posit that stories about him were known and circulated earlier. In that, I have little doubt that some of the Abraham traditions now included in the text have deeper tradition-historical origins that go back to the pre-exilic era.[336]

Instead of dating and formation, what matters, from the functionalist perspective, is the recognition that the present formation of Israel's ancestry as the history of Abraham, Isaac, and Jacob is a Judahite invention.[337] The seminal observation in this regard is that, earlier, northern Israelites did not necessarily reckoned Abraham as their ancestor.[338] They may have known him, as a southern ancestral figure but not as Israel's forefather.[339] Again, source critics may point to the Abra-

---

334 Hence, Kratz (p. 273) states, "The two monarchies appear in a non-stately garb, united under the roof of the one national God Yhwh, and made brothers in the genealogical system of the tradition of tribes and families. 'Israel' is not yet the 'all Israel' of the later Deuteronomistic and Chronistic tradition, but the son of Abraham and Isaac and the father of Judah."

335 Blum's recent simplification of his model is a good illustration of this trend. Blum originally surmised two stages, pre-exilic *Vg1* and exilic *Vg2*, but simplified his model to a single exilic *Vg* in his retake of the Bethel episode. Erhard Blum, "Noch Einmal: Jakobs Traum in Bethel–Genesis 28,10–22," in *Rethinking the Foundations: Historiography in the Ancient World and in the Bible: Essays in Honour of John Van Seters*, ed. Steven L. McKenzie and Thomas Römer, BZAW 294 (Berlin: Walter de Gruyter, 2000), 33–54.

336 Granted, one can debate the dating of the first written version of the *Vg*, but either way, it is difficult to deny that the Abraham tradition includes pre-exilic traditions rooted in southern locales. Especially, the traditions included in the Abraham-Lot cycle appear to carry old traditions that have little to do with exilic interests. See Finkelstein and Römer, "Comments on the Historical Background of the Abraham Narrative," 9–17.

337 Not incidentally, the establishment of the ancestral triad, Abraham-Isaac-Jacob, is also considered late. E.g., Köckert, *Vätergott und Väterverheissungen*; Raymond Jacques Tournay, "Genèse de la triade « Abraham-Isaac-Jacob »," *RB* 103 (1996): 321–36; Römer, "Abraham Traditions in the Hebrew Bible Outside the Book of Genesis," 177–78. As for the argument of the tribalized Israel as Judah's invention, see Tobolowsky, *The Sons of Jacob and the Sons of Herakles*.

338 See Hong, "Abraham, Genesis 20–22, and the Northern Elohist." Cf. e.g., Kratz, *The Composition of the Narrative Books*, 269.

339 Conversely, not the same can be said of the Judahite perception of Jacob. As I have argued in Part I, I understand Judahites carrying deep-seated longing for Israel, and I see them ardently pursuing acceptance into the family of Jacob/Israel. See Section 2.3 above.

ham segment in the E source, but as I discussed above, E is northern only within the strictly source-critical rationale. Seen from the basic tradition-historical framework, the Abraham traditions as a whole must belong to the South.[340] If the ancestral triad is not original but the product of Judah's redefinition of Israel's ancestral past, that begs the question of its *effect*, how this new root transforms the subsequent ancestral history.

The relationship between Jacob and Abraham must be understood in terms of mythic plurality. When multiple figures are featured, either heroes or gods, mythologists ask for social complexity behind the stories, assuming that each figure would represent specific group of people and their order indicating the present power dynamic between them. The fact that Abraham is almost dispensable in Israel's ancestral myth further corroborates this point. There is no question Abraham later arose to prominence in Jewish and Christian circles, but it is Jacob who is firmly established as the eponymous ancestor of Israel (Gen 32:25–33/ 35:20) and the father of the twelve tribes (Gen 29:31–30:24/ 35:22b–26). As I shall demonstrate in Chapter 9, the pre-P Jacob narrative could function as a self-sufficient ancestral myth for the Northern Kingdom.

Many biblical readers and critics remain surprisingly reluctant to relinquish the idea that Abraham was a foundational figure for "all Israel," even in the face of compelling critical observations. Yet, seen from an instrumentalist perspective, giving up this idea becomes a portal to unveil the profound political implications behind this reshaping of the past.

8.3 Abraham and David as Judah's Twin Prototypes

The significance of understanding Abraham as the southern prototype set against Jacob in the North is further bolstered by considering their parallel dynamics with David and Jeroboam I in the monarchic history.[341] As discussed above (Section 2.3), the DtrH and the Pentateuch work together towards a shared objective, to promote Judah's leading role in Israel. In both, one finds a dynamic that the southern addition completely reconfigures the underlying northern tradition. In DtrH, David and Jeroboam, both as founding monarchs (royal prototypes), represent the southern and northern kingdoms. Both figures, in their respective realms, were hailed as heroes. However, their legacies starkly diverge. David, with all his flaws,

---

340 Hong, "Abraham, Genesis 20–22, and the Northern Elohist."
341 For basic observations on the close link between Abraham and David, refer to Clements, *Abraham and David*, 47–60; Bernard Gosse, "Abraham and David," *JSOT* 34 (2010): 25–31, https:// doi.org/10.1177/0309089209346346.

is lionized as the ideal king, while Jeroboam stands as the archetypal sinner. If we postulate that the narratives of David and Solomon were later interpositions into a text that originally featured Jeroboam as a leader like Moses,[342] then the Davidic narrative does not merely blend in. It fundamentally overshadows and reshapes the existing narrative. David's elevation as the hero recast Jeroboam into his antithesis.

This polarization is echoed in the dynamic between Abraham and Jacob.[343] Both function as Israel's founding ancestors (ancestral prototypes) – one southern and the other northern. Abraham is presented as the first ancestor marking the inaugural claim to the land. If we accept that Jacob originally was hailed as a singular ancestor among Israelites, without Abraham, the introduction of Abraham into the lineage is consequential. With Abraham's rise to prominence, Jacob's distinguished status subtly fades. Simply, Abraham and David function as twin prototypes, ancestral and royal, in Judah's identity discourse.[344] Together, they shape Judah's narrative identity securing Judah's principal position. This focus on asserting primacy in origin traditions seems to be a central tactic in Judah's identity politics against Israel.

---

342 While reconstructing the original historical or narrative context in which Jeroboam was portrayed as a Moses-like liberator from a Pharaoh-like tyrant proves challenging, the subsequent framing within the David-Solomon narrative is undeniable. Positioned opposite David, Jeroboam becomes the emblematic bad king of Israel. See Alison L. Joseph, *Portrait of the Kings: The Davidic Prototype in Deuteronomistic Poetics* (Minneapolis: Fortress, 2015).

343 Surely, it is no coincidence that Abraham and David are linked to Hebron and Jerusalem, whereas Jacob and Jeroboam are connected to Bethel, Penuel, and Shechem. These locales are imbued with religious and political significance, which carry serious identity-defining forces for Judah and Israel. Furthermore, Jerusalem and Bethel are polar opposites in religious significance. Jerusalem is the site of Yhwh's temple built by David and Bethel is painted as the home of Jeroboam's glaring apostasy. See my studies "The Golden Calf of Bethel and Judah's Mimetic Desire of Israel"; "Bethel, Dark Woods, and Taboo: 1 Kings 13 as a Cautionary Tale," *BibInt* 31 (2023): 292–310, https://doi.org/10.1163/15685152-20221718; "Bethel between Inclusion and Exclusion in Judah's Identity Negotiation," *RB* 131 (2024): 321–39.

344 My claim is not that the Abraham tradition was from the beginning created exclusively as clan Judah's ancestral myth. It is widely observed that the Abraham tradition appears to be a compilation of diverse traditions associated with this figure centered around Hebron. For discussion of early southern traditions included in the Abraham tradition, see Finkelstein and Römer, "Comments on the Historical Background of the Abraham Narrative," 9–17. Clearly, Abraham does not align directly with the clan Judah. My claim rather is that the Abraham tradition was *adopted* by the Judahites and they employed it as a means of expressing their southern identity set against northern identity expressed in the Jacob tradition. I posit that narratives exhibit tremendous adaptability. While stories are tools to articulate identity, there is not a fixed or permanent link between a tale and a group. As political landscapes shift, different groups can stake claim on a single narrative (see Section 7.2).

8.4 Conclusion

This sets the stage for our ensuing exploration of the making of the Abrahamic Israel. When we approach the tales of Jacob and Abraham as distinct ancestral traditions rooted in the northern and southern regions respectively, their role as identity narratives for these rival groups becomes evident. Their eventual fusion into a coherent narrative, then, is laden with profound implications about the shifts in collective identity, particularly from Judah's perspective. I contend that the Judahites, in painting a revised tableau of the ancestral past of the Abrahamic Israel, were not merely weaving a tale into another, but were strategically asserting their own significance and pivotal role in the genesis of Israel. The following sections will delve into the original Jacob narrative, discerning its intended function within the Northern Kingdom, and then illustrate how the Judahites astutely reshaped this narrative to serve their own objectives.

9 Jacob: From an Indigenous Hero to Israel's Father

The rest of the book focuses on reevaluating the significance of the Abrahamic expansion of the underlying Jacob tradition. In order to accomplish this, I first have to identify the pre-P Jacob narrative, which allegedly has functioned as a self-sufficient ancestral myth for the Northern Kingdom (=*Jakoberzählung*), prior to the Abrahamic expansion taking place within the Judean ancestral history (=*Väter-geschichte*). I move one step further and claim that this tradition originally be-longed to the indigenous population that would later constitute part of "Israel." Scholars have long observed vestiges of non-Yahwistic culture in the ancestral tradi-tion,[345] but they largely dismissed them as a result of a semi-nomadic group's assimilation into sedentary culture.[346] With the growing recognition from material findings that there is no clear division between Israel and its neighbors, and the biblical depiction of an external group's conquest of the indigenous as a myth, I believe a more radical approach is called for.[347]

My understanding of the social construction of a collective identity paves the way for this shift in perspective. As illustrated in Chapter 7, I operate on the fundamental assumption that "Israel" is a social construct. The true makeup of the Israelites encompasses various popular segments, a complexity their claimed unity continually masks.[348] I posit that each segment held their distinct stories. As these segments came together as a collective, their tales coalesced into a cohesive narrative. This unified narrative then laid the discursive foundation for their shared identity. From this viewpoint, I see no better candidate than the Jacob

---

345 For a concise analysis of interpreting the figure Jacob in its distinct cultural and religious backdrop, see Hans-Jürgen Zobel, "יַעֲקֹב/יַעֲקֹב ya'aqōḇ/ya'aqôḇ," in *Theological Dictionary of the Old Testament*, ed. Johannes Botterweck and Helmer Ringgren, trans. David E. Green, vol. 6 (Grand Rapids, MI: Eerdmans, 1990), 193–201.

346 See among others, Alt, "The God of the Fathers." Against this view, Mendenhall and Gottwald have presented a significant challenge, portraying the Israelites primarily as peasants oppressed by Canaanite city-states, leading to their revolt and subsequent retreat to the societal fringes. George E. Mendenhall, "The Hebrew Conquest of Palestine," *BA* 25 (1962): 66–87, https://doi.org/ 10.2307/3210957; Gottwald, *The Tribes of Yahweh*. Cf. Gösta W. Ahlström, *Who Were the Israelites?* (Winona Lake, IN: Eisenbrauns, 1986). However, the role of the Jacob tradition as the narrative of this indigenous segment of Israel has not been a focal point in their theoretical framework.

347 See discussion in Finkelstein and Mazar, *The Quest for the Historical Israel*, 59–98; Grabbe, *Ancient Israel*, 120–30. See also Mark G. Brett, "Israel's Indigenous Origins: Cultural Hybridity and the Formation of Israelite Ethnicity," *BibInt* 11 (2003): 400–412, https://doi.org/10.1163/15685150 3322566813.

348 Cf. Gottwald, *The Tribes of Yahweh*, 239–41.

https://doi.org/10.1515/9783111376554-009

story to represent the type of narrative that would have belonged to the indigenous popular segment of Israel. Alongside the Exodus narrative, which illustrates Israel's external origins, the two narratives capture the dynamic tension between Israel's dual personas.[349] The *Bene Ya'aqob*,[350] as reflected in the Jacob story, is a rather playful, innocent, and ordinary people who strived to live harmoniously with their neighbors.

I illustrate how the Jacob story, a folk tradition of the indigenous *Bene Ya'aqob*, was integrated into Israel's dual origin myth (Jacob-Moses), before subsequently incorporated into Judah's ancestral narrative (Abraham-Jacob). The fact that the current text is a product of successive appropriations of preexisting narratives highlights the versatility and adaptability of identity narratives, which enables the story's continued resonance and significance for diverse readership.[351]

9.1 Jacob Story in the Present Text

The present form of the Jacob story is apparently designed to function within the broader ancestral history as a segment of the *toledot* structure that spans the entire Genesis (and possibly until Num 3:1).[352] A close examination reveals that the present text is an adapted version of what was originally designed to function as a self-contained tale of a trickster hero Jacob. There are various literary devices, including the *toledot* formula, that facilitated this adjustment.

---

349 I deliberately use the term "indigenous" instead of "Canaanite" as I believe that the ideologically constructed "Canaan" as depicted in the text never truly existed. Nonetheless, I will employ the term "Canaanite" when discussing the ideological baggage associated with it, especially when addressing how later authors, such as P, leveraged this concept for ideological purposes.

350 I employ the term *Bene Ya'aqob* in its basic sense, denoting the supposed tradent group of the Jacob story. Traditional scholars have often concentrated on uncovering the historical identity of this group, but my objective diverges from that path. I regard them primarily as a logical necessity, a representative group essential for the production and transmission of the story as their origin story. As this group integrated into Israel, I assume, the Jacob narrative subsequently became woven into the collective past of Israel. Cf. Lemaire's identification of *Bene Ya'aqob* with the non-Yahwist group that Joshua tried to convert in Shechem (Josh 24). André Lemaire, "Les Benê Jacob: Essai d'interprétation historique d'une tradition patriarcale," *RB* 85 (1978): 333–37; idem, "La haute Mésopotamie et l'origine des Benê Jacob," *VT* 34 (1984): 96, https://doi.org/10.1163/156853384X00115. In addition, Gottwald (*The Tribes of Yahweh*, 34–41) refers to the "Jacob group" and "Moses group" to denote distinct segments of the proto-Israelites who later became Israelites.

351 For a foundational exploration of how biblical texts continue to renew its relevance in terms of the interplay between *traditum* and *tradition*, see Michael A. Fishbane, *Biblical Interpretation in Ancient Israel* (Oxford: Clarendon, 1985), 6–19.

352 See Matthew A. Thomas, *These Are the Generations: Identity, Covenant, and the "Toledot" Formula*, LHBOTS 551 (London: T&T Clark, 2011).

THE TOLEDOT OF ISAAC

TITLE: Opening of Toledot of Isaac	25:19
1. EXPOSITION	25:20–34
A) Twin brothers born	25:20–26
Note on Parental preference	25:27–28
B) Jacob purchases birthright from Esau	25:29–34
Isaac and Abimelech after famine	26:1–33
Note on Esau's wife	26:34–35
2. INCITING MOMENT: Jacob steals blessing	27:1–46
3. COMPLICATION: Jacob sent to Laban	28:1–5
Note on Esau's new wife	28:6–9
4. DEVELOPMENT: Jacob in Haran	28:10–32:3
A. Bethel incident	28:10–22
B. Friendly preliminary meeting	29:1–14
C. Meeting with Laban and a contract	29:15–20
D. Deception by Laban	29:21–30
X. Jacob's children	29:31–30:24
D'. Deception by Jacob	30:25–31:16
C'. Meeting with Laban and a dispute	31:17–42
B'. Friendly departure and covenant	31:43–32:1
A'. Mahanaim incident	32:2–3
5. CRISIS: Preparing to meet Esau	32:4–24
6. CLIMAX: Wrestling with a man	32:25–33
7. DENOUEMENT: Jacob reconciles with Esau	33:1–17
FINAL SUSPENSE: Dinah incident; Jacob expelled	33:18–34:31
CONCLUSION: Jacob journeys back home	35:1–27
TERMINUS: Ending of Toledot Isaac's death	35:28–29

The overall narrative reads reasonably well as a life journey of Jacob, the son of Isaac and Abraham. Yet one can identify secondary layers imposed upon the underlying Jacob tradition.[353] First, the Priestly layer is noticeable.[354] The *toledot* notes at the beginning and end (25:19; 35:28–29) position this narrative within the larger *toledot* structure, and a number of notes on genealogy and itinerary (25:20, 26b;

---

353 The structure presented above is a slightly modified version taken from my unpublished doctoral dissertation. K. P. Hong, "Towards the Hermeneutics of Responsibility: A Linguistic, Literary, and Historical Reading of Genesis 28:10–22" (Ph.D. diss., Claremont Graduate University, 2011), 151.

354 See now Finkelstein and Römer, "Comments on the Historical Background of the Jacob Narrative," 334–35.

33:18a; 35:22b–27) provide pertinent information to the Priestly text. Other than that, narrative materials are sparse, except for a series of notes that reframe Jacob's flight as a betrothal journey (26:34–35; 27:46; 28:1–9) and another Bethel account (35:6–15) that features an alternative explanation for the reception of the name "Israel." It is apparent that these added layers contribute to reframing the original Jacob tradition within the larger Priestly corpus; however, none of them is essential to its core narrative.

Second, the expansion at the end of the Jacob narrative is outstanding. The secondary nature of Gen 34–35 is widely acknowledged, demonstrated in the conspicuous doubling of the arrival report (Gen 33:17–18). It appears evident that Jacob's journey was intended to conclude in Gen 33:17 at Succoth.[355] The second arrival report at Shechem in 33:18 functions as an introduction to Gen 34 that takes place in Shechem and subsequent events in Gen 35, which concludes with the *toledot* ending in 35:27–29, thereby serving the Priestly interest to complete the *toledot* cycle.[356] In the structure above, the influence of this added material is unmistakable, as it obscures the original ending, transmuting what must have originally been a climactic resolution of the Jacob-Esau rivalry into a convoluted denouement, with a laborious extension of the concluding sequence. It is reasonable to surmise that the redactors responsible for these inclusions were not chiefly preoccupied with enhancing the narrative presentation; their concerns lied somewhere else.

Third, sporadic non-P layers tie the Jacob tradition with the preceding Abraham tradition. Most notable is the Isaac tradition in Gen 26 whose secondary nature is widely recognized. Abraham's presence in the non-P Jacob tradition is limited to a few passages about Jacob's ancestral deity (Gen 28:13; 31:42, 53; 32:9). Undoubtedly, each of these notes functions as a linking device that connects the

---

355 See Claus Westermann, *Genesis 12–36* (Minneapolis: Augsburg, 1985), 527; Kratz, *The Composition of the Narrative Books*, 268.

356 Here, I disagree with Finkelstein and Römer ("Comments on the Historical Background of the Jacob Narrative," 336), who interpret Gen 34 as part of the post-P, possibly anti-Samaritan, addition. In my view, the role of Gen 34 within the Priestly text must be taken into account. As the main thrust of the narrative plot (driven by the Jacob-Esau conflict) has been finally resolved at the end of Gen 33, the original narrative must come to an end there, as Jacob settles at Succoth (Gen 33:17). Instead, the Dinah incident in Gen 34 provides a reason for further journey-making. A redactor introduced the Dinah incident here, following an abrupt relocation of Jacob from Succoth to Shechem (Gen 33:18–19). After the incident, Jacob is forced out of Shechem, which leads to the divine order, "return to Bethel" (Gen 35:1). At Bethel, another encounter with El Shaddai takes place, which is instrumental in shaping the way the Priestly author wishes to conclude the Isaac *toledot* (Gen 25:19–35:29) upon his eventual return to his father's home, with the death report of Isaac (Gen 35:27–29). It seems evident to me how the forceful addition of Gen 34 serves the Priestly author's overall plan.

Jacob story to the larger Abrahamic narrative; however, they are dispensable in the core structure of the Jacob story. As an example, in the current form of the Bethel theophany (Gen 28:10–22), Yhwh transmits the Abrahamic promise of land and progeny to Jacob (Gen 28:13), which seems out of place in the narrative.[357] Given that Jacob was a refugee fleeing from his vengeful brother, it seems unlikely that Yhwh found this as the fitting moment to transmit this great ancestral promise. What Jacob needed most at that moment was a promise of protection, stated in 28:15, suggesting that the Abrahamic promise was a later insert.[358] Naturally, Jacob makes no mention of the promise of land and progeny, but only the guidance when he wakes up and responds to the dream.

Notably, most of these additions relate to the southern Judean orientation, either linked to the Abraham and Isaac traditions or the Priestly ideology. What this indicates is clear. These are the primary instruments employed by the Judean redactors who incorporated the Jacob story into the expanded narrative framework of Judah's ancestral history of Abraham-Isaac-Jacob, and then, subsequently into the larger Priestly corpus.

---

357 Unlike the Abraham story, promise of land and progeny plays no inherent role in the Jacob story. The promise of progeny is rooted in Abraham's infertility and the land in Abraham's foreign origin. Neither applies to Jacob. As I shall further argue below (Section 9.4), Jacob is not depicted as foreign. Instead, his life is driven by the pursuit of blessing.

358 Furthermore, the Bethel theophany (Gen 28:10–22) is currently presented as Jacob's first encounter with his ancestral deity of Abraham and Isaac, but its earlier form most likely was meant to function as a grand revelation of the God of Israel to the ancestor of Israel, comparable to Yhwh's appearance to Moses at Horeb. Moses's encounter with Yhwh is also linked to "the God of the fathers," but most scholars agree that the linking is secondary. Within the independent Exodus tradition, Moses's encounter was likely to be presented as the first revelation of Yhwh, who would become the God of the people that Moses later liberated from Egypt. Likewise, given the etiological nature of the episode, it is improbable that the deity appearing at Beth-El was Yhwh, let alone the God of Abraham. "Yhwh will be my God" (Gen 28:21) may be an odd way to vow to one's ancestral deity; it would fit better if the deity were unknown to him, like it was to Moses. Modern scholars might attribute this to Jacob's decision to *personally* embrace his family deity, but I suggest that such an individualistic perspective is out of place in Jacob's cultural context. Just as Moses has a pivotal revelation at the onset of his journey, Jacob also receives a divine revelation that determines the course of his life and the future of his descendants.

9.2 Pre-P Jacob Story as Northern Israel's Identity Narrative

Removing all these devices through a literary-critical means discloses the default plot structure of the self-contained pre-P Jacob story which allegedly functioned as an ancestral myth for the Israelites in the Northern Kingdom.[359]

DEFAULT PLOT STRUCTURE OF JACOB STORY

1. EXPOSITION
   A) Twin brothers born
   B) Jacob purchases birthright from Esau
2. INCITING MOMENT: Jacob steals blessing
3. COMPLICATION: Jacob exiled
4. DEVELOPMENT: Jacob in Haran [Story within a Story]
   A. Departure and divine encounter at Bethel
      B. Jacob settles in Laban's house
         C. Deception by Laban and Jacob's two wives
            D. Wives' competition and Jacob's children
         C'. Deception by Jacob and Jacob's wealth
      B'. Jacob departs from Laban's house
   A'. Jacob's second divine encounter at Mahanaim
5. CRISIS: Jacob has to face Esau
6. CLIMAX: Jacob's nocturnal wrestle with a divine being
7. CONCLUSION: Jacob reconciles with Esau

Traditional critics were largely focused on identifying the historical entities behind each character, and whether they admitted it or not, their readings often reduced this exhilarating tale to a historical source. This frequently led to the oversimplification of the narrative into a simplistic binary framework where Jacob represented the sedentary group and Esau the nomadic one.[360] However, I propose we shift our attention to the innate nature of this story, which should be the starting point for interpreting any literary work anyway, as Gunkel has originally envisioned it.[361] Before applying a historical perspective, we should appreci-

---

359 This is not to claim that we can definitively reconstruct *the* Jacob tradition in its original pre-P form, as I think the Jacob story existed only in multiple, fluid forms. I simply posit that the presented structure offers a glimpse into *a* version of the Jacob legend familiar to the general populace of the Northern Kingdom, as reflected in texts like Hos 12.

360 See, e.g. Noth, *Pentateuchal Traditions*, 96–99.

361 It is unfortunate that Gunkel's profound appreciation for the literary nature of biblical narratives has been overshadowed by the historical focus of both his own and subsequent scholarship. Whenever I revisit his monumental Genesis commentary, I am reminded of his exception-

ate it as what it is, as a splendid folktale. Its tightly woven structure and entertaining features suggest that it could have functioned as a captivating story, written down or not.

Right from the beginning, the readers are made aware that this is a story of fraternal rivalry, which indeed constitutes the overarching framework of the narrative. The narrative begins with the birth of the twin brothers, and they are meant to conflict and struggle with each other.[362] The narrator's bias towards the younger is evident. Providing the divine promise that warrants the younger's supremacy, "the elder shall serve the younger" (Gen 25:23), the readers are guided to side with Jacob in the following fraternal confrontation. Even before birth, the hero is summoned to adventure. The birth report adds another dimension to the rivalry theme: "with his hand gripping Esau's heel; so he was named Jacob" (Gen 25:26).[363] His existential quality, divinely revealed, is engrained in his name, which perhaps can mean, "he tricks!" or even "he will be a trickster" (cf. Jer 9:6).[364] Moreover, information on parental preference (Gen 25:27–28) sets the stage for the following narrative. One becomes a hunter and the other a tent dweller. The father "loves" the first – though not for the character but for the game; the mother loves the second – without a specified reason.[365] The reader's position is further pushed towards Jacob's side by the following scene in which Esau is depicted as a negligent character who, the narrator says, "despises" the birthright (Gen 25:34).

---

al literary sensitivity. See the introduction to Hermann Gunkel, *Genesis*, trans. Mark E. Biddle (Macon, GA: Mercer University Press, 1997).

362 An extraordinary birth scene with a supernatural prediction about the new-born is one of the characteristic features of a hero story. Most cultures have a set of typical birth scenes. In Korean myth, for instance, one of the dominant types is the myth of a hero born from an egg. Because eggs are often identified with the Sun, divine (solar) authority is given to the newborn hero. See James Huntley Grayson, *Myths and Legends from Korea: An Annotated Compendium of Ancient and Modern Materials* (London: Routledge, 2000); Hyung Il Pai, *Constructing "Korean" Origins: A Critical Review of Archaeology, Historiography, and Racial Myth in Korean State-Formation Theories*, Harvard East Asian Monographs 187 (Cambridge, MA: Harvard University Asia Center, 2000).

363 This birth scene bears remarkable similarity with the birth of Perez and Sera in Gen 38:27–30, which indicates the use of a common narrative motif of strife between two closely related clans.

364 Certainly, this is rooted in popular etymology. For discussion of the potential authentic etymology of the name Jacob, lost in biblical tradition, particularly concerning the likelihood of its initial association with a theophorous name, such as "Jacob-El," see Zobel, "יַעֲקֹב/יַעֲקֹב ya'aqōḇ/ ya'aqôḇ," 188–90.

365 The lack of explanation for Rebekah's preference breaks the parallelism with the previous colon, arguably a deliberate literary devise inviting the reader to fill the gap.

The basic outline of the story roughly follows Campbell's hero's journey.[366] Jacob's stealing of the paternal blessing from Esau (Gen 27) is presented as a momentous incident within the whole narrative. Here, his mother Rebekah is featured as a helper.[367] As the sole recipient of the prophecy (Gen 25:23), she uses her knowledge to actively bring it into fruition. The hero initially refuses the call, but the helper forces him to follow. Like the divine prediction, the younger trumps the older and receives the paternal blessing. Yet the narrative does not end there. Contrary to the expectations of readers, the triumphant Jacob is forced to go into exile. The readers now know this story will conclude only when the supplanter returns to resolve this conflict. As the protagonist embarks on a journey, God appears and promises guidance (Gen 28:15). God is still with the protagonist despite his trickery and the resulting flight. This is not a typical moral or religious tale.

As the hero passes the threshold and journeys into the land of Arameans, a lengthy story within a story is launched (Gen 29–31). In this adventure, the hero's transformation takes place. It commences with a typical encounter with a woman at the well, Rachel (Gen 29:1–14a). She leads him to the house of Laban, whom Jacob was seeking, and later becomes Jacob's wife. Over the course of twenty years, Jacob struggles with Laban, who turns out to be a more skilled trickster, who exploits Jacob's affection for Rachel, manipulating it to retain him for an extended period to serve his own interests. The readers now understand the source of Rebekah's naturally displayed cunning maneuvers and recognize the trickster nature that runs in Jacob's blood. But at the same time, the readers also become concerned that Laban may pose a challenge for Jacob, as he had already outwitted him in their first encounter. Contrary to expectations, Jacob emerges victorious despite the initial setback, securing wives, sons, and property before departing Laban's house.[368]

---

366 Joseph Campbell, *The Hero with a Thousand Faces*, Bollingen Series 17 (New York: Pantheon Books, 1949). See also Edward L. Greenstein, "The Fugitive Hero Narrative Pattern in Mesopotamia," in *Worship, Women, and War: Essays in Honor of Susan Niditch*, ed. John J. Collins, T. M. Lemos, and Saul M. Olyan, BJS 357 (Providence, RI: Brown University, 2015), 17–35. Cf. Hendel's critical stance against the structuralist pursuit of universal traits in hero stories of myth, epic, and legend as discussed in Ronald S. Hendel, *The Epic of the Patriarch: The Jacob Cycle and the Narrative Traditions of Canaan and Israel*, HSM 42 (Decatur, GA: Scholars Press, 1987), 133–35.
367 Cf. Brett's depiction of Rebekah as a trickster in *Genesis: Procreation and the Politics of Identity*, 88–89.
368 One recognizes the same pattern in the Moses tradition. Moses was forced into a forty-year exile in the wilderness after committing a murder (despite his seemingly justifiable act to protect his people). In the wilderness, Moses the Egyptian transforms into a true leader of Israel. A theophany in the desert plays a critical part in this transformation. Jethro, albeit in different ways, also serves as the helper.

As the Jacob-Laban narrative comes to an end, the suspended Jacob-Esau narrative resumes. The night before the eventual reunion with his arch-nemesis, Jacob has another significant encounter with a divine being. Without knowing, Jacob becomes the eponymous ancestor of Israel. His superhuman effort to obtain the blessing is engraved in the name "Israel" that he receives after the wrestle: "you have striven with God and with humans, and have prevailed" (Gen 32:29). This is no mere transformation of Jacob's character. With Jacob receiving "Israel" as his name, what could have been originally an identity narrative of mere *Bene Ya'aqob* is made serviceable as an identity narrative for *Bene Yisrael*.

With the divine blessing at hand, Jacob's reunion with Esau turns out surprisingly amicable.[369] With the central narrative tension resolved, the entire story comes to an end. The final section of the story has been extensively reworked through later additions, making it difficult to accurately reconstruct the earlier ending.[370] Nonetheless, for our purpose, we can suffice with noting that the cli-

---

369 Speaking of the "amicable" reunion, I cannot help but share an exciting recent classroom discussion. One of my students, Lee Ji-eun, pointed out that 220 is one of the "amicable numbers" and wondered if there might be a significance to this scene of amicable reunion. She explained that amicable numbers are pairs of numbers where each number is the sum of the divisors of the other number (excluding itself), and 220 and 284 just so happen to be the classic example:

The factors of 220 are 1, 2, 4, 5, 10, 11, 20, 22, 44, 55, and 110, which add up to 284.
The factors of 284 are 1, 2, 4, 71, and 142, which add up to 220.

With a smirk on my face, I responded playfully that Jewish interpreters were probably already aware of this, taking the opportunity to introduce Jewish interpretive heritage and its profound use of Gematria. I added that it would be intriguing if we could locate the number 284 in the text. As I was about to continue, Hwang Byung-joon, a student seated next to Ji-eun, interrupted me with a mischievous grin and exclaimed, "Professor, I think I found 284!" He went on to explain how he had added up all the numbers of the living creatures specifically mentioned in the text (Gen 32:13–23), which totaled 568. By dividing this number by 2, he arrived at the magic number of 284.

Animals:
– Goats 220 + Sheep 220 + Camels 30 + Cows 40 + Bulls 10 + Donkeys 30 = Total 550.
Humans:
– 11 sons of Jacob + 4 wives + 3 servants leading the herds = Total 18.
550 animals + 18 humans = 568/2=284.

I still do not know what to make of this, but at least, I know I have Kabbalists in my class who could see beyond what Abraham Azulai, a renowned sixteenth-century Kabbalist, could see: "Our ancestor Jacob prepared his present in a wise way. This number 220 is a hidden secret, being one of a pair of numbers such that the parts of it are equal to the other one 284, and conversely. And Jacob had this in mind; this has been tried by the ancients in securing the love of kings and dignitaries." Jeffrey Stopple, *A Primer of Analytic Number Theory: From Pythagoras to Riemann* (Cambridge: Cambridge University Press, 2003), 33.

370 E.g., see now Wöhrle, "Koexistenz durch Unterwerfung." For discussion of his thesis, see n. 410 below.

max of the pre-P Jacob story involved the nocturnal struggle and the eventual reconciliation with Esau.[371]

Without suggesting that this level marks this tradition's very origin, I simply state that this tale could effectively function as an ancestral myth for the people of North Israel. This *Israelized* Jacob story, identified above, betrays strong signs of connection to the Northern Kingdom. Jacob's life journey is firmly rooted in northern locations such as Bethel and Penuel.[372] These sites are closely linked to Jeroboam ben Nebat, the founding monarch of the Northern Kingdom of Israel.[373] Immediately after the coup, he is said to have built Shechem and Penuel (1Kgs 12:25) before establishing a national shrine at Bethel (1Kgs 12:28–29). As noted above (Sec-

---

371 Although arriving at a definitive interpretation remains a challenge, I am inclined to interpret the last scene as an illustration of Jacob's transformed trickster qualities, honed during his exile, that eventually enabled him to emerge victorious over Esau. Similar to how he took cues from his dream and tricked Laban to gain wealth with the speckled, spotted, and black flock (as against the white [= Laban!] ones), he seized the clue from the encounter with "the messengers of God" to name the place Mahanaim (מַחֲנָיִם, "two camps," Gen 32:2) and divide his family and property into "two camps (שְׁנֵי מַחֲנוֹת)" (Gen 32:8, 11). The text does not explain how this strategy helped appease Esau's supposed anger (or did it in the first place?), although I see Jacob's repeated assertion of "two camps" likely played a role. However, it is possible to speculate that the original line of narrative logic has been obscured over time during the story's transmission and development.

372 See, e.g., Blum, *Die Komposition der Vätergeschichte*, 171–75; idem, "The Jacob Tradition," in *The Book of Genesis: Composition, Reception, and Interpretation*, ed. Craig A. Evans, Joel N. Lohr, and David L. Petersen, VTSup 152 (Leiden: Brill, 2012), 207–10; Albert de Pury, "Le cycle de Jacob comme légende autonome des origines d'Israël," in *Congress Volume: Leuven 1989*, ed. John Adney Emerton, VTSup 43 (Leiden: Brill, 1991), 78–96; idem, "Situer le cycle de Jacob. Quelques réflexions, vingt-cinq ans plus tard," in *Studies in the Book of Genesis: Literature, Redaction and History*, ed. André Wénin, BETL 155 (Leuven: Peeters, 2001), 213–41; idem, "The Jacob Story and the Beginning of the Formation of the Pentateuch," in *A Farewell to the Yahwist?: The Composition of the Pentateuch in Recent European Interpretation*, ed. Thomas B. Dozeman and Konrad Schmid (Atlanta: Society of Biblical Literature, 2006), 56; Carr, *Reading the Fractures*, 204–15, 256–71, 298–300; idem, *The Formation of the Hebrew Bible: A New Reconstruction* (New York: Oxford University Press, 2011), 473–75; Finkelstein and Römer, "Comments on the Historical Background of the Jacob Narrative," 321–20; Marvin A. Sweeney, "The Jacob Narratives: An Ephraimitic Text?," *CBQ* 78 (2016): 236–55. Cf. Na'aman's recent argument ("The Jacob Story and the Formation of Biblical Israel," 112) that the pre-P Jacob story was written in the mid-sixth century Judah as a part of the larger Patriarchal narrative. Na'aman argues that only the Bethel episode belongs to the genuine northern tradition.

373 Note that Jeroboam ben Nebat is the one who fulfills Jacob's vow (Gen 28:22) to build the "house" at Bethel. Jacob did revisit Bethel in his return from Aram where he has another divine encounter. Yet, he does not fulfill his initial vow to turn the pillar into a "house" but builds an altar (35:7). He later raises another pillar (35:14), which, again, may not be seen as a belated fulfillment of his vow but as a commemoration of the latest theophany (35:9–12).

tion 8.3), these two figures, one in the ancestral and the other in the monarchal past, perform as the twin prototypes defining Northern Israel's origin and identity.

The prominence of the Joseph clans, the leading clans of the northern polity, is intrinsically woven into the default plot structure of the Jacob-Laban narrative, beginning with the very first scene. As noted, Jacob's encounter with Rachel – not Leah – at the well (Gen 29:6, 10–12) forms a betrothal type-scene in which the hero meets his love.[374] This initial setup of Jacob's falling in love with Rachel (Gen 29:18) dictates the rest of the plot, much more than Moses's encounter with Zipporah in the well (Exod 2:16–22).[375] This love gave him wives – not just one but three more – quite unexpectedly for a fugitive. This love provided a rationale for his heavily delayed return (cf. Gen 27:44). It is this love that provoked Leah's jealousy, which forced the sisters to go toe-to-toe regarding who would produce sons for Jacob.[376] It is also this love that culminates in the birth of Joseph, which forms the pinnacle of the sisters' competition.

Joseph's birth also presents the necessary backdrop for the ensuing Joseph novella, Jacob's favor of Joseph. Rachel's naming him יֹסֵף, wishing for another son (Gen 30:24), foreshadows her tragic death while giving birth to another son, Benjamin, who is also featured prominently in the subsequent narrative. Here, the fact that the Jacob narrative is followed by the Joseph narrative, not the firstborn Reuben or the clan Judah of David, cannot be taken lightly either.[377] The political overtone of this plot structure is apparent. The Joseph clans' prominence among the twelve is stressed not only in the Joseph story. It is engraved already in the narrative structure of the Jacob story that prepares what follows. Thus, the Jacob story, with the subsequent Joseph story, would have served well as propaganda for the leading Joseph clans of Northern Israel.

One can compare this with the lack of presence of Judah throughout the narrative. Other than references in the birth report (Gen 29:35) and the Priestly genealogical note (35:23–26), which could be assigned secondary to the early Jacob

---

374 Michael W. Martin, "Betrothal Journey Narratives," *CBQ* 70 (2008): 505–23.
375 For the parallel nature of the Jacob and Moses stories, see Hendel, *The Epic of the Patriarch*, 137–65. On the meeting at the well scene, pp. 152–54.
376 While some interpreters make much of Jacob's quarrel with Rachel (Gen 30:1–2), it is misleading to pose too much emphasis on it. The purpose is not to signify the break of Jacob's love but to show Rachel's frustration.
377 Granted, several scholars promote the Joseph story as diasporic literature. E.g., Römer, "The Joseph Story in the Book of Genesis: Pre-P or Post-P?" Indeed, this tale may have served the Judean diaspora in later times, but they must also explain why Joseph is selected to continue the chosen line instead of Judah in the first place. It makes more sense that the Joseph story had its place together with the Jacob story earlier in Northern Israel, which has later found a renewed use as diasporic literature.

tradition,[378] Judah is absent throughout the Jacob story. It appears that Judah in the South was negligible for Israel's self-perception, which is comparable to Judah's absence in early traditions like Judg 4.[379] Judah's absence also contrasts with Jacob's presence strongly felt in the Abraham narrative, which I shall discuss below. In short, the pre-P Jacob narrative likely served as Northern Israel's self-contained ancestral myth, independent of the Abraham tradition. Yet we also saw hints that suggest a deeper, pre-Israelite origin of the Jacob story, a topic I intend to explore in greater detail soon.

9.3 Jacob and Exodus Traditions within Northern Israel

Before delving deeper, it is necessary to situate the Jacob story within the broader context of Northern Israel's mythic foundation. As we discussed above (Section 5.2.1), the Jacob narrative did not constitute the sole origin myth for the northern Israelites. The Exodus/Moses story played a seminal role in defining the identity of the Israelites, or "who we are."[380] In fact, the Exodus narrative dominates the religious identity of the people of Yhwh, in which Jacob is not conceived as a model figure (e.g., Hos 12:2–4; Jer 9:4, "for all your kin are supplanters" = כִּי כָל־אָח עָקוֹב יַעְקֹב).[381] Although the two are now combined into a coherent narrative, critics have long recognized the independent origins and fundamentally distinct characteristics of these tradition blocks.[382]

The Exodus/Moses story starts with a group of slaves emerging from Egypt, encountering their God in the wilderness, who subsequently leads them to a habitable land. The shared experience of the Exodus acts as a primary method for constructing a new identity, molding the people of Yhwh from a "mixed multitude" (Exod 12:38).[383] This is not to say that this "Moses group"[384] actually came

---

378 For the latest argument for the late dating of the birth report of Jacob's sons, see Tobolowsky, *The Sons of Jacob and the Sons of Herakles*.

379 This point stands even if one adds the Exodus tradition to Northern Israel's origin myths. The "Israel" constructed in the dual origin myths is defined as Jacob's descendants who migrated to and escaped from Egypt and returned to their homeland after encountering and making a covenant with Yhwh at Sinai. Judah is dispensable in this core narrative, although later attempts tried to preserve Judah's position in both parts.

380 See de Pury, "Le cycle de Jacob comme légende autonome des origines d'Israël," 95–96; Finkelstein and Römer, "Comments on the Historical Background of the Jacob Narrative," 329.

381 Cf. Finkelstein and Römer, "Comments on the Historical Background of the Jacob Narrative," 322.

382 E.g., de Pury, "Le cycle de Jacob comme légende autonome des origines d'Israël," 95–96.

383 Schmid, *Genesis and the Moses Story*, 146.

384 Cf. Gottwald, *The Tribes of Yahweh*, 35–41; Frank Moore Cross, "Reuben, the Firstborn of Jacob: Sacral Traditions and Early Israelite History," in *From Epic to Canon: History and Literature in Ancient Israel* (Baltimore: Johns Hopkins University Press, 1998), 67.

out of Egypt. It is simply that, over time, certain segments in Israel somehow developed a sense of their origins by participating into a narrative that depicted Israel's Egyptian origin.[385] Genealogical connections play a minimal role in this narrative. This identity narrative primarily focuses on the shared history of the Hebrew slaves' liberation and Yhwh's election: "we" were nobody until Yhwh chose us, delivered us, and guided us to the land. Consequently, election is a critical aspect of this identity narrative, which necessitates a covenantal duty of the people to their God. Put simply, in this narrative, "Israel" is not a given but *made* out of a shared allegiance to one God.

Conversely, the ancestral Jacob story exhibits a distinct character. It celebrates Jacob's heroics not for their inherent merit, but for the consequences they have for his future descendants. Election is also a crucial component in this narrative. However, "our" election is contingent upon God's choice of Jacob. The election is naturally transmitted to his descendants. Thus, it is evident that the two origin stories differ in nature.[386] The Exodus narrative portrays Israel as foreign founders,[387] while the Jacob story emphasizes Israel's ancestral heritage in the land.

In this regard, Konrad Schmid's contribution has been most significant.[388] Schmid has emphasized the distinct nature of the two origin traditions, championing them as Israel's dual origin myths.[389] However, the framework of his approach remained fundamentally traditional, which prevented him from realizing the tremendous social implications of his observation. Instead, he settles for using it as a means to determine the date of the supposed merging of the two traditions. His proposal that this foundational combination did not take place until the era of P may be cutting-edge within critical scholarship, but still, its significance is confined to literary-critical agendas.[390]

---

385 Cf. discussion in Grabbe, *Ancient Israel*, 92–98.
386 See Hutchinson and Smith, *Ethnicity*, 6–7.
387 Cf. Irad Malkin, "Foreign Founders: Greeks and Hebrews," in *Foundation Myths in Ancient Societies: Dialogues and Discourses*, ed. Naoíse Mac Sweeney (Philadelphia: University of Pennsylvania Press, 2015), 20–40.
388 See discussion in Section 7.3 above.
389 Schmid, *Genesis and the Moses Story*, 92–151. See also de Pury, "Le cycle de Jacob comme légende autonome des origines d'Israël," 93.
390 See n. 292 above. Schmid's late dating scheme, which is becoming symptomatic of today's literary critics, did not permit him to engage with the seminal stage of the formation of Israel's identity. Schmid, *Genesis and the Moses Story*, 129. I have reviewed this with regards to matters of Israel's identity formation (Section 7.4.). He thus confines the dynamic between the dual origin myths to the Persian period identity formation, assigning their interplay to the today's increasingly overused *golah* versus *'am ha'aretz* contestation. He also aligns the ancestral tradition with Judah in the South and the Exodus tradition with Israel in the North, a proposition I find unconvincing given the Jacob tradition's apparent northern orientation. True, this late Persian context

Instead, the dual origin myths in Israel appear indicative of the dialogic nature of any social identity. No social identity can be constructed by a single voice; society always consists of diverse perspectives, and it is their negotiation that shapes "who we are." As origin myths with distinct characteristics, these traditions could coexist within a society as negotiating voices, neither entirely connected nor entirely severed, a constant source of negotiation. Like any other polity, Israel was composed of diverse popular elements. Irrespective of their actual origins, complex socio-economic dynamics lead some groups to identify with indigenous markers, while others align with external indicators. While some texts take a critical stance towards the indigenous, others adopt a more lenient perspective that embraces them. Negotiation between these perspectives constituted major facets of Israel's ongoing identity negotiation that oscillated between its two personas – indigenous and external. In this regard, the Jacob story's indigenous nature is particularly pronounced.

9.4 Jacob, Canaan, and Israel's Indigenous Persona

Thus far, we delineated the pre-P Jacob narrative, which sets the stage for our ensuing examination of its reorientation by the Judahite Abrahamic expansion. Yet, before moving on, I choose to dig deeper into the potential pre-Israelite Jacob tradition. Rather than employing literary-critical methods, I aim to search for vestiges of an ancient, pre-Israelite Jacob tradition, highlighting how the Self and Others are portrayed in the story. I do this because I believe it is crucial to recognize that Northern Israel's Jacob myth was not their own creation but rather their adaptation of an indigenous tradition, one with a far richer heritage. While it is unattainable to fully and precisely reconstruct this foundational tradition, acknowledging its existence is pivotal, as it profoundly influences our interpretation of its subsequent adaptations.

Scholars well versed in contemporary archaeological findings generally acknowledge that Israel's roots are embedded in the southern Levantine cultural milieu, but few biblical critics have delved deeper to pose a necessary question: what is the identity narrative that belonged to the indigenous segment within

---

may have found the dynamic useful in its own right, but I doubt that the insider-outsider dynamic in the text first originated during the Persian period.

His late dating also resulted in an overemphasis on the independence between the two tradition blocks, prompting him to assert that the ancestral and Exodus/Moses traditions were literarily and conceptually independent throughout the monarchic Israelite period. As I presented a detailed critique elsewhere, however, I find this argument neither pragmatic nor productive. See Hong, "Genesis and Exodus as Conceptually Independent, Competing Origin Myths?"

Israel? This question is undoubtedly radical. Yet, if we are to genuinely explore the implications of embracing Israel's Canaanite origin and aim to reconcile this with the deep-rooted indigenous characteristics embedded in what we now call the *Israelite* tradition, posing this question becomes a necessity.

Aside from sporadic Yahwistic overlays, traces of the imbued El religion are evident in the Jacob tradition.[391] The sheer fact that this group assumed the El name demands serious consideration.[392] This makes it difficult to deny that El was the chief deity of the group that called themselves as "Israel."[393] Thus, deliberations on the Yhwh-worshipping group's adoption of this El name, or the El group's embrace of Yhwh, are unlikely to yield a conclusive answer from a conventional standpoint. The prevalence of El-associated theophoric elements, such as El-Bethel (Gen 31:13, 35:7) and El-Elohe-Israel (Gen 33:20), is particularly challenging. However, when we acknowledge Israel's Canaanite origin, it becomes difficult to overlook the most straightforward interpretation – that the prevalence of El in its ancestral myth underscores Israel's profound indigenous heritage.

Moreover, names that appear to include "Jacob" – such as *Ya'akob-'el* – are attested in materials found in Egypt, Mesopotamia, and Palestine, throughout the second millennium.[394] Early critics primarily aimed to use these references to validate the historical Jacob,[395] which was inevitably unsuccessful.[396] As a result, inter-

---

391 Naturally, this posed significant difficulties for biblical interpreters. E.g., Alt, "The God of the Fathers"; William Foxwell Albright, *Yahweh and the Gods of Canaan: A Historical Analysis of Two Contrasting Faiths* (London: Athlone, 1968); Frank Moore Cross, "'Ēl and the God of the Fathers," in *Canaanite Myth and Hebrew Epic: Essays in the History of the Religion of Israel* (Cambridge, MA: Harvard University Press, 1973), 13–43; Mark S. Smith, *The Early History of God: Yahweh and the Other Deities in Ancient Israel* (San Francisco: Harper & Row, 1990), 1–12; idem, *The Origins of Biblical Monotheism: Israel's Polytheistic Background and the Ugaritic Texts* (New York: Oxford University Press, 2001), 135–48; Theodore J. Lewis, *The Origin and Character of God: Ancient Israelite Religion through the Lens of Divinity* (New York: Oxford University Press, 2020), 73–118.

392 For proposed etymologies, refer to Hans-Jürgen Zobel, "יִשְׂרָאֵל yiśrā'ēl," in *Theological Dictionary of the Old Testament*, ed. Johannes Botterweck and Helmer Ringgren, trans. David E. Green, vol. 6 (Grand Rapids, MI: Eerdmans, 1990), 399–401.

393 E.g., Smith, *The Early History of God*, 7; idem, *The Origins of Monotheism in the Bible*, 146–47.

394 See Zobel, "יַעֲקֹב/יַעֲקוֹב ya'aqōḇ/ya'aqôḇ," 189.

395 E.g., Harold Henry Rowley, *From Joseph to Joshua: Biblical Traditions in the Light of Archaeology* (London: Published for the British Academy by the Oxford University Press, 1950), 35–37; Donald B. Redford, *Egypt, Canaan, and Israel in Ancient Times* (Princeton, NJ: Princeton University Press, 1993), 107–10. For the most recent study, see Ronald A. Geobey, "Joseph the Infiltrator, Jacob the Conqueror? Reexamining the Hyksos–Hebrew Correlation," *JBL* 136 (2017): 23–37, https://doi.org/10.1353/jbl.2017.0001.

396 See discussion in Thompson, *The Historicity of the Patriarchal Narratives*, 36–51. Above all, the transliterations of the Egyptian term vary, and scholars have struggled to reach a consensus

est in these references also appeared to wane. Nonetheless, for our purpose, they underscore that "Jacob" was a prevalent semitic name long before the emergence of Israel.[397] From this, to posit the existence of a pre-Israelite Jacob story is not a far reach.[398] A narrative featuring the trickster hero Jacob, who, guided by El encountered at Bethel, outsmarts his adversaries and is ultimately bestowed the name Israel at Penuel, could aptly serve as an origin tradition for *Bene Ya'aqob*.

In the ensuing analysis, I will elucidate the indigenous heritage woven into the Jacob tradition by critically examining its portrayals of the Self and Others. This endeavor is closely connected to my understanding of identity as a social construct and narratives as a critical tool in shaping it. Seeing narratives as instruments for shaping "who we are," these portrayals become keys to unlocking the social realia the narrative aimed to construct.

9.4.1 Self in Jacob Story

I must begin with reiterating that the narrative does not shy away from an explicit portrayal of Jacob as a trickster figure.[399] Every observation we have made about Jacob's trickster traits in the pre-P stage is best understood as remnants of the underlying pre-Israelite tradition. His name and birth scene (Gen 25:24–26)

---

on correlating them with Hebrew names. That lack of consensus posed further challenges. See, e.g., S. Yeivin, "Ya'qob'el," *JEA* 45 (1959): 16–18, https://doi.org/10.2307/3855458. The problem is more evident with the alleged name of Joseph. See Lysander Dickerman, "The Names of Jacob and Joseph in Egypt," *The Old Testament Student* 7 (1888): 182, https://doi.org/10.1086/469990.

397 Albright comments on *ya'qob-'el*: "The name Ya'qob el is the same as that of the Patriarch Jacob, but was certainly common in the second millennium, and probably has no connexion with him. It is, however, possible that Jacob's connextion with Transjordan is partly based upon a combination with this name, which afterwards disappeared from the sources." W. F. Albright, "The Jordan Valley in the Bronze Age," *AASOR* 6 (1924): 19 n. 17, https://doi.org/10.2307/3768510. See also Raymond Weill, "L'Installation des israélites en Palestine et la légende des patriarches," *RHR* 87 (1923): 69–120; idem, "L'Installation des israélites en Palestine et la légende des patriarches," *RHR* 88 (1923): 1–44; G. A. Danell, *Studies in the Name Israel in the Old Testament* (Uppsala: Appelbergs Boktrykeri-A.-B., 1946), 43.

398 For the plausibility of a pre-monarchic date for the early Jacob tradition, see de Pury, "Le cycle de Jacob comme légende autonome des origines d'Israël," 93.

399 As an ancestral figure, Jacob stands in stark contrast to Moses. It raises the question of how this tale of a trickster became a foundational narrative for Israel's identity, who initially crafted this story, or which groups subsequently recognized their collective identities within this trickster tale. God's choice of Jacob, despite his problematic character, posed great difficulties for biblical interpreters, but it apparently posed no issue for its intended audience. Cf. Susan Niditch, *A Prelude to Biblical Folklore: Underdogs and Tricksters* (Urbana, IL: University of Illinois Press, 2000), 93–125.

testify to his wily character, and his ensuing life journey does not betray that expectation. This is a story of an underdog who gets the best of his superior rivals. He cheats and steals, yet he is not rejected but chosen. Esau the firstborn, conversely, is rejected for no obvious reason. Although the Christian doctrine of God's election of fallible humans has somewhat eased out the problem, God's questionable choice remains an enduring topic of theological debate.

Biblical scholars tried various ways to assign this atypical narrative to certain social segments, such as de Pury's claim that it belonged to the tribal elites of the countryside (or *'am ha'aretz*), which he contrasted with the "Yahweh-only movement" behind the Exodus tradition.[400] But who were the "tribal elites?"[401] In accounting for this dissenting segment, biblical scholars were reluctant to venture beyond the presumed boundary of "Israel." Yet we know that calling Jacob, or Abraham, an Israelite is as off the mark as calling the first believers of Jesus Christians. There is a transitional phase where establishing fixed identity categories is not feasible. We can say that Jacob and his descendants morphed into what we know as Israel, but who they were before that and how exactly to understand the process of "becoming Israel" is difficult to articulate.

If one acknowledges Israel's Canaanite origin, however, it is not a significant leap from there to consider Jacob as an indigenous hero who was later reimagined as Israel's father. This shift in perspective not only helps to resolve the theological paradox surrounding Jacob's deceitful character but also offers a simpler way to reconcile all the indigenous features imbued in its narrative world.

---

400 See de Pury, "Le cycle de Jacob comme légende autonome des origines d'Israël," 92.

401 Noth (*Pentateuchal Traditions*, 87–91) holds a very different perspective, viewing Jacob's trickster trait as a secondary development in the East Jordan traditions, contrasting it with the West Jordan Jacob tradition rooted in Shechem and Bethel. He contends that the East Jordan Jacob embodies a more "worldly" (p. 91) character in contrast to the more sacral nature of the West Jordan Jacob. Noth describes, "In these stories we find the pleasure of characterizing human types, the portrayal of successful human cleverness and guile, and, on the other hand, human rashness and folly – in short, everyday human behavior now comes openly into the foreground. Obviously we have here a later kind of narrative, which is distinct from the older sacral style of tersely composed narratives concerning God's revelations and promises to the 'patriarchs.' The East Jordan Jacob is really no longer a 'patriarch' at all in the original sense; nor is he a tribal personification in the sense formerly presumed in scholarly circles, for a 'tribe of Jacob' is not involved. He is, rather, a type that characterizes the whole people and their life" (p. 91). Here, Noth's premise is that this *secularized* version emerged from Israel's assimilation into indigenous culture, an assumption directly challenged in this book. Additionally, his claim that the East-Jordanian Jacob-Laban-Esau cycle is a later work (p. 88) rests on a dubious assumption, akin to Gunkel's (*Genesis*, xxx–xxxiv), that such a well-developed story could not have originated in the earlier period.

Although detailing the process of his *conversion* proves challenging,[402] it also helps us better understand the widespread disapproval of this ancestral figure in biblical literature.

Apparently, not all social segments of Israel felt proud of such indigenous heritage. The aversion to Jacob's indigenous persona is particularly pronounced in the prophetic and Priestly circle, quite understandably so. Hence, in the words of Dtr, who represents one of the hawkish voices in Israel's social discourse, the lingering indigenous persona is seen as the product of Israel's original sin – a failure to drive out the Canaanites (e.g., Josh 17:12–13; Judg 3:1–7). However, this may have been a way to minimize the problem as a minor failure in the past when reality was much bigger that touches upon Israel's often-masked true identity. For the religious elites, suppressing this innate identity was a longstanding issue, and this tension between the two personas became the ultimate source of Israel's schizophrenia.

Israel's innermost struggle is poignantly illustrated in Hosea's impassioned call for return (Hos 12:7–8).

> But as for you (Jacob),[403] return to your God,
> hold fast to love and justice,
> and wait continually for your God.
> A trader (כְּנַעַן) in whose hands are false balances,
> he loves to oppress.

Scholars have analyzed this text for centuries, yet the prevailing notion that Israel is distinct from Canaan has hindered them from recognizing what seems transparent in the text. The prophet Hosea presents a negative portrayal of Jacob. The striking juxtaposition of Jacob as a wily figure (Hos 12:3–5) alongside Canaan as a deceitful merchant (Hos 12:8) is most noteworthy. Sweeney remarks,

> He calls Israel, "Canaan" [NRSV: "trader"], which is frequently taken as a reference to Phoenician merchants (cf. Zeph 1:11; Ezek 16:29; 17:4) based upon the imagery of false scales and riches gained through trade in the balance of the verse. But the label also expresses Hosea's rhetorical goals by labeling Israel as the Canaanites who were displaced from the land at the conquest led by Joshua. Israelite tradition labels the Canaanites as those people who were removed from the land by YHWH for immoral action, and Hosea employs this label as a means to make his point that Israel is now immoral and subject to a similar punishment if it does not change.[404]

---

402 Cf. Mendenhall, *The Hebrew Conquest of Palestine*, 84; Gottwald, *The Tribes of Yahweh*, 555–83.

403 Jacob is the antecedent that is referenced multiple times in verses 3–6.

404 Marvin A. Sweeney, *The Twelve Prophets*, vol. 1, Berit Olam (Collegeville, MN: Liturgical Press, 2000), 123.

This depiction merely follows the Bible's final presentation and its forceful exclusion of Canaan from the boundaries of "Israel" through intense othering. But what if Hosea was revealing the innermost struggle of the people of Israel? Both Jacob and Canaan share the same traits of cunning and craftiness, traits the prophet endeavored to restrain. Rather than dismissing this as mere rhetoric, I suggest that Hosea's juxtaposition of Jacob and Canaan underscores a genuine perception within the prophetic circle about Israel's Canaanite heritage.[405]

When we liberate Jacob from the overbearing religious and ethical framework that constrains him, however, one can see that the self-presentation in this story is rather healthier one. Despite the moral flaws evident in this character, the narrative addresses them head-on instead of concealing them. Jacob's missteps act as pivotal learning moments, not only for him but also for the audience, aiding him and his descendants in discerning the boundaries between good and bad. It is precisely for this reason that tricksters are regarded as culture heroes.[406] Hence, Jacob would make the perfect star of Hyde's *Trickster Makes the World*. Overall, Jacob is portrayed as a playful figure who, despite his trickery, rarely causes significant harm to others. Esau ultimately becomes a powerful man, and Laban also benefits from Jacob's service. In the end, the story concludes with a peaceful pact and a secure boundary for each group. Reflecting on this, one must question whether the story itself is as dangerous and threatening as its imposing religious framework would have us believe. Jacob's whimsical nature might set him apart from model religious figures like Moses, Elijah, or Daniel, but he has his own space for recognition.

9.4.2 Others in Jacob Story and Israel's Outer Boundary

The indigenous nature is also found in the Jacob story's depiction of Others.[407] The Jacob story features not many Others, but two major figures, Esau and Laban,

---

405 I think my perspective is shaped by a personal journey that swayed between initial unease towards Korea's indigenous heritage and a growing appreciation for it. There was a phase when I drifted away from our ancestral culture, influenced to perceive it as at odds with the principles of Christianity. The infiltration of Western culture and lifestyles cast a shadow on the traditions and practices intrinsic to our Eastern identity. This overlay was sometimes abrupt, at other times gradual, where the vibrant hues of Korean cultural tapestry dimmed amidst the gleaming allure of Western modernity. As a result, I constantly find myself navigating between my Korean heritage and Christian identity, a delicate process of rediscovery and reevaluation.

406 Lewis Hyde, *Trickster Makes This World: Mischief, Myth, and Art* (New York: Farrar, Straus and Giroux, 1998).

407 The Others play an essential role in identity narratives, providing important information about the social context from which the narrative emerged. Laurence J. Silberstein and Robert

define the outer boundary of the identity drawn by Jacob's journey. When read as the Northern Kingdom's origin myth, Esau and Laban are made to represent Edom and Aram, the two ethnic kingdoms that share Israel's northern and southern borders. Naturally, the discussion among historical critics regarding Esau and Laban has centered on their referential value to the kingdoms of Edom and Aram, with the aim of identifying the period that align with the narrative portrayal of their relationship with Jacob/Israel.[408] However, scholars have encountered challenges in interpreting this narrative as a political allegory reflective of the monarchic era.

While Aram presents less difficulty given its prominence as a neighboring entity during the monarchic era of the Northern Kingdom, Edom poses a more complex challenge.[409] On the other hand, scholars have struggled to find a period when the Northern Kingdom was inferior to Edom.[410] Generally, Edom was in a

---

L. Cohn, eds., *The Other in Jewish Thought and History: Constructions of Jewish Culture and Identity*, New Perspectives on Jewish Studies (New York: New York University Press, 1994); Ehud Ben Zvi and Diana V. Edelman, eds., *Imagining the Other and Constructing Israelite Identity in the Early Second Temple Period*, LHBOTS 456 (London: Bloomsbury T&T Clark, 2014).

408 For important studies that examined Edom and Aram as Israel's Others, see Bert Dicou, *Edom, Israel's Brother and Antagonist: The Role of Edom in Biblical Prophecy and Story*, JSOTSup 169 (Sheffield: JSOT Press, 1994); Elie Assis, "From Adam to Esau and Israel: An Anti-Edomite Ideology in 1 Chronicles 1," *VT* 56 (2006): 287–302, https://doi.org/10.1163/156853306778149629; Dominic S. Irudayaraj, *Violence, Otherness and Identity in Isaiah 63:1–6: The Trampling One Coming from Edom*, LHBOTS 633 (London: T&T Clark, 2017); Dustin Nash, "Edom, Judah, and Converse Constructions of Israeliteness in Genesis 36," *VT* 68 (2018): 111–28, https://doi.org/10.1163/15685330-12341317; Dalit Rom-Shiloni, "When an Explicit Polemic Initiates a Hidden One: Jacob's Aramaean Identity," in *Words, Ideas, Worlds: Biblical Essays in Honour of Yairah Amit*, ed. Athalya Brenner-Idan and Frank Polak, Hebrew Bible Monographs 40 (Sheffield: Phoenix Press, 2012); Omer Sergi, Manfred Oeming, and Izaak J. de Hulster, eds., *In Search for Aram and Israel: Politics, Culture, and Identity*, Orientalische Religionen in der Antike 20 (Tübingen: Mohr Siebeck, 2016); Omer Sergi, "Jacob and the Aramaean Identity of Ancient Israel between the Judges and the Prophets," in *The Politics of the Ancestors: Exegetical and Historical Perspectives on Genesis 12–36*, ed. Mark G. Brett and Jakob Wöhrle, FAT 124 (Tübingen: Mohr Siebeck, 2018), 283–305; Wöhrle, "Koexistenz durch Unterwerfung."

409 See, e.g., Sweeney, "The Jacob Narratives: An Ephraimitic Text?," 249–51.

410 See Finkelstein and Römer, "Comments on the Historical Background of the Jacob Narrative," 331–32. Jakob Wöhrle ("Koexistenz durch Unterwerfung") interprets the Jacob-Esau narrative as an etiology of the later people of Israel and Edom and delves into the political undertones embedded in the story. Wöhrle postulates that the initial rendition of the Jacob story ended with Esau's expulsion following Jacob's successful procurement of his father's blessing. He surmises that the present version of the narrative, wherein Jacob willingly submits to Esau, is the result of subsequent editorial interventions (pp. 318–20), which he attributes to the late seventh century. Wöhrle identifies this narrative shift as indicative of Israel's diplomatic endeavors to cultivate a cordial rapport with Edom. He notes that in contrast to the dynamics with Moab/Ammon, Edom and Israel shared a congenial alliance during this period (pp. 321–24). Wöhrle views this histori-

weaker position to Israel. Even if there was a phase when Edom held greater power, such intermittent dominance hardly justifies the outright portrayal of Jacob as an underdog. In fact, Edom is more frequently depicted as Judah's neighbor, for apparent reasons.[411] Yet even in relation to Judah, Edom was a minor entity, reportedly gaining independence only in the ninth century BCE (2Kgs 8:20–22). While there have been continued conflicts (e.g., 2Kgs 14:7–10), there is no record of either side obtaining a complete dominance over the other.[412] This does not align well with the depiction of Esau in relation to Jacob.[413]

I believe this challenge primarily arises from attempts to anchor the narrative within the monarchic context. While one can agree that this narrative has evolved to fit later contexts for different purposes, that does not mean its foundational structure was conceived against the backdrop of those later settings.[414] In this re-

---

cal revisionism as a calculated attempt to advocate for a "renewed, harmonious bond between the two neighboring nations" (p. 320).

Wöhrle's analysis provides an intriguing perspective, shedding light on the multifaceted dimensions of the biblical narrative. Nevertheless, the strength of Wöhrle's interpretation hinges upon his unique critical reconstruction of the original text, a stance that, in my estimation, does not possess the robust evidence required for unreserved acceptance. In deconstructing the narrative into separate elements, however, Wöhrle undermines the duality inherent in Jacob's role as the trickster. While Wöhrle expounds on the political implications of Jacob's submission, drawing analogies with various Near Eastern contexts (pp. 318–20), I question the need to delve so meticulously into the motivations behind a younger brother's submission to an elder sibling. Familial tales often spotlight intense sibling rivalries, but they can also underscore profound bonds of kinship. Ultimately, it is crucial to perceive Jacob's submission in tandem with the overarching prophecy of the younger's eventual dominance – a fate the audience anticipates to unfold, even in the face of his present submission.

411 As for North Israel's alleged dominion over Edom in the eighth century, see Israel Finkelstein, "Jeroboam II in Transjordan," *SJOT* 34 (2020): 19–29, https://doi.org/10.1080/09018328.2020.1801910.

412 Cf. Sweeney, "The Jacob Narratives: An Ephraimitic Text?," 251–52.

413 Some scholars today suggest that Kuntillet Ajrud provides evidence for the Jacob-Esau tradition's eighth-century BCE background. However, the simple phrases "Yhwh of Samaria" and "Yhwh of Teman" are too weak to support this argument. See Finkelstein and Römer, "Comments on the Historical Background of the Jacob Narrative," 331–32; Matthias Köckert, "Wie wurden Abraham- und Jakobüberlieferung zu einer »Vätergeschichte« verbunden?," *HeBAI* 3 (2014): 65–66, https://doi.org/10.1628/219222714X13994465496866. While the cryptic pictograms and inscriptions on the pithoi are intriguing, one must caution against placing too much weight on them. See now Zeev Meshel, *Kuntillet 'Ajrud (Horvat Teman): An Iron Age II Religious Site on the Judah-Sinai Border* (Jerusalem: Israel Exploration Society, 2012).

414 Cf. Na'aman ("The Jacob Story and the Formation of Biblical Israel," 98), who posits a post-exilic date. However, in articulating this perspective, Na'aman seems to exaggerate the "bitter enmity" between Jacob and Esau to distance it from the monarchic era. He also contends that Aram's hostile position to Israel during the monarchic era is incongruent with the text's depiction of Aram's familial ties with Israel.

gard, one must not forget that the text features Esau and Laban, not Edom and Aram, which implies that the narrative has been adapted to suit the later monarchic contexts.[415] By positing that the foundational structure of the Jacob tradition dates back to a pre-Israelite era, we no longer need to search for a monarchic context that fits Jacob's seeming weaker status to Esau. Instead, one can see that this story is structured as a folk tradition of *Bene Ya'aqob* in which the underdog Jacob's triumph over Esau and Laban is celebrated. The main focus of this tale is not the identities of these characters but the way our hero secured victory against them.

This has implications to another tendency to attribute narrative segments to distinct geographic locales, a practice deeply rooted in tradition-historical scholarship. For example, Martin Noth understood the present narrative as a combination of the East Jordanian Jacob-Esau-Laban cycle and the West Jordan local traditions of Shechem and Bethel.[416] Noth viewed the East Jordan Jacob as relatively "alien" tradition, which needed to be *Israelized*. According to him, the Penuel episode (Gen 31:23–33) epitomizes the process where Jacob is not only renamed Israel but also adopts several Israelite ethnic markers.[417]

There are issues here. On one hand, while Noth suggests that the more "sacral" West Jordan traditions of Shechem and Bethel are closer to what we know as Israelite traditions compared to the more "worldly" ones of East Jordan,[418] one must question if there is anything that is truly "Israelite" about these traditions. These sites are recognized for the theophoric names El-Elohe-Israel (Gen 33:20) and El-Bethel (Gen 31:13, 35:7). These might imply a sacral nature, but they are hardly intrinsic to the "Israel" that we know in the Bible. It is more likely that these names were rooted in the self-identification of El-worshipping groups, signifying "IsraEl" in connection with these ancient Canaanite cultic sites.

---

415 Regarding the secondary nature of Laban's identification as an Aramean, see now Sergi, "Jacob and the Aramaean Identity of Ancient Israel," 293–94. Esau's connection with Edom/Seir has been debated more. See discussion in Dicou, *Edom, Israel's Brother and Antagonist*, 137–39. See also Noth, *Pentateuchal Traditions*, 95.

416 Noth, 79–101.

417 Noth, 100–101. Similarly, Finkelstein and Römer view the Penuel episode as a representation of the integration between the East Jordan *Bene Ya'aqob* and the West Jordan *Bene Yisrael*. They assert that the *Bene Ya'aqob* traditions, originating in the eleventh and tenth centuries BCE, was transported to Bethel by the eighth century and were subsequently adopted by the people of Jeroboam II's kingdom. Finkelstein and Römer, "Comments on the Historical Background of the Jacob Narrative," 324–26, esp. n. 33. While I concur that the Penuel episode is imbued with significant identity reformulation, I question whether its importance can be fully grasped when confined to the literary context of the Jacob tradition. This is a complex issue that I intend to address separately in the future.

418 See n. 401 above.

On the other hand, the Transjordanian orientation is not the most pronounced element for either the Jacob-Laban or Jacob-Esau cycle. In the present form, the border that separates Jacob and Laban is set in Gilead (Gen 31:1–54), whereas the border between Jacob and Esau is marked by Seir (Gen 33:16–17).[419] However, apart from the treaty-making events with Laban and Esau, no other prominent Transjordan locations play important roles in the remainder of the narrative. Granted, Mahanaim (Gen 32:2–3) and Penuel (32:23–33) appear at the end of the Jacob-Laban narrative; yet, these appear more representative of a transitional area that connects the two sides of Jordan, rather than being emblematic of the Transjordan region. Aside from these, the rest of the Jacob-Laban narrative unfolds in the city of Nahor,[420] far removed from the Transjordan area,

---

[419] Noth (*Pentateuchal Traditions*, 95) posits that Esau's residence was set in the area around Mahanaim and Penuel, before he is subsequently linked to Edom/Seir in the southern area.

[420] The exact location of the city of Nahor, where Laban resides, remains a matter of debate. The city is referred to by various names in biblical texts, including Haran (Gen 11:31; 12:4–5; 27:43; 28:10; 29:4), Paddan-aram (Gen 25:20; 28:2, 5, 6, 7; 31:18; 33:18; 35:9, 26; 46:15, all in P), and Aram-Naharaim (Gen 24:10, Μεσοποταμίαν in LXX). Each of the three designations suggests that the region in question is situated in Syria. Based on the name Haran, scholars have proposed two possible locations: Hauran in southern Syria and Harran in upper Mesopotamia. For instance, Finkelstein and Römer ("Comments on the Historical Background of the Jacob Narrative," 322–23), who suppose a pre-P Jacob tradition dating to the eighth century BCE, initially consider this to refer to Harran of Assyria but ultimately favor the original version indicating Aram. Likewise, Köckert ("Wie wurden Abraham- und Jakobüberlieferung," 65 n. 103) draws from the textual evidence and concludes that it points to Hauran of Syria. He has two points. Firstly, Gen 29:1 characterizes the location as "the land of the people of the east." Here, the region is defined from the perspective of the Cisjordan inhabitants, referring to the area east of their land. This is a rather abstract and subjective designation. Secondly, Gen 31:22–23 suggests that Jacob's caravan took ten days to reach Gilead, which suggests that this area was within Aram, located east of Gilead.

I agree with many of these points, but, ultimately, determining the precise location is not crucial for my purpose. Both sites were associated with Aram anyway, although the latter ultimately falls under Assyrian control playing a prominent part in the empire's final era. Moreover, I doubt that "Haran" in ancient Israelites' perception was rigidly tied to either of these sites. Instead, I find it plausible that the name Haran could be employed as a general reference for the larger Aram region, without specific delineation. Bear in mind that one should not assume that ancient people's perception of locales aligns with our own. Unlike moderns, whose perception is oriented in maps that provide linear boundaries and a bird's-eye view of the region, ancient people conceived areas from tended to conceive borders and boundaries more ambiguously, as their understanding of locations was based on points rather than lines. Put simply, the concept of a linear boundary was unrefined; instead, borders were perceived as marginal zones radiating from centers. See Hastings Donnan and Thomas M. Wilson, *Borders: Frontiers of Identity, Nation and State* (Oxford: Berg, 1999); Alexander C. Diener, *Borders: A Very Short Introduction* (New York: Oxford University Press, 2012).

whereas the Jacob-Esau tradition is otherwise characterized by a notable absence of geographic orientation.[421]

Thus, from my perspective, placing emphasis on the East and West Jordan binary is not particularly productive in understanding the early Jacob tradition.[422] Archaeological findings that emphasize the highlands east and west of the Jordan as a "single cultural unit within which agro-pastoral sedentary communities and more mobile population maintained constant interaction" further cast doubt on the validity of a rigid dichotomy.[423]

I propose to see the Jacob tradition as a reflection of the lives of indigenous people residing in the general area of Syria-Palestine, encompassing both sides of the Jordan, with Laban and Esau reflecting much more figurative and abstract representation as Others of *Bene Ya'aqob*. Note in this regard that the names within the tale – Jacob, Esau, and Laban – carry certain figurative resonance. Jacob is the "heeler (יַעֲקֹב)," Esau is the "red (אֱדֹמוֹנִי)" and "hairy (שֵׂעָר)," and Laban is the "white (לָבָן)." The narrative further incorporates Leah and Rachel, representing "cow" and "ewe" respectively, likely symbols of fertility, who eventually produce many children for Jacob.[424] Then, this folk tale narrates how the "heeler" cunningly outmaneuvers, or heels, the favored "red," leveraging both the red (Gen 25:30) and the hairy (Gen 27:11–23) traits of his rival. The "white" initially deceives the "heeler" by offering him the "cow" instead of the desired "ewe." Yet, the heeler turns this to his advantage as the "cow" bears him more children. Later, he outsmarts the "white" using a ruse that involves the white and speckled (Gen 30:25–43).

It is notable that more remote Others, such as Mesopotamia and Egypt, are absent in the Jacob narrative. While Laban the "white" could be associated with the region of Syria, there is no indication of Others located further north and east, like those representing Babylonia or Persia. Egypt, a significant Other in both the Joseph and Exodus narratives (as well as the Abraham narrative), is conspicuously absent in the Jacob story.[425] There are simply no mentions of regions south of Seir. Consequently, the geographic scope of the Jacob narrative is

---

421 Noth (*Pentateuchal Traditions*, 94) remarks, "the core of the entire Jacob-Esau story is devoid of any indication of place."

422 Scholars have further attempted to separate the Jacob-Laban and Jacob Esau into northern and southern Transjordan traditions or assigning them into different periods. Yet such attempts are unproductive, as they are so intricately intertwined that disentangling them would damage the present narrative structure. See Noth, *Pentateuchal Traditions*, 94.

423 Sergi, "Jacob and the Aramaean Identity of Ancient Israel," 292.

424 See Noth, *Pentateuchal Traditions*, 94.

425 Cf. Franz V. Greifenhagen, *Egypt on the Pentateuch's Ideological Map: Constructing Biblical Israel's Identity*, LHBOTS 361 (London: Bloomsbury, 2003).

largely confined to the Syria-Palestine area, without a substantial reference to major international powers.

This corresponds with the symbolic representations of Laban and Esau we have examined earlier. While not directly associated with specific political entities, these characters could serve as implicit geographical indicators to general areas surrounding Jacob's homeland, which seems to align roughly with the central Palestinian region. Laban the "white" is emblematic of the northern snow-capped mountainous terrains,[426] while Esau the "red" is reflective of the distinctive red soil found in the regions south of the Dead Sea. This suggests that the story was designed to address issues pertaining to regional politics within Syria-Palestine.[427]

This observation resonates well with the depiction of Jacob's connection to the land in the narrative. Unlike Abraham, whose identity as a resident alien in the land is emphasized (Gen 20:13; 23:4; 24:7),[428] Jacob is not portrayed as a sojourner in the land. Instead, his life journey is defined by his forced exile and eventual return to the homeland. Naturally, the perception of the land and its indigenous population is different. As an alien, Abraham owns no land, which makes the land promise a prominent motif.[429] Yet Jacob has no yearning for the land, and the land promise plays little role.[430] What he lacks is the birthright, and what he desires is the paternal blessing. The right to the land appears innate, contingent upon the acquisition of the birthright (Gen 27:27–29). Likewise, the indigenous peoples are not subject to harsh condemnation, with all such negative perceptions coming from later texts.[431] Unlike the Exodus narrative, where "Isra-

---

426 The color "white" aligns well with western Syria, distinguished by its mountainous terrain, including the coastal mountains along the Anti-Lebanon mountains. In fact, "Lebanon (לְבָנוֹן)" means "white" aptly describing the snow-capped peaks in the region. See Marvin A. Sweeney, *Tanak: A Theological and Critical Introduction to the Jewish Bible* (Minneapolis: Fortress, 2012), 72. However, this association is less fitting for eastern Syria, which is largely defined by plateau and desert landscapes. Thus, the characterization of "white" is applicable only in a broader, more generalized sense.

427 Yet the Jacob story could have been meant to function in tandem with its sequel, the Joseph story, which focuses predominantly on addressing international concerns involving Egypt.

428 Ska, "The Call of Abraham," 51–52.

429 Cf. scholarly observations of the indigenous character of Abraham in the early southern tradition. Römer, "Abraham Traditions in the Hebrew Bible Outside the Book of Genesis."

430 Cf. Noth, *Pentateuchal Traditions*, 90.

431 Shechem in Gen 34 is imbued with a derogatory perception of the indigenous people, but this part is likely a late addition. Recent scholars argue this as part of the Hexateuch redaction. See now Finkelstein and Römer, "Comments on the Historical Background of the Jacob Narrative," 336; Stephen Germany, "The Hexateuch Hypothesis: A History of Research and Current Approaches," *CurBR* 16 (2018): 131–56, https://doi.org/10.1177/1476993x17737067. Esau's marriage with indigenous women also receives criticism, but such perception is likely added in the

el" is defined by othering the inhabitants in the land (like Canaanites, Hittites, or Amorites), internal Others *within* Palestine play little role in the Jacob tradition before the Priestly retouching. The land is not depicted as being inhabited by abominable Others that "we" need to drive out. Instead, "we" are in the land and the land is perceived as "ours," and there is no need to demonize its inhabitants or assert ownership over it. This could be explained in various ways, but, to me, it suggests the intrinsic connection between *Bene Ya'aqob* and the land. There is no emphasis on demonizing its occupants or asserting a new claim of ownership.

9.5 Conclusion

The Jacob narrative began as a tale of the trickster hero Jacob, the progenitor of *Bene Ya'aqob*. The exact identity of *Bene Ya'aqob* remains elusive, but it is evident that they constituted a notable segment of what eventually became "Israel." This playful character employs wit to secure the right to the land, all under the guidance of El. While difficult to prove, this underdog tale seems more reflective of those marginalized by the powerful Canaanite city-states, rather than serving as a narrative for those who held dominance in the region. Regardless, the way the people behind the story negotiated their identity with their neighbors, Laban and Esau, was largely nonviolent and good-humored. Jacob may not have been a conventional hero, but he managed to secure the boundary of the habitable land for his descendants, making him a hero for ordinary people.

A significant portion of those who would later identify as "Israelites" belonged to these indigenous people. Alongside them, their stories too were embraced, gradually becoming an integral strand woven into the tapestry of Israel's mythic past. The incorporated story continually underwent necessary adaptation, and with it, the perception of Jacob and its people also changed gradually. The story's clear geographic focus on key northern sites of the central highland, their Yahwistic conversion, and its plot structure emphasizing the leadership of the Joseph clans all point to the subsequent efforts made for Israelite adaptation.

The fusion of the Jacob and Exodus traditions into a cohesive narrative, establishing the dual origin myths of Israel, epitomizes the negotiation between the dual personas of Israel. While the scholarly discussion has centered on determining when this merging took place, such concerns are peripheral to my objective.[432] Whether combined or not, these two narratives consistently engaged in a

---

Priestly layer (Gen 26:34–35, 28:1–5; 6–9), which redefines Jacob's exile as a journey for a proper wife.

432 Still, it should be clear by now that I prefer an earlier date, contrasting the emergent viewpoint that attributes the combination to the Priestly author.

dialogue. Despite the consistent efforts of the Yhwh-only group behind the Exodus tradition, the deeply ingrained indigenous culture was never entirely subdued or purged. It continually reemerged and challenged the program of total transformation, and the very presence of the Jacob tradition in our Bible stands testament to its enduring resilience.

It is against this backdrop that I aim to examine the impact and significance of Judah's Abrahamic expansion. The introduction of the Abraham tradition to Northern Israel's dual origin myths marked a radical transformation, casting new light and shadows upon both Jacob and Exodus traditions.

10 Abraham and Forward Expansion of Israel's Past: A Perspective from Ancient Korean History

Since the establishment of the Rendtorff-Blum model, an examination of the Judahite reworking of the earlier Jacob tradition has been routinely treated by redaction-critical studies. Yet scholarly interests have been largely fixed on literary-critical matters, with less attention devoted to the social implications behind the merging of traditions. What do we make of the expansion of Israel's ancestral past from Jacob to Abraham-Isaac-Jacob in terms of Judah's identity negotiation? I contend that this forward expansion of Israel's history, in the southern edition of the book of Genesis, represents a pivotal identity project undertaken by the Judahites.[433] This is no mere product of traditional or literary growth but rather a critical discursive attempt to rewrite Israel's past. Such significance has been overlooked largely because of the enormous success of this reformulation.[434] Most readers of the Bible have come to accept the reinvented past, i.e., the Abrahamic Israel, as a given. What is required is a functional analysis of the Abrahamic reframing of the Jacob tradition to lay bare its consequence to Judah's imagination of "who we are."

Reimagining a nation's origin in response to a changed political dynamic is a common phenomenon. As reviewed above (Section 7.2), no origin myth merely conveys or preserves the fixed past. It rewrites the past to suit needs of the present. Take, for instance, how Bruce Lincoln describes functionality of myths:

> Consider, for instance, what happens when individuals rally groups around themselves in a situation of conflict. To take an arbitrary example, when a man of lineage 1 struggles with a man of lineage 2, they invoke Ancestors 1 and 2, respectively, that is, the apical ancestors from whom they and all members of their lineages claim descent-but not more remote antecedents nor others more proximate. When the time arrives to make peace, however, they invoke Ancestor A together: the figure through whose recollection may be formed that social group in which they are reunited.[435]

Lincoln here highlights the incredible flexibility of the past that caters to the ever-changing interests and demands of the present. Lincoln then provides a

---

433 Cf. Van Seters, *In Search of History*, 359–62.
434 Similarly, Davies (*In Search of 'Ancient Israel,'* 114) has remarked: "The ideological triumph of the biblical story is to convince that what is new is actually old. It has been successful to the point of establishing a virtually unchallenged premise of biblical scholarship."
435 Lincoln, *Discourse and the Construction of Society*, 20.

https://doi.org/10.1515/9783111376554-010

striking illustration of the "strategic tinkering with the past" taken place between the Nuer, a people of the Nilotic Sudan, and their neighboring Dinka people,[436] introducing Evans-Pritchard's classic field work.[437]

In this chapter, I present a similar case of rewriting the past in Korean ancient history as a point of comparison that highlights the function of the Abrahamic expansion of Israel's ancestral past in terms of Judah's identity reformation.

10.1 Dangun and Multiple Kingdoms in Ancient Korea

Like Israel, Korea purports to be a highly homogenous ethnic group and yet includes politically divergent subgroups located in specific regions. Even within South Korea, lingering regional tensions persist, often resurfacing during significant political events, such as Presidential elections. That may be true for any modern nation, like in the U.S. What is special in Korea is that the regional division has much deeper root, often of thousands of years of political conflict. With rises and falls, coalitions and ruptures of many political entities left us with elaborate stories and histories at each stage. These stories reflect residues of the on-going political interests and struggles of the people of the time; thus, it presents great examples of how the world of story reflects and interacts with the world of reality. The Period of the Three Kingdoms and the ensuing eras of the unified monarchy in Korean history are particularly noteworthy. These periods demonstrate notable similarity with the monarchic era of Israel and Judah, particularly with regard to the transitional era when the political division between Israel and Judah dissolved. Judah remained a singular political authority from the late eighth century until its fall in the early sixth century BCE. Of significance is the similar dynamic in which rewriting ancestry served the needs of the newly established unified kingdom. It is certain that a comparison of such divergent parties entails a danger of generalization. Yet with due caution, it may expand new perspectives to the old, familiar phenomenon.

10.1.1 Myth of One Father

Koreans have long maintained a remarkably high sense of ethnic homogeneity. As discussed above (Section 2.2.), the tragic rupture of North and South Korea

---

436 Lincoln, 21–23.
437 E. E. Evans-Pritchard, *The Nuer: A Description of the Modes of Livelihood and Political Institutions of a Nilotic People* (Oxford: Clarendon, 1940).

demonstrates that the sense of ethnic unity is barely strong enough as a force to retain political unity.[438] Despite the political division, the people of the two Koreas still take it for granted that they are one people, at least ethnically. Ethnic studies inform how a sense of ethnic unity is constructed. According to Hutchinson and Smith, several key elements construct the sense of one people: (1) a common proper name, (2) a myth of common ancestry, (3) shared historical memories, (4) one or more elements of common culture, (5) a link with a homeland, and (6) a sense of solidarity.[439] Korean people share many of these elements that bind them together and provide a sense of oneness.[440] Perhaps the most tangible among them include a common language,[441] a relatively segregated homeland in the Korean peninsula, and recent shared historical memories, particularly of collective strife against common enemies, such as Mongolia, China, and Japan. Yet, the sense of unity provided by these elements was not given from the beginning. It rather is a product of a long social life, during which original diversity in smaller scales has been flattened out.

---

438 In South Korea, the longing for reunification has been persistent since the division after the Korean War. However, as the war generation gives way to successors with no direct experience of the conflict and no tangible connection to North Korea's people and land, this sentiment seems to be gradually waning. For a recent report on this, see Jiyoon Kim et al., *South Korean Attitudes toward North Korea and Reunification*, Asan Report (Seoul: The Asan Institute for Policy Studies, 2015), http://en.asaninst.org/contents/south-korean-attitudes-toward-north-korea-and-reunification/ [retrieved 12. 06. 2017]

439 Hutchinson and Smith, *Ethnicity*, 6–7. The list is a summary prepared by Hutchinson and Smith citing the thesis of R. A. Schermerhorn, *Comparative Ethnic Relations: A Framework for Theory and Research* (Chicago: University of Chicago Press, 1978), 12.

440 Unlike in Israel, religion has not been the mainstay of Korean homogeneity. Buddhism and Confucianism have been the predominant religions in Korea, with Christianity emerging more recently. However, all these religions originated from outside Korea. While Buddhism has occasionally played a unifying role in Korean history, it does not fundamentally underpin Korea's ethnic unity.

441 Today, Koreans speak a language distinct from those of neighboring nations, serving as a cornerstone in fostering and solidifying a sense of national identity. However, pinpointing when Koreans adopted this unique and standardized language is debatable. Historical linguistics highlights its unique and isolated characteristics, yet significant dialectic variations persist across provinces. For instance, the differences between *Jeju* Island and mainland Korea are so marked that they can obstruct mutual understanding. In ancient times, these regional disparities were likely even more pronounced. Conversely, residents in the border areas often communicate with people of neighboring territories with relative ease. This suggests that relying solely on language as an inherent ethnic identifier can be misleading. Language, after all, is fluid and dynamic, evolving and adapting in response to sociopolitical changes, rather than serving as a static ethnic marker. The contemporary uniformity and distinctiveness of the Korean language may primarily be a result of extended standardization following political unification.

Playing a pertinent role in instilling the sense of unity among Koreans is a shared origin myth: the legend of Dangun (=Tangun, Tan'gun).[442] According to ancient legend, Dangun is the son of Hwanung, the son of the celestial deity Hwanin, who descended from heaven to the Korean peninsula, though the exact location of his descent remains a matter of dispute. The legend goes that the divine ruler was approached by a tigress and a she-bear who pleaded him to turn them into human. He put them to a test and ordered them to incarcerate themselves in a cave in which they were only allowed to consume garlic and wormwood. The tigress failed the test, but the she-bear endured. The she-bear transformed into a woman after twenty one days. Hwanung married her and the son born of this union was Dangun who later established the Kingdom of Chosŏn in 2333 BCE[443] at Pyongyang;[444] he allegedly ruled the kingdom for 1500 years before he finally turned into a mountain god at the age of 1908.[445]

A mythical undertone is evident, and most Koreans do not take this legend to be a historical fact, and historians continue to debate if the Kingdom of Chosŏn that Dangun allegedly founded can be considered as Korea's political origin.[446] This story yet continues to play a pivotal role in maintaining a sense of unity among Koreans. The question is when this figure began serving this role in the collective mind of the Korean people. I often raise this question about when Koreans began to perceive themselves as one people in my undergraduate classes. Whenever I do so, I see many puzzled faces staring back at me. Apparently, this question seldom occurred to college students. It is not that they took this myth to be a historical account but that the alleged claim of unity behind the myth has been taken for granted. Yet, it does not take long for my students to realize the point and acknowledge that the sense of unity, of whatever kind, could not have existed from the beginning of a social and political life of the early settlers who first migrated into the Korean peninsula. There must have been a period from

---

442 The myth of Dangun is introduced in *Samguk yusa*. Seth, *A Concise History of Korea*, 128. For an English translation, see Iryŏn, *Samguk Yusa: Legends and History of the Three Kingdoms of Ancient Korea*, trans. Tae Hung Ha and Grafton K. Mintz (Seoul: Yonsei University Press, 1972), 32–33. For a brief introduction, see Grayson, *Myths and Legends from Korea*, 30–62.

443 Calculating from this date, Koreans customarily speak of and take pride in the long history (five thousand years) of their country.

444 Indeed, the capital city of North Korea. While this city may be widely known for its frequent feature in world news these days, not many know that Pyongyang has been the center of the Great Revival in 1907 and often called Korea's new Jerusalem, before the center of Korean Christianity migrated into Seoul after the Korean War. See Robert E. Buswell Jr. and Timothy S. Lee, eds., *Christianity in Korea* (Honolulu: University of Hawaii Press, 2006), 316–17.

445 Iryŏn, *Samguk Yusa*, 33.

446 See Pai, *Constructing "Korean" Origins*.

which this story began to occupy the minds of the Korean people of disparate origins and function as a basis for unifying them. My students know this because at the heart of Korean ancient history lies the Three Kingdoms Period, in which multiple kingdoms ruled different parts of the Korean peninsula. Further, they all know for a certainty that these kingdoms existed as independent political entities, with frequent military conflicts that are well documented, not only in textbooks but also in films and other popular media. Students gradually understand that the sense of one people, "the Han people" as we call ourselves in Korea today,[447] does not have as long a history or as tangible a basis as they have presumed. Scholars in fact still debate when the concept of one people originated in Korean history. It was not until the beginning of the united monarchy, which began in the seventh century CE, that the political union, which is a prerequisite for a sense of unity, arose in the Korean peninsula. Most scholarly contentions debating the time when the sense of the ethnic unity emerged in Korea highlight this era. To better understand the significance of this alleged unification, we need to briefly outline the history of the Period of the Three Kingdoms that preceded it.[448]

10.1.2 Period of the Three Kingdoms

Sometime in the first half of the first millennium, three kingdoms emerged and dominated the political affairs in the land of Korea: Koguryŏ, Paekche, and Silla (see Tab. 2 in 4.1.).[449] Koguryŏ ruled the northern part of the peninsula and a significant part of Manchuria (northeast China and north of Korean peninsula).[450] It was a strong kingdom that protected Korea's northern border from the major

---

447 This "Han (韓)" is different from the "Han (漢)" of Han Chinese, discussed above in Chapter 5.

448 To follow a history of a foreign country is a difficult task. I have no intention to bombard unnecessary details in this discussion. Rather, my presentation will be brief, selective, and sketchy. For more details, one may want to consult other resources. Several versions of Korean history are now available in English. Seth, *A Concise History of Korea*; Jinwung Kim, *A History of Korea: From "Land of the Morning Calm" to States in Conflict* (Bloomington: Indiana University Press, 2012); Keith L. Pratt, *Everlasting Flower: A History of Korea* (London: Reaktion Books, 2006); Kyung Moon Hwang, *A History of Korea: An Episodic Narrative*, Palgrave Essential Histories (Basingstoke: Palgrave Macmillan, 2010).

449 See the map of the Three Kingdoms Period (Fig. 2) in Section 4.1.1. According to *Samguk Sagi*, the three kingdoms had their origins in the first century BCE, but this early date may be debatable. For more details, Seth, *A Concise History of Korea*, 29–50.

450 This is the same area that I have described as the home of the Manchu clan that later founds the Qing dynasty discussed above in Chapter 6.

powerhouses of China, Mongol, and several nomadic clans, such as Khitan. The other two kingdoms divided the southern part of the Peninsula, Paekche on the western and Silla on the eastern side. The territory of Paekche largely corresponds with the modern province of Jeolla-do and Silla with Kyonsang-do.[451]

During the Period of the Three Kingdoms, each kingdom enjoyed political independence and separate group identities. Each kingdom occupied their own lands and had different names, cultures and dialects, as well as origin myths pertaining to the birth of their eponymous ancestors. One must not downplay the effect of their political independence in favor of the alleged ethnic, cultural, and linguistic affinities. The idea of mutual affinities is mostly late and imposed upon the early period when they were yet to develop a sense of one people. I am not denying that these peoples, living in a relatively isolated environment within the peninsula, share more commonality against outsiders such as China and Japan. However, their relative commonality and distinctness from outsiders should not obstruct their sense of independence and political rivalry on a smaller scale. Group identity is a social function that is relative and situational. During the Period of the Three Kingdoms, each kingdom posed a serious threat to the others, leading to their distinctiveness being salienced at the expense of any shared commonalities, unless the three kingdoms were forced into a situation in which they had to fight against a common enemy. During the entire Period of the Three Kingdoms, however, one hardly finds an occasion in which the three Korean kingdoms allied together against an external threat, similar to how the Israelite tribes occasionally did before the rise of the monarchy. The way in which the three kingdoms united is instructive in this regard. As will be observed in later sections, Silla united the three kingdoms. Yet Silla's unification, and the destruction of the other two countries, was made possible only through the alliance and military aid from the Tang Empire of China (618–907 CE), a complete outsider.[452] The fact that Silla was willing to make an alliance with the others to conquer Paekche and Koguryŏ may indicate that the people of Silla had not yet developed a sense of one people with Paekche and Koguryŏ, at least not to the degree that would halt their political gains.

Against this backdrop, the fact that each kingdom maintained elaborate stories of the mysterious birth of their founders must be considered in a serious manner. I shall not go into details about each of the origin legends, which will

---

451 Even within modern South Korea, residues of the division persist between the two southern provinces, Jeolla-do and Kyongsang-do, which inherited the territories of ancient kingdoms of Paekche and Silla respectively. Though their relations have been further marred by more recent political incidents, the fundamental division between the two regions has a much longer history.
452 Seth, *A Concise History of Korea*, 47.

unnecessarily complicate our discussion. It is sufficient to note that each kingdom maintained its own origin myths that apparently functioned as a basis to maintain its individual group identity. Given the assertion provided in ethnic studies that a sense of ethnic unity is not factual but a social construct, the implications of their separate origin stories should not be overlooked. Apparently, these stories were used within their group reinforcing their independent social identity.

By embracing these stories, each kingdom drew a line between Them and Us and expressed its independent identity as a separate people. Participation in a story constitutes an important act of forming a group identity. By accepting a story as one's own, one participates in the collective experience depicted in it and accepts values expressed in it. Participating in a story of a historical incident, even of a distant past to which participants have no physical connections, provides them a sense of solidarity. Participating in a story of a common ancestor instills them a sense of fictive kinship. This is how a nation is built or maintained. The rise of a common identity as one people of Korea arrived late on the scene not as an inherent and natural trait but out of the necessity of an altered political setting of the new era of unity.

10.1.3 Unification and the Myth of Dangun

After centuries of political confrontation and coexistence,[453] a new era of unity emerged. Silla eventually overcame the others and united the three kingdoms in the latter half of the seventh century CE, opening the new era of the united monarchy in the Korean peninsula: the United Silla (=late Silla). The United Silla prospered for a while but soon exhausted its life and succumbed to another kingdom Koryŏ, a dynasty founded by the purported remnants of the old Koguryŏ (in 918 CE).[454] The Koryŏ dynasty lasted for about 500 years,[455] enduring a tumultuous era of frequent invasions, most notably from the Mongol Empire that swept the entire continent of Asia.

---

453 There were frequent shifts in their political rivalries, which were also inherently related to the external power dynamics in larger East Asia, of which China and Central Asians, such as Mongols, were major participants. Japan later loomed large in East Asia but at this point was largely isolated, though frequent exchanges are documented with southern kingdoms in the Korean peninsula.

454 The name "Korea," or "Corea," derives from this period.

455 When Koryŏ finally fell, it was replaced by another dynasty, Chosŏn that lasted until the dawn of the modern era, marked by the tragic onset of Japanese colonial infiltration. See Seth, 241–78.

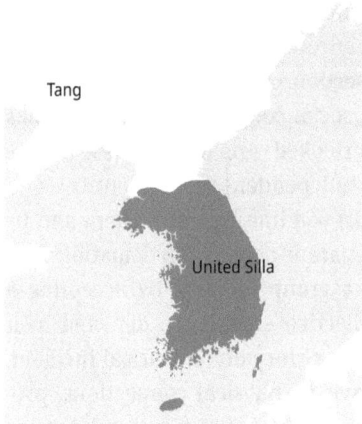

Fig. 3: Unification by Silla (668 CE).

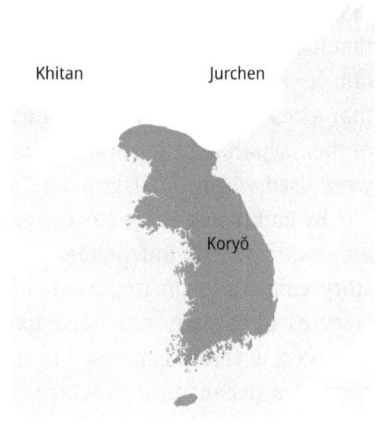

Fig. 4: Emergence of Koryŏ (918 CE).
Illustrations by Kim Minji.

It was in this time of unity when the myth of Dangun appeared in the ancient historiography of Korea. The legend was first featured in one of the major historical works of Koryŏ, *Samguk yusa* (*Memorabilia of the Three Kingdoms*), written at the end of the 13th century CE by a Buddhist monk Iryŏn.[456] The myth appears to be a part of the resources that the author gathered because the source material, though not extant today, is clearly cited. Regardless of its origin, however, what we do know is that it was by the time of Koryŏ, that the myth began to occupy a space in the collective minds of the people of Korea. Even though it was known during an earlier time, the myth was at least not foregrounded as the default basis for their group identity. What prompted this myth to be elevated to the central position of the collective memory of the past?[457]

When separate groups are forced to merge into a single group, factions among constituent elements of its population pose a constant threat to the unity and coexistence within the new order. Efforts to offset factions and unify popular basis emerge as crucial tasks of domestic politics. To that end, the past provides an ideal space.[458] As discussed above, the past is not a fixed space. In response to the changed political landscape, the past is reimagined, rewritten, and refo-

---

456 Seth, 128.
457 I am not arguing that this process of legitimation began immediately with the establishment of the kingdom. In fact, *Samguk yusa* appeared quite later and many consider it as being part of collective efforts against the Mongol invasion in the 13th century CE. For the invasion of the Mongol Empire, see Seth, 118–21.
458 See Lincoln, *Discourse and the Construction of Society*, 27–29.

cused for serving the interests of a political reality. My purpose is to demonstrate what type of space Dangun created for the era of the united monarchy. One can speculate that such efforts began with the United Silla, but no written historiography from that period has been preserved. Fortunately, two major historical works from Koryŏ are available, which provide a direct witness to how ancestral myth played a role in Koryŏ's historiography in reorienting the past.[459]

One of the unique features of *Samguk yusa* is the manner in which this history begins. *Samguk yusa*, despite its title (*Memorabilia of the Three Kingdoms*), does not begin its history with the three kingdoms. It begins with an account of Dangun, tracing the history of Korea back to the prehistorical era.[460] This story functions as a preface to the history of the three kingdoms that follow. This mythical preface, regardless of the original intent of the author, has left lasting impressions on the collective consciousness of the Korean people, serving as a focal point for their common origin. Two points require our attention.

First, Dangun becomes the father of all three kingdoms. The efficacy of the Dangun myth comes out of its claim for the foundational, prehistorical era. The Period of the Three Kingdoms belongs to the historical era that is well-occupied by notable figures and historical events in people's mind. Combining the history of the three kingdoms into one may have been an effective means to bolster Koryŏ's status as the heir of all three kingdoms, thus nurturing a sense of unity. Still, little could be done in terms of its actual contents of history, which is fraught with conflicting relations among the three kingdoms. Against this, the realm of prehistory has distinct advantages. Its space, less densely populated by memories, is more malleable to a historian's shaping. Thus, legendary, if not fictive, characters, events, or relations can be more easily established in that space. Furthermore, anteriority usually supports significance in history.[461] Being early, not to mention being the first, bestows right and authority. By promoting a mythic figure Dangun, the historian creates a space of primordial unity at the beginning of

---

459 The other major historical work along with *Samguk yusa* is *Samguk sagi* (*History of the Three Kingdoms*). See Seth, *A Concise History of Korea*, 15–16, 100–102. Completed in 1145 CE, this is the more official version of Koryŏ's history composed by Kim Bushik, a prominent official and scholar in Koryŏ dynasty. Unlike *Samguk yusa*, which begins its historical presentation as early as the Dangun era, *Samguk sagi* begins with the period of the Three Kingdoms and comprises detailed history of each of the three kingdoms that predated Koryŏ and the United Silla. The structure in itself may indicate the historian's interest to unite disparate peoples into one by demonstrating that Koryŏ inherits all three kingdoms. It is an effective means to rally support from the three sectors within its popular basis.

460 In fact, human habitation in the Korean peninsula predates the period of Dangun. Archaeology reveals that the remains of the Paleolithic habitation is found in North East Korea and has been dated back 400,000 years. See Seth, *A Concise History of Korea*, 10.

461 See n. 472 below.

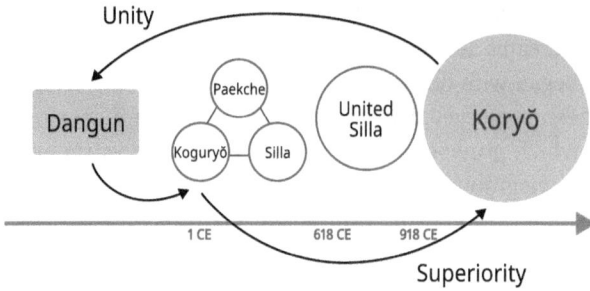

Fig. 5: Function of Dangun Myth. Illustration by Kim Minji.

history. The seed of unity is planted, ahead of the historical era, and by doing so, any political division afterward is pre-emptively oriented to the initial unity.

Second, another feature of *Samguk yusa*'s use of Dangun is that he is depicted as the father of Jumong, the founder of the kingdom of Koguryŏ, one of the Three Kingdoms. This information is featured in a separate section of the royal chronicles. The narrative account of Jumong features a comment as well regarding his potential kinship tie with Dangun through his maternal line.[462] The origin and significance of these notes are debated, but at least one could posit that there has been an effort to connect Jumong's lineage with Dangun one way or the other. In another tradition, Jumong's father is cited as Hemosu who is, like Dangun, depicted as a heavenly figure as well. Then, these may well be variant traditions that attempt to stress Jumong's heavenly origin. Such attempts to establish a fictive kinship between Jumong and Dangun have serious implications for Koryŏ that purports to inherit the legacy of the old, mighty kingdom of Koguryŏ in the Period of the Three Kingdoms. The name "Koryŏ" in fact was nothing but the alternative name used together with Koguryŏ, already attested by the 5th century CE.[463] That is, the founders of this new dynasty named their country after the old kingdom of Koguryŏ/Koryŏ. For the kingdom of Koryŏ, which needed to overcome the long legacy of the incumbent Silla, then, claiming unity through Dangun provided an implicit legitimation to their supremacy by means of an underlying claim of Dangun's connection with the founder of Koguryŏ, whose legacy they claim to inherit.

When such a story is received by people, its reception shapes people's viewpoint. It becomes part of a collective memory that affects the sense of identity. One's identity is shaped by a series of participation in stories and memo-

---

462 Iryŏn, *Samguk Yusa*, 45.
463 The distinction between the old Koguryŏ and the late Koryŏ is artificial, one introduced by historians to avoid confusion.

ries.[464] What I am pointing out is an apparent dynamic in which the rewritten past serves the political needs of a later time and eventually fossilizes into a tangible part of people's identity.

10.2 Functionality of Abraham's Principal Position

I admit that the analogy between ancient Korea and Israel may not be entirely in consonance. Despite differences in detail, however, there is some common ground between Koryŏ and Judah in the aftermath of Samaria's fall. On the one hand, Koryŏ and Judah needed grounds to unite disparate elements within the kingdom.[465] At the same time, they required a basis that would distinguish them from the incumbent hegemony (i.e., Silla for Koryŏ and Northern Israel for Judah) and underscore their unique and superior identities. These needs constitute the two ends of the symmetry within which the basic structure of their origin myths is constructed. In Korea, Dangun plays a major role in addressing these two-fold needs for Koryŏ. In Israel's ancestral history, it is Abraham who accomplishes this dual role for Judah.[466] Similar to how Dangun creates a space of union in the collective memory where a common origin of all three kingdoms is planted in the period preceding the era of division, Abraham, placed ahead of Jacob, serves the same purpose in the Israelite genealogy. Further, just as Koryŏ underscores their supremacy by genealogically linking their father Jumong (the founder of Koguryŏ that Koryŏ claims to inherit) with Dangun, Judah does so by putting Abraham, whose inherent tie with the southern clans is no secret, ahead of Jacob.[467]

---

464 To be sure, people do not buy into every story. People resist strange, unfamiliar stories. It is yet observed that certain circumstances function as a catalyst for willing participation. A common external threat is among the most notable catalyst of such. It consolidates solidarity among disparate parties within a group. It is no accident that *Samguk yusa* was composed during the most serious national crisis of Koryŏ in the face of the Mongol invasion. Seth, *A Concise History of Korea*, 122.

465 Cf. Na'aman, "The Jacob Story and the Formation of Biblical Israel," 118–19.

466 Some of these roles are mirrored in David, and the function of Abraham in ancestral history is matched by that of David in monarchic history. David constructs a golden era during the early years of the Israelite monarchy. Abraham constructs a space in Israel's genealogy in which the father of the south functions as the progenitor of Israel and neighboring kingdoms. By positioning the golden era of David at the outset of the monarchic history and attributing the blame for its tragic rupture to Northern Israel, the Deuteronomistic History legitimizes Judah's claim to inherit Israel's legacy.

467 These reworkings of the past also resemble the Assyrian scribes' redirection of the earlier Babylonian tradition that we have discussed in Section 3.2. above. After Sennacherib's conquest of Babylonia, Assyrian scribes reworked Enūma Eliš, the foundational Babylonian epic of creation. One of the decisive changes made by this Assyrian reworking is that the Babylonian god

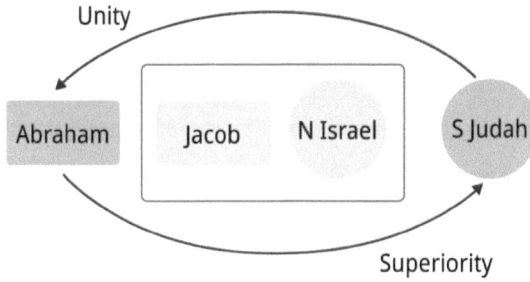

Fig. 6: Function of Abraham Narrative. Illustration by Kim Minji.

The functional import of the present position of Abraham ahead of Jacob cannot be stressed more.[468] The era of Jacob is already occupied with stories of Jacob and his household. Within this era, Judah might claim the right to belong to Jacob's household or membership with the early tribal league, but they could never escape the shade of Jacob, a popular northern figure, with whom they had a less tie, if at all, than northern tribes. Judah did strive to attain that position, which is reflected in the Judean redactional layers of the Jacob narrative.[469] Still, despite their efforts, the supreme position of the Joseph clans that are embedded in the plot structure is hardly affected.

In addition, placing Abraham ahead of Jacob provided a much more proactive and radical way of redefining Israel's past.[470] Rather than continue to work

---

Marduk was replaced by Assyrian Ashur. Furthermore, Ashur is spelled AN.ŠAR, the name of a god who preceded Marduk in the Babylonian theogony. See Na'aman, "The Israelite-Judahite Struggle for the Patrimony," 12. For a detailed discussion, see W. G. Lambert, "The Assyrian Recension of Enūma Eliš," in *Assyrien im Wandel der Zeiten*, ed. Hartmut Waetzoldt and Harald Hauptmann, HSAO 6 (Heidelberg: Heidelberger Orientverlag, 1997), 77–79. The ramifications of this reworking are apparent: it not only solidifies Assyria's place in the Mesopotamian mythical world but also legitimizes Assyria's supremacy over Babylonia. Just as Assyrian scribes elevated the status of their god, Judean scribes placed Abraham at a higher position than Jacob in genealogy.

468 For a more detailed discussion, see Hong, "The Deceptive Pen of Scribes," 437–41. Cf. Na'aman, "The Israelite-Judahite Struggle for the Patrimony."

469 In the larger scale, the very fact that Judeans did not choose to forget so many northern traditions of Jacob, Moses, Hosea, and Elijah, evinces their willingness to participate in this old heritage and ultimately appropriate it as their own. I personally very much appreciate the triumph of this inclusive stance over against the exclusionary one that might have expunged much of the Israelite heritage.

470 It is not implied here that this difference must have resulted from, or can be literary-critically traced back to, two different layers of redactions. Cf. Carr, *Reading the Fractures*, 203–4.

around the densely populated space occupied by the story of Jacob, Judahites began to explore a space prior to Jacob's generation by planting and cultivating stories of their own. That is to say, in addition to revising the existing Jacob tradition to serve their interests, the Judahite redactors inserted their own Abraham tradition at the foundation of Israel's ancestral past. By adding the Abraham tradition ahead of the Jacob story,[471] the Judahite redactors paved the way for one of the most radical reformulations of Israel's past. The ancestral history of Israel is radically reframed around Abraham. With the exalted state of Abraham, a southern father, Judah now has a space to claim its supremacy over the northern tribes. Jacob may still be remembered as the eponymous ancestor of Israel, but Abraham takes over the founding place as the *first* father of Israel.[472] He thus takes the first space of what later becomes a formulaic expression the triad of the Israelite ancestry, "Abraham, Isaac, and Jacob." In this newly structured genealogy, Judahites could find a way to redefine their identity without wiping out, or forgetting, the memory of Jacob. Israel is redefined and Jacob's role is qualified. As such, the Judean revision's two-track program ensures Judah's membership in Israel, and, at the same time, justifies Judah's leading role in it. Abraham, *our* father, is claimed as the founding figure of Israelite ancestry.

I stress the innovative nature of this reformulation in terms of Judah's identity formation. For the Judahites, this is one of the decisive moments in which they expressed their bold imagination of their collective Self as the new Israel, which was facilitated by a creative rewriting of the past.[473] While the earlier northern tradition was preserved, it served as a foundation for the newly envisioned ancestral past. This foundation, however, underwent a dramatic transformation with the integration of the Abraham tradition. I see this an invention of the past, not in the sense that all the stories were fictive, but in the sense that the significant impact of the rewriting of Israel's past must be recognized. To be sure, a rewritten

---

471 Evidence suggests that Abraham emerged late, compared to Jacob, in biblical tradition. See, e.g., Römer, "Abraham Traditions in the Hebrew Bible Outside the Book of Genesis."

472 Cf. Ska's intriguing discussion of Abraham's advanced age. In explaining Abraham's considerable age as a striking narrative trait, he ("Essay on the Nature and Meaning of the Abraham Cycle," 34) observes, "The reason is most likely cultural. In the ancient world and in the biblical world an old man is venerated, honoured, but he can hardly be argued with. No doubt for this reason he was chosen as Israel's first ancestor to the detriment of Jacob." This might sound perplexing to some, considering Abraham's current prominence in Israel's genealogy. However, when set against an earlier context in which they were independent competing figures, it suddenly becomes more comprehensible that Abraham's venerable age might have played a role as a contributing factor.

473 Cf. a similar observation in Ska, "Essay on the Nature and Meaning of the Abraham Cycle," 35.

history may not have immediately affected the collective memory of the past. But when this reformulation of the ancestral history by the hand of southerners later formed the foundation of the Torah, as authoritative religious text, it began to decisively influence those who conceive themselves as Abraham's descendants. Slowly and steadily, the once independent and competing fathers of Israel and Judah began to co-inhabit individuals' minds as Israel's common past.[474] Eventually, Abraham shares not only a place in Israel's ancestry as one of the fathers but the leading position in it. This is a revolution in Judah's self-definition. Judah no longer is a minor party that always was under the shadow of the dominant northern neighbor,[475] who owned decorated past stories such as Jacob, Moses, and Elijah. No longer mere spectators of the prominent Yahwistic heritage to their north, the Judahites began to perceive themselves as the new Israel, the rightful heir to the Yahwistic covenant.[476]

The consequence of the Abrahamic expansion has been tremendous, which I shall detail in the following chapter. This restructuring of Israel's past, situated at the outset of the Torah, was so effective that it thereafter dictated readers' understanding of Israel such that without Abraham, Israelite identity became unthinkable.[477] Abraham, who was virtually non-existent as a father figure in early biblical literature,[478] emerges as the central figure in post-Hebrew Bible literature, including the Christian New Testament. In due time, the Abrahamic circumcision grows into the foundational identity marker of Jewishness, and the significance given to this rite as an identity marker has everything to do with its embryonic position (Gen 17).[479]

Finally, our discussion has important implications for dating the Abrahamic tradition. While most critics today stress the exilic background of the Abraham narrative, the polemical nature inherent in the choice and placement of Abraham

---

474 In the apocryphal literature, the attention given to Abraham (33 times) increased almost comparably to that of Jacob (43 times), and then, in the New Testament, Abraham occurs 69 times and Jacob 26 times. This perhaps signifies a growing reputation of Abraham as the founding ancestor of Israel.

475 Finkelstein and Silberman, *The Bible Unearthed*, 146–50.

476 Na'aman, "The Israelite-Judahite Struggle for the Patrimony"; Hong, "The Deceptive Pen of Scribes."

477 Cf. Joachim Schaper, "Torah and Identity in the Persian Period," in *Judah and the Judeans in the Achaemenid Period*, ed. Oded Lipschits, Gary N. Knoppers, and Manfred Oeming (Winona Lake, IN: Eisenbrauns, 2011), 27–38.

478 See, e.g., Römer, "Abraham Traditions in the Hebrew Bible Outside the Book of Genesis," 159–80; Hong, "Abraham, Genesis 20–22, and the Northern Elohist," 337.

479 See Matthew Thiessen, *Contesting Conversion: Genealogy, Circumcision, and Identity in Ancient Judaism and Christianity* (New York: Oxford University Press, 2011).

is hardly justified by its exilic dating. It has been argued that living up to the inclusive spirit of the Persian period, Abraham served as the "ecumenical" ancestral figure.[480] It is undoubtedly true that the Judeans had gone into subsequent stages of identity struggle, and I believe Abraham became a major vehicle through whom the progress of that struggle was expressed.[481] The more inclusive and lenient boundary of the Abrahamic covenant and the generic quality of his faith or covenantal commitment would emerge as a fitting alternative in the exilic setting. It was again Abraham's faith through which this exilic boundary maintenance for a more inclusive and lenient identity was expressed.[482] Abraham eventually grew into a big tree under whose shade all those who claim to share his faith would nest. He became the father not only of Israel and Judah but of *all* who came to live in the land. I also agree that the current Abraham narrative in its literary form may date to the exilic and post-exilic period.

It is still necessary, however, to point out that this exilic dating would lead to misunderstanding if it were taken to mean that Abraham's "ecumenical" character was the reason that Abraham was initially brought into Israel's ancestral narrative. The post-exilic inclusive spirit might well explain the ecumenical character came to embrace in its present form but it falls short of doing justice to the Abrahamic expansion of the Patriarchal narrative and its underlying polemical nature against the Jacob tradition. The point I am trying to make is that before Abraham became the name through which the exilic Judean identity expansion took place, there must have been a prior moment in which the once independent Abraham tradition was combined with the Jacob tradition, even though this initial stage is difficult to trace in the literary-critical level.

10.3 Conclusion

In this chapter, I have highlighted the consequences of Judah's "strategic tinkering with the past." Placing Abraham ahead of Jacob was one of the most critical

---

480 See, e.g., de Pury, "Abraham: The Priestly Writer's 'Ecumenical' Ancestor."

481 The broadened boundary of the Abrahamic *oikumene*, which now includes Egypt and Arab, fits well into the diaspora identity of the exilic Judean community. Yet, this hardly implies that such a boundary expansion could not have been achieved by Jacob. Note Jacob's exile to Mesopotamia and return to the land. He also has an Egyptian connection established through Joseph. Had Northern Israel survived instead of Judah, hypothetical as it may be, the post-exilic version of Israel's ancestry might not have needed Abraham at all. Jacob would have made a perfect archetype for the exile and return to the land.

482 But as I shall demonstrate in the following chapter, the seeming lenient boundary entails another side that limits the promised line only to Abraham's descents and is exclusionary to all others.

moves made by the Judahites who needed a new past that supports their newly found identity as the leading clan of Israel. The Jacob story, once standing alone as the founding myth of the tribes of Israel, came to be framed within Abraham's lineage, promise, and covenant. While traditional scholars viewed this change merely in terms of traditional and literary growths, I highlighted its functionality in terms of Judah's identity formation. Rewriting the past cannot be taken separate from the on-going identity negotiation of the present.

A comparison with ancient Korean history has highlighted the crucial role bestowed upon Abraham in his present position in Israel's ancestral history. The memory of the common founder Dangun planted in the prehistorical realm, prior to the historical era of the Period of the Three Kingdoms, provides a space used frequently by later groups in search of a basis for unity. Likewise, Abraham provides an analogous space for the Judahites who strived to overcome their inferiority vis-a-vis their northern counterpart. A particular emphasis has been placed on the political implications of Abraham's preceding Jacob in the genealogical order. The origin story of the once rival kingdom is now subordinated to Abraham's lineage, which provides a basis for Judah's claim for supremacy. The bold idea that Yhwh has selected Judah and Jerusalem to replace Israel has fundamentally reshaped Judah's self-perception.

11 From Jacob to Abraham: Preliminary Observations

Abraham's bestowed principal position in Israel's lineage inevitably has repercussions, intended or not, on the ensuing Jacob narrative. Such consequences demand scrutiny due to their potential ramifications on Judah's identity discourse against Israel. While traditional critics have recognized the Abrahamic expansion, as repeatedly noted, they have mainly approached it in terms of tracing formation history. Naturally, the resultant framing effect on the once-autonomous northern identity narrative has not been their primary concern, let alone its consequences for the Judean identity formation.[483] Some recent studies have explored the Abraham tradition in terms of identity formation, yet most investigations have been situated in the exilic context, a setting not prominent for the supposed North-South dynamic.[484]

By pivoting focus from text formation to identity formation, and from the text's growth to its functionality, we can unlock a wealth of untapped insights. My objective is not to present a novel reconstruction of the text's growth; but I will probe deeper than the final text, relying on rich assets of critical scholarship on its historical development. I seek to show that these literary developments are not just neutral compilations of historical data, but critical discursive endeavors to construct a past that has a profound impact on their present social dynamics and self-perceptions. By examining the impact of these textual reworkings against the intergroup dynamic between Judah and Israel, we can better understand the transformative effect of the Abrahamic reorientation on the underlying Jacob tradition.[485]

11.1 Abraham and Jacob

Compared to the Jacob narrative, the Abraham narrative often seems disjointed and lacking a cohesive plot structure. It appears that disparate local traditions are loosely combined around the theme of Abraham's lack of progeny.[486] Further-

---

483 But see Finkelstein, *The Forgotten Kingdom*, 141–42.

484 E.g., de Pury, "Abraham: The Priestly Writer's 'Ecumenical' Ancestor"; Jean-Louis Ska, "Essay on the Nature and Meaning of the Abraham Cycle (Gen 11:29–25:11)," in *Exegesis of the Pentateuch: Exegetical Studies and Basic Questions*, FAT 66 (Tübingen: Mohr Siebeck, 2009), 23–45. See discussion in Section 7.4.

485 Similarly, Ska ("Essay on the Nature and Meaning of the Abraham Cycle") has made some analogous observations, mainly with regards to Moses, but not against Jacob.

486 See discussion in Ska, 23–24. As for the underlying traditions, I concur with scholars who posit the existence of older, pre-exilic Abraham traditions, though confidently restoring them

https://doi.org/10.1515/9783111376554-011

more, when viewed as identity narratives, the Abraham and Jacob traditions differ fundamentally, each displaying distinct characteristics. While both stories construct the collective Self through the retelling of the ancestor's heroic life journey, Jacob is portrayed as a folk hero whose heroics defy moral standards, whereas Abraham is depicted as an exemplary figure of faith. The Abraham narrative is structured with a distinct set of identity markers, including the promise, covenant, obedience, and circumcision. This new foundation transforms the superstructure built upon it, and a new preface alters the way the subsequent narrative is interpreted. By placing the Abraham narrative at the beginning of the ancestral myth of Israel, the rest of the ancestral narrative and, indeed, the remainder of the biblical presentation, are reframed. Below, I highlight key strategies employed in this process and demonstrate how the Abrahamic expansion served Judah's "strategic tinkering with the past,"[487] redefining what it means to be "Israel."

11.1.1 Pre-occupation: Abraham was there first

Jacob and Abraham, as ancestral prototypes, represent symbolic values modeled after them for their descendants. In that regard, Abraham is not an accepting and forgiving grandfather to Jacob. Instead, he reclaims most of the values Jacob had once stood for, leaving his grandson little to represent.

11.1.1.1 Abraham Claims Jacob's Land Right

To begin with, scholars have observed a curious tendency in which Abraham journeys through sites featured in the Jacob tradition as if Abraham claims his prior connections to these places.[488] While their concern was mostly framed with-

---

remains elusive. For such attempts, see Blum, *Die Komposition der Vätergeschichte*, 273–89; Thomas Römer, "Recherches actuelles sur le cycle d'Abraham," in *Studies in the Book of Genesis: Literature, Redaction and History*, ed. André Wénin, BETL 155 (Leuven: Peeters, 2001), 193–210; Matthias Köckert, "Die Geschichte der Abrahamüberlieferung," in *Congress Volume: Leiden, 2004*, ed. André Lemaire, VTSup 109 (Leiden: Brill, 2006), 117–28; Finkelstein and Römer, "Comments on the Historical Background of the Abraham Narrative," 9–17; Oded Lipschits, Thomas Römer, and Hervé Gonzalez, "The Pre-Priestly Abraham Narratives from Monarchic to Persian Times," *Semitica* 59 (2017): 284–95, https://doi.org/10.2143/SE.59.0.3239913.

487 Lincoln, *Discourse and the Construction of Society*, 21.

488 See, e.g, de Pury, "Le cycle de Jacob comme légende autonome des origines d'Israël," 94; Schmid, *Genesis and the Moses Story*, 268; Köckert, "Wie wurden Abraham- und Jakobüberlieferung," 53–55; Finkelstein and Römer, "Comments on the Historical Background of the Abraham Narrative," 18; idem, "Comments on the Historical Background of the Jacob Narrative," 333.

in the matter of traditional and literary combination of the two tradition blocks,[489] I construe this as part of a strategic move in terms of Judah's identity politics, which I call "pre-occupation."

Immediately after receiving the divine commission (Gen 12:1–3), Abram departs Haran and migrates into the land. Initially, Abram arrives at Shechem, specifically at the oak of Moreh, and builds an altar there (Gen 12:7). He then moves down to Bethel and builds an altar between Bethel and Ai (Gen 12:8).[490] After a brief sojourn in Egypt (Gen 12:10–20), he returns to Bethel. Eventually, he moves down to Hebron (Gen 12:4–13:18). In this itinerary, Bethel and Shechem are major northern sites that are closely linked to Jacob, but they play a minor role within the rest of the Abraham narrative. Bethel is mentioned only once again in Gen 13:3, where it simply refers back to the initial remark in Gen 12:8 without adding new information. Shechem never appears again. Thus, the significance of Abram's entry to the land through these sites is not apparent within the scope of the Abraham narrative.[491] However, its importance is immediately evident when compared to Jacob's journey. Abram's journey repeats Jacob's itinerary in his travel back home from Haran (Gen 33–35).[492] Shechem is one of the places Jacob initially settles in following his arrival from Haran/Paddan-aram (Gen 33:18). After

---

489 Thus, e.g., Köckert's comprehensive review ("Wie wurden Abraham- und Jakobüberlieferung," 55) of the places in the Abraham tradition ends with a simple remark on literary dependence: "Während die Orte Bethel und Sichem sowie die Reisen in der Substanz der Jakobüberlieferung fest verankert sind, erscheinen sie in der Abrahamüberlieferung nur als episodenhafte Vorschaltung vor die ältere Abraham-Lot-Erzählung. Sie sind also offenkundig von Jakob auf Abraham übertragen worden."

490 Finkelstein and Römer ("Comments on the Historical Background of the Abraham Narrative," 18) observe that "Bethel and Ai" demonstrates an effort to prevent Abraham from worshipping at the unauthorized Bethel sanctuary. However, could it be that their perspective is, albeit indirectly, influenced by Jewish exegetes who have long been troubled by Jacob's failure to pay homage to Jerusalem in his way to Bethel? See, e.g., Rashi's remark in M. Rosenbaum and A. M. Silbermann, eds., *Pentateuch with Targum Onkelos, Haphtaroth and Rashi's Commentary*, vol. 1 (Jerusalem: Silbermann Family, 1973), 133. On the significance of the altar building, see Wolfgang Zwickel, "Die Altarbaunotizen im Alten Testament," *Bib* 73 (1992): 533–46, https://doi.org/10.2143/BIB.73.4.3215035; Siegbert Riecker, "Ein theologischer Ansatz zum Verständnis der Altarbaunotizen der Genesis," *Bib* 87 (2006): 526–30, https://doi.org/10.2143/BIB.87.4.3189068.

491 See Köckert, "Wie wurden Abraham- und Jakobüberlieferung," 53.

492 Scholars have long noted that the Abraham tradition parallels the Jacob story. That parallel nature has normally been seen as a redactional device used to mold the Abraham tradition into the Jacob story. E.g., Albert de Pury, *Promesse divine et légende cultuelle dans le cycle de Jacob: Genèse 28 et les traditions patriarcales*, Études bibliques (Paris: Gabalda, 1975), 82; Römer, "Abraham Traditions in the Hebrew Bible Outside the Book of Genesis," 178. Yet the striking level of parallels suggests that an implicit polemic against Jacob's founding role lies beneath the surface text.

the conflict with the Shechemites forced his family to move out, Jacob returns to Bethel (Gen 35:1–5). On his way, Jacob buries foreign idols under the terebinth near Shechem (הָאֵלָה אֲשֶׁר עִם־שְׁכֶם), which alludes to Abram's oak of Moreh (אֵלוֹן מוֹרֶה). Like Abram, Jacob's journey ends at Hebron, where he reunites with Isaac (Gen 35:27–29). Although there are differences in details, such as Bethel vs. Bethel and Ai,[493] the overall similarity is too striking to overlook. The effect is clear: regardless of what transpires in these places *later* (in narrative time) in Jacob's eventful life, Abraham is depicted as having been there first. I interpret this as part of the Judean author/redactor's literary campaign against the existing northern tradition. Like Assyrian kings march through town after town in a *palû* campaign, Abraham strides through Jacob's lands and claims them. I read this as an indication of the Abraham narrative's competitive edge over Jacob, a sentiment not reciprocated in the Jacob tradition. This aligns with my overarching contention regarding Judah's sense of inferiority, an observation that will consistently emerge in our ensuing discussions.

The same point applies to Haran. In the present text, Haran is associated with both Abraham and Jacob, which could potentially serve specific functions. Within the Jacob narrative, Haran is introduced as Jacob's maternal homeland (Gen 27:43; 28:10; 29:4). Rebekah sends Jacob to Laban, who is introduced as "Laban my brother in Haran" (Gen 27:43). Later, when Jacob arrives at Haran, he asks the people there about "Laban the son of Nahor" (Gen 29:5). Biblical readers already know this Nahor as Abraham's brother, but that connection is made only in the Priestly genealogy (Gen 11:26–29; 22:20–23).[494] By presenting Nahor as Abram's brother, P effectively adopts Laban the "Aramean" (Gen 25:20) into the Terah family.[495] Before the Priestly genealogy, Rebekah and Laban were known as family members of Nahor, who was yet to be related to Abraham. Then, making Abraham depart from Haran (Gen 12:1–5) carries a specific effect on Jacob. I contend that asserting Abraham's Aramean origin must be viewed in relation to Jacob's innate Aramean heritage.[496] Haran is pre-emptively defined as Abraham's

---

493 On the significance of "Bethel and Ai" as the border of the two kingdoms, see Wolfgang Zwickel, "Der Altarbau Abrahams zwischen Bethel und Ai (Gen 12 f.)," *BZ* 36 (1992): 207–19, https://doi.org/10.1163/25890468-03602005; Köckert, "Wie wurden Abraham- und Jakobüberlieferung," 54.
494 Bethuel is missing here. He is introduced as the father of Laban and Rebekah only in P (Gen 22:22; 25:20) and in Gen 24 during Eliezer's journey to acquire Isaac's wife. In fact, he makes no appearance in the pre-P Jacob narrative. This may have been part of P's efforts to combine Jacob and Abraham's genealogical pasts. Curiously in the MT of Gen 11:31, Nahor is left out of those who accompanied Terah out of Ur. Some Greek manuscripts thus add "and Nahor."
495 Cf. Köckert, "Wie wurden Abraham- und Jakobüberlieferung," 48.
496 Köckert ("Wie wurden Abraham- und Jakobüberlieferung," 65) sees it the opposite way. Jacob's maternal land originally was Hauran in southern Syria ("the land of the East" in Gen 29:1), which has been changed to Harran (in *Vätergeschichte*). This was to align Jacob's Hauran with

land before it is later presented as Jacob's maternal homeland.[497] Jacob's journey to his maternal land, a place where he is trained and matures into a superior trickster, is redefined as a journey to the land of Abraham.[498] Resultantly, all that Jacob achieves in Haran can now be reinterpreted as the fruition of the Abrahamic promise just passed onto him (Gen 28:13–14).

The implications become more significant when seen against recent scholarly observations that in early southern tradition, Abraham was viewed as an autochthonous figure.[499] Scholars find support for this notion in prophetic literature such as Ezek 33:24 and Isa 51:2; 63:16, where Abraham is not portrayed as a figure of foreign origin but is perceived in relation to land ownership.[500] If they are right, these observations suggest that rediscovering Abraham's home at Haran could be seen as the first step to de-emphasize his autochthonous status, which was later completed with a further extension to Ur of Mesopotamia. Here, it is important to recognize the difference between these extensions. The extension to Haran primarily targets Jacob's Aramean heritage, while the subsequent extension to Ur is set in the context of the *golah*'s identity politics against *'am ha'aretz*.[501]

Abram's home Harran, which he assumes existed in the now lost pre-P tradition before Gen 12:1. In doing so, he can argue that both Abram and Jacob are turned into models for the *golah*. See n. 501.

497 One might argue that Haran was merely a temporary stop for Terah's family, but the departure report, which mentions the numerous possessions and people that Abram acquired there (Gen 12:5), implies that it was more than just a stopover.

498 In this regard, Eliezer's betrothal journey to Abraham's hometown, "Aram-naharaim the city of Nahor" (Gen 24:10), plays a similar role. This well-designed episode is a late addition and is presented in a way that is quite similar to Jacob's journey to Haran. See Alexander Rofé, "An Inquiry into the Betrothal of Rebekah," in *Die Hebräische Bibel und ihre zweifache Nachgeschichte: Festschrift für Rolf Rendtorff zum 65. Geburtstag*, ed. Erhard Blum, Christian Macholz, and Ekkehard Stegemann (Neukirchen-Vluyn: Neukirchener Verlag, 1990), 27–40; idem, "The Admonitions Not to Leave the Promised Land in Genesis 24 and 26 and the Authorization in Genesis 46," in *The Post-Priestly Pentateuch: New Perspectives on Its Redactional Development and Theological Profiles*, ed. Federico Giuntoli and Konrad Schmid, FAT 101 (Tübingen: Mohr Siebeck, 2015), 177–84; Ska, "The Call of Abraham and Israel's Birth-Certificate," 52. I also see this as part of the pre-occupation strategy. Eliezer's journey to Nahor's town is apparently composed later than Jacob's, yet it is now placed before the Jacob tradition, thus prefiguring all that Jacob does by Abraham's servant.

499 Römer, "Abraham Traditions in the Hebrew Bible Outside the Book of Genesis."

500 See discussion in Ska, "The Call of Abraham and Israel's Birth-Certificate," 60; Römer, "Abraham Traditions in the Hebrew Bible Outside the Book of Genesis," 161–73; Köckert, "Wie wurden Abraham- und Jakobüberlieferung," 65; Finkelstein and Römer, "Comments on the Historical Background of the Abraham Narrative," 10–12.

501 Hence, I disagree with Köckert ("Wie wurden Abraham- und Jakobüberlieferung," 64–65), who forces this into the *golah* versus *'am ha'aretz* framework. He posits that the people in the

11.1.1.2 Abrahamic Promise Foreshadows Jacob

Abraham's pre-occupation is not limited to the spatial realm; he receives a divine promise (Gen 12:1–3) and enters into a covenantal relationship with Yhwh (Gen 15:18; 17:1–21). Within the narrative logic of the Judean ancestral history (*Vätergeschichte*), Abraham is presented as the first recipient of Yhwh's promise and covenant partnership.[502] The promise encompasses not only the land, but also the progeny, without which Jacob could not have existed. It is well-established that the promise scheme has been instrumental in stitching together the originally independent ancestral tradition blocks into a coherent whole.[503] The effect of the Abrahamic promise layer on the subsequent Jacob narrative cannot be underestimated. In the Jacob narrative, the promise held minimal significance; its central motif rather was blessing – paternal and divine.[504] Abraham owns the promise of Yhwh, and Jacob must now seek his share from it. Accordingly, note the positioning of the transmission of the Abrahamic promise to Jacob (Gen 28:13–14). Immediately after embarking on his exile, Yhwh appears and provides him the ancestral promise of the land and progeny. From this point on, the challenge for Jacob is not only to assert his legitimacy as the firstborn but also the worthiness as the recipient of the Abrahamic promise.

This promise is echoed at the end of Jacob's journey. As Jacob returns from Paddan-aram, the Priestly author concludes the narrative by giving the name "Israel" (Gen 35:10) and presenting the list of his twelve sons (Gen 35:23–26). As such, by the end of this journey, the seeds for what will eventually grow into the "great nation" (Gen 12:2) are sown, the significance of which I will discuss in short. This effectively connects the Jacob narrative to the promise initially given to Abraham. By weaving Jacob's journey with the overarching promise scheme, the Priestly author reinforces Abraham's founding role and underscores the significance of the promise as the primary driving force behind the narrative. Ska

---

land upheld the idea of an indigenous Abraham to reinforce their claim to the land, and creating an external origin for Abram in Haran was a strategic move by the *golah* to negate their claim and use him as their model. However, for that purpose, relocating him to Ur (Gen 11:31) would have made more sense. So why include another departure report from Haran (Gen 12:1)? Cf. Jean-Louis Ska, "The Call of Abraham and Israel's Birth-Certificate (Gen 12:1–4a)," in Exegesis of the Pentateuch: Exegetical Studies and Basic Questions, FAT 66 (Tübingen: Mohr Siebeck, 2009), 43. Also refer to my discussion of Ska's view in n. 530.

502 This point is well demonstrated in Ska, "The Call of Abraham and Israel's Birth-Certificate."

503 See Rendtorff, *Process of Transmission*; Ska, "The Call of Abraham and Israel's Birth-Certificate."

504 As Carr (*Reading the Fractures*, 228) has observed, "whereas almost all of the (late) references featuring Abraham and Isaac occur in some connection with the promise theme [...] there is no such unambiguous reference to the promise in the datable references to Jacob."

has put it most dramatically: "For the author of Gen 12:1–4a the act of obedience that leads the patriarch to an unknown land is the act of the birth of a people. On Abraham's obedience depends the future of Israel. It really is a founding moment in 'history.'"[505]

11.1.2 Negation: Abraham Denies Jacob

11.1.2.1 Abraham Tames Trickster Jacob

As Israel's new ancestral prototype, Abraham embodies a new set of prototypical values that redefine what it requires to be "Israel." Above all, Abraham is remembered for his faith and patience.[506] Abraham receives a divine promise from the beginning of his life journey (Gen 12:1–3), the fulfillment of which he must wait despite the lack of an heir. The gap between the promised ideal and the heirless reality propels the narrative forward. His struggle to cope with the hopeless reality gives rise to Ishmael (Gen 16), but that turns out to be an essential lesson that appears to have helped him pass the eventual test at Moriah (Gen 22). When God orders him to surrender the promised son, Abraham proves his righteousness by submitting Isaac, demonstrating his faithfulness to God's providence, who had earlier saved Ishmael (Gen 21:14–21).

From this perspective, Jacob is perhaps the last in line as a model ancestor. He lacks the patience that defines Abraham's life. Instead, Jacob's dogged pursuit of birthright makes him comparable with Lot, whose pursuit of what is desirable in the eyes led to a catastrophic ending (Gen 13:10–13; 19:24–25). Then, what the Abraham narrative *does* to the Jacob narrative as a frame is comparable to how most cultures sanitize and moralize trickster tales. When placed after the Abraham narrative, the trickster features of Jacob make for a moralized reading, which discourages readers from entertaining the trickster's wiliness. As discussed above, I understand the Jacob tale earlier in North Israel served as an ancestral myth that described how Jacob, the underdog, overcame Esau and Laban and emerged as the recipient of divine favor. If Jacob's life is symbolized by his persistent desire for blessing, Abraham's life is characterized by his faithfulness to Yhwh's promise. Placed after Abraham, Jacob's crafty behavior is now cast in a negative light by Abraham's life story. Abraham is depicted as a model devotee of Yhwh, whose perseverance in faith cemented his position as the holder of Yhwh's promise (Gen 22:16–18). The effect of becoming Abraham's grandson can-

---

505 Ska, "The Call of Abraham and Israel's Birth-Certificate," 55.
506 Ska, "Essay on the Nature and Meaning of the Abraham Cycle," 33–34.

not be underestimated. Abraham denies Jacob's principal traits as a folk hero.[507] The original audience of the northern Jacob tradition would not have viewed the new position given to their ancestor as a favorable development for their collective self-esteem.

11.1.2.2 Abraham Questions Underdog Jacob

Jacob's being the second son was integral to his underdog identity in the original version. Now as the potential heir of Abraham's chosen lineage, however, his lack of birthright turns into major deficiency. Birthright is a surprisingly dominating principle in the Abraham narrative. While many Christian readers would consider Abraham as a model of faith, it would be misleading to read the original Abraham story as delineating an inclusive boundary that is open to believing gentiles, as St. Paul interpreted it (Rom 4:1–5). Pauline theology asserts that whoever follows Abraham's faith, even the deceitful Jacob, is eligible to be embraced as part of God's people. After all, what matters is faith, not work. However, it must be acknowledged that this is a product of Paul's revolutionary reception of Abraham, not necessarily coinciding with the intrinsic meaning of the Abraham narrative.

When Abram "believed (וְהֶאֱמִן)," it was considered "righteousness (צְדָקָה)" (Gen 15:6).[508] However, it is unclear if God's choice of Abraham over others was made solely based on his faith. Throughout his life, Abraham had to prove his faith, but it is fair to say that God's choice of Abraham preceded his proving so.[509] Hence, one may have a theological debate as to on what basis God has chosen Abraham, but frequently overlooked behind the idea of God's choice is that Abra-

---

507 Similarly, scholars have often observed how Moses of Exodus domesticates Jacob in the present juxtaposition of the originally independent origin myths. E.g., de Pury, "Le cycle de Jacob comme légende autonome des origines d'Israël," 96.

508 The nature of Abram's belief and Yhwh's recognition is open to interpretation. Christian readers tend to interpret it from the Pauline perspective of universal significance, but the intended meaning of both acts was likely to have been limited to the specific circumstance of Yhwh's election of Abram. As Nahum Sarna (*Genesis: The Traditional Hebrew Text with the New JPS Translation*, JPS Torah Commentary [Philadelphia: Jewish Publication Society, 1989], 113) remarks, Abram remained steadfast despite challenges. Yhwh reckoned his act of faith as a "merit" worthy of reward, which manifested in the form of the subsequent covenant-making.

509 Cf. Ska ("Essay on the Nature and Meaning of the Abraham Cycle," 35) stresses that, when it comes to Gen 22:15–18, Abraham's obedience preceded Yhwh's promise. However, Ska's observation cannot be taken as a definitive claim, considering that Yhwh's promise appeared earlier in Gen 12:1–3.

ham was the firstborn of the chosen line and its implications.[510] In the present text, Abraham is introduced by the genealogy of Shem (Gen 11:10) and is the son of Terah (Gen 11:26). Terah had two other sons, Nahor and Haran, but the text makes little effort to justify God's choice of Abraham over against them. Was the same opportunity given to Nahor and Haran to prove their faith? We never know, given the paucity of narrative information available on Terah's family. However, the same point can be elaborated on concerning Abraham's two sons, Ishmael and Isaac. Compare Abraham with the fate of Ishmael, the firstborn but ultimately "diselected" by God. Ishmael's birthright was forsaken not because he failed to prove his faith. In fact, he was never given a chance to do so. Despite the birth of Ishmael, Yhwh promised another son who would be the heir of the chosen line (Gen 18:9–15). It is fair to say that Ishmael simply lied outside God's plan.[511] Given the stress on Sarah's role here, it is difficult to deny that the reason for Yhwh's diselection of Ishmael was due to his *impure* maternal line.[512] This motif of purity in lineage is more fully developed in P, but one cannot neglect that its foundation is already established at the non-P level.

Therefore, qualification is needed to the nature of Abraham's alleged test of faith. Unlike the Pauline interpretation, Abraham's "faith" is not necessarily

---

510 E.g., Ska (pp. 33–42) offers an extensive description of Abraham's obedience, fidelity, and observance of the Torah, but he does not address Abraham's status as Terah's firstborn or the possible implication of purity ideology.

511 Phyllis Trible, *Texts of Terror: Literary-Feminist Readings of Biblical Narratives* (Philadelphia: Fortress, 1984), 19.

512 Christian theologians may take issues with my discussion on Abraham's election, but I have no intention to initiate a theological debate here. My aim is to make a simple point concerning the literary effect of his election on the subsequent Jacob narrative. Intended or not, the narrative of Isaac's election and Ishmael's rejection entails consequences that can be interpreted, or abused, in line with purity ideology. It is so because the same motif of purity of lineage appears to be at work in accounting for the diselection of Esau, the lawful heir of Isaac and Rebekah.

See, e.g., Rom 9:6–13, where Paul incorporates the purity ideology inherent in the election of Isaac and Jacob (in contrast to Ishmael and Esau) as a foundation for his theology of Christian election, turning Isaac and Jacob as symbols for those chosen by God. The interpretations of this text by Christian theologians reveal that purity ideology persists albeit in different forms. Consider how the Swiss biblical commentator Frédéric Louis Godet (*Commentary on St. Paul's Epistle to the Romans*, trans. A. Cusin, vol. 2 [Edinburgh: T&T Clark, 1881], 147) reshapes the purity ideology of pure/impure into a carnal/spiritual dichotomy, employing it as a basis for his doctrine of Christian election over Jews: "But could Isaac and his race, though proceeding from Abraham, and that through the intervention of a divine factor, be regarded without any other condition as real children of God? Evidently not; for if the faith of Abraham himself ceased to belong to them, they became again a purely carnal seed. It must then be foreseen that the same law of exclusion which had been applied to Ishmael, in favour of Isaac, would anew assert its right even within the posterity of the latter."

presented as a criterion for the election of gentiles. The test itself was a privilege given to Abraham, the promise holder (Gen 12:1–3). The beneficiary of the promise here remains limited to the chosen line. Ishmael, Lot, and others are embraced as Abraham's family members, and will be blessed for that.[513] However, from the outset, they were excluded from the promised line, which is limited to the lawful heir of Abraham and Sarah. At the non-P level, the motif of purity in lineage is only implied, and I have no intention to overemphasize its importance at this level. Nevertheless, one can safely judge that the governing principle behind Yhwh's choice was hereditary, which the text does not even attempt to clarify. Against this principle, Jacob cannot trump Esau, no matter how magical and marvelous a trickster he proves to be. His chance is even lower than Isaac's because, unlike Ishmael who was born to an Egyptian woman, Esau is a legitimate son of Isaac and Rebekah.

The motif of purity in lineage in the Abrahamic frame suffocates the innate folk grammar of the Jacob story that enabled the audience to hail the adventure of the trickster hero. As a folk hero, Jacob was predetermined as the winner of the competition despite being the underdog. All the circumstantial indications of the hero's illegitimacy, including his being the second son, functioned as part of the narrative device that intended to add dramatic effects to the eventual triumph of the underdog. Indeed, Jacob's supremacy is anticipated from the beginning of the narrative (Gen 25:23), immediately after depicting him as the second son. From his birth, Jacob gains the sympathy of the Israelite audience, who are built to side with their forefather over against the father of the rival Edom. Nevertheless, the hero must endure a period of exile, a transformative period that prepares the underdog for his rise. His dramatic success in obtaining the paternal blessing leads to his own exile; but there, Jacob matures into the father of "Israel." The Israelite tribes were born there in exile, and his struggle with Laban (the helper turned opponent) trained him to become a stronger trickster. Eventually, Jacob returns triumphantly as the one who "has striven with God and with men, and has prevailed" (Gen 32:28).

In this narrative grammar, Jacob's lack of birthright was not portrayed as a legal issue that needed to be legitimized. However, when placed after the Abraham narrative, Jacob's illegitimacy as heir to the ancestral promise is brought to

---

513 Brett (*Genesis: Procreation and the Politics of Identity*, 49–85) contends that Ishmael (and Hagar) is not entirely dismissed in the narrative and Abram is not depicted as faultless. Indeed, certain elements within the text seem to challenge the superficial perspective I have presented here. I also concede that the Bible, unlike its neighboring culture, does not always uphold birthright, as seen in the cases of Cain, Esau, and Manasseh (pp. 37–38). Still, in Abraham's case, his birthright is honored *despite* his flaws unlike others.

the forefront, and Yhwh's election of Jacob is fundamentally challenged. As a result, Jacob's status as an ancestral figure is made awkward by the precedent set by his grandfather. According to the governing principle of the Abraham narrative, there appears to be no way for Jacob to inherit the promise line without some radical intervention. It is against this backdrop that it becomes important to observe how Abraham is depicted as a pure source that ultimately purifies the impure Jacob into a worthy heir of the divine promise.

11.1.3 Purification: Abraham Provides Pure Wives for Jacob

The motif of pure lineage finds clearer expressions in the Priestly corpus.[514] To begin with, Ishmael's rejection is made more explicit. Despite Abraham's willingness to make Ishmael his successor (Gen 17:18), Yhwh makes it clear that he is not the chosen one: "No, but your wife Sarah shall bear you a son ... I will establish my covenant with him as an everlasting covenant for his offspring after him" (Gen 17:19). By emphasizing Sarah as the mother of the promised son, the text points to Hagar as the reason for Ishmael's rejection. P's introduction of the circumcision as the new identity marker for Yhwh's everlasting covenant with Abraham's offspring reinforces the motif of pure lineage.[515] Only the son born between Abraham and Sarah, the promised line, will be the rightful heir of the "everlasting covenant" (Gen 17:7) signified by circumcision, a new Priestly identity marker

---

514 E.g., E. A. Speiser, *Genesis*, AB 1 (Garden City, NY: Doubleday, 1964), 216.

515 Brett (*Genesis: Procreation and the Politics of Identity*, 63–64) highlights that all members of Abraham's household, including foreigners, are invited for circumcision, which he interprets as a sign that the circumcision rite is not as exclusive as commonly believed. Jakob Wöhrle ("The Integrative Function of the Law of Circumcision," in *The Foreigner and the Law: Perspectives from the Hebrew Bible and the Ancient Near East*, ed. Reinhard Achenbach, Rainer Albertz, and Jakob Wöhrle, BZABR 16 [Wiesbaden: Harrassowitz Verlag, 2011], 71–87) also makes a similar argument highlighting the inclusive function of circumcision. I can understand what Brett and Wöhrle are aiming at in their fresh interpretations; however, in cases like this, there is always an opposing side to the argument. Brett aims to emphasize that Ishmael and Hagar did receive their due, and thus the text is not entirely exclusive. This is correct, but saying so could be perceived as a veiled compliment, if seen from the perspective of the deprived, suggesting "this should be enough for you." Ishmael may be circumcised before Isaac, but his circumcision only affords him a basic in-group status. He can never achieve the status of heir within the chosen line. As firstborns, Ishmael and Esau's expectations surpass mere avoidance of rejection; they seek recognition for their birthright. Thus, they would likely find little solace in not being rejected. The violence inherent in God's choice of Abraham and Sarah's line finds eloquent expression in Trible (*Texts of Terror*, 9–35), though mainly through the perspective of Hagar. In effect, Hagar's expulsion bears striking similarities to Ezra's marriage crisis. Cf. Brett, 61.

(Gen 17:10–14).[516] Among the Israelite ancestors, Isaac is the first to be circumcised on the eighth day after birth (Gen 21:4), which raises further suspicion about Jacob's legitimacy. Jacob's circumcision is not even mentioned.[517]

This Priestly purity ideology further renders Jacob illegitimate as the promised heir. Jacob's rejection only serves as a backdrop to promote Abraham as Jacob's remedy. The motif of purity in lineage is strategically implemented in the Priestly layers of the Jacob narrative. First, the narrator casts doubt on Esau's rightful state by highlighting his Hittite wives as the source of Rebekah's frustration (Gen 26:34–35, 27:46).[518] Like Ishmael's demotion for his maternal line, Esau's Hittite wives are repeatedly targeted as a problem.[519] Implied is blame that they contaminate the purity of the chosen line. Second, the Priestly text adds another commission that redefines Jacob's exile as a journey to find a proper wife from his ancestral land in Paddan-aram to amend Esau's marriage crisis (Gen 28:1–5). As a result, what was earlier conceived as Jacob's fugitive exile is redefined as a betrothal journey for a proper wife, which reinforces the narrative logic that justifies Jacob's election over Esau. Third, Jacob's reception of the name "Israel," originally the sign of the hero's ultimate triumph (Gen 32:29), is redefined as the reward after his successful return from the betrothal journey (Gen 35:9–15); the list of his sons immediately follows the accomplishment of his mission (35:22b–26). As a result, technically speaking, Esau is disqualified for his improper wives, and Jacob is promoted as the lawful heir of the promised line. Like Sarah's mater-

---

516 Furthermore, Moab and Ammon are denounced for being the children of improper relations between father and daughter. In a sense, both Ishmael and Lot, the two proximate Others in the Abraham story, are rejected on the basis of the principle of purity in lineage. Interest in the "pure" line is further evinced in Gen 20, in which scholars have long observed an apologetic undertone that tries to ensure that the matriarch was not defiled by the foreign ruler (Gen 20:6). E.g., Gerhard Von Rad, *Genesis: A Commentary*, Rev. ed., OTL (Philadelphia: Westminster, 1972), 230. Cf. Heard, *The Dynamics of Diselection*, 80. However, consider Brett's observation (*Genesis: Procreation and the Politics of Identity*, 52–53) that Abraham's episode in Gen 20 can also be interpreted negatively, with his endogamy effectively parodied as similar to Lot's incest. Thus, I see that there are competing claims coexisting in the text.

517 In the Jacob tradition, circumcision is mentioned only in Gen 34, within the context of contempt for the indigenous people of Shechem as uncircumcised. The anachronistic remark, which considers "Israel" as an established group entity, also indicates the lateness of this text. See Finkelstein and Römer, "Comments on the Historical Background of the Jacob Narrative," 336.

518 Brett (*Genesis: Procreation and the Politics of Identity*, 88) contends that this was not Rebekah's true motive, but rather part of her ploy, as a trickster herself, to manipulate Isaac to further her cause.

519 Similarly, see Finkelstein and Römer, "Comments on the Historical Background of the Jacob Narrative," 335 n. 83.

nal line secured Isaac's birthright, Jacob needs Leah and Rachel, who elevate him above Esau. Additionally, the pure wives are provided in Haran, the ancestral land that, as argued, has been made to be preoccupied by Abraham.[520] Simply put, Jacob is made illegitimate only for Abraham to be promoted as the ultimate prescription. A curiously familiar line of rhetoric emerges. How many times do we hear that Israel is to be saved by Judah and Jerusalem (or David) in biblical literature?

11.1.4 Extension: Abraham Exiled from the Land

A major change implemented in P is the extension of Abraham's homeland to "Ur of the Chaldeans." As a member of Terah's family, Abram is said to have accompanied Terah who initiated a journey from Mesopotamia to the land of Canaan (Gen 11:27–32).[521] As widely observed, the redundancy of the two departure reports suggests that two different traditions are harmonized in the present text (cf. Acts 7:2).[522] Critics' discussion on the redundancy has played out mainly in terms of source delineation;[523] however, I consider it important to pay heed to the function of this extension of Abraham's origin.

As noted above (Section 11.1.1.1), in the earlier tradition, Abraham may have been construed as an indigenous figure. Later in the pre-P level, Abraham's home is identified with Haran, either in Syria or upper Mesopotamia.[524] In contrast, lower Mesopotamia, after the initial appearance, is not mentioned again in the rest of

---

520 There is no doubt that this point is accentuated by P, who prepared this argument by stressing Esau's Hittite wives (Gen 26:34–35; 27:46). However, the search for a proper wife is intertwined with the motif of fleeing from Esau at the pre-P level as well. Without it, the extended Haran narrative makes little sense.

521 The source delineation of Gen 11:27–12:9 is seriously debated. Cf. Ronald Hendel, "Abram's Journey as Nexus: Literarkritik and Literary Criticism," *VT* 69 (2019): 567–93, https://doi.org/10.1163/15685330-12341383.

522 E.g., Speiser, *Genesis*, 80–81; Claus Westermann, *Genesis: A Commentary*, trans. John Scullion (Minneapolis: Augsburg, 1984), 139–40; Ska, "The Call of Abraham and Israel's Birth-Certificate," 49; Köckert, "Wie wurden Abraham- und Jakobüberlieferung," 48–49.

523 Scholars have repeatedly noted the difficulty in the source delineation in these texts. See, e.g., Westermann, *Genesis 12–36*, 136.

524 Indeed, in Genesis 12 and onward, Haran is consistently depicted as Abraham's ancestral home. He is living there when receiving commission (Gen 12:1) to leave his "land (אָרֶץ)," "kindred (מוֹלֶדֶת)," and "father's house (בֵּית אָב)." This idea is reiterated in Genesis 24. Abraham's sending Eliezer to "my land (אָרֶץ) and my kindred (מוֹלֶדֶת)" (Gen 24:4), which is identified as "Aram-naharaim (אֲרַם נַהֲרַיִם)" and "the city of Nahor" (Gen 24:10).

the Abraham narrative or in the subsequent ancestral tradition.[525] Thus, while the notion of Abraham's origin in Ur is prevalent in later traditions (Gen 15:7; Neh 9:7; Acts 7:2), it does not seem to be an intrinsic part of the early Abraham tradition.

Then, we can examine the effect of this redefinition of Abraham's origin. Chronologically, this forward expansion extends the Abraham narrative further back into the mythic past, cultivating an era of Terah's generation and beyond. Geographically, this account traces Abraham's roots back to lower Mesopotamia, extending his origin one step further from Haran to Ur. The Priestly author/redactor was not interested in detailing Terah's life in Mesopotamia.[526] Their purpose was much grander, using Terah as a gateway to the entire epoch of Primeval history.[527] This is a radical shift, which must be understood from the standpoint of the Judean exile.[528] By prefacing the ancestral tradition with primordial accounts that reflect the influence of Mesopotamian creation myths, a vast mythic space was opened up for the exiled Judeans to reimagine their origin in relation to the new cultural impetus brought about by their exilic context.

Identity narratives rely on binary oppositions, defining the extremes of their symbolic world and delineating the scope of the mythic space. By simplifying complex realities into neat oppositions, these narratives draw clear lines between Us and Them. The unity of Us and the difference from Them are maximized. Hence, it is noteworthy how this forward expansion reshuffles the existing binary oppositions upon which "Israel" had been defined.

Us	:	Them
Mesopotamia	:	Canaan
Diaspora	:	Homeland
golah	:	*'am ha'aretz*
Pure	:	Impure
South	:	North
Abraham	:	Jacob

A comprehensive analysis of the implications of this overhaul is beyond the scope of this chapter. Instead, I will present some basic observations regarding the alternations it generated, as well as the possibilities it opened up for diverse future audiences to explore.

---

525 Cf. ארם נהרים in the MT is rendered Μεσοποταμία in the LXX.
526 Instead, the gap is filled in by later rabbinic literature that famously depicts Abraham as an idol smasher. E.g., Genesis Rabbah 38:13.
527 See Köckert, "Wie wurden Abraham- und Jakobüberlieferung," 65 n. 104.
528 Either from Hauran in southern Syria or Harran in upper Mesopotamia. Cf. Köckert, 65.

First, Judah's collective Self is transposed to lower Mesopotamia. By imagining Abraham's Mesopotamian origin, the Judean exiles can perceive their ultimate roots in the land they now reside.[529] In constructing identity, the position of the Self is critical. Mesopotamia, the diaspora, is construed as "our" home, creating a new and complex dynamic with the homeland. This diasporic Self sets a new vantage point for the whole narrative that follows. The new location of the Self requires a new definition of Us. Judah's collective Self is further distanced from the land, yes, the land originally claimed by Jacob. Previously (in the pre-P level), the objective of the Abraham tradition was to surpass Jacob. The focus now shifts dramatically, as if Abraham, inspired by a newly discovered vision, leaves farther away from the land, effectively resetting the place of departure for his descendants.

The significance of the reorientation is particularly relevant in terms of the Judean exile's efforts to redefine "Israel" in relation to the land.[530] For every ethnic group, a real or imagined link with the homeland is a key element in constructing "who we are."[531] As the people's perception of the land changes, the

---

529 Is it possible that some of them employed this notion to assert that Abraham was present in this land long before the Achaemenid Persians arrived? For some Korean Americans seeking recognition as genuine American, emphasizing their forefathers' early immigration dates, let us say possibly earlier than some other Irish immigrants, could provide a foundation for demanding recognition. Similarly, it seems plausible that some Judean exiles might have been willing to use the idea of Abraham's Chaldean origin as a means to reimagine their own identities. While this might not have altered social perceptions, it could have affected their self-esteem. Would it be far-fetched to suggest that such an inclination towards social assimilation made myths about figures like Daniel or Esther valuable in resisting and countering that? Cf. Ahn's discussion on the second and third generations as to how they navigate the complexities of their dual identity, assimilating into the mainstream and eventually find the place as their new home. John J. Ahn, *Exile as Forced Migrations: A Sociological, Literary, and Theological Approach on the Displacement and Resettlement of the Southern Kingdom of Judah*, BZAW 417 (Berlin: Walter de Gruyter, 2011).
530 Ska ("Essay on the Nature and Meaning of the Abraham Cycle," 43) makes a similar observation: "The prescriptions that Abraham keeps are the ones that are dear to the group that came back from exile and finally imposed themselves on Jerusalem. It is probable that at an early stage this group appealed to the exodus as the 'founding myth' to justify its claims. Then, because of the opposition of the 'people of the land', the 'gôlâ' reinterpreted the figure of Abraham to make him the first 'pilgrim' coming from Mesopotamia, a journey that prefigured the return of the exiles. In this way the 'gôlâ' deprived its opponents of a weighty argument. Abraham was in fact more the father of the returning exiles than of those who had stayed in the country." In comparison with my reading, how he narrows the potential impact of the Abrahamic expansion to the *golah* vs. *'am ha'aretz* confrontation appears apparent. Cf. n. 501. I have endeavored to demonstrate that a deeper root for this exists, extending all the way back to Judah's struggle with Israel (Abraham vs. Jacob), as well as its subsequent manifestations in various forms.
531 See Hutchinson and Smith, *Ethnicity*, 6–7.

role of the land in constructing Us is redefined. Such changes are well evidenced in the identity struggles of many diasporic communities.[532] For instance, seeking to redefine Us in relation to the distant homeland often generates a complex perception of the land and its current inhabitants. That is precisely what happened to the *golah*'s perception of the homeland.[533] The land is profaned by sin, requiring a period of purification (e.g., Jer 25:11–12; Isa 40:1–2; Ezek 36:24–25). This gives rise to a myth of the empty land, which further requires denying those who remained there.[534] They are rendered non-existent or profane and need to be wiped out. The purged land is for Us, who endured the period of purification in exile. This is the core of the *golah*'s identity program, and one can see that the purity ideology plays a central role.

In the book of Ezra, this ideology is promoted by the concept of "the holy seed," which is exclusively linked to the *golah* community (Ezra 9:2).[535] Like Abraham, the *golah* is conceived as those who came from Mesopotamia. The people of the land can be, if possible, purified only by joining the *golah* (Ezra 6:21). A fundamental affinity is recognized with the othering scheme employed against the remnants of Samaria, who had been defiled by the Assyrian policy of forced migration (2Kgs 17). It is not coincidental that the *golah* highlights the *'am ha'aretz*'s alleged connection to those mix-blooded northerners (Ezra 4:2) when they argue their exclusive right to build the new temple. The likelihood that the *golah*'s purity was tainted in the exile is willfully ignored, a point that requires further elaboration.[536]

Second, the rediscovery of Abraham's Mesopotamian origin further distinguishes him from Jacob, by distancing Israel's true origin from Jacob's land and its indigenous identity. In the homeland-diaspora dialectic, Abraham is associated with

---

532 See, e.g., Shlomo Sand, *The Invention of the Land of Israel: From Holy Land to Homeland*, trans. Geremy Forman (London: Verso, 2012).

533 For the historical development of this idea, see Rom-Shiloni, *Exclusive Inclusivity.*

534 Cf. Hans M. Barstad, *The Myth of the Empty Land: A Study in the History and Archaeoloogy of Judah During the "Exilic" Period*, Symbolae Osloenses. Fasc. Supplet. 28 (Oslo: Scandinavian University Press, 1996).

535 For recent studies, see Katherine Southwood, "The Holy Seed: The Significance of Endogamous Boundaries and Their Transgression in Ezra 9–10," in *Judah and the Judeans in the Achaemenid Period*, ed. Oded Lipschits, Gary N. Knoppers, and Manfred Oeming (Winona Lake, IN: Eisenbrauns, 2011), 189–224; Willa Mathis Johnson, *The Holy Seed Has Been Defiled: The Interethnic Marriage Dilemma in Ezra 9–10*, Hebrew Bible Monographs 33 (Sheffield: Phoenix Press, 2011); E. Allen Jones, "Who Is the Holy Seed?: Purity and Identity in the Restoration Community," *JSOT* 45 (2021): 515–34, https://doi.org/10.1177/0309089220963428.

536 I cannot help but ponder that the *golah*'s obsessive preoccupation with purity may have been a means to mask their own feelings of impurity and mixed heritage, inescapable while residing in a foreign land. Without question, Abraham serves as a model for Ezra.

the diaspora/pure, while Jacob is identified with the land/impure.[537] The ultimate source of Abraham's pure line is traced back to Ur, which is farther away from the land. Jacob may claim a connection to Haran through his maternal line, but he has no relation to lower Mesopotamia. This new orientation complements the existing dichotomy that aligns Abraham with faith/promise/purity and Jacob with wiliness/ underdog status/impurity. If Abraham's pure line was earlier rooted in the promise, now it takes on a tangible geographic orientation through his Mesopotamian origin. Just as those who remained in the land had to be separated from the unclean land and purified by joining the "holy seed," Jacob's impure lineage can only be purified by the Abrahamic line that originated in Ur. As such, Abraham becomes the proto-type of the pure *golah* community, while Jacob is demoted as a model for the impure *'am ha'aretz*. Nehemiah exemplifies this reorientation by identifying Abra-ham's departure from Ur as the beginning of Israel, with Jacob being entirely forgotten (Neh 9:7–8). The erasure of Jacob aligns with the myth of the empty land; just as the existence of those who remained in the land is denied, their father figure, symbolic as it may be, is erased in their recollection of the past.[538]

All these observations do not imply rigid or permanent changes; they merely highlight new potential interpretive paths emerging in the context of identity politics. In the "Us versus Them" paradigm that pervaded identity debates, the *golah*'s burgeoning affiliation with "Abraham from Ur" forcefully pushes "Jacob in the land" at the polar opposite, imbuing him with the symbolic weight of representing "those who remained in the land."[539]

---

537 Once again, it is important to emphasize that this dialectic is not meant to encompass the entire scope of homeland-diaspora relations. As Bedford's research on Ezra-Nehemiah illustrates, the relationship between the Jewish diaspora and their homeland was intricate and multifaceted, defying reduction to simple dichotomies like "Us vs. Them" or "Insiders vs. Outsiders." See Peter Bedford, "Diaspora: Homeland Relations in Ezra-Nehemiah," *VT* 52 (2002): 147–65, https://doi.org/ 10.1163/156853302760013820.

538 Cf. recent studies, Yitzhak Lee-Sak, "Polemical Propaganda of the Golah Community against the Gibeonites: Historical Background of Joshua 9 and 2 Samuel 21 in the Early Persian Period," *JSOT* 44 (2019): 115–32, https://doi.org/10.1177/0309089218762286; William Krisel, *Judges 19–21 and the "Othering" of Benjamin: A Golah Polemic against the Autochthonous Inhabitants of the Land?*, OtSt 81 (Leiden: Brill, 2022).

539 The operating systems of Mac and Windows offer a compelling illustration of how symbols and designs can polarize in opposition. One of the most recognizable aspects of Windows' user interface is the iconic "Start" button, traditionally placed at the bottom-left corner. Mac OS, in contrast, positions its equivalent – the Apple logo – at the top-left corner of the screen. Addition-ally, icons stack up from left to right in Windows, while in Mac OS they do so from right to left. These differences carry no inherent meaning. Rather, decisions likely arose from each company's pursuit to differentiate its identity from the other. Over time, what might have begun as arbitrary choices rooted in differentiation become deeply ingrained markers of each brand's identity, creating a distinct user interface that loyalists of each camp cherish and defend.

11.2 Excursus: Abraham and Moses

Abraham's influence extends also to Moses, another major figure rooted in the North. Although this is not the central focus of this book, I will briefly outline how Abraham also impacts Moses's standing, thereby redefining both indigenous and external personas of Israel.

First, shortly after Abraham migrates to the Promised Land, he journeys down to Egypt, confronts and overcomes danger, then escapes and returns to the land (Gen 12:10–20). This exodus narrative of Abraham is significant with regards to Moses. Although the future enslavement and liberation of Israel from Egypt is not mentioned, a clear allusion is made.[540] A famine forces Abraham/Israel to leave the land and migrate into Egypt. There they suffer but escape the crisis by God's deliverance and find their way back to the land.[541] Again, the effect is evident: Abraham undergoes an exodus himself before Jacob/Israel does.[542] In the same vein, Gen 15 also establishes a connection between Abraham and Moses. Specifically, it draws a parallel between Abraham's exodus from Ur (Gen 15:7) and Moses's exodus from Egypt (Gen 15:13–14), positioning Moses's as the second exodus under the model of Abraham's first exodus.[543] This parallel is reinforced

---

540 Köckert, "Wie wurden Abraham- und Jakobüberlieferung," 50 n. 35.

541 Recently, there has been considerable debate among scholars regarding Gen 15, with many arguing that its allusion to Exodus serves as a basis for assign it a post-P text. See among others, John Ha, *Genesis 15: A Theological Compendium of Pentateuchal History*, BZAW 181 (Berlin: Walter de Gruyter, 1989); Thomas Römer, "Gen 15 und Gen 17. Beobachtungen und Anfragen zu einem Dogma der 'neueren' und 'neuesten' Pentateuchkritik," *DBAT* 26 (1990): 32–47; Jan Christian Gertz, "Abraham, Mose und der Exodus: Beobachtungen zur Redaktionsgeschichte von Gen 15.," in *Abschied vom Jahwisten: Die Komposition des Hexateuch in der jüngsten Diskussion*, ed. Jan Christian Gertz, Konrad Schmid, and Markus Witte, BZAW 315 (Berlin: Walter de Gruyter, 2002), 63–81; Christoph Levin, "Jahwe und Abraham im Dialog: Genesis 15," in *Gott und Mensch im Dialog: Festschrift für Otto Kaiser zum 80. Geburtstag*, ed. Markus Witte, BZAW 345 (Berlin: Walter de Gruyter, 2004), 237–57; Matthias Köckert, "Gen 15: Vom »Urgestein« der Väterüberlieferung zum »theologischen Programmtext« der späten Perserzeit," *ZAW* 125 (2013): 25–48, https://doi.org/10.1515/zaw-2013-0003. Although it is true that a direct reference to Israel's exodus from Egypt is confined to Gen 15, Gen 12 encompasses all the details that allude to the exodus event as well.

542 Römer has observed Abraham and Moses as competing figures. Yet he does not use Gen 12:10–22 as Abraham's prefiguring Moses's exodus event. See Thomas Römer, "Abraham and Moses, A (not so) Friendly Competition," in *And God Saw That It Was Good (Gen 1:12): The Concept of Quality in Archaeology, Philology and Theology*, ed. Filip Čapek and Petr Sláma, Beiträge zum Verstehen der Bibel 42 (Zürich: Lit Verlag, 2020), 99–109.

543 In comparison, Ska ("Some Groundwork on Genesis 15," in *Exegesis of the Pentateuch: Exegetical Studies and Basic Questions*, FAT 66 [Tübingen: Mohr Siebeck, 2009], 79) notes that the two Exodus events are in conflicting relations within the present text: "On the one side, God brought Abraham out of Ur of the Chaldaeans to give him the land and on the other he brings

by their linkage to the Abrahamic covenant established in this chapter, which extends to Moses and culminates at Sinai (Exod 19:1–6).

Ska has also noted the connection between the Abrahamic promise of a "great nation (גּוֹי גָדוֹל)" and the fulfillment formula in Gen 12:4a, which is ultimately realized through Moses. In Gen 46:3, the promise of a great nation is conveyed to Jacob, thus establishing a link between Abraham and Moses as Jacob journeys to Egypt. Ska goes on to highlight that precedence is given to Abraham when Moses appeals to Yhwh, urging to remember the promise made to Abraham (Exod 32:13). He explains,

> The meaning of these texts is quite clear: Israel's ancestor is not Moses but Abraham. Conversely, the members of the "great nation" are the descendants of Abraham and not only the descendants or disciples of Moses. Perhaps it is possible to see in these statements the desire to place Abraham and Moses in relation to each other and to show that Abraham has priority over Moses in one fundamental point. In other words, to find the roots of the people of Israel we have to go back beyond the exodus and the Mosaic institutions to Abraham's first migration, to his faith, his obedience and the divine promises made to him.[544]

As such, Abraham is promoted as the model who prefigures both Jacob's life journey and the subsequent Exodus of Moses. In doing so, nearly every important facet of Israel's subsequent history is modeled after Abraham's foundational adventure.

Second, the Priestly transposition of Abraham's origin to Ur redefines Israel's external identity and, thereby, further reinforces the shift from Moses to Abraham. Beforehand, Israel's external origin was defined by the Exodus narrative, which traced Israel's origin to the liberated slave group from Egypt. Now, with the Abraham's Mesopotamian origin rediscovered, the earliest phase of Israel's history is relocated to Mesopotamia. Even before they came to Canaan and forced out of it to Egypt, they were in Mesopotamia. The Exodus myth no longer is the sole memory that defines Israel's external persona; it exists only in tension with a new founding memory of Abraham's Mesopotamian origin.[545] This aligns effectively with a rigorous effort to reframe the *golah*'s return migration as the second exodus, an observation that biblical scholars have consistently made.[546] Conse-

---

Israel out of Egypt to give it the land. The first affirmation loses its force when the second one is added to it."

544 Ska, "The Call of Abraham and Israel's Birth-Certificate," 59.

545 The Exodus myth, which once held a formative position in identifying Israel's origin in Egypt, could be pejoratively redefined as a period of deviation caused by Jacob's emigration from the land.

546 See now Jeon, *From the Reed Sea to Kadesh*, 50 with references.

quently, the significance of the exodus from Egypt is counterbalanced by the refreshed importance of the exodus from Mesopotamia.

11.3 Making of the Abrahamic Israel

The Abrahamic expansion completely redesigns Israel's dual origin myths, both its indigenous and external aspects. The Jacob tradition, which depicts Israel in relation to experiences inside the land, is now bookended by traditions linked to Israel's external origins – of Mesopotamia and Egypt. Ultimately, the once-balanced insider-outsider identity paradigm of Northern Israel (see Section 9.3) is reframed by the motif of Mesopotamian repatriation and the *golah*'s purity ideology. Consequently, the notion of Israel's Mesopotamian origin and Babylonia as a second home for Jews are firmly established. When we compare this to its putative original form, the extent of the changes introduced becomes apparent. Let me briefly outline the evolution of the Jacob story by identifying the contested boundaries that the story at its each level aimed to defend, modify, or reinforce.

11.3.1 From Indigenous Jacob to Israel's Dual Origin Myths

The Jacob tradition originated as the identity narrative of *Bene Ya'aqob*, an indigenous group residing in the land. The extent of the narrative Self aligns with the geographic boundary of the land, with Esau and Laban demarcating its borders. Since this group came to form part of Israel, their stories also were incorporated into Israel's tradition.

As disparate popular elements merge and coalesce to form the people of Israel, the Jacob tradition appears to be put into dialogue with the Exodus narrative. In this negotiation of identity, the Jacob tradition is set to represent Israel's indigenous identity, while the Exodus narrative represents its external identity.

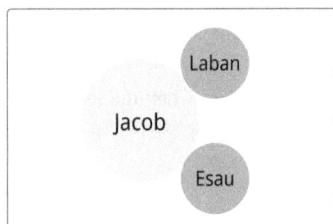

Fig. 7: Self and Others in Pre-Israelite Jacob Narrative. Illustration by Kim Minji.

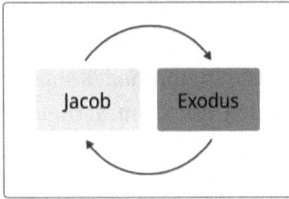

Fig. 8: Jacob in North Israel's Origin Myths. Illustration bry Kim Minji.

Although the two voices may contest severely at times, both eventually contribute to Israel's societal discourse on defining "who is Israel."

The Jacob and Exodus narratives are fundamentally distinct identity narratives, and their dialogue could be a rough one, understandably so. Throughout biblical literature, we observe a conflict between two perspectives. While the surface narrative emphasizes the exclusive worship of Yhwh, an underlying impulse to return to indigenous cultural traditions continually reappears. What we see in the presently juxtaposed two narratives is a clash of two different cultures, and I see their debate constitutes a major part of Israel's ingroup negotiation. Despite their contestation, however, these narratives *together* defined the outer boundary of Israel's newly found identity. The goal of this negotiation is to strike a balance between the two personas of Israel, no matter how severe the contention becomes. This is what I mean by saying that the Jacob and Exodus narratives served as the dual origin myths of the people of Israel. It is against this backdrop that the significance of the Abrahamic Israel must be analyzed.

11.3.2 Pre-P Judahite Reformulation

Judah's reformulating the existing Jacob-Exodus tradition operates in two stages. In the pre-P level, the southern Abrahamic tradition is inserted into the beginning of the ancestral tradition, making him the forefather of Jacob. At this stage, the contested boundary shifts to the dynamic between Abraham and Jacob.

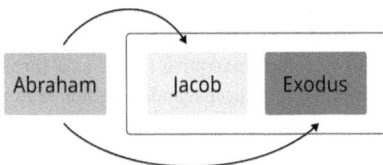

Fig. 9: Function of pre-P Abraham addition. Illustration by Kim Minji.

Abraham targets Jacob, reacts to his journey, and usurps his status. As detailed in this chapter, the focus was displayed through strategies of pre-occupation and negation, with the goal of trumping Jacob and establishing Abraham's superiority. At this level, Abraham is from Haran. The Haranide Abraham archetype foreshadows Jacob, while Abraham's eiso- and exodus foreshadow Moses. Such maneuvers mirror the ambitious spirit characteristic of the time of Josiah. Similar to Josiah's alleged northern campaign, whether real or imagined,[547] the aspiration is directed towards the North. This period of ambition aims to elevate Judah's status by promoting Abraham's importance in the symbolic world of Israel.

11.3.3 Priestly Renovation

As Judah found themselves in exile, the desire for supremacy over Israel waned in the face of more pressing needs of the moment. The traditional Priestly level attests to this shift.

In the Priestly level, two central aspects of reformulation have been analyzed: purification and extension. The new focus is on differentiating the pure Israel – here, in exile – from the contaminated one – there, in the land. This entails initiating a radical identity project that reimagines their newfound home in Babylonia as the birthplace of Israel by tracing Abraham's origin to Ur. This ambitious

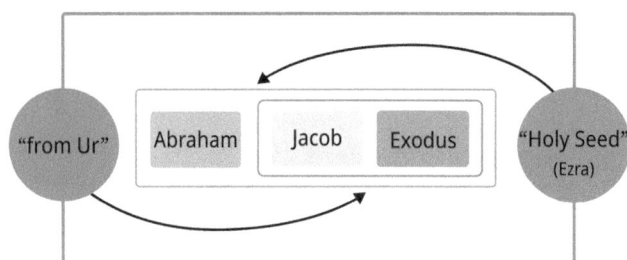

Fig. 10: Framing Effect of Priestly Abraham extension to Mesopotamia. Illustration by Kim Minji.

---

547 As noted, scholars have long debated the historical veracity of Josiah's purported reform. See n. 231 for discussion. However, the argument presented here remains valid whether the reform was real or purely a literary construct. If the entire reform narrative serves as a form of propaganda, the focus should be on how those responsible for the propaganda envisioned the reform and portrayed the desecration of Bethel as the culmination of the reform process. If the primary contributors to this narrative were individuals who had migrated from the North, it raises the question of how the construction of the propaganda can be explained within this context.

project redefined Abraham as the model repatriate, shifting the focus to promoting the *golah*'s status against the people of the land. The key motif at this stage is "exile and return," not only for Abraham but also for Jacob. The new frame foregrounds Jacob's exile and return, backgrounding his original trickster features. Even Moses's exodus from Egypt is subsumed into the model of exile and return pre-emptively set by Abraham. Now, the entire Pentateuch can be read as a story of return migration to the land.

Intriguingly, this redesigned past also serves as the ideological basis for Ezra's program. Ezra's return precisely rehearses the path of Abraham's journey (Ezra 7:1–10). Scholars have long noted that Ezra's return is projected as a second exodus, but I stress that that is only a partial picture. Ezra not only vampirizes Moses, he also turns Abraham and Jacob (of the Priestly text) to the model repatriates, models set in Israel's founding era. In addition, both Abraham and Jacob are co-opted to support Ezra's endogamous identity project. Although many scholars cite Mosaic stipulations against intermarriage with Canaanites (e.g., Deut 7:1–6; 23:3–7) as the basis for Ezra's exclusionary program,[548] the Priestly Abraham and Jacob traditions offer a more tangible example. These traditions highlight the rejection of Ishmael and Esau due to impure marriages, underscoring the importance of endogamy for the "holy seed." Such narratives inherently exclude the people of the land and reinforce the concept of a pure lineage.

11.4 Conclusion

Jacob and Abraham's cohabitation in Israel's ancestry is neither natural nor friendly. Rather, this partnership is a product of Judah's stringent efforts to redefine their past, which was destructive to earlier northerners' imagination of the past. While the traditional critics tended to attribute this combination of Abraham and Jacob traditions to an individual – whether a redactor, theologian, or historian – I find it unlikely that their decision was made in isolation from ongoing social negotiation. The act of combining literary traditions cannot be separated from the influence of the negotiation on "who we are."

Equally important to discerning *who* was behind the combination and *when* it took place is understanding its *effect*. The addition of the Abraham narrative is not an innocent act of preserving past traditions. As a result of this combination, Israel's ancestral past is radically redefined around Abraham, qualifying Jacob's foundational role. Abraham prefigures Jacob by pre-emptively occupying Jacob's

---

548 See, e.g., Katherine Southwood, *Ethnicity and the Mixed Marriage Crisis in Ezra 9–10: An Anthropological Approach* (Oxford: Oxford University Press, 2012), 75–78.

lands. Abraham is portrayed as a model of piety and the ultimate holder of Yhwh's promise. This casts doubt on Jacob's trickster character, whose crafty victory is redefined in light of the Abrahamic promise. His transformation into the promised heir is enabled only by the betrothal journey that provided pure wives provided by Abraham's homeland. Eventually, Abraham is plucked off from Jacob's land, rediscovering his true origin in Mesopotamia. Abraham's Mesopotamian origin reshuffles both the indigenous and external sides of Israel's identity, which provides a new foundation for the *golah*'s identity project.

In all, I have endeavored to demonstrate the deeper roots of Judah's Persian-period identity program. Judah's post-exilic identity reformation did not emerge out of a vacuum; identity exists only in a continuum of constant negotiation. Encounters with new Others and rapidly changing international circumstances certainly brought about what amounts to identity explosion for Judah, but the preceding stages of identity formation were equally vital for the later stage to exist. Only through a deep comprehension of their origins can we gain a comprehensive and nuanced understanding of Judah's ongoing identity project. Biblical texts have undergone multiple stages of development, propelled in part by Israel's and Judah's identity struggles, which resulted in a complex and multifaceted text with conflicting portrayals of the Self and Others. Ironically, it is the very versatility and adaptability of the competing identity discourse imbedded in the text that perhaps have made the narrative so effective and resonant for countless readers who can identify with its numerous facets. Reflecting on the far-reaching consequences of this ancient tradition, it is enlightening to understand that it all began with Judahites' quest for survival and identity recognition. The debt we owe them is immeasurable.

12 Conclusion: Judah's Desire and Our Desire

Returning to my initial questions: What was Judah's self-perception with regards to Israel, and how did the Israelites perceive Judah? I posed these questions because I believed in the significance of the subjective side of one's self-perception and its impact on one's social behaviors. My answer to these questions, as presented in this book, can be summarized as follows: Judahites claimed they were part of Israel, but the Israelites thought differently. For an extended period, Judahites lived under the shade of their powerful northern neighbor, which harbored a longing for Israel. Yet they were never fully embraced by the Israelites. The sense of rejection only intensified their longing. This gap between the ideal and reality fostered a deep-seated desire for Judah to be like Israel, which I argued, was a driving force behind Judah's rigorous appropriation of Israel.

By this, I challenge the enduring assumption that Judah and Israel ultimately shared a common origin. While an increasing number of scholars acknowledge them as separate kingdoms, this idea of innate unity permeates every subset of biblical scholarship's centuries-long efforts to understand Israel's origin and history. Simply acknowledging their independence in the political sphere does not remove all traces of this foundational assumption. I am not suggesting that the assumption is entirely wrong; rather, my emphasis has been that this transcends simple binaries of right and wrong. It pertains more to shifting perceptions than to static reality. The pull of ethnic unity can be invincible in some instances, but in others, it can be elusive. Merely stating that Judah was either a kin group to Israel or a separate entity cannot fully grasp this changing perception. Instead, I gave more weight to the alternative path that the Judahites forged this ancient connection with the intent of appropriating Israel's rich heritage that they lacked. I posit that my somewhat ambiguous answer provides a more effective framework to grapple with Judah's complex relationship with Israel.

If one were to ask whether Judah had connections to the Israelites, of course, one cannot deny them. Yet the problem is, then, the same must be true to other neighboring entities. Thus, rather than grappling with the elusive question of historical origins, my focus was on discerning the extent of changes that took place during Judah's adoption of Israel and the resultant contrasts between Judah's Israel and Ephraim's Israel. A mere binary framing of the issue falls short in addressing the complex dynamics that molded the evolving portrait of "Israel."

In that regard, I posited that reimagining the past was a pivotal strategy in implementing this identity takeover, illustrated by the Abrahamic expansion of the underlying Jacob tradition. Yet, that does not mean Judah's real Self was completely overshadowed or replaced; instead, it signified the creation of a new

https://doi.org/10.1515/9783111376554-012

hybrid Self, adding layers of complexity to the presentation of "biblical Israel." Consequently, I contend that the perceived unity between Israel and Judah, as evident in the current form of the text – or the "Abrahamic Israel" – is not an inherent reality but a construct born out of Judah's aspirations, which in turn, stemmed from Judah's inferior status in relation to Israel. Traditional view that saw the transmission of the Israelite legacy to Judah as a natural process,[549] as Judah being the sole remnant of Israel, falls short of taking into account the intricate psychological aspects of their complex relationships. Recognizing this alternative trajectory could pave the way for deeper insights into this critical stage in Israel's transformation.

12.1 On Functional Approach

Exploring the social dynamics and perceptions that underpin the relationship between Judah and Israel, I came to appreciate the instrumentalist perspective as more suitable than the dated primordialism. The construction of any group identity is a result of continuous social negotiations regarding our collective sense of Self, encompassing reflections on our origins, our present circumstances, and our aspirations for the future. Again, challenging the primordial unity of "Israel" serves not as an end in itself. It rather is a means to question how and when the "one Israel" as we know it was constructed and how the present text functioned as a discursive tool in that process.[550] The positive outcome of this perspective is that it compels me to meticulously examine the strategies Judah employed constructing its own ideal of "Abrahamic Israel."

In today's postmodern society, it is not uncommon to come across a challenging voice to fixed concepts and ideas, including the collective identities of groups or nations, such as in Shlomo Sand's controversial book *The Invention of the Jewish People*.[551] However, it is worth noting how Sand's critiques have vehemently defended the concept of one Jewish people, still relying on ideas such as tangible genetic markers of Jewish ancestry. This highlights how deeply ingrained

---

549 Of course, the claim is not that scholars have failed to recognize the Judahite orientation of the Abraham narrative. They have indeed identified all of the formational aspects I focused on. The key point here is that despite their recognition of the same data, they have not explored the transformative changes introduced by the additional material to the existing narrative and its impact on Israel's perception of its ancestral past and collective Self.

550 Indeed, the text undeniably carries numerous indications of primordial unity between Judah and Israel. The real question, however, is determining if these indications stem from historical facts or serve as discursive tools for constructing an ideal.

551 Shlomo Sand, *The Invention of the Jewish People*, trans. Yael Lotan (London: Verso, 2010).

the belief in the unity of ethnic groups is in the popular setting.[552] Thus, I see benefits in construing Jewishness, and also Koreanness, fundamentally as social constructs.[553] Again, this is not to say that the facts (of shared history, culture, and language) are lacking, but that fiction plays an equally important role in shaping these identities.

Unlike the elusive task of restoring the earliest Israel and Judah, observing the text as Judah's discursive attempts to reimagine the past redirects our attention from the historical past behind the text to the text itself, not as an artifact but as a discursive tool for identity formation of the historical present. I understand "Israel" as a dynamic notion that has been constantly contested. I therefore embrace the plurality of "Israels" in the Bible as reflections of the reality in negotiation. Judah's constructed Israels, both Abrahamic and pan-Israelite, constituted only part of many voices in negotiation with "Israel" in reality. This resists the temptation to neatly align different conceptions of Israel by time and space. Biblical historians may want to pinpoint Israel's genesis to specific groups and chart their evolution into subsequent political entities. Yet the reality was likely far more complex and ambiguous. My contention is that the present text's indecisiveness mirrors that contested reality, not an oversight or the redactors' failure to reconcile them. If so, what we need to do is not to figure out which period fits this and that concept and how to align them to different eras, but to use them to better understand how different voices served as discursive means in attempting to construct different "Israels," which worked together to make up the "biblical Israel" in the present text.

I have therefore highlighted that before Abraham enlisted himself as the ecumenical father of many, he was first the unforgiving forefather of Jacob; the "Abrahamic expansion," first and foremost, was part of the larger identity project through which Judah aimed to take over Israel's legacy. To underscore this, I delved into the transformative effects brought about by positioning Abraham's story at the root of Israel's ancestry. Observations on the distinct characteristics of the Abraham and Jacob traditions as identity narratives led me to recognize Abraham's strategic placement and significance within Judah's identity narrative, an aspect overlooked by scholars who viewed their combination as a "natural growth." I suggested that Abraham's principal position in Israel's ancestry is not

---

552 See, e.g., Harry Ostrer, *Legacy: A Genetic History of the Jewish People* (New York: Oxford University Press, 2012).

553 I want to emphasize that my intention is not to provoke my fellow Jewish and Israeli colleagues. This same principle applies to my Korean identity, whose constructed nature I also acknowledge. This recognition holds even though the Korean people have maintained their homeland, and their language and culture have remained relatively isolated for over a millennium.

based on historical accuracy, but rather on Judah's longing to shape their past in that manner. By remembering Abraham as the founding father of Israel, the Judahites fundamentally reframed the construction of "Israel." In this way, remembering is, indeed, "re-membering." At the end of the day, however, appropriating the other's legacy leaves a sense of shame and vulnerability, which seemingly prompted Judah to adopt a defensive measure of excessively vilifying Israel as a way of seeking justification for their act of appropriation.

In comparison to the other competing models (discussed in Chapter 3), the appropriation model places greater emphasis on the functionality of ancestral traditions as identity narratives. Naturally, it offers the most radical perspective on Judah's motivations for adopting Israel's identity. Most scholars, from past to present, tend to see a greater continuity between Judah and Israel than I posit, which they use as a basis to explain Judah's unlikely assumption of Israel's identity. However, in doing so, they must face the challenge of explaining away the ensuing discrepancy with the reality of division. Instead, I aimed to underscore that sometimes, the sheer intensity of desire, fueled by a sense of inferiority, is all it takes for one to appropriate the legacy and identity of a superior neighbor. With this, I believe I have made a cogent case that addresses most of the complexities surrounding Judah's appropriation of Israel. Of course, this does not mean that my claim negates all other propositions. Each model possesses its own merits, and one can see my proposition can supplement other models. Thus, others might simply incorporate insights from my proposition to supplement their existing arguments. That is, even if there was a North-South mediation, through refugees or Benjaminites, or the textual depiction of David's supposed dominion over Israel had a real foundation, or this appropriation emerged as a later Judean development in the post-exilic era, the core assertion stands: Judah's perceived inferiority had some influence on the process.

Yet, I am convinced that a more comprehensive shift towards the appropriation model is warranted. Foremost, my model effectively unravels the conundrum of how Judah vilified Israel while simultaneously adopting its legacy – a challenge not addressed adequately by other models. While Judah's contradictory sentiments towards Israel are not easily explained through straight reasoning, things begin to align, when viewed through the lens of mimetic rivalry of enemy brothers. The inferior Self's desire for the superior, while outwardly resenting them, serves as an apt illustration of this contradictory state, which I attempted to apply to Judah's psychological state in relation to Israel.

This change in perspective carries tremendous implications. If I were to pinpoint the primary contribution of my study within the historical-critical framework, it would be a call to fully reassess the northern legacy in Judah's Bible, building on the foundation established by Daniel Fleming. As Fleming, along with his predecessors, has shown, virtually every part of biblical literature bears the legacy of Northern Israel. If so, the transformative effect of the Abrahamic expansion to the original Jacob tradition, as I illustrated in this book, should be applied to other segments of the Bible, including its foundation myths, historical accounts, and prophetic writings – all viewed as facets of Judah's identity project, implemented on the space of the past, present, and future.

Consider the book of Hosea as an illustration. Undoubtedly, this text originated from the North. But when integrated into Judah's prophetic collection, does this book stay true to its northern original? While I concur that only minimal alterations have been made, perhaps subtle mentions of David and the like (Hos 3:5), the interpretation of the significance of this slight reorientation, and the meaning of the resultant Judahite version of Hosea, can differ dramatically based on one's understanding of the takeover. Rather than viewing it as a mere natural transmission between brethren, this book can be perceived as having undergone a radical transformation when received by the readership of opposite political orientation. In particular, consider Hosea's oracle of judgement against Ephraim/Israel (e.g., Hos 1:9; 4:1–6 and others). Would its significance in Judah remain consistent with Hosea's original intentions? Hosea likely intended his message as a desperate call for "return" (e.g., Hos 5:15; 6:1–3; 10:12; 12:6; 14:1–3). Yet, the Judahites likely viewed it as an affirmation of YHWH's rejection of Israel in favor of Judah. If this was central to the reasons for the book's initial embracement in Judah, how would the historical Hosea have reacted to such a view? Delving into such questions is inevitably speculative, but it underscores the complexity in understanding the nature of Judah's appropriation of Israel's heritage. Specifically, this issue hinges on the implications of altering the intended scope of discourse.[554]

---

554 Let me further illustrate this point by means of another Korean analogy. During the 1970s under South Korea's military regime, a robust resistance movement emerged. In the ideologically divided backdrop of the Korean peninsula, the rhetoric from this resistance sometimes appeared, or was portrayed, as leaning towards pro-North propaganda. Thus, these activists were often branded as threats to national security and charged with pro-North and anti-national criminals. In such a divided landscape, the multifaceted narratives get reduced to simplistic binaries, but the true situation is not as stark. When North Korea co-opts these sentiments for its propaganda, for instance, presenting them as proof of their regime's superiority and implying endorsement from these activists, the narrative instantly takes a twist. Criticizing South Korea's regime does not automatically mean endorsing North Korea. Many of them would have felt offended by North Korea's rhetoric. However, the implications of the North Korean agency's rhetoric extend beyond mere offense to the activists; it can significantly jeopardize their standing in South Korea, especially when they face accusations of violating National Security Law from their own government. The key takeaway is that in situations involving multiple political entities, political discourse should be assessed within its native societal context. Is this not applicable to the book of Hosea, which was primarily intended for Ephraim/Israel?

When a narrative stretches beyond its intended scope of discourse, its significance inevitably gets skewed due to the contrasting perceptions of the involved parties.

This may be a single example, but it does hint at the breadth of reevaluation needed when addressing matters related to North-South transitions. Having a renewed understanding of Judah's relationship with Israel, we are compelled to undertake a sweeping examination of the entire Bible, from the vantage point of Judah's identity project. The implications of such investigations might surpass what traditional critics have previously outlined in terms of historical evolution, especially in comprehending the essence of "biblical Israel."

12.2 On Contextual Approach

Historical-critical readers might believe the aforementioned review adequately captures the essence of the book. However, my study delves deeper than just the historical implications. There is a reason why I have presented what some might see as a simple, and well-known, historical thesis – that Judah and Israel were independent entities – in this complex and distinct way. While many might primarily focus on the "what's new?" question in this approach, I contend that the path to that conclusion, the "how I got there," holds equal significance. There are several key aspects through which my context informed my investigation.

While many scholars assume the ethnic unity of Judah and Israel, my context made me question the tangible implications of this perceived unity. Particularly in times of political upheaval, the purported unity can prove ineffective. Given this, the general assumptions scholars make about northern traditions and migrants finding their way to Jerusalem to eventually restore ancient unity was approached with caution. Just a few decades after the North's purported attempt to overthrow the Davidic throne (Isa 7:6) and amid the Assyrian crisis, it is more likely that Judah and Israel operated independently, mainly driven by their singular interests for survival. It is conceivable that some remnants of Israel considered seeking refuge in Jerusalem to be in line with their best interests despite recent conflicts. However, this does not necessarily imply that they were welcomed or were granted significant influence, let alone being given a dominant role in shaping Judah's future direction. In supporting this idea, I have drawn parallels from the Korean context, providing a foundation for more informed hypotheses regarding the potential impact refugees would likely have had in the host society.

To address the central question of how independent Judah came to adopt the name of Israel, I leaned into historical parallels found in Korea's interactions with

China. I highlighted Korea's vassal relationship with China in antiquity, pointing out one phase in history where Koreans exhibited a surprising tendency for voluntary submission, even going so far as to refer to themselves as the "little China." Furthermore, I cited instances where China's marginal Others, especially the Manchus, upon conquering the Chinese mainland, embraced China's esteemed name. By drawing parallels with discussions on New Qing History, I underscored the possibility that biblical scholars might have been overly focused on Judah's "Israelization," inadvertently missing out on the significance of Judah's hybrid identity.

Fundamentally, my inclination to adopt the notion of inferiority is ingrained in my context. This perspective, whether familiar or foreign to others, has always resonated with me as the apt lens for understanding the Judah-Israel relations. Korea, traditionally overshadowed in East Asian geopolitics and marred by a history of relentless conflicts, has for long grappled with a sense of inferiority. However, this sentiment has been transformed into a driving force, propelling Korea to overcome its troubled past and now serving as a model for many developing countries. This perhaps guides me to empathize more closely with the "inferior" Judah. Additionally, Judah's apparently paradoxical actions echo the typical contradictions of a mimetic Self, a sentiment all too familiar to me. While emulating other countries has underpinned Korea's success, it has also left us grappling with a less-than-favorable self-image that we struggled to overcome. At the same time, I understand that the imitating Self is not merely a mindless echo without its own aspirations. The inherent drive to outdo the original is a ubiquitous impulse, and when directed aptly, it becomes a potent force for success. This perhaps explains why painting Judah purely as a passive entity does not sit right with me.

I intentionally avoided using Western examples; not only am I less familiar with them, but I also did not want to position my self as seeking their validation.[555] I trust that readers can draw their own relevant analogies, an approach this study actively promotes. I also wanted to demonstrate that each culture owns its unique resources to shed light on issues presented in the Bible and its history. It continues to surprise me that Western scholars assume their culture maintains

---

555 To be honest with myself, I cannot ignore an inherent resistance I feel towards certain academic practices. My students routinely grapple with unfamiliar examples in the texts I assign them to study, as authors include references foreign to our context. I have yet to come across Western writers who consciously use diverse examples for a wider audience. Consequently, my students often find themselves googling these examples to fully engage with the material. I am aware that such assignments might make them feel deficient, and for that, I bear responsibility as well. It is not that they lack understanding; they are simply made to work with materials not tailored for their perspective.

a closer affinity with the biblical, or *Oriental*, world than people from other parts of the world. Although Western civilization integrated Hebraism early as a fundamental component of their world, there is no denying that their understanding of it was skewed by the Greco-Roman framework from the outset. I know critical scholars have been diligently working to address such biases; I merely say that perspectives from East Asia, and many other contexts, could contribute to and diversify their efforts. Unless one claims direct access to the ancient Israelite context, which is largely elusive to most, any interpretation of the Bible embodies inherent prejudices and biases external to the text and its world, making them all *contextual* studies.

This is my way to engaging with readers who might interpret the term "contextual" in the book's subtitle as an invitation to sideline my study against their "normative" ones. Characterizing my study as contextual does not imply that theirs is non-contextual. In fact, it invites consideration towards the opposite. We need to ponder what leads them to believe that their studies are not contextual, and what underlies that perception. How does this perception differ from the Greek perception of ἔθνη, the Roman view of Barbarians, and China's perception of animal Others? I cannot help but point out a striking commonality among these cases. While they have clearly defined terms for Others, the corresponding term for Us is either lacking or vague. There was simply no need to define Us, as it was taken for granted. But how much Our boundary making owes to Their presence out there has not been well recognized. This, I believe, reveals a symptomatic lack of self-awareness among Western scholars regarding the extent to which their normative Self shapes their interpretations. Throughout human history, and across diverse cultures and settings, those at the center struggled to acknowledge that the very definition and existence of Us is contingent upon the othering of Them. Without the perceived threat of the Others (a construct both then and now), their true selves – riddled with internal discord and tensions alleviated only by this othering – might have faced disintegration far earlier.[556]

Of course, no assertion of superiority is implied here for my contextual study over other *contextual* studies, Western included. My point is simply that incorporating divergent perspectives can offer additional lenses to understand the text, thereby only enriching our comprehension of this multifaceted text. Venturing down this less-trodden path, I am exhilarated to demonstrate that my Korean identity, and my East Asian heritage, instead of posing barriers, unfold rich potentials. I hope my own candid contextual reading, and the unfamiliar, but useful, interpretation that ensues, prompts readers to reconsider the unexamined prejudices they may have been unknowingly adopting.

---

556 Cf. Edward W. Said, *Orientalism* (New York: Pantheon Books, 1978).

12.3 History and Identity

Another notable distinction of my study from traditional scholarship is its adoption of identity formation, instead of history, as the primary lens to scrutinize the past. This is not to suggest an either-or situation. Identity formation inherently possesses historical aspects, and I have drawn extensively from historical-critical scholarship, perhaps more than any other biblical scholar who employed identity formation as a frame. This altered viewpoint, nonetheless, introduces nuances, some profoundly influencing my approach. Allow me to briefly outline the ramifications of this shift of emphasis.

First, using identity formation as the primary lens enables me to transcend traditional divisions in biblical studies, allowing for greater fluidity across the conventional boundaries that compartmentalize segments of the Bible. Historically, the Patriarchal and monarchic periods might appear distinct and distant from each other. Yet, identity formation provides a lens to see them in one stroke, all combined in terms of the effect it produces. I understand identity formation entails past, present, and future; and they work together for a common goal of shaping collective identity. Such a viewpoint allows me to understand Judah's relationship with Israel, a subject typically limited to Israel's historical literature, based on the growth of ancestral narratives.[557]

Secondly, employing identity discourse as a frame empowers me to fluidly navigate its preceding and subsequent discourses, in a more continuous and broader scheme. I am fully aware that this may be viewed as lacking methodological control in the viewpoint of today's literary critics, who have gradually moved into posing greater emphasis on tangible texts than problematic "traditions." However, focusing solely on the text – whether its final form or supposed written precursors – poses its own challenges. These extant texts are merely snapshots in the larger, ongoing discursive process that produced them. Before the Jacob story was ever committed to papyrus or parchment, there existed traditions or stories about Jacob.

---

557 In this grand scheme, connections emerge with canonical criticism, particularly echoing Sanders' notion of canon and community. James A. Sanders, *Canon and Community: A Guide to Canonical Criticism*, Guides to Biblical Scholarship (Philadelphia: Fortress, 1984). This perspective also bridges to biblical theology, a discipline that paints with broader strokes. Biblical theologians, Christian and Jewish, have increasingly employed a dialogic mode of investigation, which resonates well with the notion of identity negotiation inherent in my study. See Walter Brueggemann, *Theology of the Old Testament: Testimony, Dispute, Advocacy* (Minneapolis: Fortress, 2012); Sweeney, *Tanak: A Theological and Critical Introduction to the Jewish Bible*. While Old Testament theology examines Israel's identity vis-à-vis God, an identity discourse approach widens this scope, examining Israel's identity and boundaries within an expansive social framework.

Literary critics focus their inquiry on texts and their development, because their goal is to understand their origins and evolution. For them, stepping beyond what can be reconstructed through literary-critical methods is deemed methodologically unsound. Thus, when I discuss the Jacob story within the early monarchic period, critics would ask which text I am referring to, whether the story was already textualized at that time, or if reconstructing the text from that era is even possible. As I discussed above, it is impossible to precisely reconstruct the text by that early time; we cannot prove if a written material on the Jacob story existed by then. Yet, my problem is that the difficulty in precise reconstruction does not mean stories of Jacob were unknown to early Israelites.

Here, my fundamental premise makes a difference. I operate on the assumption that humans are storytelling animals and, as social and political entities emerge, they rely on narratives to imbue their communities with meaning, boundaries, and identity. Therefore, it becomes essential for me to investigate the narratives employed by the people of the Northern Kingdom to articulate their collective origins. In other words, what mythic support system underpinned their social cohesion as a community? That is to say, even if literary critics can substantiate that the Jacob text as we have it today is a product of the late exilic or post-exilic period, I am still interested in examining how an earlier version of the Jacob story functioned as a foundational element of their mythic past. While we may not be able to reconstruct that earlier version with precision, both internal factors (such as the narrative's plot structure) and external evidence (such as references to Jacob in early literature like Hosea) together attest that Jacob occupied a significant place in Israel's collective imagination of the ancestral past since the pre-exilic period. Critics might say they agree with me in principle, but my concern is with the actual practice of scholarship. Once scholars became skeptical about the possibility of reconstructing a monarchic version of the ancestral stories, research on earlier periods in relation to these ancestral narratives practically vanished – as if the Jacob story only became significant or available in the post-exilic era, which I find misleading. Even if the present form of the Jacob narrative came from a text of a later period, we should ask whether the plot of the story was crafted expressly for the audience of that time or whether it was a renarration of a story originating from an earlier period.

Thirdly, by framing the matter on identity formation, we forge a direct connection between the biblical text and its readership. Judah's act of claiming Israel was not a singular event. Historically, numerous attempts have been made to redefine and stake a claim on "Israel." Through the lens of identity formation, we draw a line that connects Judah's initial claim of Israel to myriad subsequent endeavors of the same nature, stretching to contemporary times. To elaborate, the rewriting of Israel's past may have been the Judahites' desperate attempts to seek legitimation for their desired supremacy through their Abrahamic connection. However, in doing so, they inadvertently opened the door for numerous other "Judahs" to follow their path. This includes Korean Christians, who could not be more foreign to "Israel": the gentiles of gentiles. Yet, even Korean Christians living in the twenty-first century can claim to ultimately inherit Abraham and be part of God's chosen people because of the sustained efforts to redefine Israel triggered by Judah's initial attempt.

The history of Judaism can be characterized as a continuous effort to define and defend the boundary of "Israel." The advent of Christianity brought a new layer to this dynamic, as it sought to redefine "Israel," but now under the banner of the Church.[558] The mutual struggle to define their respective identities has, in fact, served to crystallize the core elements of each tradition. Each faith, in contesting and reacting to the other, has shaped its counterpart in ways that would have been inconceivable in isolation. In due course, Christians established a discursive system that allowed them to graft themselves onto the larger tree of "Israel," even to the point of considering themselves the "true Israel," not unlike how Judah once related to Israel. Two millennia of interpretive strategies that redefined "Israel" by Paul, Luther, Calvin, and many others have allowed Christians, including Korean, to take a leap of faith and embrace a Christian identity, despite so many barriers. Inheriting Abraham was an important part of this leap of faith. Paul's role cannot be exaggerated in redefining God's chosen people by foregrounding faith. Yet, it must also be emphasized that major tools for Paul's renarration of the salvation history – mainly through Adam and Abraham – were provided by Judah's seminal efforts to redefine "Israel," first against Northern Israel and then later against the exilic context.

Simply, Judah's discursive strategies to claim Israel's identity is forever embedded in the text, inviting new readers to participate in them. Even my own journey mirrors Judah's initial effort to incorporate Israel. I see no intrinsic distinction between Judah's endeavor to appropriate Israel and my personal struggle as a Christian to contextualize the Hebrew Bible as Christian scripture. The impetus for Christians to claim the Old Testament as their identity narrative, of course, is not any tangible ethnic tie to the "Israel" described therein. Instead, it is the aspiration to be counted among "God's chosen" that drives them to engage with a narrative originally not their own.

---

558 Ahlström, *Who Were the Israelites?*, 117 n. 45.

12.4 Us and Them

Reflection on my identity must prompt reflections on the Others. To wrap up, I would like to touch on the practical implications of this research in our time of extremism. Recently, Erich S. Gruen, in *Rethinking the Other in Antiquity*,[559] offered a nuanced exploration of how ancient civilizations, especially in the Greco-Roman context, perceived and represented the Other. Contrary to the simplistic depictions of the Other as merely barbaric or exotic, Gruen underscores the multifaceted nature of these relationships. He posits that, while there might have been an ideological impetus to emphasize differences for various reasons, internal perspectives often reveal a recognition of shared values and a subtle appreciation for the Other. This complexity mirrors my argument that overt distinctions mask deeper shared realities, hinting at the intricate interplay of differentiation and assimilation. My research underscores the extent to which the constructed aspects of our identity stem from adopting the narratives of Others. It emphasizes the pivotal role that incorporating the stories of Others plays in shaping our self-perception. In essence, our existence is interwoven with the cultures and narratives of those around us.

A crucial observation to make is that, practically speaking, there is not any noticeable distinction between my personal narratives and acquired narratives when it comes to defining "who I am." I hold memories from individual experiences, as well as shared recollections of significant historical events, such as the Korean War or Japanese colonialism. While I have not lived through the war or colonialism firsthand, immersing myself in the collective memory of these events has an impact on me as profound as my personal experiences. In the same vein, reflecting on Abraham's faith introduces another dimension of my adopted memory, shaping the religious side of my Self. Each of these memories resonates with me as authentic part of "who I am." This might elucidate why I was initially drawn to interpret these traditions more as identity narratives rather than mere history. It presented a medium through which I could genuinely connect to these narratives. While history might discriminate me as a gentile, if measured by the degree of my eagerness to integrate the narrative identities these stories offer, I am equally qualified. This perspective also underscores how and why my challenging the Abraham tradition as a myth might disturb some Korean evangelical Christian students more profoundly than it might trouble some secular Jews. The depth of the connection one feels to a narrative identity is not governed by its factual basis but by the weight of importance one assigns to the narrative.

---

559 Erich S. Gruen, *Rethinking the Other in Antiquity*, Martin Classical Lectures (Princeton, NJ: Princeton University Press, 2011).

It is against this backdrop that I must comment on my discussion on Israel's origin in Canaan, the ultimate Other in biblical world view. Some readers might have wondered about the emphasis I placed on Israel's Canaanite origins when my overall thesis primarily concerns Judah's appropriation of Israel; however, this aspect has pragmatic underpinnings to my argument. By recognizing Israel's Canaanite origins, we see that there was a deeper layer to Judah's appropriation of Israel: Israel desired Canaan before Judah desired Israel.[560] As I argued, the permeation of Canaanite culture in the Jacob tradition signifies more than nomadic Israel assimilating into the new sedentary culture they encountered. Instead, Israel, or at least its majority, grew out of Canaan and later sought to differentiate themselves from it. If this is how Israel emerged, it indicates a profound connection to the Canaan they ostensibly abhorred. This is exactly the same dynamic that we observed in the way Judah later desired/resented Israel.

In this way, history indeed repeats itself. I have long been fascinated by this recurrent pattern, a sentiment I have conveyed in a previous publication in the context of Judah's relationship with Israel.[561] On top of that, I now see that the issue transcends that particular moment in history, serving as the backdrop for the enduring debate between the two seminal voices (of identity discourse) that make up and continually redefine "Israel."[562] Such appropriation has been a recurrent process throughout the history of Abrahamic religions and continues to manifest in varied forms across diverse locales today. The creation of countless "Israels" involved a desired Self (in ideal) and a lacking Self (in real), which necessitated self-promotion through identification, assimilation, or appropriation. Central to each iteration of this identity appropriation is the longing to be recognized within God's peoplehood, driven more by a desire for belonging than by any direct link to its origin. Among many other new "Israels," Korean Christians stand as one of the latest in line. While the extent might vary, the fundamental nature of Judah's appropriation of Israel mirrors that of Korean Christians asserting an Israel identity.

This is the essence of the message I share with my students in my final class on the Pentateuch, a session I deeply cherish. I turn a semester long study of the Pentateuch into an arena of discussion as to what it means for us, Asian Christians,

---

560 Using this phrasing might suggest clear boundaries between Israel and Canaan, as well as between Israel and Judah. That is not my intent. While limited by expression, my argument has been that these relationships are more nuanced than commonly perceived. In essence, Israel's ties to Canaan may be closer, and its bond with Judah more distant, than traditionally believed.
561 See Hong, "The Deceptive Pen of Scribes," 440.
562 The debate permeates biblical literature, extending beyond the juxtaposition of Genesis and Exodus narratives, which I shall delve into in future works.

to read and internalize the narratives of Abraham, Jacob, and Moses, questions first introduced at the beginning of the course. This touches upon the meaning of belief, how we have embraced an unlikely scenario of conversion, internalizing this narrative and using it to reconceive "who we are." Recognizing the unlikelihood of this *conversion* opens up our eyes to recognize centuries of interpretive endeavors that paved this path.

Acknowledging that group identities are constructed, often by the appropriation of Others' narratives, can help prevent the abuse of power often stems from a misguided sense of unity. While nations often promote the idea of an innate, primordial unity to their citizens, we get to see this contradicts social-scientific observations on how nation is built, not given. Recognizing that our sense of unity is forged out of societal imperatives for survival and security can encourage a more measured use of the sentiment of exclusive unity. Understanding that our past was once constructed suggests that it can be reshaped again, and in novel ways. It is crucial to recognize that Others too have their beliefs rooted in shared origins, which at times encroach or challenge our own claims. Yet, understanding how we became "who we are" can usher in a more wholesome relationship with Others, who also need to seek affirmation in their narrative identities as fervently as we do in ours.

Bibliography

Adler, Jonathan M., Lauren M. Skalina, and Dan P. McAdams. "The Narrative Reconstruction of Psychotherapy and Psychological Health." *Psychotherapy Research* 18 (2008): 719–34. https://doi.org/10.1080/10503300802326020.

Ahlström, Gösta W. *Who Were the Israelites?* Winona Lake, IN: Eisenbrauns, 1986.

Ahn, John J. *Exile as Forced Migrations: A Sociological, Literary, and Theological Approach on the Displacement and Resettlement of the Southern Kingdom of Judah.* BZAW 417. Berlin: Walter de Gruyter, 2011.

Albright, W. F. "The Jordan Valley in the Bronze Age." *AASOR* 6 (1924): 13–74. https://doi.org/10.2307/3768510.

Albright, William Foxwell. *Yahweh and the Gods of Canaan: A Historical Analysis of Two Contrasting Faiths.* London: Athlone, 1968.

Alt, Albrecht. "Die Heimat des Deuteronomium." In *Kleine Schriften zur Geschichte des Volkes Israel*, vol. 2: 250–75. München: C. H. Beck, 1953.

Alt, Albrecht. *Essays on Old Testament History and Religion.* Oxford: Blackwell, 1966.

Alt, Albrecht. "The God of the Fathers." In *Essays on Old Testament History and Religion*, 1–66. Oxford: Blackwell, 1966.

Alt, Albrecht. "The Formation of the Israelite State in Palestine." In *Essays on Old Testament History and Religion*, 172–237. Oxford: Blackwell, 1966.

Alter, Robert. *The David Story: A Translation with Commentary of 1 and 2 Samuel.* New York: W. W. Norton, 1999.

Anderson, Benedict. *Imagined Communities: Reflections on the Origin and Spread of Nationalism.* Rev. ed. London: Verso, 2006.

Assis, Elie. "From Adam to Esau and Israel: An Anti-Edomite Ideology in 1 Chronicles 1." *VT* 56 (2006): 287–302. https://doi.org/10.1163/156853306778149629.

Assmann, Jan. "Communicative and Cultural Memory." In *Cultural Memory Studies: An International and Interdisciplinary Handbook*, edited by Astrid Erll and Ansgar Nünning, 109–18. Media and Cultural Memory 8. Berlin: Walter de Gruyter, 2008.

Assmann, Jan. *Cultural Memory and Early Civilization: Writing, Remembrance, and Political Imagination.* New York: Cambridge University Press, 2011.

Avigad, Nahman. *Discovering Jerusalem.* Nashville: Thomas Nelson, 1983.

Baden, Joel S. *J, E, and the Redaction of the Pentateuch.* FAT 68. Tübingen: Mohr Siebeck, 2009.

Baden, Joel S. *The Composition of the Pentateuch: Renewing the Documentary Hypothesis.* New Haven: Yale University Press, 2012.

Bang, Yong-chul. "The Outbreak and Characteristics of Goguryeo Revival War." *Daegu Historical Review* 133 (2018): 115–49. https://doi.org/10.17751/DHR.133.115 [방용철. "고구려 부흥전쟁의 발발과 그 성격." 대구사학 133].

Barstad, Hans M. *The Myth of the Empty Land: A Study in the History and Archaeoloogy of Judah During the "Exilic" Period.* Symbolae Osloenses. Fasc. Supplet. 28. Oslo: Scandinavian University Press, 1996.

Bar-Tal, Daniel. *Shared Beliefs in a Society: Social Psychological Analysis.* Thousand Oaks, CA: Sage, 2000.

Barth, Fredrik, ed. *Ethnic Groups and Boundaries: The Social Organization of Culture Difference.* Boston: Little, Brown and Co., 1969.

Bedford, Peter. "Diaspora: Homeland Relations in Ezra-Nehemiah." *VT* 52 (2002): 147–65. https://doi.org/10.1163/156853302760013820.

https://doi.org/10.1515/9783111376554-013

Ben Zvi, Ehud. "Who Knew What?: The Construction of the Monarchic Past in Chronicles and Implications for the Intellectual Setting of Chronicles." In *Judah and the Judeans in the Fourth Century B.C.E*, edited by Oded Lipschits, Gary N. Knoppers, and Rainer Albertz, 349–60. Winona Lake, IN: Eisenbrauns, 2007.

Ben Zvi, Ehud. "Chronicles and Its Reshaping of Memories of Monarchic Period Prophets: Some Observations." In *Prophets, Prophecy, and Ancient Israelite Historiography*, edited by Mark J. Boda and Lissa M. Wray Beal, 167–88. Winona Lake, IN: Eisenbrauns, 2013.

Ben Zvi, Ehud, and Diana V. Edelman, eds. *Imagining the Other and Constructing Israelite Identity in the Early Second Temple Period*. LHBOTS 456. London: Bloomsbury T&T Clark, 2014.

Berlejung, Angelika. "Family Ties: Constructed Memories about Aram and the Aramaeans in the Old Testament." In *In Search for Aram and Israel: Politics, Culture, and Identity*, edited by Omer Sergi, Manfred Oeming, and Izaak J. de Hulster, 355–77. Orientalische Religionen in der Antike 20. Tübingen: Mohr Siebeck, 2016.

Berquist, Jon L. "Constructions of Identity in Postcolonial Yehud." In *Judah and the Judeans in the Persian Period*, edited by Oded Lipschits and Manfred Oeming, 53–66. Winona Lake, IN: Eisenbrauns, 2006.

Bhabha, Homi K. *The Location of Culture*. London: Routledge, 1994.

Blum, Erhard. *Die Komposition der Vätergeschichte*. WMANT 57. Neukirchen-Vluyn: Neukirchener Verlag, 1984.

Blum, Erhard. *Studien zur Komposition des Pentateuch*. BZAW 189. Berlin: Walter de Gruyter, 1990.

Blum, Erhard. "Noch Einmal: Jakobs Traum in Bethel–Genesis 28,10–22." In *Rethinking the Foundations: Historiography in the Ancient World and in the Bible: Essays in Honour of John Van Seters*, edited by Steven L. McKenzie and Thomas Römer, 33–54. BZAW 294. Berlin: Walter de Gruyter, 2000.

Blum, Erhard. "The Jacob Tradition." In *The Book of Genesis: Composition, Reception, and Interpretation*, edited by Craig A. Evans, Joel N. Lohr, and David L. Petersen, 181–211. VTSup 152. Leiden: Brill, 2012.

Bohnet, Adam. "Ruling Ideology and Marginal Subjects: Ming Loyalism and Foreign Lineages in Late Chosŏn Korea." *Journal of Early Modern History* 15 (2011): 477–505. https://doi.org/10.1163/157006511X604013.

Bond, George C., and Angela Gilliam, eds. *Social Construction of the Past: Representation as Power*. One World Archaeology 24. London: Routledge, 1994.

Brett, Mark G. *Genesis: Procreation and the Politics of Identity*. London: Routledge, 2000.

Brett, Mark G. "Israel's Indigenous Origins: Cultural Hybridity and the Formation of Israelite Ethnicity." *BibInt* 11 (2003): 400–412. https://doi.org/10.1163/156851503322566813.

Broshi, Magen. "Expansion of Jerusalem in the Reigns of Hezekiah and Manasseh." *IEJ* 24 (1974): 21–26.

Brubaker, Rogers. *Ethnicity Without Groups*. Cambridge, MA: Harvard University Press, 2004.

Brubaker, Rogers, and Frederick Cooper. "Beyond 'Identity.'" *Theory and Society* 29 (2000): 1–47. https://doi.org/10.1023/A:1007068714468.

Brueggemann, Walter. *First and Second Samuel*. Interpretation. Louisville, KY: John Knox, 1990.

Brueggemann, Walter. *Theology of the Old Testament: Testimony, Dispute, Advocacy*. Minneapolis: Fortress, 2012.

Bruner, Jerome S. *Acts of Meaning*. Cambridge, MA: Harvard University Press, 1990.

Buccellati, Giorgio. *Cities and Nations of Ancient Syria; an Essay on Political Institutions with Special Reference to the Israelite Kingdoms*. Rome: Istituto di Studi Del Vicino Oriente, Università di Roma, 1967.

Buswell Jr., Robert E., and Timothy S. Lee, eds. *Christianity in Korea*. Honolulu: University of Hawaii Press, 2006.

Calhoun, Craig. "Nationalism and Ethnicity." *Annual Review of Sociology* 19 (1993): 211–39. https://doi.org/10.1146/annurev.so.19.080193.001235.

Campbell, Joseph. *The Hero with a Thousand Faces*. Bollingen Series 17. New York: Pantheon Books, 1949.

Carr, David. "Narrative and the Real World: An Argument for Continuity." *History and Theory* 25 (1986): 117–31. https://doi.org/10.2307/2505301.

Carr, David M. *Reading the Fractures of Genesis: Historical and Literary Approaches*. Louisville, KY: Westminster John Knox, 1996.

Carr, David M. *The Formation of the Hebrew Bible: A New Reconstruction*. New York: Oxford University Press, 2011.

Carrico, Kevin. *The Great Han: Race, Nationalism, and Tradition in China Today*. Berkeley, CA: University of California Press, 2017.

Chen, Jian. *China's Road to the Korean War: The Making of the Sino-American Confrontation*. New York: Columbia University Press, 1994.

Choi, Ho-won. "Geommojam and Anseung Forces of Goguryeo and Their Relationship with and Perception of Silla." *Sillasahakpo* 49 (2020): 171–206 [최호원. "고구려 검모잠·안승 세력과 대신라관계 인식." 신라사학보 49].

Chung, Sun-Yoh. "The Goguryo Refugees Who Move to the Silla Kingdom – Focused on the Settlers in Bodeokguk." *History and Discourse* 56 (2010): 71–106 [정선여. "신라로 유입된 고구려 유민의 동향." 역사와 담론 56].

Cinnirella, Marco. "Exploring Temporal Aspects of Social Identity: The Concept of Possible Social Identities." *European Journal of Social Psychology* 28 (1999): 227–48. https://doi.org/10.1002/(SICI)1099-0992(199803/04)28:2<227::AID-EJSP866>3.0.CO;2-X.

Clements, R. E. *Abraham and David: Genesis XV and Its Meaning for Israelite Tradition*. SBT 2/5. Naperville, IL: Allenson, 1967.

Cohen, Anthony P. *The Symbolic Construction of Community*. Chichester: E. Horwood and Tavistock, 1985.

Collingwood, R. G. *An Autobiography*. London: Oxford University Press, 1939.

Condor, Susan. "Social Identity and Time." In *Social Groups and Identities: Developing the Legacy of Henri Tajfel*, edited by W. P. Robinson, 285–315. International Series in Social Psychology. Oxford: Butterworth-Heinemann, 1996.

Coote, Robert B. *In Defense of Revolution: The Elohist History*. Minneapolis: Fortress, 1991.

Cornell, Stephen. "That's the Story of Our Life." In *We Are a People: Narrative and Multiplicity in Constructing Ethnic Identity*, edited by Paul R. Spickard and W. Jeffrey Burroughs, 41–53. Philadelphia: Temple University Press, 2000.

Cross, Frank Moore. *Canaanite Myth and Hebrew Epic: Essays in the History of the Religion of Israel*. Cambridge, MA: Harvard University Press, 1973.

Cross, Frank Moore. "'Ēl and the God of the Fathers." In *Canaanite Myth and Hebrew Epic: Essays in the History of the Religion of Israel*, 13–43. Cambridge, MA: Harvard University Press, 1973.

Cross, Frank Moore. *From Epic to Canon: History and Literature in Ancient Israel*. Baltimore: Johns Hopkins University Press, 1998.

Cross, Frank Moore. "Reuben, the Firstborn of Jacob: Sacral Traditions and Early Israelite History." In *From Epic to Canon: History and Literature in Ancient Israel*, 53–72. Baltimore: Johns Hopkins University Press, 1998.

Crossley, Pamela Kyle. *A Translucent Mirror: History and Identity in Qing Imperial Ideology*. Philip E. Lilienthal Asian Studies Imprint. Berkeley, CA: University of California Press, 1999.

Crouch, Carly L. *The Making of Israel: Cultural Diversity in the Southern Levant and the Formation of Ethnic Identity in Deuteronomy*. VTSup 162. Leiden: Brill, 2014.

Crouch, Carly L. *Israel and Judah Redefined: Migration, Trauma, and Empire in the Sixth Century BCE*. Society for Old Testament Study Monographs. Cambridge: Cambridge University Press, 2021.

Cumings, Bruce. "American Orientalism at War in Korea and the United States: A Hegemony of Racism, Repression, and Amnesia." In *Orientalism and War*, edited by Tarak Barkawi and Keith Stanski, 39–64. New York: Columbia University Press, 2012.

Danell, G. A. *Studies in the Name Israel in the Old Testament*. Uppsala: Appelbergs Boktrykeri-A.-B., 1946.

Davies, Philip R. *In Search of 'Ancient Israel.'* JSOTSup 148. Sheffield: JSOT Press, 1992.

Davies, Philip R. "The Origin of Biblical Israel." *JHebS* 5 (2005): 1–14. https://doi.org/10.5508/jhs.2005.v5.a17.

Davies, Philip R. "The Origin of Biblical Israel." In *Essays on Ancient Israel in Its Near Eastern Context: A Tribute to Nadav Na'aman*, edited by Yaira Amit, Ehud Ben Zvi, Israel Finkelstein, and Oded Lipschits, 141–48. Winona Lake, IN: Eisenbrauns, 2006.

Davies, Philip R. *The Origins of Biblical Israel*. LHBOTS 485. New York: T&T Clark, 2007.

Davies, Philip R. "The Trouble with Benjamin." In *Reflection and Refraction*, edited by Robert Rezetko, Timothy H. Lim, and W. Brian Aucker, 93–111. VTSup 113. Leiden: Brill, 2007.

Dickerman, Lysander. "The Names of Jacob and Joseph in Egypt." *The Old Testament Student* 7 (1888): 181–85. https://doi.org/10.1086/469990.

Dicou, Bert. *Edom, Israel's Brother and Antagonist: The Role of Edom in Biblical Prophecy and Story*. JSOTSup 169. Sheffield: JSOT Press, 1994.

Diener, Alexander C. *Borders: A Very Short Introduction*. New York: Oxford University Press, 2012.

Donnan, Hastings, and Thomas M. Wilson. *Borders: Frontiers of Identity, Nation and State*. Oxford: Berg, 1999.

Dozeman, Thomas B., and Konrad Schmid, eds. *A Farewell to the Yahwist?: The Composition of the Pentateuch in Recent European Interpretation*. Atlanta: Society of Biblical Literature, 2006.

Duncan, John B. "Confucianism in the Late Koryŏ and Early Chosŏn." *Korean Studies* 18 (1994): 77–102. https://doi.org/10.1353/ks.1994.0015.

Duncan, John B. *The Origins of the Choson Dynasty*. Seattle: University of Washington Press, 2000.

Eberstadt, Nick. *Korea Approaches Reunification*. Armonk, NY: M. E. Sharpe, 1995.

Edelman, Diana. "Hezekiah's Alleged Cultic Centralization." *JSOT* 32 (2008): 395–434. https://doi.org/10.1177/0309089208092.

Edelman, Diana V., and Ehud Ben Zvi, eds. *Remembering Biblical Figures in the Late Persian and Early Hellenistic Periods: Social Memory and Imagination*. Oxford: Oxford University Press, 2013.

Elliott, Mark C. *The Manchu Way: The Eight Banners and Ethnic Identity in Late Imperial China*. Stanford, CA: Stanford University Press, 2001.

Emerton, J. A. "Some Problems in Genesis XXXVIII." *VT* 25 (1975): 338–61. https://doi.org/10.1163/156853375X00656.

Engel, John D., Joseph Zarconi, Laura L. Pethtel, and Sally A. Missimi. *Narrative in Health Care: Healing Patients, Practitioners, Profession, and Community*. Oxford: Radcliffe, 2008.

Eriksen, Thomas Hylland. *Ethnicity and Nationalism: Anthropological Perspectives*. 3rd ed. London: Pluto, 2010.

Erikson, Erik H. *Identity, Youth, and Crisis*. New York: W. W. Norton, 1968.

Erll, Astrid, and Ansgar Nünning, eds. *Cultural Memory Studies: An International and Interdisciplinary Handbook*. Media and Cultural Memory 8. Berlin: Walter de Gruyter, 2008.

Evans-Pritchard, E. E. *The Nuer: A Description of the Modes of Livelihood and Political Institutions of a Nilotic People*. Oxford: Clarendon, 1940.

Fairbank, John King, and Ta-tuan Ch'en, eds. *The Chinese World Order: Traditional China's Foreign Relations*. Harvard East Asian Series 32. Cambridge, MA: Harvard University Press, 1968.

Finkelstein, Israel. "The Date of the Settlement of the Philistines in Canaan." *TA* 22 (1995): 213–39. https://doi.org/10.1179/tav.1995.1995.2.213.

Finkelstein, Israel. "The Archaeology of the United Monarchy: An Alternative View." *Levant* 28 (1996): 177–87. https://doi.org/10.1179/lev.1996.28.1.177.

Finkelstein, Israel. "Hazor and the North in the Iron Age: A Low Chronology Perspective." *BASOR* 314 (1999): 55–70. https://doi.org/10.2307/1357451.

Finkelstein, Israel. "The Settlement History of Jerusalem in the Eighth and Seventh Century BC." *RB* 115 (2008): 499–515. https://doi.org/10.2143/RBI.115.4.3206463.

Finkelstein, Israel. "A Great United Monarchy?: Archaeological and Historical Perspectives." In *One God, One Cult, One Nation: Archaeological and Biblical Perspectives*, edited by Reinhard Gregor Kratz and Hermann Spieckermann, 3–28. Berlin: Walter de Gruyter, 2010.

Finkelstein, Israel. "Saul, Benjamin and the Emergence of 'Biblical Israel': An Alternative View." *ZAW* 123 (2011): 348–67.

Finkelstein, Israel. *The Forgotten Kingdom: The Archaeology and History of Northern Israel*. ANEM 5. Atlanta: Society of Biblical Literature, 2013.

Finkelstein, Israel. "Jeroboam II in Transjordan." *SJOT* 34 (2020): 19–29. https://doi.org/10.1080/09018328.2020.1801910.

Finkelstein, Israel, Yuval Gadot, and Lidar Sapir-Hen. "Pig Frequencies in Iron Age Sites and the Biblical Pig Taboo: Once Again." *UF* 49 (2018): 109–16.

Finkelstein, Israel, and Amihai Mazar. *The Quest for the Historical Israel: Debating Archaeology and the History of Early Israel*. Edited by Brian B. Schmidt. ABS 17. Atlanta: Society of Biblical Literature, 2007.

Finkelstein, Israel, and Eli Piasetzky. "The Iron Age Chronology Debate: Is the Gap Narrowing?" *NEA* 74 (2011): 50–54. https://doi.org/10.5615/neareastarch.74.1.0050.

Finkelstein, Israel, and Thomas Römer. "Comments on the Historical Background of the Abraham Narrative: Between 'Realia' and 'Exegetica.'" *HeBAI* 3 (2014): 3–23. https://doi.org/10.1628/219222714X13994465496820.

Finkelstein, Israel, and Thomas Römer. "Comments on the Historical Background of the Jacob Narrative in Genesis." *ZAW* 126 (2014): 317–38. https://doi.org/10.1515/zaw-2014-0020.

Finkelstein, Israel, and Neil Asher Silberman. *The Bible Unearthed: Archaeology's New Vision of Ancient Israel and the Origin of Its Sacred Texts*. New York: Free Press, 2001.

Finkelstein, Israel, and Neil Asher Silberman. *David and Solomon: In Search of the Bible's Sacred Kings and the Roots of the Western Tradition*. New York: Free Press, 2006.

Finkelstein, Israel, and Neil Asher Silberman. "Temple and Dynasty: Hezekiah, the Remaking of Judah and the Rise of the Pan-Israelite Ideology." *JSOT* 30 (2006): 259–85. https://doi.org/10.1177/0309089206063428.

Finley, M. I. *The Use and Abuse of History*. London: Chatto and Windus, 1975.

Fishbane, Michael A. *Biblical Interpretation in Ancient Israel*. Oxford: Clarendon, 1985.

Fiskesjo, Magnus. "The Animal Other: China's Barbarians and Their Renaming in the Twentieth Century." *Social Text* 29 (2011): 57–79. https://doi.org/10.1215/01642472-1416091.

Flanagan, James W. "Judah in All Israel." In *No Famine in the Land: Studies in Honor of John L. McKenzie*, edited by James W. Flanagan and Anita Weisbrod Robinson, 101–16. Missoula, MT: Scholars Press, 1975.

Fleming, Daniel E. *The Legacy of Israel in Judah's Bible: History, Politics, and the Reinscribing of Tradition*. New York: Cambridge University Press, 2012.

Fleming, Daniel E. "The Bible's Little Israel: Terminological Clasts in a Compositional Matrix." *HeBAI* 10 (2021): 149–86. https://doi.org/10.1628/hebai-2021-0011.

Fohrer, Georg. "Der Vertrag zwischen König und Volk in Israel." *ZAW* 71 (1959): 1–22. https://doi.org/10.1515/zatw.1959.71.1-4.1.

Friedman, Richard Elliott. *Who Wrote the Bible?* New York: Summit Books, 1987.

Gadamer, Hans Georg. *Truth and Method*. 2nd ed. London: Continuum, 2004.

Geary, Patrick J. *Before France and Germany: The Creation and Transformation of the Merovingian World*. New York: Oxford University Press, 1988.

Geertz, Clifford. *The Interpretation of Cultures: Selected Essays*. New York: Basic Books, 1973.

Geobey, Ronald A. "Joseph the Infiltrator, Jacob the Conqueror? Reexamining the Hyksos–Hebrew Correlation." *JBL* 136 (2017): 23–37. https://doi.org/10.1353/jbl.2017.0001.

Germany, Stephen. "The Hexateuch Hypothesis: A History of Research and Current Approaches." *CurBR* 16 (2018): 131–56. https://doi.org/10.1177/1476993x17737067.

Gertz, Jan Christian. "Abraham, Mose und der Exodus: Beobachtungen zur Redaktionsgeschichte von Gen 15." In *Abschied vom Jahwisten: Die Komposition des Hexateuch in der jüngsten Diskussion*, edited by Jan Christian Gertz, Konrad Schmid, and Markus Witte, 63–81. BZAW 315. Berlin: Walter de Gruyter, 2002.

Gertz, Jan Christian, Konrad Schmid, and Markus Witte, eds. *Abschied vom Jahwisten: Die Komposition des Hexateuch in der jüngsten Diskussion*. BZAW 315. Berlin: Walter de Gruyter, 2002.

Gertz, Jan C., Bernard M. Levinson, Dalit Rom-Shiloni, and Konrad Schmid, eds. *The Formation of the Pentateuch: Bridging the Academic Cultures of Europe, Israel, and North America*. Tübingen: Mohr Siebeck, 2016.

Geus, C. H. J. de. *The Tribes of Israel: An Investigation into Some of the Presuppositions of Martin Noth's Amphictyony Hypothesis*. Studia Semitica Neerlandica 18. Assen: Van Gorcum, 1976.

Geva, Hillel, ed. *Jewish Quarter Excavations in the Old City of Jerusalem: Conducted by Nahman Avigad, 1969–1982*. Vol. 1. Jerusalem: Israel Exploration Society, 2000.

Ginsberg, Harold Louis. *The Israelian Heritage of Judaism*. TSJTSA 24. New York: Jewish Theological Seminary of America, 1982.

Girard, René. *Deceit, Desire, and the Novel: Self and Other in Literary Structure*. Baltimore: Johns Hopkins University Press, 1965.

Girard, René. "Mimesis and Violence: Perspectives in Cultural Criticism." *Berkshire Review* 14 (1979): 9–19.

Girard, René. *A Theater of Envy: William Shakespeare*. Odéon. New York: Oxford University Press, 1991.

Giuntoli, Federico, and Konrad Schmid, eds. *The Post-Priestly Pentateuch: New Perspectives on Its Redactional Development and Theological Profiles*. FAT 101. Tübingen: Mohr Siebeck, 2015.

Gnuse, Robert Karl. *The Elohist: A Seventh-Century Theological Tradition*. Eugene, OR: Cascade Books, 2017.

Godet, Frédéric Louis. *Commentary on St. Paul's Epistle to the Romans*. Translated by A. Cusin. Vol. 2. 2 vols. Edinburgh: T&T Clark, 1881.

Gosse, Bernard. "Abraham and David." *JSOT* 34 (2010): 25–31. https://doi.org/10.1177/0309089209346346.

Gottwald, Norman K. *The Tribes of Yahweh: A Sociology of the Religion of Liberated Israel, 1250–1050 B.C.E.* Maryknoll, NY: Orbis, 1979.

Grabbe, Lester L. *Ancient Israel: What Do We Know and How Do We Know It?* Rev. ed. London: Bloomsbury T&T Clark, 2017.

Graupner, Axel. *Der Elohist: Gegenwart und Wirksamkeit des Transzendenten Gottes in der Geschichte.* WMANT 97. Neukirchen-Vluyn: Neukirchener Verlag, 2002.

Grayson, James Huntley. *Myths and Legends from Korea: An Annotated Compendium of Ancient and Modern Materials.* London: Routledge, 2000.

Greenstein, Edward L. "The Fugitive Hero Narrative Pattern in Mesopotamia." In *Worship, Women, and War: Essays in Honor of Susan Niditch,* edited by John J. Collins, T. M. Lemos, and Saul M. Olyan, 17–35. BJS 357. Providence, RI: Brown University, 2015.

Greifenhagen, Franz V. *Egypt on the Pentateuch's Ideological Map: Constructing Biblical Israel's Identity.* LHBOTS 361. London: Bloomsbury, 2003.

Gruen, Erich S. *Culture and National Identity in Republican Rome.* Cornell Studies in Classical Philology 52. Ithaca, NY: Cornell University Press, 1992.

Gruen, Erich S. *Rethinking the Other in Antiquity.* Martin Classical Lectures. Princeton, NJ: Princeton University Press, 2011.

Guillaume, Philippe. "Jerusalem 720–705 BCE: No Flood of Israelite Refugees." *SJOT* 22 (2008): 195–211. https://doi.org/10.1080/09018320802661184.

Gunkel, Hermann. *Genesis.* Translated by Mark E. Biddle. Macon, GA: Mercer University Press, 1997.

Ha, John. *Genesis 15: A Theological Compendium of Pentateuchal History.* BZAW 181. Berlin: Walter de Gruyter, 1989.

Halbwachs, Maurice. *The Collective Memory.* New York: Harper & Row, 1980.

Halbwachs, Maurice. *On Collective Memory.* The Heritage of Sociology. Chicago: University of Chicago Press, 1992.

Hamori, Esther J. "Echoes of Gilgamesh in the Jacob Story." *JBL* 130 (2011): 625–42. https://doi.org/10.2307/23488271.

Handy, Lowell K. "Hezekiah's Unlikely Reform." *ZAW* 100 (1988): 111–15.

Haran, Menahem. "Behind the Scenes of History: Determining the Date of the Priestly Source." *JBL* 100 (1981): 321–33. https://doi.org/10.2307/3265957.

Hasel, Gerhard F. *The Remnant: The History and Theology of the Remnant Idea from Genesis to Isaiah.* 2nd ed. Berrien Springs, MI: Andrews University Press, 1974.

Hasel, Michael G. "Israel in the Merneptah Stela." *BASOR* 296 (1994): 45–61. https://doi.org/10.2307/1357179.

Heard, R. Christopher. *The Dynamics of Diselection: Ambiguity in Genesis 12–36 and Ethnic Boundaries in Post-Exilic Judah.* SemeiaSt 39. Atlanta: Society of Biblical Literature, 2001.

Hendel, Ronald. "Abram's Journey as Nexus: Literarkritik and Literary Criticism." *VT* 69 (2019): 567–93. https://doi.org/10.1163/15685330-12341383.

Hendel, Ronald S. *The Epic of the Patriarch: The Jacob Cycle and the Narrative Traditions of Canaan and Israel.* HSM 42. Decatur, GA: Scholars Press, 1987.

Hobsbawm, Eric, and Terence Ranger, eds. *The Invention of Tradition.* Past and Present Publications. Cambridge: Cambridge University Press, 1983.

Hong, K. P. "Towards the Hermeneutics of Responsibility: A Linguistic, Literary, and Historical Reading of Genesis 28:10–22." Ph.D. diss., Claremont Graduate University, 2011.

Hong, Koog P. "The Deceptive Pen of Scribes: Judean Reworking of the Bethel Tradition as a Program for Assuming Israelite Identity." *Bib* 92 (2011): 427–41. https://doi.org/10.2143/BIB.92.3.3188816.

Hong, Koog P. "Abraham, Genesis 20–22, and the Northern Elohist." *Bib* 94 (2013): 321–39. https://doi.org/10.2143/BIB.94.3.3186154.

Hong, Koog P. "Once Again: The Emergence of 'Biblical Israel.'" *ZAW* 125 (2013): 278–88. https://doi.org/10.1515/zaw-2013-0017.

Hong, Koog P. "Abraham, Our Father, the Father of All: A Perspective from Ancient Korean History." *JSOT* 43 (2019): 371–84. https://doi.org/10.1177/0309089217734731.

Hong, Koog P. "Genesis and Exodus as Conceptually Independent, Competing Origin Myths?" *ZAW* 133 (2021): 427–41. https://doi.org/10.1515/zaw-2021-4001.

Hong, Koog P. "United yet Divided: Reading Judah and Israel in the Context of Two Koreas." In *The Oxford Handbook of the Bible in Korea*, edited by Won W. Lee, 304–18. Oxford: Oxford University Press, 2022.

Hong, Koog P. "Bethel, Dark Woods, and Taboo: 1 Kings 13 as a Cautionary Tale." *BibInt* 31 (2023): 292–310. https://doi.org/10.1163/15685152-20221718.

Hong, Koog P. "The Golden Calf of Bethel and Judah's Mimetic Desire of Israel." *JSOT* 47 (2023): 359–71. https://doi.org/10.1177/03090892231168657.

Hong, Koog P. "Bethel between Inclusion and Exclusion in Judah's Identity Negotiation." *RB* 131 (2024): 321–39.

Hurowitz, Victor Avigdor. "Babylon in Bethel-New Light on Jacob's Dream." In *Orientalism, Assyriology and the Bible*, edited by Steven W. Holloway, 436–48. Hebrew Bible Monographs 10. Sheffield: Phoenix Press, 2006.

Hurvitz, A. "The Evidence of Language in Dating the Priestly Code." *RB* 81 (1974): 24–56.

Hutchinson, John, and Anthony D. Smith, eds. *Ethnicity*. Oxford Readers. Oxford: Oxford University Press, 1996.

Hwang, Kyung Moon. *A History of Korea: An Episodic Narrative*. Palgrave Essential Histories. Basingstoke: Palgrave Macmillan, 2010.

Hyde, Lewis. *Trickster Makes This World: Mischief, Myth, and Art*. New York: Farrar, Straus and Giroux, 1998.

Irudayaraj, Dominic S. *Violence, Otherness and Identity in Isaiah 63:1–6: The Trampling One Coming from Edom*. LHBOTS 633. London: T&T Clark, 2017.

Iryŏn. *Samguk Yusa: Legends and History of the Three Kingdoms of Ancient Korea*. Translated by Tae Hung Ha and Grafton K. Mintz. Seoul: Yonsei University Press, 1972.

Ishida, Tomoo. *The Royal Dynasties in Ancient Israel: A Study on the Formation and Development of Royal-Dynastic Ideology*. BZAW 142. Berlin: Walter de Gruyter, 1977.

Jang, Byung-jin. "Stories of Goguryeo described in Tomb Epitaphs Made for the Goguryeo Refugees in Dang." *Quarterly Review of Korean History* 117 (2020): 225–56. https://doi.org/10.35865/YWH.2020.09.117.225 [장병진. "고구려 유민 묘지명의 고구려 관련 전승과 그 계통." 역사와 현실 117].

Jauss, Hans Robert. *Aesthetic Experience and Literary Hermeneutics*. Theory and History of Literature 3. Minneapolis: University of Minnesota Press, 1982.

Jauss, Hans Robert. *Literaturgeschichte als Provokation*. Frankfurt am Main: Suhrkamp, 1970.

Jauss, Hans Robert. *Toward an Aesthetic of Reception*. Theory and History of Literature 2. Minneapolis: University of Minnesota Press, 1982.

Jenkins, Richard. *Social Identity*. 3rd ed. Key Ideas. London: Routledge, 2008.

Jeon, Jaeyoung. *From the Reed Sea to Kadesh: A Redactional and Socio-Historical Study of the Pentateuchal Wilderness Narrative*. FAT 159. Tübingen: Mohr Siebeck, 2022.

Johnson, Willa Mathis. *The Holy Seed Has Been Defiled: The Interethnic Marriage Dilemma in Ezra 9–10*. Hebrew Bible Monographs 33. Sheffield: Phoenix Press, 2011.

Jones, E. Allen. "Who Is the Holy Seed?: Purity and Identity in the Restoration Community." *JSOT* 45 (2021): 515–34. https://doi.org/10.1177/0309089220963428.

Jones, Siân. *The Archaeology of Ethnicity: Constructing Identities in the Past and Present*. London: Routledge, 1997.

Joniak-Luthi, Agnieszka. *The Han: China's Diverse Majority*. Studies on Ethnic Groups in China. Seattle: University of Washington Press, 2015.

Jonker, Louis. "Textual Identities in the Books of Chronicles: The Case of Jehoram's History." In *Community Identity in Judean Historiography: Biblical and Comparative Perspectives*, edited by Gary N. Knoppers and Kenneth A. Ristau, 197–217. Winona Lake, IN: Eisenbrauns, 2009.

Jonker, Louis, ed. *Texts, Contexts and Readings in Postexilic Literature: Explorations into Historiography and Identity Negotiation in Hebrew Bible and Related Texts*. FAT 2/53. Tübingen: Mohr Siebeck, 2011.

Joseph, Alison L. *Portrait of the Kings: The Davidic Prototype in Deuteronomistic Poetics*. Minneapolis: Fortress, 2015.

Kang, David C. *East Asia Before the West: Five Centuries of Trade and Tribute*. Contemporary Asia in the World. New York: Columbia University Press, 2010.

Keating, Michael. *Nations Against the State: The New Politics of Nationalism in Quebec, Catalonia, and Scotland*. Basingstoke: Palgrave Macmillan, 1996.

Kim, A Ram. "Beyond the 38th Parallel, Across the Sea, to Hallasan – The Settlement Process and the Lives of North Korean Refugees." *Critical Studies on Modern Korean History* 35 (2016): 207–51 [김아람. "38선 넘고 바다 건너 한라산까지, 월남민의 제주도 정착 과정과 삶." 역사문제연구 35].

Kim, Gwiok. *The Life Experiences and Identities of North Korean Migrant Settlers: A Grassroots Study of North Korean Migrant Settlers*. Seoul: Seoul National University Press, 1999 [김귀옥. 월남민의 생활 경험과 정체성: 밑으로부터의 월남민 연구. 서울: 서울대학교 출판부, 1999].

Kim, Gwiok. *Separated Families, Neither "Anti-Communist Fighters" nor "Communists"...: A New Perspective on the Issue of Separated Families*. Seoul: Yukbi, 2004 [김귀옥. 이산가족, '반공전사'도 '빨갱이'도 아닌...: 이산가족 문제를 보는 새로운 시각. 서울: 역사비평사, 2004].

Kim, Hyun Chul Paul. "'The Myth of the Empty Exile': A Comparative Exploration into Ancient Biblical Exile and Modern Korean Exile." *JSOT* 45 (2020): 45–64. https://doi.org/10.1177/0309089219875157.

Kim, Hyung-Jin. "For First Time Since 2010, South Korea Defense Report Doesn't Refer to North Korea as 'Enemy'," USA Today, 15. 01. 2019, https://www.usatoday.com/story/news/world/2019/01/14/south-korea-north-korea-relations-no-enemy-designation/2578073002/ [accessed 30. 05. 2019].

Kim, Jinwung. *A History of Korea: From "Land of the Morning Calm" to States in Conflict*. Bloomington: Indiana University Press, 2012.

Kim, Richard E. *The Martyred*. New York: G. Braziller, 1964.

Kim, Sebastian C. H., and Kirsteen Kim. *A History of Korean Christianity*. New York: Cambridge University Press, 2015.

Kim, Su-Jin. "Recognition of Goguryeo by Bureaucrats in Tang Dynasty Through the Epitaphs of Displaced People in Goguryeo." *Humanities Studies East and West* 54 (2018): 41–84 [김수진. "고구려 유민 묘지명에 나타난 당인 관인의 '高句麗' 인식." 동서인문학 54].

Kim, Uriah Y. *Decolonizing Josiah: Toward a Postcolonial Reading of the Deuteronomistic History*. Sheffield: Sheffield Phoenix Press, 2005.

Kim, Uriah Y. *Identity and Loyalty in the David Story: A Postcolonial Reading*. Sheffield: Sheffield Phoenix Press, 2008.

Kim, Yong-bok, ed. *Minjung Theology: People as the Subjects of History*. Singapore: Christian Conference of Asia, 1981.

Kim, Youngmin. "Reconsidering Sinocentrism In Late Choson Korea." *The Journal of Korean History* 162 (2013): 211–52 [김영민. "조선중화주의의 재검토: 이론적 접근." 한국사연구 162].

Kim, Yung Suk, and Chin-ho Kim, eds. *Reading Minjung Theology in the Twenty-First Century: Selected Writings by Ahn Byung-Mu and Modern Critical Responses*. Eugene, OR: Pickwick, 2013.

Kirk, Alan. "Social and Cultural Memory." In *Memory, Tradition, and Text: Uses of the Past in Early Christianity*, edited by Alan Kirk and Tom Thatcher, 1–24. SemeiaSt 52. Atlanta: Society of Biblical Literature, 2005.

Knauf, Ernst Axel. "Bethel: The Israelite Impact on Judean Language and Literature." In *Judah and the Judeans in the Persian Period*, edited by Oded Lipschits and Manfred Oeming, 291–349. Winona Lake, IN: Eisenbrauns, 2006.

Knohl, Israel. *The Sanctuary of Silence: The Priestly Torah and the Holiness School*. Minneapolis: Fortress, 1995.

Knoppers, Gary N. *Two Nations under God: The Deuteronomistic History of Solomon and the Dual Monarchies. Vol. 1. The Reign of Solomon and the Rise of Jeroboam*. HSM 52. Atlanta: Scholars Press, 1993.

Köckert, Matthias. *Vätergott und Väterverheissungen: Eine Auseinandersetzung mit Albrecht Alt und seinen Erben*. FRLANT 142. Göttingen: Vandenhoeck & Ruprecht, 1988.

Köckert, Matthias. "Die Geschichte der Abrahamüberlieferung." In *Congress Volume: Leiden, 2004*, edited by André Lemaire, 103–28. VTSup 109. Leiden: Brill, 2006.

Köckert, Matthias. "Gen 15: Vom »Urgestein« der Väterüberlieferung zum »theologischen Programmtext« der späten Perserzeit." *ZAW* 125 (2013): 25–48. https://doi.org/10.1515/zaw-2013-0003.

Köckert, Matthias. "Wie wurden Abraham- und Jakobüberlieferung zu einer »Vätergeschichte« verbunden?" *HeBAI* 3 (2014): 43–66. https://doi.org/10.1628/219222714X13994465496866.

Köckert, Matthias. *Von Jakob zu Abraham: Studien zum Buch Genesis*. FAT 147. Tübingen: Mohr Siebeck, 2021.

Kratz, Reinhard Gregor. "Israel als Staat und als Volk." *ZTK* 97 (2000): 1–17.

Kratz, Reinhard Gregor. *The Composition of the Narrative Books of the Old Testament*. Translated by John Bowden. London: T&T Clark, 2005.

Kratz, Reinhard Gregor. "Israel in the Book of Isaiah." *JSOT* 31 (2006): 103–28. https://doi.org/10.1177/0309089206068845.

Kratz, Reinhard G. *Historical and Biblical Israel: The History, Tradition, and Archives of Israel and Judah*. Translated by Paul Michael Kurtz. Oxford: Oxford University Press, 2015.

Krisel, William. *Judges 19–21 and the "Othering" of Benjamin: A Golah Polemic against the Autochthonous Inhabitants of the Land?* OtSt 81. Leiden: Brill, 2022.

Kwon, Chang-hyeok. "A Review of Silla's Strategy to Support Goguryeo Revival Movement in 670–673." *Sillasahakpo* 51 (2021): 165–205 [권창혁. "670~673년 신라의 고구려 부흥운동 지원 전략에 대한 검토." 신라사학보 51].

Kwon, Jinkwan, and Volker Küster, eds. *Minjung Theology Today: Contextual and Intercultural Perspectives*. Contact Zone 21. Leipzig: Evangelische Verlagsanstalt, 2018.

Kye, Seung Bum. "A Criticism of the Contemporary Korean Scholarship on the Chosŏn Elites' View of the Chinese Confucian Culture (zhonghua) in the 1600s to the 1800s." *The Journal of Korean History* 159 (2012): 265–94 [계승범. "조선후기 조선중화주의와 그 해석 문제." 한국사연구 159].

Lambert, W. G. "The Assyrian Recension of Enūma Eliš." In *Assyrien im Wandel der Zeiten*, edited by Hartmut Waetzoldt and Harald Hauptmann, 77–79. HSAO 6. Heidelberg: Heidelberger Orientverlag, 1997.

Langlois, John D., ed. *China Under Mongol Rule*. Princeton, NJ: Princeton University Press, 1981.

Lee, Gyu-ho. "Dang's Policy to Deal with Goguryeo Refugees, and the Situation of the Refugees." *Quarterly Review of Korean History* 101 (2016): 141–72 [이규호. "당의 고구려 유민 정책과 유민들의 동향." 역사와 현실 101].

Lee, Je-hun. "Leaders of Two Koreas Engage in Perilous Game of Chicken," Hankyoreh, 05. 01. 2023, https://english.hani.co.kr/arti/english_edition/e_northkorea/1074579.html [accessed 20. 01. 2023].

Lee, Ji Young. *China's Hegemony: Four Hundred Years of East Asian Domination*. New York: Columbia University Press, 2016.

Lee, Mi Kyoung. "Silla's Policy for Ruling Bodeokguk." *Daegu Historical Review* 120 (2015): 101–32. https://doi.org/10.17751/DHR.120.101 [이미경. "신라(新羅)의 보덕국(報德國) 지배정책." 대구사학 120].

Lee, Min Jin. *Pachinko*. New York: Grand Central Publishing, 2017.

Lee, Woongbee. "The North and South Korean gold medal ping pong pals separated forever," BBC News, 10. 02. 2018, https://www.bbc.com/news/av/world-asia-42999448/ [accessed 30. 05. 2019].

Lee-Sak, Yitzhak. "Polemical Propaganda of the Golah Community against the Gibeonites: Historical Background of Joshua 9 and 2 Samuel 21 in the Early Persian Period." *JSOT* 44 (2019): 115–32. https://doi.org/10.1177/0309089218762286.

Lemaire, André. "Les Benê Jacob: Essai d'interprétation historique d'une tradition patriarcale." *RB* 85 (1978): 321–37.

Lemaire, André. "La haute Mésopotamie et l'origine des Benê Jacob." *VT* 34 (1984): 95–101. https://doi.org/10.1163/156853384X00115.

Lemche, Niels Peter. *Early Israel: Anthropological and Historical Studies on the Israelite Society Before the Monarchy*. VTSup 37. Leiden: Brill, 1985.

Lemche, Niels Peter. *The Israelites in History and Tradition*. Library of Ancient Israel. London: SPCK, 1998.

Lemche, Niels Peter. "Did a Reform like Josiah's Happen?" In *The Historian and the Bible: Essays in Honour of Lester L. Grabbe*, edited by Philip R. Davies and Diana V. Edelman, 11–18. LHBOTS 530. New York: T&T Clark, 2010.

Lemche, Niels Peter. "Too Good to Be True? The Creation of the People of Israel." *WO* 50 (2020): 254–74. https://doi.org/10.13109/wdor.2020.50.2.254.

Lemche, Niels Peter. *Back to Reason: Minimalism in Biblical Studies*. Discourses in Ancient near Eastern and Biblical Studies. Sheffield: Equinox, 2022.

Leonard-Fleckman, Mahri. *The House of David: Between Political Formation and Literary Revision*. Minneapolis: Fortress, 2016.

Levenson, Jon Douglas. *Sinai and Zion: An Entry into the Jewish Bible*. New Voices in Biblical Studies. Minneapolis: Winston, 1985.

Levin, Christoph. *Der Jahwist*. FRLANT 157. Göttingen: Vandenhoeck & Ruprecht, 1993.

Levin, Christoph. "Jahwe und Abraham im Dialog: Genesis 15." In *Gott und Mensch im Dialog: Festschrift für Otto Kaiser zum 80. Geburtstag*, edited by Markus Witte, 237–57. BZAW 345. Berlin: Walter de Gruyter, 2004.

Levin, Yigal. "Joseph, Judah and the 'Benjamin Conundrum.'" *ZAW* 116 (2004): 223–41.

Lewis, Theodore J. *The Origin and Character of God: Ancient Israelite Religion through the Lens of Divinity*. New York: Oxford University Press, 2020.

Lincoln, Bruce. *Discourse and the Construction of Society: Comparative Studies of Myth, Ritual, and Classification*. New York: Oxford University Press, 1989.

Linville, James Richard. *Israel in the Book of Kings: The Past as a Project of Social Identity*. JSOTSup 272. Sheffield: Sheffield Academic Press, 1998.

Lipschits, Oded, Thomas Römer, and Hervé Gonzalez. "The Pre-Priestly Abraham Narratives from Monarchic to Persian Times." *Semitica* 59 (2017): 261–96. https://doi.org/10.2143/SE.59.0.3239913.

Liverani, Mario. *Israel's History and the History of Israel*. London: Equinox, 2005.

Lohfink, Norbert. "Culture Shock and Theology: A Discussion of Theology as a Cultural and a Sociological Phenomenon Based on the Example of a Deuteronomic Law." *BTB* 7 (1977): 12–22. https://doi.org/10.1177/014610797700700104.

Mac Sweeney, Naoíse, ed. *Foundation Myths in Ancient Societies: Dialogues and Discourses.* Philadelphia: University of Pennsylvania Press, 2015.

Machinist, Peter. "Literature as Politics: The Tukulti-Ninurta Epic and the Bible." *CBQ* 38 (1976): 455–82.

Machinist, Peter. "Outsiders or Insiders: The Biblical View of Emergent Israel and Its Contexts." In *The Other in Jewish Thought and History: Constructions of Jewish Culture and Identity*, edited by Laurence J. Silberstein and Robert L. Cohn, 35–60. New Perspectives on Jewish Studies. New York: New York University Press, 1994.

Machinist, Peter. "The Rab Šāqēh at the Wall of Jerusalem: Israelite Identity in the Face of the Assyrian 'Other.'" *HS* 41 (2000): 151–68. https://doi.org/10.1353/hbr.2000.0039.

MacKay, Joseph. "The Nomadic Other: Ontological Security and the Inner Asian Steppe in Historical East Asian International Politics." *Review of International Studies* 42 (2016): 471–91. https://doi.org/10.1017/S0260210515000327.

Maeir, Aren. "On Defining Israel: Or, Let's Do the Kulturkreislehre Again!" *HeBAI* 10 (2021): 106–48. https://doi.org/10.1628/hebai-2021-0010.

Malamat, Abraham. "Organs of Statecraft in the Israelite Monarchy." *BA* 28 (1965): 34–65. https://doi.org/10.2307/3211054.

Malešević, Siniša. *The Sociology of Ethnicity.* London: Sage, 2004.

Malkin, Irad. "Foreign Founders: Greeks and Hebrews." In *Foundation Myths in Ancient Societies: Dialogues and Discourses*, edited by Naoíse Mac Sweeney, 20–40. Philadelphia: University of Pennsylvania Press, 2015.

Malkki, Liisa. "Context and Consciousness: Local Conditions for the Production of Historical and National Thought among Hutu Refugees in Tanzania." In *Nationalist Ideologies and the Production of National Cultures*, edited by Richard G. Fox, 32–62. American Ethnological Society Monograph Series 2. Washington, DC: American Anthropological Association, 1990.

Martin, Michael W. "Betrothal Journey Narratives." *CBQ* 70 (2008): 505–23.

Mayes, A. D. H. *Israel in the Period of the Judges.* London: S.C.M. Press, 1974.

McAdams, Dan P. "The Psychology of Life Stories." *Review of General Psychology* 5 (2001): 100–122. https://doi.org/10.1037/1089-2680.5.2.100.

McCarter, P. Kyle. *II Samuel: A New Translation with Introduction, Notes, and Commentary.* AB 9. Garden City, NY: Doubleday, 1984.

McKay, J. W. "Man's Love for God in Deuteronomy and the Father/Teacher–Son/Pupil Relationship." *VT* 22 (1972): 426–35. https://doi.org/10.1163/156853372X00181.

Mendenhall, George E. "The Hebrew Conquest of Palestine." *BA* 25 (1962): 66–87. https://doi.org/10.2307/3210957.

Meshel, Zeev. *Kuntillet 'Ajrud (Horvat Teman): An Iron Age II Religious Site on the Judah-Sinai Border.* Jerusalem: Israel Exploration Society, 2012.

Mettinger, Tryggve N. D. *King and Messiah: The Civil and Sacral Legitimation of the Israelite Kings.* ConBOT 8. Lund: LiberLäromedel/Gleerup, 1976.

Miller, James C. "Ethnicity and the Hebrew Bible: Problems and Prospects." *CurBR* 6 (2008): 170–213. https://doi.org/10.1177/1476993x07083627.

Millward, James A., Ruth W. Dunnell, Mark C. Elliott, and Philippe Forêt, eds. *New Qing Imperial History: The Making of Inner Asian Empire at Qing Chengde.* London: Routledge, 2004.

Milstein, Sara J. *Tracking the Master Scribe: Revision Through Introduction in Biblical and Mesopotamian Literature.* New York: Oxford University Press, 2016.

Monroe, Lauren A. S. *Josiah's Reform and the Dynamics of Defilement: Israelite Rites of Violence and the Making of a Biblical Text.* Oxford: Oxford University Press, 2011.

Monroe, Lauren. "On the Origins and Development of Greater Israel." *HeBAI* 10 (2021): 187–227. https://doi.org/10.1628/hebai-2021-0012.

Monroe, Lauren, and Daniel E. Fleming. "Earliest Israel in Highland Company." *NEA* 82 (2019): 16–23. https://doi.org/10.1086/703322.

Monroe, Lauren, and Daniel E. Fleming, eds. "Israel before the Omrides." *HeBAI* 10 (2021): 97–227. https://doi.org/10.1628/hebai-2021-0009.

Moore, Megan Bishop, and Brad E. Kelle. *Biblical History and Israel's Past: The Changing Study of the Bible and History.* Grand Rapids, MI: Eerdmans, 2011.

Mullaney, Thomas S. *Critical Han Studies: The History, Representation, and Identity of China's Majority.* New Perspectives on Chinese Culture and Society 4. Berkeley, CA: University of California Press, 2012.

Mullen, E. Theodore, Jr. *Narrative History and Ethnic Boundaries: The Deuteronomistic Historian and the Creation of Israelite National Identity.* SemeiaSt. Atlanta: Scholars Press, 1993.

Mullen, E. Theodore, Jr. *Ethnic Myths and Pentateuchal Foundations: A New Approach to the Formation of the Pentateuch.* SemeiaSt. Atlanta: Scholars Press, 1997.

Müller, Reinhard, and Cynthia Edenburg. "A Northern Provenance for Deuteronomy? A Critical Review." *HeBAI* 4 (2015): 148–61. https://doi.org/10.1628/219222715X14453513581333.

Na'aman, Nadav. "The Debated Historicity of Hezekiah's Reform in the Light of Historical and Archaeological Research." *ZAW* 107 (1995): 179–95. https://doi.org/10.1515/9781575065694-025.

Na'aman, Nadav. "When and How Did Jerusalem Become a Great City? The Rise of Jerusalem as Judah's Premier City in the Eighth-Seventh Centuries B.C.E." *BASOR* 347 (2007): 21–56. https://doi.org/10.1086/BASOR25067021.

Na'aman, Nadav. "Saul, Benjamin and the Emergence of 'Biblical Israel' (Part 1)." *ZAW* 121 (2009): 211–24. https://doi.org/10.1515/ZAW.2009.014.

Na'aman, Nadav. "Saul, Benjamin and the Emergence of 'Biblical Israel' (Part 2)." *ZAW* 121 (2009): 335–49. https://doi.org/10.1515/ZAW.2009.023.

Na'aman, Nadav. "The Growth and Development of Judah and Jerusalem in the Eighth Century BCE: A Rejoinder." *RB* 116 (2009): 321–35. https://doi.org/10.2143/RBI.116.3.3206430.

Na'aman, Nadav. "The Israelite-Judahite Struggle for the Patrimony of Ancient Israel." *Bib* 91 (2010): 1–23. https://doi.org/10.2143/BIB.91.1.3188850.

Na'aman, Nadav. "The Jacob Story and the Formation of Biblical Israel." *TA* 41 (2014): 95–125. https://doi.org/10.1179/0334435514Z.00000000032.

Nash, Dustin. "Edom, Judah, and Converse Constructions of Israeliteness in Genesis 36." *VT* 68 (2018): 111–28. https://doi.org/10.1163/15685330-12341317.

Nicholson, Ernest W. *Deuteronomy and Tradition.* Philadelphia: Fortress, 1967.

Nicholson, Ernest W. *The Pentateuch in the Twentieth Century: The Legacy of Julius Wellhausen.* Oxford: Clarendon, 1998.

Nicholson, Ernest W. "Reconsidering the Provenance of Deuteronomy." *ZAW* 124 (2012): 528–40. https://doi.org/10.1515/zaw-2012-0037.

Niditch, Susan. *A Prelude to Biblical Folklore: Underdogs and Tricksters.* Urbana, IL: University of Illinois Press, 2000.

Noth, Martin. *Das System der zwölf Stämme Israels.* Darmstadt: Wissenschaftliche Buchgesellschaft, 1930.

Noth, Martin. *The History of Israel.* 2nd ed. New York: Harper & Row, 1960.

Noth, Martin. *A History of Pentateuchal Traditions.* Englewood Cliffs, NJ: Prentice Hall, 1972.

Oboler, Suzanne. *Ethnic Labels, Latino Lives: Identity and the Politics of (Re)Presentation in the United States.* Minneapolis: University of Minnesota Press, 1995.

Ostrer, Harry. *Legacy: A Genetic History of the Jewish People.* New York: Oxford University Press, 2012.

Pai, Hyung Il. *Constructing "Korean" Origins: A Critical Review of Archaeology, Historiography, and Racial Myth in Korean State-Formation Theories*. Harvard East Asian Monographs 187. Cambridge, MA: Harvard University Asia Center, 2000.

Park, Jongmin, Young-Ju Jung, Ho Jun Joo, and Hyeon Woo Kim. "How Has the Republic of Korea Viewed 'North Korea' and 'Reunification' Over the Past 20 Years?" *Korean Journal of Journalism & Communication Studies* 64 (2020): 161–201. https://doi.org/10.20879/kjjcs.2020.64.6.005 [박종민, 정영주, 주호준, 김현우. "대한민국은 지난 20년간 '북한'과 '통일'을 어떻게 보았는가? 언론 보도 빅데이터 분석 및 국민 인식 종단연구." 한국언론학보 64].

Patterson, Lee E. *Kinship Myth in Ancient Greece*. Austin: University of Texas Press, 2010.

Perdue, Peter C. *China Marches West: The Qing Conquest of Central Eurasia*. Cambridge, MA: Belknap, 2005.

Pfoh, Emanuel. *The Emergence of Israel in Ancient Palestine: Historical and Anthropological Perspectives*. Copenhagen International Seminar. Abingdon, Oxon: Routledge, 2009.

Pratt, Keith L. *Everlasting Flower: A History of Korea*. London: Reaktion Books, 2006.

Pury, Albert de. *Promesse divine et légende cultuelle dans le cycle de Jacob: Genèse 28 et les traditions patriarcales*. 2 vols. Études bibliques. Paris: Gabalda, 1975.

Pury, Albert de. "Le cycle de Jacob comme légende autonome des origines d'Israël." In *Congress Volume: Leuven 1989*, edited by John Adney Emerton, 78–96. VTSup 43. Leiden: Brill, 1991.

Pury, Albert de. "Abraham: The Priestly Writer's 'Ecumenical' Ancestor." In *Rethinking the Foundations: Historiography in the Ancient World and in the Bible: Essays in Honour of John Van Seters*, edited by Steven L. McKenzie and Thomas Römer, 163–81. BZAW 294. Berlin: Walter de Gruyter, 2000.

Pury, Albert de. "Situer le cycle de Jacob. Quelques réflexions, vingt-cinq ans plus tard." In *Studies in the Book of Genesis: Literature, Redaction and History*, edited by André Wénin, 213–41. BETL 155. Leuven: Peeters, 2001.

Pury, Albert de. "The Jacob Story and the Beginning of the Formation of the Pentateuch." In *A Farewell to the Yahwist?: The Composition of the Pentateuch in Recent European Interpretation*, edited by Thomas B. Dozeman and Konrad Schmid, 51–72. Atlanta: Society of Biblical Literature, 2006.

Rawski, Evelyn Sakakida. *The Last Emperors: A Social History of Qing Imperial Institutions*. Berkeley, CA: University of California Press, 1998.

Redford, Donald B. *Egypt, Canaan, and Israel in Ancient Times*. Princeton, NJ: Princeton University Press, 1993.

Rendtorff, Rolf. *The Problem of the Process of Transmission in the Pentateuch*. Translated by J. J. Scullion. JSOTSup 89. Sheffield: Sheffield Academic Press, 1990.

Rhoads, Edward J. M. *Manchus and Han: Ethnic Relations and Political Power in Late Qing and Early Republican China, 1861–1928*. Studies on Ethnic Groups in China. Seattle: University of Washington Press, 2000.

Riecker, Siegbert. "Ein theologischer Ansatz zum Verständnis der Altarbaunotizen der Genesis." *Bib* 87 (2006): 526–30. https://doi.org/10.2143/BIB.87.4.3189068.

Ritchie, Donald A. *Doing Oral History*. 3rd ed. Oxford: Oxford University Press, 2014.

Ro, Johannes Unsok, and Diana Edelman, eds. *Collective Memory and Collective Identity: Deuteronomy and the Deuteronomistic History in Their Context*. BZAW 534. Berlin: Walter de Gruyter, 2021.

Robinson, Theodore H. "The Origin of the Tribe of Judah." In *Amicitiæ Corolla: A Volume of Essays Presented to James Rendel Harris, D. LITT., on the Occasion of His Eightieth Birthday*, edited by Herbert George Wood, 265–73. London: University of London Press, 1933.

Rofé, Alexander. "An Inquiry into the Betrothal of Rebekah." In *Die Hebräische Bibel und ihre zweifache Nachgeschichte: Festschrift für Rolf Rendtorff zum 65. Geburtstag*, edited by Erhard

Blum, Christian Macholz, and Ekkehard Stegemann, 27–40. Neukirchen-Vluyn: Neukirchener Verlag, 1990.

Rofé, Alexander. "The Admonitions Not to Leave the Promised Land in Genesis 24 and 26 and the Authorization in Genesis 46." In *The Post-Priestly Pentateuch: New Perspectives on Its Redactional Development and Theological Profiles*, edited by Federico Giuntoli and Konrad Schmid, 177–84. FAT 101. Tübingen: Mohr Siebeck, 2015.

Römer, Thomas. "Gen 15 und Gen 17. Beobachtungen und Anfragen zu einem Dogma der 'neueren' und 'neuesten' Pentateuchkritik." *DBAT* 26 (1990): 32–47.

Römer, Thomas. *Israels Väter: Untersuchungen zur Väterthematik im Deuteronomium und in der deuteronomistischen Tradition*. OBO 99. Freiburg, Schweiz: Universitätsverlag, 1990.

Römer, Thomas. "Recherches actuelles sur le cycle d'Abraham." In *Studies in the Book of Genesis: Literature, Redaction and History*, edited by André Wénin, 179–211. BETL 155. Leuven: Peeters, 2001.

Römer, Thomas. "Abraham Traditions in the Hebrew Bible Outside the Book of Genesis." In *The Book of Genesis: Composition, Reception, and Interpretation*, edited by Craig A. Evans, Joel N. Lohr, and David L. Petersen, 159–80. VTSup 152. Leiden: Brill, 2012.

Römer, Thomas. "The Joseph Story in the Book of Genesis: Pre-P or Post-P?" In *The Post-Priestly Pentateuch: New Perspectives on Its Redactional Development and Theological Profiles*, edited by Federico Giuntoli and Konrad Schmid, 185–201. FAT 101. Tübingen: Mohr Siebeck, 2015.

Römer, Thomas. "Abraham and Moses, A (not so) Friendly Competition." In *And God Saw That It Was Good (Gen 1:12): The Concept of Quality in Archaeology, Philology and Theology*, edited by Filip Čapek and Petr Sláma, 99–109. Beiträge zum Verstehen der Bibel 42. Zürich: Lit Verlag, 2020.

Rom-Shiloni, Dalit. "When an Explicit Polemic Initiates a Hidden One: Jacob's Aramaean Identity." In *Words, Ideas, Worlds: Biblical Essays in Honour of Yairah Amit*, edited by Athalya Brenner-Idan and Frank Polak. Hebrew Bible Monographs 40. Sheffield: Phoenix Press, 2012.

Rom-Shiloni, Dalit. *Exclusive Inclusivity: Identity Conflicts between the Exiles and the People Who Remained (6th–5th Centuries BCE)*. LHBOTS 543. London: Bloomsbury, 2013.

Rosenbaum, M., and A. M. Silbermann, eds. *Pentateuch with Targum Onkelos, Haphtaroth and Rashi's Commentary*. Vol. 1. 4 vols. Jerusalem: Silbermann Family, 1973.

Rosenwald, George C., and Richard L. Ochberg, eds. *Storied Lives: The Cultural Politics of Self-Understanding*. New Haven: Yale University Press, 1992.

Rossabi, Morris. *Khubilai Khan: His Life and Times*. Berkeley, CA: University of California Press, 1988.

Rowe, William T. *China's Last Empire: The Great Qing*. History of Imperial China. Cambridge, MA: Harvard University Press, 2010.

Rowley, Harold Henry. *From Joseph to Joshua: Biblical Traditions in the Light of Archaeology*. London: Published for the British Academy by the Oxford University Press, 1950.

Said, Edward W. *Orientalism*. New York: Pantheon Books, 1978.

Sand, Shlomo. *The Invention of the Jewish People*. Translated by Yael Lotan. London: Verso, 2010.

Sand, Shlomo. *The Invention of the Land of Israel: From Holy Land to Homeland*. Translated by Geremy Forman. London: Verso, 2012.

Sanders, James A. *Canon and Community: A Guide to Canonical Criticism*. Guides to Biblical Scholarship. Philadelphia: Fortress, 1984.

Sarna, Nahum M. *Genesis: The Traditional Hebrew Text with the New JPS Translation*. JPS Torah Commentary. Philadelphia: Jewish Publication Society, 1989.

Schaper, Joachim. "Torah and Identity in the Persian Period." In *Judah and the Judeans in the Achaemenid Period*, edited by Oded Lipschits, Gary N. Knoppers, and Manfred Oeming, 27–38. Winona Lake, IN: Eisenbrauns, 2011.

Schermerhorn, R. A. *Comparative Ethnic Relations: A Framework for Theory and Research*. Chicago: University of Chicago Press, 1978.

Schmid, Konrad. *Erzväter und Exodus: Untersuchungen zur doppelten Begründung der Ursprünge Israels Innerhalb der Geschichtsbücher des Alten Testaments*. WMANT 81. Neukirchen-Vluyn: Neukirchener Verlag, 1999 = *Genesis and the Moses Story: Israel's Dual Origins in the Hebrew Bible*. Translated by James Nogalski. Siphrut 3. Winona Lake, IN: Eisenbrauns, 2010.

Schniedewind, William M. "Jerusalem, the Late Judahite Monarchy, and the Composition of the Biblical Texts." In *Jerusalem in Bible and Archaeology: The First Temple Period*, edited by Andrew G. Vaughn and Ann E. Killebrew, 375–93. Symposium Series 18. Leiden: Brill, 2003.

Schniedewind, William M. *How the Bible Became a Book: The Textualization of Ancient Israel*. Cambridge: Cambridge University Press, 2004.

Schütte, Wolfgang. "Wie wurde Juda israelitisiert?" *ZAW* 124 (2012): 52–72. https://doi.org/10.1515/zaw-2012-0004.

Schütte, Wolfgang. *Israels Exil in Juda: Untersuchungen zur Entstehung der Schriftprophetie*. OBO 279. Fribourg: Academic Press Fribourg, 2016.

Schwartz, Baruch J. "The Priestly Account of the Theophany and Lawgiving at Sinai." In *Texts, Temples, and Traditions: A Tribute to Menahem Haran*, edited by Michael V. Fox, James L. Kugel, and Frank Moore Cross, 103–34. Winona Lake, IN: Eisenbrauns, 1996.

Schwartz, Baruch J. "Does Recent Scholarship's Critique of the Documentary Hypothesis Constitute Grounds for Its Rejection?" In *The Pentateuch: International Perspectives on Current Research*, edited by Thomas B. Dozeman, Konrad Schmid, and Baruch J. Schwartz, 3–16. FAT 78. Tübingen: Mohr Siebeck, 2011.

Sergi, Omer. "The Emergence of Judah as a Political Entity between Jerusalem and Benjamin." *ZDPV* 133 (2017): 1–23.

Sergi, Omer. "Jacob and the Aramaean Identity of Ancient Israel between the Judges and the Prophets." In *The Politics of the Ancestors: Exegetical and Historical Perspectives on Genesis 12–36*, edited by Mark G. Brett and Jakob Wöhrle, 283–305. FAT 124. Tübingen: Mohr Siebeck, 2018.

Sergi, Omer. "Israelite Identity and the Formation of the Israelite Polities in the Iron I–IIA Central Canaanite Highlands." *WO* 49 (2019): 206–35. https://doi.org/10.13109/wdor.2019.49.2.206.

Sergi, Omer. "(Re)Constructing Identities in the Bronze and Iron Age Levant: Introduction." *WO* 49 (2019): 146–50. https://doi.org/10.13109/wdor.2019.49.2.146.

Sergi, Omer. "Saul, David, and the Formation of the Israelite Monarchy: Revisiting the Historical and Literary Context of 1 Samuel 9–2 Samuel 5." In *Saul, Benjamin, and the Emergence of Monarchy in Israel: Biblical and Archaeological Perspectives*, edited by Joachim J. Krause, Omer Sergi, and Kristin Weingart, 57–91. AIL 40. Atlanta: SBL Press, 2020.

Sergi, Omer. *The Two Houses of Israel: State Formation and the Origins of Pan-Israelite Identity*. Atlanta: SBL Press, 2023.

Sergi, Omer, Manfred Oeming, and Izaak J. de Hulster, eds. *In Search for Aram and Israel: Politics, Culture, and Identity*. Orientalische Religionen in der Antike 20. Tübingen: Mohr Siebeck, 2016.

Seth, Michael J. *A Concise History of Korea: From Antiquity to the Present*. 2nd ed. Lanham, MD: Rowman & Littlefield, 2016.

Shin, Eun-yi. "The Foundation and Meanings of Bodeokguk." *Daegu Historical Review* 132 (2018): 237–73. https://doi.org/10.17751/DHR.132.237 [신은이, "보덕국의 탄생과 그 의미." 대구사학 132].

Silberstein, Laurence J., and Robert L. Cohn, eds. *The Other in Jewish Thought and History: Constructions of Jewish Culture and Identity*. New Perspectives on Jewish Studies. New York: New York University Press, 1994.

Ska, Jean-Louis. *Exegesis of the Pentateuch: Exegetical Studies and Basic Questions*. FAT 66. Tübingen: Mohr Siebeck, 2009.

Ska, Jean-Louis. "Essay on the Nature and Meaning of the Abraham Cycle (Gen 11:29–25:11)." In *Exegesis of the Pentateuch: Exegetical Studies and Basic Questions*, 23–45. FAT 66. Tübingen: Mohr Siebeck, 2009.

Ska, Jean-Louis. "Some Groundwork on Genesis 15." In *Exegesis of the Pentateuch: Exegetical Studies and Basic Questions*, 67–81. FAT 66. Tübingen: Mohr Siebeck, 2009.

Ska, Jean-Louis. "The Call of Abraham and Israel's Birth-Certificate (Gen 12:1–4a)." In *Exegesis of the Pentateuch: Exegetical Studies and Basic Questions*, 46–66. FAT 66. Tübingen: Mohr Siebeck, 2009.

Smith, Anthony D. *Nationalism and Modernism: A Critical Survey of Recent Theories of Nations and Nationalism*. London: Routledge, 1998.

Smith, Anthony D. *The Ethnic Origins of Nations*. Oxford: Blackwell, 1987.

Smith, Mark S. *The Early History of God: Yahweh and the Other Deities in Ancient Israel*. San Francisco: Harper & Row, 1990.

Smith, Mark S. *The Origins of Biblical Monotheism: Israel's Polytheistic Background and the Ugaritic Texts*. New York: Oxford University Press, 2001.

Smith, Mark S. *God in Translation: Deities in Cross-Cultural Discourse in the Biblical World*. FAT 57. Tübingen: Mohr Siebeck, 2008.

Somers, Margaret R. "The Narrative Constitution of Identity: A Relational and Network Approach." *Theory and Society* 23 (1994): 605–49. https://doi.org/10.1007/BF00992905.

Southwood, Katherine. "The Holy Seed: The Significance of Endogamous Boundaries and Their Transgression in Ezra 9–10." In *Judah and the Judeans in the Achaemenid Period*, edited by Oded Lipschits, Gary N. Knoppers, and Manfred Oeming, 189–224. Winona Lake, IN: Eisenbrauns, 2011.

Southwood, Katherine. *Ethnicity and the Mixed Marriage Crisis in Ezra 9–10: An Anthropological Approach*. Oxford: Oxford University Press, 2012.

Sparks, Kenton L. *Ethnicity and Identity in Ancient Israel: Prolegomena to the Study of Ethnic Sentiments and Their Expression in the Hebrew Bible*. Winona Lake, IN: Eisenbrauns, 1998.

Speiser, E. A. *Genesis*. AB 1. Garden City, NY: Doubleday, 1964.

Stager, Lawrence E. "Forging an Identity: The Emergence of Ancient Israel." In *The Oxford History of the Biblical World*, edited by Michael David Coogan, 123–75. New York: Oxford University Press, 1998.

Stopple, Jeffrey. *A Primer of Analytic Number Theory: From Pythagoras to Riemann*. Cambridge: Cambridge University Press, 2003.

Stulman, Louis. "Encroachment in Deuteronomy: An Analysis of the Social World of the D Code." *JBL* 109 (1990): 613–32. https://doi.org/10.2307/3267366.

Subotić, Jelena. "Narrative, Ontological Security, and Foreign Policy Change." *Foreign Policy Analysis* 12 (2016): 610–27. https://doi.org/10.1111/fpa.12089.

Sun, Weiguo. "An Analysis of the 'Little China' Ideology of Chosŏn Korea." *Frontiers of History in China* 7 (2012): 220–39. https://doi.org/10.3868/s020-001-012-0012-5.

Sweeney, Marvin A. *The Twelve Prophets*. Vol. 1. 2 vols. Berit Olam. Collegeville, MN: Liturgical Press, 2000.

Sweeney, Marvin A. *King Josiah of Judah: The Lost Messiah of Israel*. Oxford: Oxford University Press, 2001.

Sweeney, Marvin A. *Tanak: A Theological and Critical Introduction to the Jewish Bible*. Minneapolis: Fortress, 2012.

Sweeney, Marvin A. "The Jacob Narratives: An Ephraimitic Text?" *CBQ* 78 (2016): 236–55.

Thiessen, Matthew. *Contesting Conversion: Genealogy, Circumcision, and Identity in Ancient Judaism and Christianity*. New York: Oxford University Press, 2011.

Thiselton, Anthony C. "Reception Theory, H. R. Jauss and the Formative Power of Scripture." *SJT* 65 (2012): 289–308. https://doi.org/10.1017/S0036930612000129.

Thomas, Matthew A. *These Are the Generations: Identity, Covenant, and the "Toledot" Formula.* LHBOTS 551. London: T&T Clark, 2011.

Thompson, Thomas L. *The Historicity of the Patriarchal Narratives: The Quest for the Historical Abraham.* BZAW 133. Berlin: Walter de Gruyter, 1974.

Thompson, Thomas L. *The Mythic Past: Biblical Archaeology and the Myth of Israel.* New York: Basic Books, 1999.

Thompson, Thomas L. *Early History of the Israelite People: From the Written & Archaeological Sources.* Brill's Scholars' List. Leiden: Brill, 2000.

Tobolowsky, Andrew. *The Sons of Jacob and the Sons of Herakles: The History of the Tribal System and the Organization of Biblical Identity.* FAT 2/96. Tübingen: Mohr Siebeck, 2017.

Tobolowsky, Andrew. "Israelite and Judahite History in Contemporary Theoretical Approaches." *CurBR* 17 (2018): 33–58. https://doi.org/10.1177/1476993X18765117.

Tobolowsky, Andrew. *The Myth of the Twelve Tribes of Israel: New Identities Across Time and Space.* Cambridge: Cambridge University Press, 2022.

Tournay, Raymond Jacques. "Genèse de la triade « Abraham-Isaac-Jacob »." *RB* 103 (1996): 321–36.

Trible, Phyllis. *Texts of Terror: Literary-Feminist Readings of Biblical Narratives.* Philadelphia: Fortress, 1984.

Van Seters, John. *Abraham in History and Tradition.* New Haven: Yale University Press, 1975.

Van Seters, John. *In Search of History: Historiography in the Ancient World and the Origins of Biblical History.* New Haven: Yale University Press, 1983.

Van Seters, John. *Prologue to History: The Yahwist as Historian in Genesis.* Louisville, KY: Westminster John Knox, 1992.

Vansina, Jan. *Oral Tradition as History.* Madison, WI: University of Wisconsin Press, 1985.

Vaux, Roland de. *The Early History of Israel.* Philadelphia: Westminster, 1978.

Von Rad, Gerhard. *Genesis: A Commentary.* Rev. ed. OTL. Philadelphia: Westminster, 1972.

Wegner, Daniel M., and Robin R. Vallacher, eds. *The Self in Social Psychology.* New York: Oxford University Press, 1980.

Weill, Raymond. "L'Installation des israélites en Palestine et la légende des patriarches." *RHR* 87 (1923): 69–120.

Weill, Raymond. "L'Installation des israélites en Palestine et la légende des patriarches." *RHR* 88 (1923): 1–44.

Weinfeld, Moshe. *Deuteronomy and the Deuteronomic School.* Oxford: Clarendon, 1972.

Weinfeld, Moshe. *The Place of the Law in the Religion of Ancient Israel.* VTSup 100. Leiden: Brill, 2004.

Weingart, Kristin. *Stämmevolk – Staatsvolk – Gottesvolk?: Studien zur Verwendung des Israel-Namens im Alten Testament.* FAT 2/68. Tübingen: Mohr Siebeck, 2014.

Weingart, Kristin. "What Makes an Israelite an Israelite? Judean Perspectives on the Samarians in the Persian Period." *JSOT* 42 (2017): 155–75. https://doi.org/10.1177/0309089216677664.

Welch, Adam Cleghorn. *The Code of Deuteronomy: A New Theory of Its Origin.* London: J. Clarke & Co., 1924.

Westad, Odd Arne. *Empire and Righteous Nation: 600 Years of China-Korea Relations.* Cambridge, MA: The Belknap Press of Harvard University Press, 2021.

Westermann, Claus. *Genesis: A Commentary.* Translated by John Scullion. Minneapolis: Augsburg, 1984.

Westermann, Claus. *Genesis 12–36.* Minneapolis: Augsburg, 1985.

Whitelam, Keith W. *The Invention of Ancient Israel: The Silencing of Palestinian History.* New York: Routledge, 1996.

Whitelam, K. W. "'Israel Is Laid Waste; His Seed Is No More': What If Merneptah's Scribes Were Telling the Truth?" In *Virtual History and the Bible*, edited by J. Cheryl Exum, 8–22. Leiden: Brill, 2000.

Williamson, H. G. M. "The Concept of Israel in Transition." In *The World of Ancient Israel: Sociological, Anthropological, and Political Perspectives*, edited by R. E. Clements, 141–61. Cambridge: Cambridge University Press, 1989.

Wöhrle, Jakob. "The Integrative Function of the Law of Circumcision." In *The Foreigner and the Law: Perspectives from the Hebrew Bible and the Ancient Near East*, edited by Reinhard Achenbach, Rainer Albertz, and Jakob Wöhrle, 71–87. BZABR 16. Wiesbaden: Harrassowitz Verlag, 2011.

Wöhrle, Jakob. "Koexistenz durch Unterwerfung: Zur Entstehung und politischen Intention der vorpriesterlichen Jakoberzählung." In *The Politics of the Ancestors: Exegetical and Historical Perspectives on Genesis 12–36*, edited by Mark G. Brett and Jakob Wöhrle, 307–27. FAT 124. Tübingen: Mohr Siebeck, 2018.

Wright, Jacob L. *David, King of Israel, and Caleb in Biblical Memory*. New York: Cambridge University Press, 2014.

Wright, Jacob L. *War, Memory, and National Identity in the Hebrew Bible*. Cambridge: Cambridge University Press, 2020.

Wright, Mary C., ed. *China in Revolution: The First Phase, 1900–1913*. New Haven: Yale University Press, 1968.

Yeivin, S. "Yaʿqobʾel." *JEA* 45 (1959): 16–18. https://doi.org/10.2307/3855458.

Yoreh, Tzemah L. *The First Book of God*. BZAW 402. Berlin: Walter de Gruyter, 2010.

Zarakol, Ayşe. "Ontological (In)Security and State Denial of Historical Crimes: Turkey and Japan." *International Relations* 24 (2010): 3–23. https://doi.org/10.1177/0047117809359040.

Zevit, Ziony. "Converging Lines of Evidence Bearing on the Date of P." *ZAW* 94 (1982): 481–511. https://doi.org/10.1515/zatw.1982.94.4.481.

Zhao, Gang. "Reinventing China: Imperial Qing Ideology and the Rise of Modern Chinese National Identity in the Early Twentieth Century." *Modern China* 32 (2006): 3–30. https://doi.org/10.1177/0097700405282349.

Zobel, Hans-Jürgen. "יַעֲקֹב/יַעֲקֹב yaʿaqōḇ/yaʿaqōḇ." In *Theological Dictionary of the Old Testament*, edited by Johannes Botterweck and Helmer Ringgren, translated by David E. Green, 6:186–208. Grand Rapids, MI: Eerdmans, 1990.

Zobel, Hans-Jürgen. "יִשְׂרָאֵל yiśrāʾēl." In *Theological Dictionary of the Old Testament*, edited by Johannes Botterweck and Helmer Ringgren, translated by David E. Green, 6:307–420. Grand Rapids, MI: Eerdmans, 1990.

Zwickel, Wolfgang. "Der Altarbau Abrahams zwischen Bethel und Ai (Gen 12 f.)." *BZ* 36 (1992): 207–19. https://doi.org/10.1163/25890468-03602005.

Zwickel, Wolfgang. "Die Altarbaunotizen im Alten Testament." *Bib* 73 (1992): 533–46. https://doi.org/10.2143/BIB.73.4.3215035.

Modern Authors Index

https://doi.org/10.1515/9783111376554-014

Subject Index

https://doi.org/10.1515/9783111376554-015

Scripture Index

Genesis

11:10   187
11:26   187
11:26–29   182
11:27–12:9   191
11:27–32   183, 191
11:31   158, 182, 184
12   191, 196
12:1   183, 191
12:1–3   181, 184–186, 188
12:1–5   182
12:2   184
12:4–5   158
12:4–13:18   181
12:4a   197
12:7   181
12:8   181
12:10–20   181, 196
12:10–22   196
12–50   129
13:3   181
13:10–13   185
15   196
15:6   186
15:7   192, 196
15:13–14   196
15:18   184
16   185
17   176
17:1–21   184
17:7   189
17:10–14   190
17:18   189
17:19   189
18:9–15   187
19:24–25   185
19:30–37   88
20   190
20:6   190
20:13   160
20–22   126
21:4   190
21:14–21   185
22   185
22:15–18   186

22:16–18   185
22:20–23   182
22:22   182
23:4   160
24   182, 191
24:4   191
24:7   160
24:10   158, 183, 191
25:19   138
25:19–35:29   138, 139
25:20   138, 158, 182
25:23   142, 143, 188
25:24–26   151
25:26   142
25:26b   138
25:27–28   142
25:30   159
25:34   142
26:34–35   139, 161, 190, 191
26–35   131
27   143
27:11–23   159
27:27–29   160
27:43   158, 182
27:44   146
27:46   139, 190, 191
28:1–5   161, 190
28:I–9   139
28:2   158
28:5   158
28:6   158
28:6–9   161
28:7   158
28:10–22   140
28:10   158, 182
28:13–14   183, 184
28:13   139, 140
28:15   140, 143
28:21   140
28:22   145
29:1–14a   143
29:1   158, 182
29:4   158, 182
29:5   182
29:6   146

https://doi.org/10.1515/9783111376554-016